Seeing with the
Eyes of the Heart

Seeing with the Eyes of the Heart

CULTIVATING A SACRAMENTAL IMAGINATION IN AN AGE OF PORNOGRAPHY

EDITED BY ELIZABETH T. GROPPE

The Catholic University of America Press
Washington, D.C.

The paper used in this publication meets the minimum
requirements of American National Standards for Information
Science—Permanence of Paper for Printed Library Materials,
ANSI Z39.48-1984.
∞

Cataloging-in-Publication Data available from the
Library of Congress
ISBN 978-0-8132-3289-8

No one has ever seen God.
Yet if we love one another,
God remains in us,
and his love is brought
to perfection in us.

—1 JN 4:12

CONTENTS

ILLUSTRATIONS

Illustrations can be found between book pages 82 and 83.

Seeing with the Eyes of the Heart

ELIZABETH T. GROPPE

Introduction ⇜ "Seeing with the Eyes of the Heart" (Eph 1:18)

Imagine that it is the first century and that you live in Ephesus, a community nestled amongst fertile fields on the coast of the Aegean Sea in a region we know today as Turkey. A fresh, crisp breeze blows off the azure waters and tousles your hair as you walk through the streets of a city that was the birthplace of the philosopher Heraclitus. Visible between the street and the sea despite the walls of the city enclosure is the Temple of Artemis, a columned structure that Philo of Byzantium declared to be one of the seven wonders (*theamatōn*, or "things to be seen") of the world.[1] Its white marble was quarried by slave labor and then carved in exquisite detail by the finest craftsmen and the result is dazzling. In the month of Artemesion, the statue of the golden figure of Artemis that resides within the Temple is carried in a procession by Ionians clad in garments dyed violet, purple, yellow, crimson, flame-orange, and sea-green.[2]

You do not tarry, however, to gaze at the Temple or ponder these memories. Your attention is focused on what you have just heard read aloud from a letter written by someone in prison: "I do not cease to give thanks for you as I remember you in my prayers. . . . I pray that the God of our Lord Jesus Christ, the Father of glory, may give you a spirit of wisdom and revelation as you come to know him, so that, with the eyes of your heart being lit up (*pephōtismenous tous ophthalmous tēs kardias hymōn*), you may know the hope to which he has called you, what are the riches of his glorious inheritance among the saints, and what is the immeasurable greatness of this power for us who believe"

1. Kai Brodersen, ed. and trans., *Reiseführer zu den Sieben Weltwundern: Philon von Byzanz und andere antike Texte* (Frankfurt am Main: Insel, 1992), 20.

2. John and Elizabeth Romer, *The Seven Wonders of the World: A History of the Modern Imagination* (New York: Barnes & Noble Books, 2005), 129–64.

(Eph 1:16–18).[3] The enlightenment of which the letter speaks refers to the baptism that has graced you with participation in the power that raised Jesus the Christ from the dead (Eph 1:20).[4] And, in the psalms that you are learning to pray together with other Gentiles who have become members of the household of God (Eph 1:11–22), the "heart" is the center of the physical, emotional, and spiritual life (Ps 101:5, 103:15).[5]

But, of course, you do not live in Ephesus and it is not the first century. It is 2020, and the internet is a wonder of your world. In the digital culture of the twenty-first century, anyone of any age with a computer or smart phone and an internet connection can access a seemingly infinite array of texts, images, and videos at any time of day or night. Among the available digital images and videos are pornographic scenes of every conceivable kind. Social taboos once associated with pornography have attenuated, particularly among youth of the internet generation who have been socialized into what journalist Pamela Paul describes as a "pornified" culture.[6]

Studies that attempt to gauge the prevalence of pornography usage include Paul J. Wright's analysis of data from the General Social Survey, which found that 34 percent of men surveyed in the United States in the period from 2000–2010 reported viewing pornography.[7]

3. The author of the letter describes himself as "an ambassador in chains" for the sake of the mystery of the Gospel (Eph 6:19–20). The letter bears the name of Paul, but it differs in syntax and style from Corinthians and Romans and there is a debate among scholars as to whether the letter we now know as Paul's Epistle to the Ephesians was composed by Paul himself or a close associate. The audience of the letter is also uncertain, since the earliest extant manuscripts do not include reference to the Ephesians in the greeting. The letter may have been circulated among multiple communities in Asia Minor. See Peter T. O'Brien, *The Letter to the Ephesians* (Grand Rapids, Mich.: Eerdmans, 1999), 4–47. My thanks to my colleague Silviu Bunta for his assistance with translation and transliteration of the Ephesians text.

4. The grammatical form of the phrase "having the eyes of your heart enlightened" is, in the original Greek, the perfect participle, which, biblical scholar Stephen Fowl explains, invites identification of a distinct point at which the enlightening occurred, such as conversion or baptism. Stephen E. Fowl, *Ephesians: A Commentary* (Louisville, Ky.: Westminster John Knox, 2012), 58.

5. See Walter F. Taylor, *Ephesians: Augsburg Commentary on the New Testament* (Minneapolis, Minn.: Augsburg, 1985), 40.

6. Pamela Paul, *Pornified: How Pornography Is Transforming Our Lives, Our Relationships, and Our Families* (New York: Times Books, an imprint of Henry Holt, 2005).

7. Paul J. Wright, "U.S. Males and Pornography, 1973–2010: Consumption, Predictors, Correlates," *Journal of Sex Research* 50, no. 1 (2013): 65.

In a 2008 study of 813 students at 6 universities in the United States, 87 percent of young men and 31 percent of young women reported using pornography.[8] The 2016 Barna Group study *The Porn Phenomenon* commissioned by Josh McDowell's Protestant ministry found that within their U.S. population sample, 51 percent of persons ages 13 and older seek out pornography at least occasionally.[9] Among survey participants who identified as practicing Christians, pornography usage was significantly less frequent than within the survey sample at large. Whereas 8 percent of those who did not identify as practicing Christians reported seeking pornography daily, this rate among practicing Christians was 2 percent.[10] Of the practicing Christians who participated in the Barna survey, 13 percent reported seeking out pornography at least once a month, as compared to 42 percent of other participants.[11] Approximately 7 in 10 practicing Christians (72 percent) report never searching for pornography, as compared to 39 percent of those who do not practice Christianity.[12]

The Barna Group report is evidence that the practice of Christianity provides protection against pornography but that it is not an impenetrable shield, particularly among youth of the internet generation. "When 54 percent of Christian young adults ages 18 to 24 seek out porn at least occasionally," Protestant minister Josh McDowell reflects in his preface to *The Porn Phenomenon*, "and when two out of three youth pastors and more than half of senior pastors say porn is a current or past struggle, we have a genuine crisis on our hands."[13] A survey on a smaller scale at a Midwestern Catholic high school found that 48 percent of the male student participants viewed pornography one or more times a week and 36 percent reported feelings of addic-

8. Jason S. Carroll et al., "Generation XXX: Pornography Acceptance and Use Among Emerging Adults," *Journal of Adolescent Research* 23, no. 1 (2008): 16–17.

9. Barna Group, *The Porn Phenomenon: The Impact of Pornography in the Digital Age* (Ventura, Calif.: Barna Group, in partnership with Josh McDowell Ministry, 2016), 38. For a breakdown of this data by age, gender, marital status, income level, and ethnicity, see *Porn Phenomenon*, 39–45.

10. Barna, *Porn Phenomenon*, 47. Cf. 73–74.

11. Barna, *Porn Phenomenon*, 47. These figures are a composite of the data given on those who view daily, weekly, and once or twice a month.

12. Barna, *Porn Phenomenon*, 47.

13. Josh McDowell, preface to *Porn Phenomenon*, 6.

tion.[14] In the Archdiocese of Kansas City, Catholic Charities reports that nearly 50 percent of married couples who come for counseling are struggling with challenges related to pornography.[15] When Anne's spouse, Mike, began a process of recovery from porn addiction and joined a support group, Anne discovered that "wonderful, normal, good Catholic men, just like Mike, can get caught up in this addiction."[16] Nor are priests immune from this struggle, as Father John Smith (pseud.) shares in a testimony about his own experience.[17]

Exposure to pornography is now common, but theological conversation about pornography is not. For a variety of reasons, this is a topic that is difficult to discuss. It is, nonetheless, pastorally imperative to do so, and I am grateful to the contributors to this volume for their willingness to address this subject. Some have devoted major portions of their professional careers to psychological study of pornography's influence and care for those who suffer from pornography's harms. Others had the generosity of spirit to engage the topic from the vantage point of their various areas of expertise.

The composition of this book follows the publication of the United States Conference of Catholic Bishops' November 2015 statement "Create in Me a Clean Heart: A Pastoral Response to Pornography" or, in Spanish, "*Crea en Mí un Corazón Puro: Una Respuesta Pastoral a la Pornografía*."[18] The bishops intend this statement "to give a word of hope and healing to those who have been harmed by pornography and to raise awareness of its pervasiveness and harms." They explain: "In the confessional and in our daily ministry and work with families,

14. Website of the Archdiocese of Kansas City "My House" Initiative, accessed September 20, 2018, https://www.archkck.org/myhouse/stats.

15. Website of the Archdiocese of Kansas City "My House" Initiative, https://www.archkck.org/myhouse/stats.

16. Mike and Anne, "To Hell and Back," in *Delivered: True Stories of Men and Women Who Turned from Porn to Purity*, ed. Matt Fradd (San Diego, Calif.: Catholic Answers Press, 2013), 85.

17. John Smith, "Confessing My Porn Addiction: A Priest Learns to Ask for Help," *America Magazine* 216, no. 7 (April 3, 2017): 32–36. For a broader discussion of priests, religious, and seminarians who struggle with pornography, see Peter C. Kleponis, *Integrity Restored: Helping Catholic Families Win the Battle against Pornography* (Steubenville, Ohio: Emmaus Road, 2014), 161–79.

18. United States Conference of Catholic Bishops, "Create in Me a Clean Heart: A Pastoral Response to Pornography" (Washington D.C.: United States Conference of Catholic Bishops, 2015).

we have seen the corrosive damage caused by pornography—children whose innocence is stolen; men and women who feel great guilt and shame for viewing pornography occasionally or habitually; spouses who feel betrayed and traumatized; and men, women, and children exploited by the pornography industry."[19] Pornography is defined as a media form that removes "real or simulated sexual acts from the intimacy of the partners, in order to display them deliberately to third parties. It offends against chastity because it perverts the conjugal act, the intimate giving of spouses to each other. It does grave injury to the dignity of its participants (actors, vendors, the public), since each one becomes an object of base pleasure and illicit profit for others."[20] The human being, the pastoral statement emphasizes, is a person ordered to *love*; she or he is not an object to be used.[21] "Create in Me a Clean Heart" includes an overview of the Church's teaching on sexuality, chastity, and the dignity and vocation of the human person; an account of pornography as both a personal and social sin; a survey of research on pornography's wide-reaching effects on our society and culture; a discussion of pornography's influences on men, women, youth, and children; concluding words of hope and healing; and an appendix that provides readers with pastoral resources.

The pastoral statement emphasizes that "the Church's teaching on the harm and sinfulness of pornography is grounded in the greater 'yes' or affirmation of the inviolable dignity of the human person revealed fully in Christ and the gift of human sexuality and marriage in God's plan."[22] Analogously, *Seeing with the Eyes of the Heart* affirms that the Church's critique of the visual culture of pornography is grounded in an even greater "yes" to the beauty of God's creation and the visual culture of the Christian tradition. The "no" to the pornified imagination is rooted in an even greater "yes" to the sacramental imagination, and the "no" to images that degrade the human person is rooted in an even greater "yes" to images that portray the human

19. United States Conference of Catholic Bishops, introduction to "Create in Me a Clean Heart," 1.

20. *Catechism of the Catholic Church*, 2nd ed. (Washington, D.C.: United States Conference of Catholic Bishops, 2000), 2354. Cited in "Create in Me a Clean Heart," 5.

21. United States Conference of Catholic Bishops, "Create in Me a Clean Heart," 6 (emphasis original).

22. United States Conference of Catholic Bishops, "Create in Me a Clean Heart," 5.

vocation to deification (2 Pet 1:4). Some of the essays in this volume draw forth the beauty of visual culture in the Catholic and Orthodox traditions, including liturgical and sacramental practices, church architecture, iconography, frescoes, mosaics, sculptures, paintings, and illuminated biblical manuscripts. Other essays highlight practices that can nurture a sacramental imagination. These include active participation in the sacraments of the Church and the life of the ecclesial body, Eucharistic adoration, ascetic disciplines, the incorporation of Christian iconography within the home, the cultivation of memory of sacred images, and the practice of the corporal works of mercy.

This volume originated in a generous grant from the Our Sunday Visitor Institute awarded to the Division for Mission of Saint Mary's College, Notre Dame, Indiana for the purpose of the March 2015 conference "'Seeing with the Eyes of the Heart' (Eph 1:18): Cultivating a Sacramental Imagination in an Age of Pornography." Veronique Wiedower, CSC, now president of the Sisters of the Holy Cross, was at that time Vice President for Mission of Saint Mary's, and she oversaw the grant administration with the support of Patricia K. Doyle in the Office of Grant Services. I served as a consultant to the Division for Mission to coordinate the conference that brought together theologians, psychologists, a humanistic scholar, an iconographer, a scholar of Christian art, a professor of communication with expertise in media studies, and undergraduate and graduate students who responded to a nationwide invitation to submit conference paper proposals. The event would not have been possible without the generous support of multiple cosponsors, including Saint Mary's College Belles Against Violence (BAVO), Saint Mary's College Campus Ministry, Saint Mary's College Center for Spirituality, Saint Mary's College Student Affairs, the University of Notre Dame Department of Theology, the McGrath Institute for Church Life at the University of Notre Dame, Campus Ministry at the University of Notre Dame, the Center for Gender Relations at the University of Notre Dame, and the Department of History, Philosophy, and Theology at Holy Cross College. These cosponsors contributed both financial support and the time and talents of their gifted faculties and staff. Special gratitude is due to Judith R. Fean, Vice President for Mission of Saint Mary's College; Saint Mary's College Center for Spirituality Associate Director, Michelle L. Egan, and Administrative Assistant, Kathleen R. Guthrie; J. Matthew Ashley, Chair of the Department of Theology at the University of Notre Dame; John C. Cavadini, the McGrath-Cavadini Director of the McGrath Institute for Church Life at the University of Notre Dame; and David Lutz, Professor of Philosophy and Dean of Faculty at Holy Cross College. These persons made possible the convocation of the conference on the campuses of both Saint Mary's College and the University of Notre Dame and enabled the participation of students from all three of the Holy Cross educational communities in Notre Dame, Indiana.

Gail Porter Mandell, English professor and Schlesinger Chair of Humanistic Studies emerita at Saint Mary's College, spoke at the conference about the educational philosophy of Madeleva Wolff, CSC, who served for twenty-seven years as president of a Catholic college founded to serve young women. Sister Madeleva was raised in northern Wisconsin where the changing seasons and lush forests revealed to her the beauty and continuing mystery of creation. She hungrily read poetry "for beauty's sake," and the poetry that she herself wrote and published was often inspired by nature wherein she found God hidden. Her own "apostolate of beauty," as she described her vocation, included a vision for Saint Mary's College as a place where young women could receive an education that integrated intellectual, moral, and religious formation. Her emphasis on the liturgical life, the fine arts, and Christian culture were central to this vision. She oversaw the planting of gardens on the college campus and overcame significant challenges to build the Moreau Center for the Fine Arts to serve both the college and the wider community. "We wanted to build a home for beauty," she said of her mission at Saint Mary's. "I knew that of the trinity—goodness, truth and beauty, each an equation for God—beauty is the most palpable, the most irresistible. I have called it God's visibility."[23]

Take care of beauty, Sister Madeleva professed, revising an axiom of artist Eric Gill, and goodness and truth will take care of them-

23. Sister M. Madeleva, *My First Seventy Years* (New York: Macmillan, 1959), 104. Cited by Gail Porter Mandell, "Beauty Is God's Visibility: The Educational Philosophy of Sister M. Madeleva Wolff, CSC." (Paper presentation, "Seeing with the Eyes of the Heart" conference, Saint Mary's College, Notre Dame, Ind., March 27, 2015).

selves.[24] True beauty, she believed, originates from and leads back to the divine. Yet she also cautioned that beauty is "a perilous gift" that can be warped for exploitive purposes. She spoke publicly against the print and celluloid media's exploitation of young women in the 1940s and 1950s, and one can only imagine what words she would have for today's pornified culture. The exploitation of young women and young men has intensified to a degree that would likely have been inconceivable to Sister Madeleva. And yet, her insight into the hungers of the human heart still rings true: our modern world, she believed, is starved for beauty.

The volume opens with a chapter that I composed to provide context for the essays that follow. The chapter offers a reflection on the importance of visual culture in Christianity and introduces the visual culture of pornography, drawing from the work of Erica Scharrer, professor of communication at the University of Massachusetts at Amherst, who spoke at the "Seeing with the Eyes of the Heart" conference about a research project on the character of today's pornography to which she contributed. The chapter also notes briefly some of the differences between a sacramental and pornographic gaze.

Part 1 of the volume features complementary essays by Dr. Jill Manning and Dr. William M. Struthers and Kyler Mulhauser on the influence of pornography on women and men. Dr. Manning combines her expertise in psychological scholarship with her clinical experience to elucidate the manifold ways that pornography is harming both single and married women. Professor Struthers and his former graduate assistant Kyler Mulhauser draw from their own laboratory research and that of others to explain neurologically the influence of pornography on men. In the interdisciplinary spirit of this volume, Manning and Struthers integrate their psychological and neurological expertise with the wisdom of their Protestant traditions, framing their psychological exposition with reflection on the dignity of the human person created in the image of God (Gn 1:26–27) and called through Christ to covenantal relationships.

24. Gill's axiom was: "Take care of goodness and truth, and beauty will take care of itself." Sister Madeleva comments on her revision of this axiom: "I had not found this so." Sister Madeleva, *My First Seventy Years*, 104.

Part 2 explores several dimensions of the visual culture of Christianity. Orthodox iconographer Randi Sider-Rose describes the devotional use of icons in the Orthodox home and the spiritual disciplines and refined techniques that the iconographer employs to invite us into a sacralized vision of creation and the human person. Danielle M. Peters presents a historical and theological survey of Marian imagery from both the East and the West with particular attention to the way in which this heritage could protect the imagination from the intrusion of pornography and contribute to the healing of persons whom pornography has injured. Dianne Phillips elucidates Catholic visual culture of the high medieval through early modern periods with particular attention to imagery that enlists the sensual dimensions of human bodily existence to express visually God's passionate love for us and the human yearning for God.

In part 3 of the volume, sacramental theologians David W. Fagerberg and Kimberly Hope Belcher reflect on the meaning of the sacramental imagination in the context of our pornographic culture. Fagerberg exegetes the Epistle to the Ephesians's prayer that the God of glory might grant us "a spirit of wisdom and revelation" to see with the eyes of the heart the hope to which we are called (Eph 1:18). Contextualizing this passage in the Epistle's account of the history of salvation, Fagerberg emphasizes that a sacramental imagination beholds the goodness of God's creation and does not disdain the human body or human sexuality. A sacramental imagination sees, *through* the means of the good body, signs of the mystery that God desires that we become, by grace, what Christ is by nature and so enter the upward draw of redeemed eros into the divine love that flows between Father, Son, and Holy Spirit. In "Sacramental Exposure," Belcher evokes a sacramental vision that is not less but rather *more* alluring than a possessive and objectifying pornographic gaze. Reflecting on the music videos of popular R&B artist Janelle Monáe, the *Maria lactans* tradition that portrays the Virgin Mary nursing the Christ child, and the sacrament of baptism, Belcher elucidates ways that art and liturgy can be holy forms of seduction that invite an iconic gaze in which vulnerable human bodies are beheld through the prism of the all-consuming love of the crucified and risen Christ who shares and transfigures our humanity.

Part 4 probes a number of ways that the Christian tradition can support the cultivation of a sacramental imagination. Ann W. Astell offers a reflection on the Song of Songs, a biblical poem of love regarded in the early Church as a prophecy of the sacraments of Christian initiation. This powerful text, she writes, can be both preventive medicine and palliative balm in an era of pornography, forming our memory with erotic poetic imagery that symbolically represents Christ's love for the Church and each human soul and celebrates marriage and religious life as a sacramental participation in divine love. In medieval culture, Nathaniel Peters emphasizes in his chapter "Vision, Memory, and the Eucharist's Reformation of the Mind," the training of memory was not only a matter of practical necessity but also a matter of ethics and character. The Christian vocation to holiness requires that we fill the storehouse of our memory with holy things, including holy images. Peters illustrates this with an exposition of the writings of the twelfth-century Cistercian monk William of Saint Thierry, who counseled his monastic community to practice visual meditations as one means to grow in love of Christ and store this love in their memories. Boyd Taylor Coolman exegetes the multivalent meanings of Paul's exhortation that Christians should have "the mind of Christ" (1 Cor 2:16—*nous Christou* in the Greek New Testament and *sensus Christi* in the Latin Vulgate) through the prism of the teaching and tradition of the Church. He offers a liturgico-sacramental therapy for a pornographic sensibility in which Christ is both subject and object of a healing *sensus* that is acquired sacramentally and cultivated liturgically. Nicholas Ogle finds at the root of our pornified culture a loss of a teleological vision of the purpose of human embodiment. The problem with pornography, he explains, is not that it shows too much but that it shows too little, displaying a body but violating and obscuring the person in her or his dignity, intellect, and vocation to self-giving love and eternal enjoyment of God. The healing of this splitting of bodies from persons, he emphasizes, will require bodily practices exercised in charity, particularly the corporal works of mercy.

The volume concludes with reflections on the healing of vision. In part 5, we hear the voice of Jonah (pseud.), who wrote his chapter as an undergraduate student at a North American university. He shares the story of a youthful curiosity that became a habitual pornography practice that fractured his relationships with God and other persons. Through the compassionate mediation of a campus minister, he has begun to heal. He expresses his hope that the Church can be in the words of Pope Francis a "field hospital" for the many others in our society who suffer in some way because of pornography.[25] These include not only young men like himself but also young women who face both the cultural influence of pornography and social pressure to participate in pornography consumption. The conference call for papers did not result in any testimonies by young women, but accounts published elsewhere include the autobiographical reflection of Audrey Assad.[26] It is important to be mindful that women too can become habitual viewers of pornography, for it is often presumed that pornography is a "guy thing," and this can make it difficult for women to find the support that can facilitate healing.

Part 5 on the "Healing of Vision" continues with an essay by Jennifer Newsome Martin, who elucidates the pornography industry's erasure of the human person and the consequences of a culture that reduces women and men to parts of bodies. At the root of the culture of pornography, she finds a destructive anthropology and a constriction of perception that eclipses beauty's ontological and objective form. She draws from the theology of Hans Urs von Balthasar to offer as an antidote a rehabilitated transcendental theology of beauty and a Christology and theological anthropology that wed embodiment, materiality, and spirituality. John C. Cavadini draws the volume near conclusion with a reflection on pornography as an anti-sacrament. He observes that even a documentary film intended as a critique of the pornography industry participates in the pornographic culture that it challenges. The film offers no ideal of masculinity that can counter pornography's construal of manhood as domination, no framework in which sexuality has a telos, and no vision that answers to the longings of the human heart. Elucidating an image of the *Anastasis* (Resurrec-

25. Antonio Spadaro, "A Big Heart Open to God: The Exclusive Interview with Pope Francis," *America Magazine* 209, no. 8 (September 20, 2013): 24.

26. Audrey Assad, "Freedom and Fullness," in *Delivered: True Stories of Men and Women Who Turned from Porn to Purity*, ed. Matt Fradd (San Diego, Calif.: Catholic Answers Press, 2013), 33–42.

tion) that depicts the redemption in Christ of Adam and Eve, he reflects on the power of Love crucified to heal our imaginations.

This volume of scholarly essays is composed with a pastoral care and concern, and a concluding pastoral coda recapitulates some of the themes of the chapters with attention to pastoral practice. This conclusion is enriched by the reflections of readers who generously agreed to review a draft of the manuscript and offer their comments. These readers include several current and former students from two Catholic universities as well as members of the Saint Augustine Men's Group, a lay apostolate in the diocese of Fort Wayne-South Bend that supports men in living in chastity and freedom from pornography. I am grateful for their contributions.

I am most grateful as well to John B. Martino of the Catholic University of America Press who was willing to undertake a project made much more time-consuming by the inclusion of color plates and who shepherded the volume to publication. Thanks to John's support, this book includes not only reflection on Christian visual culture but also photos of exemplars from this tradition, many of which are extraordinarily beautiful. Copy editor Amy Elise Quinn carefully polished the text, and I thank also the anonymous Catholic University of America Press reviewers whose comments and recommendations significantly improved the manuscript. My former graduate assistant Olivia Seeger assisted with several bibliographic tasks. I am also deeply grateful to my department chair, Daniel Speed Thompson, and Dean Jason Pearce for granting a subvention to fund the inset with color images. The color inset raised printing costs by more than 50 percent, and it would not have been possible to include this without the generous support of the University of Dayton.

The color plates were made possible not only through the financial support of the Department of Religious Studies at the University of Dayton but also through the generosity of many others. I extend gratitude to the artists who granted permission to reproduce their beautiful work: Daniel Bonnell, Neilson Carlin, Lisa Fracica, Rev. John B. Giuliani, Brother Michael O'Neill McGrath, Suzann Miriello and her colleagues at the New Guild Studio, and Randi Sider-Rose. Jason Bourgeois and Olivia Gillingham of the University of Dayton Library assisted with research on Marian imagery with the support of University of Dayton Marian Library director Sarah B. Cahalan, and digital projects manager Ryan O'Grady photographed several works from the Marian Library collection for inclusion in this volume. Edward Brink, SM, David Coleman, and Christine Denton of Chaminade University of Honolulu made possible the inclusion of a photograph of *Ke Lede o Kaminaka* (Our Lady of Chaminade), which Dr. Coleman and the Humanities and Fine Arts division at Chaminade University commissioned from the studio of Father Damien Higgins in anticipation of the 125th anniversary of the Marianist presence in the Island of Hawaii. Other images were sourced with the support of professional staff at Alinari, Art Resource, the Benaki Museum in Athens, Bridgeman Images, the Horne Museum in Florence, the Metropolitan Museum of Art, the Museu de Bellas Artes de València, the Museum of Fine Arts in Boston, the National Gallery in London, Rijksmuseum in Amsterdam, the Staatliche Museen zu Berlin, the Snite Museum of Art at the University of Notre Dame, the University of Michigan Visual Resources Collection, the Walker Art Gallery in Liverpool, and the Yale University Art Gallery and Beinecke Rare Book and Manuscript Library. Professional photographer Christopher Humphrey and graphic designer Claire M. Groppe generously assisted with the digital formatting of the photographs of some of the images.

A photo of an *Anastasis* icon that was commissioned from iconographer Randi Sider-Rose for the occasion of the "Seeing with the Eyes of the Heart" conference appears on the cover of this book. In the Orthodox tradition, iconographers do not sign their own names on their work. "We are," Sider-Rose explains, "mere vessels, not artistic geniuses or masters. Some iconographers write on the back of an icon, 'through the hands of . . . ' or even 'through the sinful hands of.'" The *Anastasis* icon made through her hands now hangs in its irreproducible translucence on a wall of Regina Chapel at Saint Mary's College.

Orthodox iconography works with a limited array of types and themes that the women and men who practice this discipline write again and again (icons are technically "written," not painted) as they carry forward this living tradition. In Orthodoxy, there are only two icons of the Resurrection. One features the women who bring myrrh to Christ's tomb and the other depicts Christ's descent into Hades, a mystery foreshadowed in icons of the Nativity in which the Christ child lies in the dense darkness of a cave. The *Anastasis* icon on the book cover is of this second type.

The significance of this *Anastasis* icon in an age of pornography is multivalent. The Catholic Church teaches that the production or consumption of pornography with complete, deliberate consent and full knowledge of the sinful character of the act and its opposition to God's law is a mortal sin, and mortal sin that has not been repented results in a self-caused state of separation from God.[27] It is also the teaching of the Church that God so desires that every person should be saved (1 Tm 2:4) that God takes on human flesh in the person of the divine Word and descends even into Hades, extending the hand of love and mercy visible in this icon.

There are other layers of meaning in this image. In the internet age, pornography consumption is a complex reality involving not only personal moral agency but also social sin and compulsive and addictive behaviors. Dr. Peter Kleponis, a licensed clinical therapist who has established a program for supporting Catholic men in overcoming pornography addiction, emphasizes that this is "a disease similar to any other addiction, and not simply a moral failing. No one wants to become an addict. The addiction silently creeps into a man's life and soon takes over.... Many don't know what to do or to whom to turn."[28] Kleponis emphasizes the need for mercy and compassion that is evident in the icon.

Pornography can make of earthly life an inverted and twisted kind of "Hades" in which innocent persons suffer from its effects. This is evident, for example, in the relationship of some pornography production to the sexual trafficking of human persons;[29] in the accounts of children groomed for sexual abuse by deliberate exposure to pornographic films;[30] in the testimonies of spouses in marriages that por-

27. United States Conference of Catholic Bishops, "Create in Me a Clean Heart," 5; *Catechism of the Catholic Church*, nos. 1859, 1874.

28. Kleponis, *Integrity Restored*, 57.

29. See, for example, Catharine A. MacKinnon, "Pornography as Trafficking," in *Pornography: Driving the Demand in International Sex Trafficking*, ed. David E. Guinn with Julie DiCaro, 31–42 (Los Angeles, Calif.: Captive Daughters Media, 2007).

30. See, for example, Gail Dines's account of her conversation with a convicted

nography has frayed;[31] in research on pornography's effect on family life;[32] and in studies of the relation of pornography to the staggering rates of sexual violence and aggression in our society.[33] In *Smut: A Sex Industry Insider (and Concerned Father) Says Enough Is Enough,* secular author Gil Reavill invokes the theological imagery of Hades to express his experience. "'Hold back the edges of your gowns, Ladies,'" he advises, citing a line from poet William Carlos Williams, "'we are going through hell.'"[34]

"Amid the deepest shadow," Pseudo-Dionysius prays in the opening to his *Mystical Theology,* the mysteries of the Word of the triune God pour overwhelming light.[35] This light of divine love has the power to redeem our vision. In a context in which our perception of women and men may have been degraded by easily accessible hardcore pornography or by the softcore pornography so prevalent in the media that it is almost impossible to avoid, we are beckoned by the Holy Spirit to

---

child molester in her film *Pornland: How the Porn Industry Has Hijacked Our Sexuality* (North Hampton, Mass.: Media Education Foundation, 2014), DVD. The conversation can be read on pages 10–11 of a transcript of the film accessed September 20, 2018, at: http://www.mediaed.org/transcripts/Pornland-Transcripts.pdf.

31. Mike and Anne, "To Hell and Back." See also Susan Cebulko, *The Impact of Internet Pornography on Married Women: A Psychodynamic Perspective* (Youngstown, N.Y.: Cambria Press, 2007); Matt Fradd and Cameron Fradd, *Restored: True Stories of Love and Trust after Porn* (El Cajon, Calif.: Catholic Answers Press, 2015).

32. United States Conference of Catholic Bishops, "Create in Me a Clean Heart," 14–15; Jill C. Manning, "The Impact of Internet Pornography on Marriage and the Family: A Review of the Research," *Sexual Addiction & Compulsivity* 13, no. 2/3 (2006): 131–65.

33. Mary Anne Layden, Director of the Sexual Trauma and Psychopathology Program in the Department of Psychiatry at the University of Pennsylvania and a contributor to the "Seeing with the Eyes of the Heart" conference, addresses this subject in "Pornography and Violence: A New Look at the Research," in *The Social Costs of Pornography: A Collection of Papers,* ed. James R. Stoner Jr. and Donna M. Hughes (Princeton, N.J.: The Witherspoon Institute, 2010), 57–68. Jill Manning also speaks to this issue in chapter 2. Corroborating work published subsequent to her conference presentation includes Paul J. Wright and Robert S. Tokunaga, "Men's Objectifying Media Consumption, Objectification of Women, and Attitudes Supportive of Violence against Women," *Archives of Sexual Behavior* 45, no. 4 (2016): 955–64; Walter S. DeKeseredy and Marilyn Corsianos, *Violence against Women in Pornography* (New York: Routledge, an imprint of the Taylor & Francis Group, 2016).

34. Gil Reavill, *Smut: A Sex Industry Insider (and Concerned Father) Says Enough Is Enough* (New York: Sentinel, an imprint of the Penguin Group, 2005), 41.

35. Pseudo-Dionysius, "The Mystical Theology," in *Pseudo-Dionysius: The Complete Works,* trans. Colm Luibheid, The Classics of Western Spirituality (New York: Paulist Press, 1987), 135.

a healing of the imagination within the communion of a Church that Pope Francis describes as a field hospital for the wounded. The contributors to this volume invite us to a form of sacramental vision. "Rise up, work of my hands, you who were created in my image," Christ, with wounds in his hands and side, says to Adam and Eve in a Holy Saturday homily by St. Epiphanius that is cited by Paul Evdokimov in a commentary on the *Anastasis* icon. "'Let us leave here and go from pain to joy, Christ continues. The wedding hall is prepared . . . the eternal tents have been put up . . . this heavenly Kingdom which existed before the ages is now waiting for you.'"[36]

36. Epiphanius, "Homily for Holy Saturday," in Patrologiae cursus completus, series graeca, ed. Jacques Paul Migne (Paris: Migne, 1857–66), 43:440–64. Cited in Paul Evdokimov, *The Art of the Icon: A Theology of Beauty*, trans. Steven Bigham (Redondo Beach, Calif: Oakwood Publications, 1990), 323.

ELIZABETH T. GROPPE

1 ↞ Visual Cultures and the Sacramental Imagination

The chestnut-brown rabbit nibbling on green clover in the lawn outside my window has a round black and brown eye on either side of its head.[1] It eats in an alert state, surveying its surroundings with the peripheral vision afforded by eyes strategically placed to enable it to behold approaching danger. I am one of its potential predators. Humans, in contrast to rabbits, writes Diane Ackerman in *A Natural History of the Senses,* have predator eyes—that is, eyes in the front of our heads that give us the binocular vision necessary to find and follow prey. These predator eyes were well-suited to the life of gathering and hunting that sustained *Homo sapiens* for thousands of years. Most of us no longer gather or hunt for our food, but the eyes are still the "great monopolists of our senses."[2] Indeed, 70 percent of the sense receptors in the human body cluster in the eyes. The rabbit grazing on the lawn, in contrast, has large perky ears and a keener sense of hearing than I—as does the dog beside the rocking chair lolling at my son's feet. Humans and other primates are microsmatic (feeble scented) in comparison to macrosmatic canines, whose olfactory receptors outnumber ours by the hundreds of millions. "The world abounds with aromas, but we are spectacle-less," writes Alexandra Horowitz, using a visual metaphor to express our olfactory inferiority to canines.[3]

1. I am grateful to Dianne Phillips for her assistance with this chapter. The limitations and any errors that remain are my own.

2. Diane Ackerman, *A Natural History of the Senses* (New York: Vintage Books, 1990), 229. Paleontologists Donna Hart and Robert Sussman argue to the contrary that early humans were not predators but prey on the African savannah. See Donna Hart and Robert W. Sussman, *Man the Hunted: Primates, Predators, and Human Evolution* (Boulder, Colo.: Westview, 2009). It would seem that early humans were likely both.

3. Alexandra Horowitz, *Being a Dog: Following the Dog into a World of Smell* (New York: Scribner, 2016), 5.

Sight is the human creature's dominant sense. Employed in the service of our biological survival, it enabled us to find food and a mate. Yet the eye, the Christian tradition affirms, is more than just a biological organ with an evolutionary history of adaptation for survival and reproduction. It is also an organ that serves our vocation to holiness. The eye and that which it beholds figure prominently in Christianity's protological and eschatological narratives. In the first chapter of Genesis, God creates the heavens and the earth and saw that this was good (Gn 1), and God forms male and female in the divine image and likeness (Gn 1:26–27). "No one," God told Moses, "shall see me and live" (Ex 33:20), and yet one who sees Jesus Christ "sees him who sent me" (Jn 12:45). To see the glory of the Lord in a vulnerable infant or in a crucified king (Jn 19:21) requires the purification and schooling of the organ of sight. It requires learning to see sacramentally, with the eyes of the heart (Eph 1:18). The Roman Catholic Rite of Acceptance into the Order of Catechumens includes a signing of the eyes by the catechumen's sponsor or catechist as the celebrant prays, "Receive the sign of the cross on your eyes, that you may see the glory of God."[4] The predator eye can be transformed into an eye that beholds in awe the glory of the Lord.

This, mystics testify, is a vision of a glory so brilliant that it is experienced by finite, mortal human creatures as a kind of darkness. "What does it mean," probes Gregory of Nyssa (d. AD 394) in his *Life of Moses*, that "Moses entered the darkness and then saw God in it? For leaving behind everything that is observed, not only what sense comprehends but also what the intelligence thinks it sees, it keeps on penetrating deeper until by the intelligence's yearning for understanding it gains access to the invisible and the incomprehensible, and there it sees God. This is the true knowledge of what is sought; this is the seeing which consists in not seeing."[5]

The language of vision, writes theologian Hans Boersma, is uniquely suited to an account of our relationship with God, and *visio Dei* has been the privileged metaphor for our ultimate end throughout the

4. International Commission on English in the Liturgy, *Rite of Christian Initiation of Adults: Study Edition* (Chicago, Ill.: Liturgy Training Publications, 1988), 26.

5. Gregory of Nyssa, *The Life of Moses*, trans. A. J. Malherbe and E. Ferguson, The Classics of Western Spirituality (New York: Paulist Press, 1978), 94–95.

Christian tradition. This, he surmises, is because of the importance of light and vision in the eschatological narratives of Scripture, the priority of vision over other human senses, and vision's greater congruity vis-à-vis the other senses to the being of God.[6] As Dante Alighieri (d. AD 1321) ascends through the spheres of paradise, Boersma notes, words fail even this greatest of poets, who relies increasingly on vision. ("To soar beyond the human cannot be described/ in words."[7]) Vision, moreover, as understood by Augustine (d. AD 430) and others, is an active sense that unites the person seeing to the seen. When that which we behold is nothing less than the glory of God, vision can be transforming or, in Dante's terms, "transhumanizing."[8]

This ascent to a seeing that is not-seeing begins with our acts of perception of the tangible, material creation. In *On the Literal Meaning of Genesis,* Augustine articulated a trifold typology of vision that would prove influential for many centuries to come. *Visio corporalis,* or physical vision, Augustine wrote, is first in the order of human experience but last in theological significance, for the human organ of vision is inadequate to the knowledge of God. *Visio spiritualis,* or spiritual vision, is the perception of images acquired by physical vision that are held in the memory, and the use of reason and imagination to reconstruct these images with the inner eye. Through a disciplined process of purification, one can ascend to a *visio intellectualis* in which the highest faculty of the rational soul, created in the image of God, receives the illuminating grace of divine truth.[9] "Using the analogy of sight," explains historical theologian Carol Harrison, "the soul sees and knows by God's illumination, though Augustine some-

6. Hans Boersma, *Seeing God: The Beatific Vision in Christian Tradition* (Grand Rapids, Mich.: Eerdmans, 2018), 2–5.

7. "Trasumanar significar per verba non si poria." Dante Alighieri, *Paradiso,* trans. Jean Hollander and Robert Hollander, ed. Robert Hollander (New York: Doubleday, 2007), 1.70–72. Cited in Boersma, *Seeing God,* 221.

8. Boersma, *Seeing God,* 5, 219–53.

9. Augustine, *On Genesis,* vol. 1, bk. 13 in *The Works of Saint Augustine: A Translation for the 21st Century,*,ed. John E. Rotelle, trans. Edmund Hill (Hyde Park, N.Y.: New City Press, 2002), 464–65. See also Veerle Fraeters, "*Visio*/Vision," in *The Cambridge Companion to Christian Mysticism,* eds. Amy Hollywood and Patricia Z. Beckman (New York: Cambridge University Press, 2012), 178–79; Matthew Drever, *Image, Identity, and the Forming of the Augustinian Soul* (New York: Oxford University Press, 2013), 85–87.

times admits that this knowledge is more affective and sensual than rational and intellectual: 'What eye of the mind understands God? It is sufficient that, if the eye is pure, it touch Him. And if it touches, it touches with some sort of incorporeal and spiritual touch, but it does not understand' (*sermo* 117.5)."[10]

Both *what* we hold in our corporeal and spiritual eye and *how* we behold are important to the cultivation of a sacramental vision receptive to this illuminating grace. What and how we see are matters of visual culture, and the primary bearers of the visual culture of the Christian tradition are the sacraments themselves, visible and efficacious signs of the grace of Christ. Christian visual culture also includes church architecture and iconography, illuminated biblical manuscripts, family bibles placed in positions of prominence in living rooms, rosaries and scapulars, paintings, statues, liturgical vestments, monastic and religious habits, pilgrimage sites, relics, and public processions. These and other dimensions of Christian visual culture have a foundational role in shaping our imagination. I use the word "imagination" not to connote a realm of fantasy populated by the likes of Lewis Carroll's pocket-watch bearing rabbit but in the sense of theologian Francesca Aran Murphy, who writes of the "realistic imagination" that is both receptive and creative. The imagination encounters the world in all its particularities and from these realities creates metaphysically-significant patterns, forms, and narratives.[11] Philosopher Charles Taylor, in turn, speaks of the "social imaginary" as the way in which "people imagine social existence, how they fit together with others, how things go on between them and their fellows, the expectations that are normally met, and the normative notions and images that underlie these expectations."[12] Visual cultures contribute significantly to the imagination in the sense that this term is used by both Murphy and Taylor. In this chapter, I offer a very broad introduction to the important role of visual culture in Christianity and an intro-

10. Carol Harrison, "Spiritual Senses," in *Augustine through the Ages: An Encyclopedia*, ed. Allan D. Fitzgerald (Grand Rapids, Mich.: Eerdmans, 1999), 768.

11. Francesca Aran Murphy, *Christ the Form of Beauty: A Study in Theology and Literature* (Edinburgh: T & T Clark, 1995), 7–9.

12. Charles Taylor, *Modern Social Imaginaries* (Durham, N.C.: Duke University Press, 2004), 23.

duction to the visual culture of pornography.[13] I conclude with a brief reflection on some of the differences between the sacramental and pornographic gaze.[14]

Christian Visual Culture

In AD 26, Pontius Pilate, the newly appointed Roman procurator of Judea, moved his army from Caesarea to winter-quarters in Jerusalem. His troops carried a Roman standard—a pennant or flag on a pole—bearing an image of a bust of Caesar who as emperor was a focus of the imperial cult. Such standards were commonplace in Caesar's empire, but in the capital of Judea the Jews protested. They would die, they vowed, rather than transgress the law that proscribed graven images (Dt 4:15–18). According to the Jewish historian Josephus, Pilate removed the standards.[15]

It is within this context that Jesus Christ suffered under Pontius

13. The scholarly study of visual culture is an interdisciplinary reflection upon images, visual artifacts, and the practices and assumptions that shape acts of sight in their historical and cultural contexts. On the study of visual culture in the field of religion, see David Morgan, *The Sacred Gaze: Religious Visual Culture in Theory and Practice* (Berkeley, Calif.: University of California Press, 2005).

14. Following Morgan, I use the term "gaze" in a broad sense that connotes viewers, their context, and the relationship between the viewers and the person or thing that is seen, as distinct from the Lacanian use of the term to connote the power of a voyeur or a coercive or totalitarian authority. See Morgan, *Sacred Gaze*, 3.

15. "Pilate was sent by Tiberius to Judaea as procurator, and in a covert operation at night he smuggled into Jerusalem under wraps those portrait plaques of the emperor which are called standards. When day came, this excited a huge commotion among the Jews. The immediate onlookers were appalled to see what amounted to a heavy-footed desecration of their laws, which forbade the erection of any graven image in the city, and this fury in the town brought a whole crowd pouring from the countryside. They stormed off to confront Pilate in Caesarea, and begged him to remove the standards from Jerusalem and show respect for their traditions. When Pilate refused, they threw themselves face-down in a ring round his house, and stayed like that without moving for five days and nights. On the day after that Pilate took his seat on the platform in the great stadium and summoned the crowd as if he was ready to give them an answer. Instead he gave a prearranged signal for fully armed troops to surround the Jews, and they did so in a phalanx three ranks deep. The Jews were speechless with horror at this unimaginable sight, but Pilate told them that he would cut them all down if they did not accept the images of the emperor, and nodded to his soldiers to unsheathe their swords. At this, as if by tacit agreement, the entire body of Jews fell to their knees and bent their necks, shouting that they were ready to be killed rather than transgress their law. Utterly astonished at the sheer strength of their religious conviction, Pilate ordered the immediate removal of the standards from Jerusalem." Josephus, *The Jewish War*, trans. Martin Hammond (New York: Oxford University Press, 2017), 2.169–74 (pp. 108–9).

Pilate, was crucified, died, was buried, and was raised from the dead. Throughout the empire in which Christian faith would spread, images and statues of the Roman emperor and the Roman gods were commonplace in both public places and domestic households. The Roman people decorated these images with garlands, placed incense before them, carried them in processions, and entreated them with petitions for success in battle, healing from illness, and protection from famine. The images were believed to make present the powers of the gods they represented. Cyprian, bishop of Carthage (ca. AD 248–58), advised Christians to shield their line of vision from view of these images. Failing this, he prescribed tears of penitence for the cleansing of the eyes.[16]

"You shall not make for yourself an idol or a likeness of anything in the heavens above or on the earth below or in the waters beneath the earth," God enjoins the people Israel (Ex 20:4). Judaism is often said to be "aniconic," but it would be more precise, Steven Fine explains, to describe the Jewish tradition as "anti-idolic."[17] In fidelity to God, idolatry is fiercely resisted, but there is an appreciation in the Jewish tradition for the importance of visual culture. Ben Sirah extols the splendor of the garments of the high priest (Sir 45:6–13), Josephus describes the Temple as unsurpassed in its magnificence, and the scrolls of the Torah have an iconic place in synagogue worship.[18] In 1920, British archeologists discovered the remains of Dura-Europos, a settlement founded by the Seleucid dynasty in 303 BC high above the western bank of the Euphrates River in the region we know today as Syria.[19] Dura-Europos was razed by the Persians in AD 245, and the extraordinary remains unearthed between 1920–37 include a synagogue whose interior walls were covered from floor to ceiling with sophisticated visual compositions including scenes of the binding of Isaac, Moses at

16. "We should hear from the penitent frequent sighs, we should see once more faithful tears streaming from their eyes. In this way those very same eyes which have sinfully looked upon the heathen images may by their weeping make satisfaction to God and efface the crimes which they have unlawfully perpetrated." Cyprian, Epistle 31.7.1, in *Letters 28–54*, vol. 2 of *The Letters of St. Cyprian of Carthage*, trans. G. W. Clarke (New York: Newman Press, 1984), 38.

17. Steven Fine, *Art and Judaism in the Greco-Roman World: Toward a New Jewish Archaeology* (New York: Cambridge University Press, 2010), 69–70.

18. Fine, *Art and Judaism*, 65–69.

19. Clark Hopkins, *The Discovery of Dura-Europos* (New Haven, Conn.: Yale University Press, 1979).

the burning bush, the camp in the wilderness, Elijah on Mount Carmel, Ezekial and the dry bones, and scenes from other biblical narratives (Fig. 1-1). This archeological discovery has enabled scholarly reflection about the antecedents of this remarkable imagery and the liturgical and didactic purposes that it served.

The oldest surviving works of Christian imagery date to the beginning of the third century. During the reign of Emperor Commodus, who was more tolerant of Christianity than some of his predecessors, Christians acquired land outside the walls of the city of Rome to build an underground burial site, and they painted its subterranean walls with conventional images from Roman funerary art (flowers, fruits, birds), classical motifs imbued with Christian significance (such as a shepherd, a boat, an anchor, a praying figure, a banquet), and biblical scenes including Abraham's near-sacrifice of Isaac, Moses striking water from the rock, the baptism of Christ, the healing of the paralytic, and Jonah rising from the belly of the whale. In the catacombs and on stone coffins of this era, similar scenes reappear with a growing repertoire of images. Robin M. Jensen, a historian of both art and the Christian tradition, explains that these compositions are of a relatively low quality and style compared to Roman wall painting of this period, yet "these artworks demonstrate that Christians valued and used visual art, at least from the time that we may identify objects and spaces that were openly Christian-owned."[20]

Compelling evidence of this comes from the excavations at Dura-Europos, where archeologists unearthed just 200 meters from the mural-covered synagogue walls (Fig. 1-1) a Christian house church dated to AD 249 that was carefully moved to the Yale Art Gallery and there reconstructed.[21] The remains of the building suggest that integral to the experience of the sacrament of Christian initiation that once took place in its baptistery were visions of David and Goliath, Simon Peter walking on water, Jesus' healing of a paralytic, a shepherd caring for a large flock of sheep, and a procession of women (Fig. 1-2).[22] Stylistic similari-

20. Robin Margaret Jensen, *Face to Face: Portraits of the Divine in Early Christianity* (Minneapolis, Minn.: Fortress, 2005), 3.

21. Viewable on the website of the Yale University Art Gallery, accessed September 20, 2018, http://media.artgallery.yale.edu/duraeuropos/.

22. For a history of the interpretation of these images and original reflection, see

ties between the wall paintings of the Dura-Europos house church and the art of the catacombs, Jensen observes, suggest the emergence of a distinctive Christian iconography that may well have been supported by the circulation of books of patterns or artistic motifs.[23] The mood of this early Christian imagery, historical theologian Margaret R. Miles observes, "is consistently peaceful" despite the periodic persecutions of imperial Rome and the reality of martyrdom.[24]

In AD 312, just one year before the Edict of Milan (AD 313) granted freedom of worship to Christians, the first buildings designed expressly for Christian worship were built in Rome: San Crisogono and San Sebastiano, the latter constructed over the site venerated as the place of burial of Saints Peter and Paul. Emperor Constantine (d. AD 337) desired to unite the empire in the Christian religion, and his patronage supported multiple new church buildings. The exterior of these buildings had the common appearance of a typical Roman assembly hall; inside, however, Miles comments, "the eye was engaged and delighted wherever it rested."[25] Worshippers in these basilicas stood in the nave, whose strong longitudinal orientation focused their attention on the altar. In the light admitted by the basilica windows, one beheld paintings, sculptures, and mosaics with a wide range of styles, materials, subjects, and themes. Miles describes the Constantinian era as a time of "excitement with a *via universalis*, a way of salvation for all people," and this "could not have been more strongly and directly reflected and communicated than it was in the architecture, the images, and the statues of Constantinian churches."[26] Eusebius, bishop of Caesarea, described a new cathedral at Tyre in northern Palestine as "a marvel of beauty, utterly breathtaking."[27] For one who stands within, he continues, such is the perfection of the design and the beauty of the individual parts that "the evidence of our eyes makes instruction through

Michael Peppard, *The World's Oldest Church: Bible, Art, and Ritual at Dura-Europos, Syria* (New Haven, Conn.: Yale University Press, 2016).

23. Jensen, *Face to Face*, 20.

24. Margaret R. Miles, *Image as Insight: Visual Understanding in Western Christianity and Secular Culture* (Boston, Mass.: Beacon Press, 1985), 47.

25. Miles, *Image as Insight*, 51.

26. Miles, *Image as Insight*, 53.

27. Eusebius, *The History of the Church from Christ to Constantine*, trans. G. A. Williamson (Middlesex, England: Penguin, 1965), X, 4.58 (p. 397).

the ears unnecessary."[28] Within the basilicas, those under instruction in the Christian faith attended only the Mass of the Catechumens, which consisted of Scripture readings, prayers, and a homily. They then moved to a side room from which they could hear but not see the offertory and the consummation of the liturgy in the Eucharist. "To see, apparently," Miles comments, "was to participate in the mass; to hear without seeing was merely to be allowed to eavesdrop, to overhear. Visual participation made the difference between outsider and member."[29]

In her analysis, the contribution of visual culture to the life of the Christian community was manifold. Basilicas drew people to the Christian faith by visible splendor.[30] Christian iconography was influenced by Roman art and included motifs from Roman culture—like the vine tendrils of Dionysius engraved on a Eucharistic chalice—enabling the convert from the gods of Rome to find familiarity in this new visual culture but also to witness the trans-signification of recognizable images.[31] At a time when books were rare and illiteracy was common, imagery was also important to instruction and formation in the Christian faith. When Bishop Serenus cast out images from the churches of Marseilles, Pope Saint Gregory the Great (ca. AD 540–604) wrote to him explaining that although images are not to be adored, they are "made use of in churches for this reason: that such as are ignorant of letters may at least read by looking at the walls what they cannot read in books."[32] Even for the literate, visual culture had an important role in the formation of Christian character. Gregory of Nyssa, Miles notes, testified that "he could not contemplate a particular depiction of the sacrifice of Abraham without tears."[33]

28. Eusebius, *History of the Church*, X, 4.42 (p. 394).

29. Miles, *Image as Insight*, 51.

30. Miles, *Image as Insight*, 57.

31. Sometimes Roman images were used in a sense diametrically opposed to their original meaning. See André Grabar, *Christian Iconography: A Study of Its Origins* (Princeton, N.J.: Princeton University Press, 1968), xlviii–xlix.

32. Gregory the Great, "Epistle CV, To Serenus, Bishop of Massilia," in vol. 13 of *Nicene and Post-Nicene Fathers*, 2nd series, eds. Phillip Schaff and Henry Wace, trans. James Barmby (Grand Rapids, Mich.: Eerdmans, 1978), 23.

33. Gregory of Nyssa, "Oratio de deitate filii et spiritus sancti," in Patrologiae cursus completus, series graeca, ed. Jacques Paul Migne (Paris: Migne, 1857–66), 46:572. Cited in Miles, *Image as Insight*, 44.

In the East, icons emerged as a distinct form of Christian visual culture. Images of Christ, Mary, saints, and martyrs were typically painted on wooden boards and could also take the form of mosaics, frescos, embroidery, or metal work. Placed not only in churches but also in homes and public places, they became a cherished part of the expression and practice of Christian faith and worship. There are various theories as to why, after centuries of acceptance, icons became in eighth century Byzantium a point of tremendous contention. Why, queries Christoph Schönborn, did Emperor Leo II remove the image of Christ that had been mounted above the main entrance to the imperial palace in Constantinople in AD 726? After reviewing the extant textual evidence, Schönborn concludes that Leo II understood himself to be a reformer akin to King Hezekiah committed to the restoration of a pure religion cleansed of idolatry. The emperor interpreted a severe earthquake in AD 726 as a sign of divine disfavor with icon veneration, and he understood his post-iconoclasm military success against Arabian incursions as a sign of renewed divine approval.[34] In 731, Pope Gregory III convened a council that defended Christian iconography and condemned iconoclasm, resulting in a breach between Rome and Constantinople. Leo II was succeeded by his son Constantine V, who convened a council in Hiereia in 754 that strengthened iconoclastic theology and practice. Those monks who continued to paint icons and to encourage their veneration suffered persecution and even death, and iconoclasm prevailed in Byzantium until the deaths of both Constantine V and his own son Leo IV (775–80). Imperial policy was reversed by Leo's widow, the Empress Irene. In AD 787, a council in Nicaea restored icon veneration with the support of a theology that distinguished the honor (*proskynesis*) given to icons and the worship (*latreia*) due to God alone. The council also articulated a Christological defense of icons: the Word of God assumed a human nature, and it is therefore not idolatrous but imperative to portray Christ visibly with line and colors made from material pigments. Icons express that

34. Christoph Schönborn, *God's Human Face: The Christ-Icon*, trans. Lothar Krauth (San Francisco, Calif.: Ignatius Press, 1994), 141–45. See also Anthony Bryer and Judith Herrin, eds., *Iconoclasm* (Birmingham: University of Birmingham, 1997); Judith Herrin, *Byzantium: The Surprising Life of a Medieval Empire* (Princeton, N.J.: Princeton University Press, 2007).

"the incarnation of the Word is genuine and not illusory."[35] They are also an expression of the reality of grace and the baptismal vocation to deification. Icons, Orthodox theologian Silviu Bunta explains,

> point to the mystery of God in me, divinity in an earthen vessel, light in darkness, everything in nothing, sinlessness in sinfulness. This is why we Orthodox made the commemoration of the triumph of the icons "the Sunday of Orthodoxy." The mystery of the icon is the ultimate mystery of experience: Christ in me. I am nothing and yet God who is everything dwells in me. I am a handful of dirt and yet the One who is beyond everything has made me his dwelling.[36]

Today, writes Orthodox bishop and theologian Kallistos Ware, "an Orthodox act of liturgical prayer is unthinkable without the presence of icons."[37]

In Western Christianity as well rich forms of visual culture continued to develop. "In late medieval Italy," for example, Dianne Phillips explains, "increasing urbanization and the rise of a prosperous merchant class coincided with the success of the mendicant orders, resulting in an efflorescence of pictoral decoration in religious and secular buildings. Fruits of these phenomena include Giotto's fresco cycles in the Arena Chapel and at San Francesco in Assisi and Santa Croce in Florence."[38] The *Catholicon* by John of Genoa (d. ca. AD 1298), a widely used reference work, articulated three reasons for the importance of Christian imagery:

> *First*, for the instruction of simple people, because they are instructed by them as if by books. *Second*, so that the mystery of the incarnation and the examples of the Saints may be the more active in our memory through being presented daily to our eyes. *Third*, to excite feelings of devotion, these being aroused more effectively by things seen than by things heard.[39]

35. Council of Nicaea, cited in Kallistos Ware, "Eastern Christendom," in *The Oxford Illustrated History of Christianity*, ed. John McManners (New York: Oxford University Press, 1992), 143.

36. Correspondence with Silviu Bunta, December 17, 2019.

37. Ware, "Eastern Christendom," 143.

38. Correspondence with Dianne Phillips, October 30, 2018.

39. John of Genoa, *Catholicon* (Venice, 1497). Cited with translation in Michael Baxandall, *Painting and Experience in Fifteenth Century Italy: A Primer in the Social History of Pictorial Style*, 2nd ed. (Oxford: Oxford University Press, 1972), 41.

In a sermon published in AD 1492, Dominican Fra Michele da Carcano cited Genoa and emphasized that "many people cannot retain in their memories what they hear, but they do remember if they see images."[40] In the words of Bishop Durandus of Mende (AD 1237–96), paintings "move the mind more than descriptions; for deeds are placed before the eyes in paintings and thus appear to be actually carrying out. But in description, the deed is done as it were by hearsay, which affects the mind less when recalled to memory."[41] This thirteenth-century pedagogical observation is supported by what we are now learning from twenty-first century cognitive science about mirror neurons and visual imagery.[42]

The apex of the visual culture of the Catholic and Orthodox traditions is the Eucharistic liturgy. Those of us accustomed to viewing works of art in galleries may be inclined to think of an ornate church as a kind of religious museum, but the frescoes or icons in a church are not "art" in the way that modern museum visitors typically conceive of this. Rather, they are an integral dimension of the liturgical and sacramental space.[43] In the early centuries of Christianity in both East and West, Robin Jensen observes, the words of biblical narratives and the images of ecclesial iconography were a composite form of expression and neither was complete without the other.[44] In the medieval church, Miles emphasizes, visual imagery served together with vivid sermons, religious dramas, and popular devotions to place Catholics

40. Fra Michele de Carcano, "*Sermo XX, De adoratione*," in *Sermones quadragesimales fratris Michaelis de Mediolano de decem preceptis* (Venice, 1492). Cited with translation in Baxandall, *Painting and Experience*, 41.

41. Durandus of Mende, *Rationale divinorum officiorum*, 3.4. Cited with translation in Miles, *Image as Insight*, 66. See William Durand, "Rationale of the Divine Offices," in vol. 2 of *A Documentary History of Art*, ed. Elizabeth Gilmore Holt (New York: Doubleday, 1957), 123.

42. See chapter 3 of this volume by Wheaton College Professor of Psychology William M. Struthers and Kyler Mulhauser.

43. On the distinction between Christian imagery and "art," see Hans Belting, *Likeness and Presence: A History of the Image before the Era of Art*, trans. Edmund Jephcott (Chicago: University of Chicago Press, 1994). On the creation of the Louvre museum after the French Revolution as a repository for former church property, see Larry Shiner, *The Invention of Art: A Cultural History* (Chicago, Ill.: University of Chicago Press, 2001), 181. In this context, religious works become "art" that is "essentially purposeless and placeless." Shiner, *Invention of Art*, 182.

44. Robin Margaret Jensen, *The Substance of Things Seen: Art, Faith, and the Christian Community* (Grand Rapids, Mich.: Eerdmans, 2004), 50.

tangibly within the drama of creation, sin, and redemption. "The medieval worshipper became, through concentrated vision, present at the nativity, the crucifixion, the resurrection, and Last Judgment."[45]

In the analysis of Cambridge Lecturer Chloë Reddaway, this is also the case in the Brancacci Chapel in the Carmelite Church of Santa Maria del Carmine, where the three walls of the sanctuary bear early Italian Renaissance frescoes painted by Masolino da Panicale, Masaccio, and Filippino Lippi between AD 1424 and 1428. These frescoes incorporate the communicant into the visual drama of the history of salvation from creation, through the events recounted in the Gospels with particular attention to the life of Saint Peter, and then into the painters' contemporary period—evident in the appearance of two fashionable Florentine men who cross a piazza with their hands hidden in their fine clothes, oblivious to the healing of a cripple and the raising of Tabitha happening in their midst (Fig. 1-3).[46] The gate of paradise glimpsed in the fresco of the expulsion of Adam and Eve from Eden joins the actual wall of the chapel (Fig. 1-4), and the painters use space and focal points in such a way that the two-dimensional pictoral plane converges with the three dimensional space of the liturgical participant (Fig. 1-5). "Physically located in the chapel, the viewer interacts with the image and its setting, and may absorb the possibility of the divine activity in the image as real potential in his own, three dimensional, world."[47] In the baptismal scene, one neophyte trembles with cold while another kneels in the water, and "flesh is visibly being redeemed" (Fig. 1-6).[48] Akin to the frescoes in the Brancacci Chapel, the murals of Holy Trinity Episcopal Cathedral, painted in our own era in Port-au-Prince, Haiti, invite the liturgical participant to enter imaginatively into the full drama of creation, sin, and redemption (Fig. 1-7). It is within this vivid panorama that the muralists depict a

45. Miles, *Image as Insight*, 67.

46. Chloë Reddaway, "Reading Hermeneutic Space: Pictorial and Spiritual Transformation in the Brancacci Chapel," in *ReVisioning: Critical Methods of Seeing Christianity in the History of Art*, eds. James Romaine and Linda Stratford, 146–65 (Cambridge: Lutterworth Press, 2014).

47. Reddaway, "Reading Hermeneutic Space," 157.

48. Reddaway, "Reading Hermeneutic Space," 159. For a contemporary reinterpretation of the Brancacci Chapel murals by Billy Ray Sandusky, see http://sites.saintmarys.edu/~sandusky/brancacci.html, accessed October 30, 2018.

joyful and colorful Haitian interpretation of the Johannine narrative of the wedding feast in Cana (Fig. 1-8).

The visual culture of Christian liturgical space is inextricable from elements that engage all of the senses. In medieval Byzantium, for example, icons were venerated amidst wafts of fragrance and smoke from burning incense and the reverberation of music and prayer. "Touch, smell, taste, and sound were part of 'seeing' an *eikon*," explains Bissera Pentcheva, a scholar of art and aesthetics. "All five senses were engaged, leading to *synaesthesis*."[49] In many medieval Italian churches, the font in the baptistery and the pulpit in the corresponding cathedral had common stylistic and iconographic elements, suggestive of the inseparability of the iconography that is seen, the water that is touched, and the Word of God that is heard.[50] Indeed, Augustine describes a sacrament as a "visible word."[51]

Vision, nonetheless, was the dominant sense organ used by participants in the Catholic liturgy at the time of the Protestant Reformation. The priest prayed the Mass in hushed tones in the Latin language that few lay people could understand, and a high point of the liturgy was the priest's visually-evident elevation of the Eucharistic Host. In Germany, Martin Luther was concerned that visual imagery in churches could be a distraction from the words of the Gospel, and, in Switzerland, Ulrich Zwingli, a professed admirer of fine art, believed that the attraction of images was so powerful that they could draw attention away from worship. Between June 20 and July 2 of 1524, Zwingli led a committee that stripped every church in Zurich of paintings, standing altars, crucifixes, statues, and reliquaries and then whitewashed the walls. And yet such is the power of images that Luther urged the inclusion of printed images in the 1534 German Bible "for the sake of

49. Bissera V. Pentcheva, *The Sensual Icon: Space, Ritual, and the Senses in Byzantium* (University Park, Pa.: Pennsylvania State University Press, 2010), 1–2.

50. Nirit Ben-Aryeh Debby, *"Nel mio bel San Giovanni, fatti per loco de' battezzatori*: Baptismal Fonts in Tuscany," in *The Visual Culture of Baptism in the Middle Ages: Essays on Medieval Fonts, Settings and Beliefs*, eds. Harriet M. Sonne de Torrens and Miguel A. Torrens (Burlington, Vt.: Ashgate, 2013), 25–27.

51. Augustine, *Jo. ev. tr.*, 15.4. Cited in Emmanuel J. Cutrone, "Sacraments," in *Augustine through the Ages: An Encyclopedia*, ed. Allan D. Fitzgerald (Grand Rapids, Mich.: Eerdmans, 1999), 744.

remembrance and better understanding,"[52] and printed images have continued to play an important role in Protestant religious education and character formation.[53] Even John Calvin, whose war against the idols emphasized that God's transcendence and invisibility proscribed any use of human-made images in worship, believed that signs of the invisible can become manifest in "living icons or images of God" of which the Word of God is the soul and the Holy Spirit the illumination who gives us eyes to see. Whereas inert figures made by human hands idolatrously attempt to make God in our own finite image, Reformation scholar Randall Zachman explains, Calvin believed that the living images of God manifest in creation, the history of Israel, and the life of Christ and the Christian community "transform the person contemplating them into the image of God, from one degree of glory to another, so that we might become more and more like God in order to be united to God."[54]

In the 1550s, in the aftermath of the Protestant Reformation, German Catholicism was, according to European art historian Jeffrey Chipps Smith, a "dispirited shell of its pre-Reformation body."[55] The Society of Jesus, established in 1540, renewed Catholicism in the German provinces by teaching catechism classes for both children and adults, building schools and churches, establishing confraternities, preaching, sponsoring public plays and processions, and renewing visual culture. The Society of Jesus produced and commissioned prints, illustrations in books, paintings, sculptures, goldsmith works, and church architecture. Jesuits, including Ignatius of Loyola (ca. 1491–1556), Jerome Nadal (1507–80), Antoine Sucquet (1574–1627), and Louis Richeome (1544–1625), believed in the power of art to engage the senses, spirit, intellect, and memory. Hubert Gerhard's monumen-

52. Martin Luther, *Luther's Works* (Philadelphia, Penn.: Fortress, 1975), 40:99. Cited in Miles, *Image as Insight*, 115.

53. See, for example, David Morgan, *Protestants & Pictures: Religion, Visual Culture, and the Age of American Mass Production* (New York: Oxford University Press, 1999).

54. Randall C. Zachman, *Image and Word in the Theology of John Calvin* (Notre Dame, Ind.: University of Notre Dame Press, 2007), 8.

55. Jeffrey Chipps Smith, *Sensuous Worship: Jesuits and the Art of the Early Catholic Reformation in Germany* (Princeton, N.J.: Princeton University Press, 2002), 1.

tal bronze group *St. Michael Vanquishing Lucifer* on the facade of St. Michael's in Munich and other works sponsored by the Jesuits, Smith explains, are "inextricably bound to the idea of *Bildung*, or Christian formation. . . . This is a long-term process of forming the devout Christian who strives for union with God—which, according to Ignatius, should be the ultimate goal of all human beings."[56]

The chapters that follow in part 2 of this volume offer reflection on Christian visual culture in much greater depth and detail. The primary point of this introductory reflection is simply that visual culture is a fundamental dimension of Christian ecclesial life, worship, and formation in the baptismal vocation to holiness. Jews and Christians were willing to give their lives rather than honor images of emperors or pagan gods, and some did make this ultimate sacrifice. Iconoclasts objected to the inclusion of imagery in liturgical spaces not because they thought images were a waste of limited resources but because they recognized the power of images and the potential for idolatrous abuse. Images attract our attention, educate us, imprint themselves on our memories, serve as crystallizing points for our emotions, influence our wills, and shape our imaginations and desires. This is patently evident in our own media-saturated era. In the electronic digital culture of the twenty-first century in which we "speak in pictures,"[57] the question is not whether our memories, wills, and desires will be shaped by visual culture, but only what kind of images will form our imaginations.

The Visual Culture of Pornography

The Greek word "*porno-graphe*" comes from the terms *graphein* (writing) and *porneia*, which means unsanctioned sexual activity. The word "pornography" as the term is used today does not appear in an English dictionary until 1857. Nonetheless, images of nude figures and explicit sexual acts can be found in Paleolithic caves, ancient Egyptian papyri (1292–1075 BC), frescoes on the walls of the city of Pompeii, and other artefacts of ancient Greek and Rome.[58] Whether or not these images

56. Smith, *Sensuous Worship*, 7.

57. Chelsea Peitz, *Talking in Pictures: How Snapchat Changed Cameras, Communication, and Communities* (Chelsea Peitz, 2017).

58. Shira Tarrant, *The Pornography Industry* (New York: Oxford University Press, 2016).

would be classified as art or as pornography as defined in Catholic teaching is contingent on the intention and function of this imagery in its cultural context.

In Western European culture, the history of pornographic imagery parallels that of technological innovation. Within decades of Johannes Gutenberg's invention of the printing press in the fifteenth century, the imprints stamped out by the new presses included illustrated narratives that spanned the gamut from the erotic to the pornographic. This development, Miles comments in *Image as Insight*, should be understood in the context of the emergence of a market economy that moved the primary locus of economic production from the home into male guilds; in the context of the professionalization of medicine, including the dissection of human cadavers approached as material objects to be utilized for the production of anatomical drawings; in the context of the persecution of women alleged to be witches that reached its height between 1550 and 1650; and in the context of the Protestant Reformation.[59] Authors, most of whom remained anonymous, wrote to amuse, arouse, and intrigue. With the development of the steam-powered rotary printing press in 1843 came the soft-porn magazines popular between 1896 and 1955, including *Wink: A Whirl of Girls*, *Flirt: A FRESH Magazine*, and *Snappy*, typically sold under the counter.[60] Louis Daguerre's invention of still photography in 1839 enabled the production of pornographic daguerreotype images as early as 1846, and, seven years after Thomas Edison's invention of the movie camera in 1889, Eugène Pirou and Albert Kirchner produced the first pornographic movies.[61] The quality of photography and film continued to improve, and the first edition of *Playboy* magazine, published in 1953, combined articles and interviews with high resolution photographs of nude women in sexually evocative poses. *Penthouse* (1965) and *Hustler* (1979) followed, each vying for readership by breaking their predecessors' limits on the kind of images that appeared on the pages of these glossy magazines.[62]

59. Margaret R. Miles, *A Complex Delight: The Secularization of the Breast, 1350–1750* (Berkeley, Calif.: University of California Press, 2008), 87–129.

60. Tarrant, *Pornography Industry*, 16.

61. Tarrant, *Pornography Industry*, 16.

62. Tarrant, *Pornography Industry*, 18–20.

Videotapes (VHS) and digital video discs (DVDs) that could be played in one's home became a new medium for pornography in the 1980s and early 1990s. These continue to be a significant pornographic medium. Between 1986 and 1996, pornographic film rental revenues from video stores increased from $75 million to $665 million.[63] In 2005, over 950 million pornographic videos were rented in the United States. Today, the internet and portable electronic devices (laptops, smart phones, etc.) are the primary means of pornography distribution. The pornography industry not only employs communications technology but also drives the development of this technology with investment in improvements in bandwidth and screen resolution. Estimates of the portion of sites on the worldwide web that are pornographic range from 4 to 12 percent.[64] In 2011, the filtering software CYBERsitter blocked 2.5 million different websites with "adult" content.[65] Computational neuroscientists Ogi Ogas and Sai Gaddam wrote a program to catalog terms entered into search engines, which they ran from July 2009 to July 2010. Their study found that among 400 million terms or phrases entered into search engines, 55 million (approximately 13 percent) had sexual content. Although not all of this sexual content was pornographic, terms entered into search engines included "hot Latina ass," "bootylicious babes," "Asian sailor orgy," and "sexy guys with bubble butts."[66] Even if one is not intentionally seeking pornography online, it may pop-up uninvited. In a 2001 Kaiser Foundation survey, 70 percent of youth ages 15–17 who participated in the study reported that they had been exposed to online pornography unintentionally while using the internet for other purposes; 23 percent indicated that this happens often or somewhat often.[67] A study

63. Steven Stack, Ira Wasserman, and Roger Kern, "Adult Social Bonds and Use of Internet Pornography," *Social Science Quarterly* 85, no. 1 (2004): 75–88.

64. Barna Group, *The Porn Phenomenon: The Impact of Pornography in the Digital Age* (Ventura, Calif.: Barna Group, in partnership with Josh McDowell Ministry, 2016), 21.

65. Ogi Ogas and Sai Gaddam, *A Billion Wicked Thoughts: What the World's Largest Experiment Reveals about Human Desire* (New York: Dutton, an imprint of the Penguin Group, 2011), 8.

66. Ogas and Gaddam, *A Billion Wicked Thoughts*, 14.

67. Henry J. Kaiser Family Foundation, "Generation Rx.Com: How Young People Use the Internet for Health Information: A Kaiser Family Foundation Survey" (December 2001), 12, accessed September 20, 2018, https://kaiserfamilyfoundation.files.wordpress.com/2001/11/3202-genrx-report.pdf.

conducted in 2005 among youth ages 10–17 in the United States found that 42 percent of those who used the internet had seen online pornography within the past year, and 66 percent of these reported only unwanted exposure.[68] Today, it is harder to avoid pornography than it once was to acquire it.

Playboy recently announced that the corporation will no longer produce magazines with photos of nude women, as these are so readily available on the internet. Photos of scantily-clad women similar to those initially published in *Playboy* are now visible on the covers of magazines in racks adjacent to candy displays in grocery store checkout lines, and imagery that could be categorized as soft pornography is common in the advertising and television programming that shapes our culture and consciousness. In just one day, writer Gil Reavill recounts, his twelve-year-old daughter watched on television a sitcom intended for "tween" youth between the ages of nine and twelve in which seven-year-old girls practicing a cheerleading routine stick out and slap their buttocks like pole dancers while squealing, "Shake it, shake it, shake it." A commercial break in the program featured an advertisement for a movie in which a female porn star moves in next door to a teenage boy. Later in the day, the family went for a drive, and in the car Reavill's daughter sang together with the rapper, whose hit music had been downloaded onto her iBook, the lyrics: "I swear to f****n' God, Dude you f****n' rock! Please, Marshall, please, let me s*** your ****."[69] Reavill's experience is one manifestation of what Pamela Paul named the "pornification" of our culture in her book *Pornified* published in 2005.[70]

In the United States and other countries, pornography has become part of mainstream culture. Roxanne Qualls, editor-in-chief at Barna Group, publisher of the 2017 study *The Porn Phenomenon: The Impact of Pornography in the Digital Age*, comments: "One of the things that

68. Janas Wolak, Kimberly Mitchell, and David Finkelhor, "Unwanted and Wanted Exposure to Online Pornography in a National Sample of Youth Internet Users," *Pediatrics* 119, no. 2 (February 2007): 247.

69. Gil Reavill, *Smut: A Sex Industry Insider (and Concerned Father) Says Enough Is Enough* (New York: Sentinel, an imprint of the Penguin Group, 2005), 21–23.

70. Pamela Paul, *Pornified: How Pornography Is Transforming Our Lives, Our Relationships, and Our Families* (New York: Times Books, an imprint of Henry Holt, 2005).

we really noticed at Barna was the vast generational difference in terms of how people of the younger generation, especially teens and young adults, are viewing pornography.... We really saw an acceptance of it. Youth say: 'Not only is it not a bad thing to do but it is pretty much an accepted reality of our lives. We talk about it with our friends and we watch it. We just assume people are watching pornography.'"[71] Three-quarters of young men ages thirteen to twenty-four surveyed in the Barna study reported talking with their friends about pornography at least occasionally. Within this three-quarters, nine out of ten "say that how they talk about porn is encouraging, accepting, or neutral."[72]

Pornography production and distribution is a major commercial enterprise. In 2006, the pornography industry produced over 13,000 new videos—almost 26 times more than the 507 new Hollywood films released in 2005.[73] In 2007, *Bloomberg Businessweek* estimated global pornography revenues to be $10 billion, a reduction of 50 percent from prior years because of the availability of free pornography on "tube" sites supported by advertisements. Approximately half of this $10 billion was generated in U.S. sales.[74] Pornography producers hold trade shows and have trade magazines, just like producers of cars or home appliances. On cable television, pornography is broadcast by home entertainment companies, and each year there are "Adult Awards" for best producers, actors, and actresses modeled on the Oscars or the Golden Globes.[75] Retailers sell "Porn Star" or "Future Porn Star" T-shirts and jerseys,[76] and internet channels exist on which one can upload one's own homemade pornographic videos. Pornographic images are also routinely produced by owners of digital technology and sent through phones and social media. Qualls notes: "We are calling

71. Roxanne Qualls, Remarks at "Set Free Global Summit" (Greensboro, N.C., April 2016), accessed September 20, 2018, https://setfreesummit.org/monday/the- porn-phenomenon-david-kinnaman-roxanne-stone/.

72. Barna Group, *Porn Phenomenon*, 9.

73. Motion Picture Association of America 2010 and Adult Video News 2006, cited in Ana J. Bridges et al., "Aggression and Sexual Behavior in Best-Selling Pornography Videos: A Content Analysis Update," *Violence against Women* 16, no. 10 (2010): 1065.

74. Paul M. Barrett, "The New Republic of Porn," *Bloomberg Businessweek*, no. 4285 (June 21, 2012): 62.

75. Tarrant, *Pornography Industry*, 47.

76. See, for example, the website of Cafepress, accessed September 10, 2018, https://www.cafepress.com/+porn-star+gifts.

this porn 2.0 … It is porn that you have generated yourself. This is a real reality for teens and young adults. 60 percent of teens and young adults have received a nude image from a text and 40 percent have sent one. This is not some small sliver of the population. This is the majority of teens and young adults."[77]

What is the character of the pornography that is now so pervasive in our culture? There are two primary genres of commercially produced pornographic videos: "features" and "gonzo." Features are narratives filmed on elaborate sets with costumed performers in which pornographic scenes are part of a broader plot line. These productions may be parodies of TV shows or films, such as *Whore of the Rings* (a perversion of J. R. R. Tolkein's *Lord of the Rings*).[78] But most of the commercial pornography produced today is "gonzo porn." These films are very inexpensive to make as they consist simply of a pornographic scene. The majority of women who appear in these films are between the ages of eighteen and twenty-five, but there are films that feature women of all ages.[79] Ogas and Gaddam's study of one internet search engine found that one in six searches for sexual content included an age-related term, most commonly some form of the word "teen."[80]

"All pornography," the United States Conference of Catholic Bishops emphasizes in their pastoral statement "Create in Me a Clean Heart," exploits "both the persons portrayed and the viewer and is devoid of love and relationship."[81] Proponents of pornography argue that its production and sale provide employment for women that can enable them to earn a livelihood, support children, or finance a college education.[82] There is little scholarly study of persons em-

77. Qualls, Remarks at "Set Free Global Summit." See also Amanda Lenhart, "Teens and Sexting: How and Why Minor Teens Are Sending Sexually Suggestive Nude or Nearly Nude Images via Text Messaging" (Washington, D.C.: Pew Research Center, 2009), accessed October 20, 2018, http://www.pewinternet.org/2009/12/15/teens-and-sexting/.

78. Tarrant, *Pornography Industry*, 32.

79. Walter S. DeKeseredy and Marilyn Corsianos, *Violence against Women in Pornography* (New York: Routledge, an imprint of the Taylor & Francis Group, 2016), 12.

80. Ogas and Gaddam, *A Billion Wicked Thoughts*, 26.

81. United States Conference of Catholic Bishops, "Create in Me a Clean Heart: A Pastoral Response to Pornography" (Washington, D.C.: United States Conference of Catholic Bishops, 2015), 10.

82. See, for example, Melissa Monet, "Pornography Does Not Harm Those Involved in Its Production," in *Pornography: Opposing Viewpoints*, ed. Melissa Monet (San Diego, Calif.: Greenhaven Press, 2002), 63–69.

ployed in the pornography industry, but the few studies that do exist indicate that women who work as actresses are five times more likely than women in the general population to be survivors of domestic violence, three times more likely to have been abused as children, and five times more likely to have been in foster care.[83] A woman's entrée into this form of employment is often shaped by very limited opportunities and traumatic childhood experiences of violation or loss.[84] Moreover, the short-term limited income that a performer receives comes at the expense of human dignity and often at the expense of mental and physical health. April Garris took work first in a strip club and then in pornography production with the encouragement of her husband, who became her manager. "I saw myself as neither valuable nor loveable but as a commodity," she reflects.[85] She recalls ignoring her own emotions, joining the other performers who were smoking marijuana as they waited for their scene to start, and feeling as if she were a puppet. "Filming was a traumatic experience ... all the while acting like you are enjoying it and wanting more, more, more.... I had no control over my own body and I was slowly losing my grip on reality."[86] The objectification of the human person that is inherent in pornography production is verbally explicit in this photo caption in a men's magazine: "I think girls are like plasticine, if you warm them up you can do anything you want with them."[87]

While all pornography disorders human relationships, it is important to be aware, as "Create in Me a Clean Heart" observes, that "the kinds of content available today are becoming increasingly coarse, violent, degrading."[88] Violent and cruel imagery itself is not new. Feminist author Andrea Dworkin, a leading voice against pornography in

83. Corita R. Grudzen et al., "Comparison of the Mental Health of Female Adult Performers and Other Young Women in California," *Psychiatric Services* 62, no. 6 (2011): 639–45.

84. DeKeseredy and Corsianos, *Violence against Women*, 71.

85. April Garris, "Beauty for Ashes," in *Delivered: True Stories of Men and Women Who Turned from Porn to Purity*, ed. Matt Fradd (San Diego, Calif.: Catholic Answers Press, 2013), 64.

86. Garris, "Beauty for Ashes," 65.

87. This and other examples of photo captions can be found in Matt Fradd, *The Porn Myth: Exposing the Reality behind the Fantasy of Pornography* (San Francisco, Calif.: Ignatius Press, 2017), 56.

88. United States Conference of Catholic Bishops, "Create in Me a Clean Heart," 10.

the 1980s, described pornography as a form of male power over women, and the evidence she offered to support this position includes a magazine photograph that she described as follows:

> The photography is captioned "BEAVER HUNTERS." Two white men, dressed as hunters, sit in a black Jeep. The Jeep occupies almost the whole frame of the picture. The two men carry rifles. The rifles extend above the frame of the photograph into the white space surrounding it. The men and the Jeep face into the camera. Tied onto the hood of the black Jeep is a white woman. She is tied with thick rope. She is spread-eagle. Her pubic hair and crotch are the dead center of the car hood and the photograph. Her head is turned to one side, tied down by rope that is pulled taut across her neck, extended to and wrapped several times around her wrists, tied around the rearview mirrors of the Jeep, brought back around her arms, crisscrossed under her breasts and over her thighs, drawn down and wrapped around the bumper of the Jeep, tied around her ankles.... The text under the photograph reads: "Western sportsmen report beaver hunting was particularly good throughout the Rocky Mountain region during the past season. These two hunters easily bagged their limit in the high country. They told HUSTLER that they stuffed and mounted their trophy as soon as they got her home."[89]

It is hard to imagine an image more degrading than this scene, yet, in the internet age, pornography has become even more transgressive.

Erica Scharrer, professor of communication at the University of Massachusetts at Amherst, spoke at the "Seeing with the Eyes of the Heart" conference about research she conducted with four colleagues to systematically document content patterns in popular twenty-first century pornographic videos with particular attention to aggression.[90] The research team of which Scharrer was part randomly selected 50 videos from films named between December 2004 and June 2005 in the top 30 of Adult Video News' monthly list of the 250 best-selling and most rented videos. These popular films had titles such as *Teen*

89. Andrea Dworkin, *Pornography: Men Possessing Women* (New York: Perigee Books, an imprint of G. P. Putnam's Sons, 1981), 25–26. That this kind of image was not an aberration is evident in Diana Russell's descriptions of cartoons found in pornography magazines published in the 1970s and 1980s. Diana E. H. Russell, *Dangerous Relationships: Pornography, Misogyny, and Rape* (Thousand Oaks, Calif.: SAGE Publications, 1998), 37–110.

90. Bridges et al., "Aggression and Sexual Behavior in Best-Selling Pornography Videos," 1065–85.

*F*** Holes*, *New Whores*, and *I'm Your Slut #3*. The scholarly team developed a methodology to code acts of physical or verbal aggression and trained coders to use this methodology with consistency. Their findings: 88.8 percent of the scenes in the films they analyzed included aggressive actions. In fifty films, there were a total of 3,375 acts of physical or verbal aggression (an average of 67.5 acts of aggression per film). The most common acts of physical aggression were spanking (which occurred 980 times), gagging (759 times), and open-hand slapping (408 times). Other acts of physical aggression included hair-pulling (276 times), choking (184 times), and holding someone in bondage or confinement (30 times). There were 632 acts of verbal aggression recorded, including insults, threats, and coercive language. Name calling (e.g., "bitch," "slut") comprised 97.2 percent of the acts of verbal aggression. Of all aggressive acts, 94.4 percent were directed toward women and 5.2 percent were directed toward men; 69.2 percent were perpetrated by men and 29.4 percent by women. In the films, 41.1 percent of the scenes include a sequence in which a man removes his male organ from a woman's rectum and then puts it uncleansed into her mouth. In 18.1 percent of the scenes, a woman is penetrated vaginally and anally by two men simultaneously. It is significant that 95.1 percent of the targets of aggression in the films responded with expressions of neutrality or pleasure to name-calling, gagging, choking, and other degrading and cruel acts, and that women were more likely to express pleasure when aggressed against than were men.[91] Pornography of this genre simultaneously eroticizes aggression and veils the pain and suffering inherent in the film's production.

Today the primary source of pornographic films is not DVD purchase or rental but the internet, and a 2018 study of the content of the most watched videos on the popular website PornHub also found high rates of explicit aggression. Using a coding methodology similar to that employed by Scharrer and her colleagues, Eran Shor and her research team found that 43 percent of the popular videos that they analyzed included visible acts of aggression. Some conveyed aggression in their very titles: for example, "Gigantic C*** Rips Skinny Bitch"

91. Bridges et al., "Aggression and Sexual Behavior in Best-Selling Pornography Videos," 1077.

and "Teeny Booper [sic] Kidnapped by Huge Black C***."[92] Among the significant contributions of Shor's research project are her findings on the portrayal of teenagers. The study found that films featuring female teenagers were about three times more likely to bear a title that suggests aggression than videos with adult female performers.[93] And, although the number of actual acts of aggression perpetrated against female teenage performers was comparable to the number of acts of aggression perpetrated against adult female performers, teenage female performers were more likely to suffer from some particular kinds of aggressive and degrading acts. "When compared with adult performers, teenage performers were more than twice (21.82 vs. 9.40%) as likely to be featured in videos featuring anal penetration, and about five times (12.73 vs. 2.56%) more likely to take part in videos featuring forceful anal penetration (with an apparent intent to cause pain). In addition, teenage performers were more likely than their adult counterparts to be part of videos in which the male performer ejaculated in their mouth or on their face (65.45 vs. 45.30%)."[94] And, as in the films studied by Scharrer and her colleagues, female performers commonly feigned pleasure or even sexual climax in aggressive scenes. Shor found that "90% of the teenage women in videos containing visible aggression displayed pleasure, compared with 54.29% when visible aggression was not present. Similarly, teenage performers displayed a sexual climax in 40.00% of the videos containing aggression in which they were featured, compared with 8.57% when visible aggression was not present."[95] The acts in aggressive scenes in which teenage female performers displayed pleasure included spanking, forceful vaginal or anal penetration, and gagging.[96]

Why is overt physical and verbal aggression so common in popular films? One explanation is that, in a market flooded with pornography, producers are vying for customers by making videos that depict what has not been seen before. At the same time, persons who have

92. Eran Shor, "Age, Aggression, and Pleasure in Popular Online Pornographic Videos," *Violence against Women* 25, no. 8 (2019): 1024.

93. Shor, "Age, Aggression, and Pleasure," 1025.

94. Shor, "Age, Aggression, and Pleasure," 1024–25.

95. Shor, "Age, Aggression, and Pleasure," 1027.

96. Shor, "Age, Aggression, and Pleasure," 1027.

viewed a lot of pornography can become desensitized to sexual scenes they have seen repeatedly and may seek out the novelty of ever-more transgressive forms.[97] "So many fans," one pornography director explains, "want to see so much more extreme stuff that I'm always trying to figure out ways to do something different. But it seems everybody wants to see a girl doing d.p. [double penetration] now or a gangbang."[98] Another pornography director describes the aggression in popular videos as a form of men "getting even" with women they desire but "cannot have."[99] Robert Jensen, professor emeritus in the School of Journalism at the University of Texas at Austin, offers another explanation: pornography and the other hyper-mediated experiences of our culture do not meet our deepest human needs, and pornography becomes more and more degrading in order to obscure this banality with cruelty.[100]

The Barna Group study *The Porn Phenomenon* found both an acceptance of pornography among large sectors of the U.S. population and a large majority of persons who believe that pornography is unethical if it portrays persons in a demeaning way or includes sexual acts that are forced or painful.[101] Why, then, are videos with high lev-

97. Sociologist and anti-pornography advocate Gail Dines writes: "Some of the worst stories I hear are from men who have become so desensitized that they have started using harder porn and end up masturbating to images that previously disgusted them. Many of these men are deeply ashamed and frightened and they don't know where it will all end. Phil told me, 'Sometimes I can't believe the porn I like. I feel like a freak,' and Anthony sees it as a 'slippery slope I never thought I would slide down. I never thought of myself as a guy who would like the really hard-core porn, but that's what happened to me.' Some speak of moving toward more violent images while others have become increasingly interested in bondage and even child porn." Gail Dines, *Pornland: How Porn Has Hijacked Our Sexuality* (Boston, Mass.: Beacon, 2010), 93–94.

98. Porn director, cited in Robert Jensen, *Getting Off: Pornography and the End of Masculinity* (Cambridge, Mass.: South End Press, 2007), 70. "Double penetration" is simultaneous vaginal and anal penetration by two men of one woman. "Gangbang" is slang for penetration by multiple men.

99. "I'd like to bring even more violence into my creations. I'd like to bring what I call erotic terror: the stabbing in the shower in *Psycho*, the ax murder in *Dementia 13*. I'd like to really show what I believe the men want to see: violence against women. I firmly believe that we serve a purpose by showing that. The most violent we can get is the cum shot in the face. Men get off behind that, because they get even with women they can't have." Cited in R. J. Stroller and I. S. Levine, *Coming Attractions: The Making of an X-Rated Video* (New Haven, Conn.: Yale University Press, 2007), 22.

100. Robert Jensen, statement in Barna Group, *Porn Phenomenon*, 104–5.

101. Barna Group, *Porn Phenomenon*, 70–71, 104.

els of aggression at the top of the popularity charts? This may mean, Jensen comments, that even those who view this kind of pornography recognize that it violates their own moral principles of respect, dignity, and equality.[102] The National Center on Sexual Exploitation emphasizes the need for education:

> We especially want people who watch pornography to know that the images they are watching are, very often, acts of real abuse against real women.... We want people to know that many women in pornography come from broken backgrounds and their tragic experiences have been used against them, conditioning them to accept abuse for the entertainment and enjoyment of the viewer. When people become educated about the multifaceted harms of pornography and about how their own pornography use is a form of participation in sexual exploitation, some start to care. The abuse and degradation inherent in all pornography, when addressed in the light of day, ignites a sense of compassion and urgency in people who do not want to stand by while others suffer.[103]

In 2016, the National Center on Sexual Exploitation (NCOSE) appealed to the United Nations Special Rapporteur on Torture to recognize the production of hardcore pornography as a form of the torture of human beings.[104]

In a time such as ours when blatant manifestations of prejudice and discrimination against people of color have led to the establishment of an ad hoc United States Conference of Catholic Bishops committee to address the sin of racism, it is also important to emphasize that the visual culture of pornography commonly includes racialized scenes.[105] For example, a genre of "Interracial" films marketed to white men features a black male "doing just about everything that can be done to a white woman's body," perpetuating myths about black

102. Robert Jensen, statement in Barna Group, *Porn Phenomenon*, 104.

103. National Center on Sexual Exploitation, statement in Barna Group, *Porn Phenomenon*, 103.

104. Haley Halverson, "Report: The Gender-Based Torture Found in the Pornography Industry" (Washington, D.C.: The National Center on Sexual Exploitation, 2016), accessed September 20, 2018, http://endsexualexploitation.org/wp-content/uploads/NCOSE_Report_UN_Final.pdf.

105. United States Conference of Catholic Bishops News Release, "U.S. Bishops Establish New Ad Hoc Committee against Racism" (Washington, D.C.: United States Conference of Catholic Bishops, August 23, 2017), accessed September 20, 2018, http://www.usccb.org/news/2017/17-149.cfm.

male sexual desire for white women, which were among the justifications given for the lynching of African American men in the United States.[106] Racialized films include *Black Bros and White Ho's* ["Ho" is slang for "hooker"] and *Blacks on Blondes*, in which a caged white man watches black men have intercourse with his wife.[107] Black men are often cast as drug dealers or criminals, perpetuating unjust cultural stereotypes.[108] There are also genres of pornography that perpetuate the stereotyped racialization of Latinas, Asians, and persons of other ethnicities. That this kind of pornography can contribute to racialized stereotyping and crime is evident in the case of a Native American woman who was raped at a highway rest stop by white male motorists who enacted a scene from a pornographic video game that caricatured General Custer.[109]

The harm perpetuated by pornography production wounds also pornography users. As chapters 2 and 3 will explain, a growing body of personal testimonies and peer-review scholarly research documents the harm that pornography may cause both female and male viewers. Of special concern is the influence of pornography on youth who are coming to maturity and forming their sexual mores in a context in which pornography is widely used as a means of sexual education or entertainment.[110] The National Center on Sexual Exploitation (NCOSE) explains: "Children are at greatest risk as research shows such exposure affects their developing brains and shapes their sexual templates. The younger and more often children are exposed to such content the more problematic it becomes." [111] Not all youth or adults exposed to

106. Gail Dines, *Pornland*, 136.

107. DeKeseredy and Corsianos, *Violence against Women*, 19.

108. Barna Group, *Porn Phenomenon*, 92–93.

109. Carole Lafavor, "Testimony XXX," in *In Harm's Way: The Pornography Civil Rights Hearings*, ed. Catharine A. MacKinnon and Andrea Dworkin (Cambridge, Mass.: Harvard University Press, 1997), 147–49. The name of the video game cited in the hearings is "Custer's Last Stand," although I suspect in fact the game's precise title was "Custer's Revenge," released in 1982.

110. On some of the effects on youth, see United States Conference of Catholic Bishops, "Create in Me a Clean Heart," 13–14; Mary Eberstadt and Mary Anne Layden, *The Social Costs of Pornography: A Statement of Findings and Recommendations* (Princeton, N.J.: The Witherspoon Institute, 2010), 27–32.

111. National Center on Sexual Exploitation (NCOSE), introduction to "Pornography: A Public Health Crisis. A Collection of Papers from Symposium Held at the U.S. Capitol on July 14, 2015" (Washington, D.C.: National Center on Sexual Exploitation,

pornography, NCOSE continues, have the same response. But pornography viewing can become compulsive, particularly among adolescents "who are more susceptible to forming addictions than adults because the dopamine neurons in their nucleus accumbens (i.e. the brain's pleasure center) are much more active and have an exaggerated plasticity in response to addictive stimulus."[112] There are studies that correlate pornography consumption with increased incidence of sexual promiscuity, STIs (sexually transmitted infections), negative body image, substance abuse, erectile dysfunction, failed relationships or divorce, and aggression and violence.[113] At the time of this writing, the legislatures of fifteen states of the union—Arkansas, Arizona, Florida, Idaho, Kansas, Kentucky, Louisiana, Missouri, Montana, Oklahoma, Pennsylvania, South Dakota, Tennessee, Utah, and Virginia—have passed resolutions that name pornography a threat to public health.[114] The Arkansas House of Representatives resolution, for example, highlights the relationship of pornography to the hyper-sexualization of prepubescent children and youth; low self-esteem and body image disorders; addictive behaviors; the normalization of sexual violence and the abuse of women and children; an increase in the demand for prostitution and sexual trafficking and sexual slavery; greater dissatisfaction with marriage; an increased incidence of marital infidelity; and a reduction in the desire to marry. The Arkansas legislature resolved that the state must recognize "the public health crisis created by pornography and the sexually toxic environment it perpetuates and acknowledge the need for education, prevention, research, and policy change at the community and societal levels in order to address the

---

2015), accessed September 20, 2018, https://endsexualexploitation.org/publichealth/#problem.

112. NCOSE, introduction to "Pornography: A Public Health Crisis."

113. NCOSE, introduction to "Pornography: A Public Health Crisis." See also NCOSE, "Pornography & Public Health: Research Summary," NCOSE website, September 8, 2016, accessed September 20, 2018, https://endsexualexploitation.org/wp-content/uploads/NCOSE_PornographyPH_RESEARCH-SUMMARY_9-8-16.pdf.

114. Fight the New Drug, "These Sixteen States Passed Resolutions Recognizing Porn as a Public Health Issue," Fight the New Drug website, May 9, 2019, accessed December 14, 2019, https://fightthenewdrug.org/here-are-the-states-that-have-passed-resolutions/ ; Eli Meixler, "Florida's House of Representatives Just Declared Pornography a Health Risk," *Time.com* (February 21, 2018), accessed September 20, 2018, http://time.com/5167792/florida-house-pornography-health-risk/.

epidemic that is harming the people of our state and our country as a whole."[115] The character of resolutions approved in other states is similar, and a number of these measures passed unanimously or with the support of an overwhelming majority of the legislative body.[116]

The Sacramental and Pornographic Gaze

Visual culture is a matter of both what we see and also *how* we see, the context in which we see, and the way in which we frame and interpret what we see. Jean-Luc Marion reflects that the same *signa* of the divine can be approached either as an idol or an icon, and so too there are works of Christian art that are susceptible to both pornographic and sacramental modes of vision.[117] There are, for example, Baroque paintings of barely clad female saints being tortured that may evoke an objectifying pornographic gaze, and Renaissance pastors preached to laywomen that paintings of the nude St. Sebastian pierced by arrows should not become an occasion for lascivious desire.[118] Although the fundamental difference between the sacramental and pornographic gaze is self-evident, I conclude this introductory chapter by articulating a few of the qualities that distinguish these two forms of vision in order to emphasize that visual culture is not only a matter of what we behold but also the manner in which we see.

Clearly, the difference between viewing pornography and viewing

115. State of Arkansas, 91st General Assembly, "House Resolution 1042: Recognizing and Finding that the Proliferation and Accessibility of Pornography Has Created a Public Health Crisis Leading to a Broad Spectrum of Individual and Public Health Impacts and Societal Harms," Regular Session 2017, accessed September 20, 2018, http://www.arkleg.state.ar.us/assembly/2017/2017R/Bills/HR1042.pdf.

116. Gary Herbert, "Governor Signs Anti-Pornography Bills Declaring Public Health Crisis," website of Utah Governor Gary Herbert, April 19, 2016, accessed October 20, 2018, https://governor.utah.gov/2016/04/20/governor-signs-anti-pornography-bills-declaring-public-health-crisis/; NCOSE, "South Dakota Unanimously Declared Pornography a Public Health Crisis," NCOSE website, February 2, 2017, accessed October 20, 2018, https://endsexualexploitation.org/articles/south-dakota-unanimously-declared-pornography-public-health-crisis/; NCOSE, "Tennessee Just Officially Recognized Pornography as a Public Health Crisis," NCOSE website, June 21, 2017, accessed October 20, 2018, https://endsexualexploitation.org/articles/the-governor-of- tennessee-just-officially-declared-pornography-a-public-health-crisis/.

117. Jean-Luc Marion, *God without Being: Hors-Texte*, trans. Thomas A. Carlson (Chicago, Ill.: University of Chicago Press, 1991), 8.

118. Correspondence with Dianne Phillips, October 30, 2018.

Christian iconography is not that pornography portrays nudity while Christian iconography does not.[119] In a mid-fourth century sarcophagus, a small, nude male child stands at the feet of Christ. This, Robin Jensen explains, is almost certainly a depiction of the resurrected Lazarus restored to childlike innocence. "Lazarus," she comments, "is nude, not only because he has lost his linen burial clothes but also because he has been reborn. In this respect he appears like Jesus, also shown as a small nude child at his baptism in early Christian art."[120] In early Christianity, adult catechumens entered the waters of the baptismal font unclothed. "Immediately, then," Bishop Cyril of Jerusalem says to the recently initiated, "upon entering, you removed your tunics. This was a figure of the 'stripping off of the old man with his deeds' (Col 3:9). Having stripped, you were naked, in this also imitating Christ, who was naked on the cross."[121] In a font that symbolizes both tomb and womb, the initiand dies to sin and becomes a new creation. "As 'partakers of Christ' (Heb 3.14)," Cyril says to the baptizands after their entire bodies have been anointed with holy chrism, "therefore, you are rightly called 'Christs,' i.e. 'anointed ones': it was of you that God said: 'Touch not my Christs.'"[122]

The sacrament of baptism is a visible and efficacious sign of a Christic grace that transcends the capacity of our human organs of perception. The screen on which I behold a pornographic image also veils an invisible reality, but this veiled reality is not an invisible grace, and herein is one of the many fundamental differences between the pornographic and sacramental gaze. Invisible beyond the pixels of a computer or phone screen is the reality of women whose employment in the pornography industry was in many cases preceded by childhood sexual abuse, financial desperation, and the false promises of the agents

119. See, for example, David Clayton, "What Is the Place of the Nude in Sacred Art?" in *The Beauty of God's House: Essays in Honor of Stratford Caldecott*, ed. Francesca Aran Murphy (Eugene, Ore.: Cascade Books, an imprint of Wipf and Stock, 2014), 232–54.

120. Robin Margaret Jensen, *Baptismal Imagery in Early Christianity: Ritual, Visual, and Theological Dimensions* (Grand Rapids, Mich.: Baker Academic, 2012), 152.

121. Cyril of Jerusalem, "The Mystagogical Lectures," vol. 2 of *The Works of Saint Cyril of Jerusalem*, trans. Leo P. McCauley and Anthony A. Stephenson, Fathers of the Church 64 (Washington, D.C.: The Catholic University of America Press, 1970), lecture 2, para. 2, p. 161.

122. Cyril of Jerusalem, "The Mystagogical Lectures," lecture 3, para. 1, p. 168.

who recruited them; this may well also be true of male actors, although emphasis in the extant literature is on the female actresses.[123] Invisible also is the reality of alcohol and drugs like Ecstasy, Cocaine, Marijuana, Xanax, Valium, and Vicodin consumed on production sets to enable actresses and actors to endure their objectification.[124] And, behind the visible expressions of neutrality or even pleasure that appear on the faces of actresses, there is in many cases the reality that the performers are in physical, emotional, mental, and spiritual pain. "When I was finished with the scene," Rachel testifies, "my throat was bleeding, I had bruises all over my body, my vagina was torn in two places, and I ended up with pink eye. I felt so weak, used, and honestly I felt like I had been raped all over again."[125] Corina describes a scene in which "the pain became too much and I was in shock and my body went limp."[126]

The sacramental gaze and pornographic gaze differ not only in the realities veiled from direct view, but also in the relationship the gaze establishes between the viewer and a vulnerable human person. In 1972, the Catholic Church restored the Rite of Christian Initiation of Adults and renewed the practice of baptism by full immersion at the Easter Vigil. Adults today are baptized clothed with a brown garment, but the baptizands still appear before the congregation in a state of vulnerability, publicly witnessing to the reality of sin and mortality and our need for grace and redemption. In this vulnerability, the baptizands follow the example of the Word of God become incarnate who knew hunger, thirst, and temptation and then suffered and died on a cross. "He suffered in actual fact," Cyril reminds the newly baptized,

123. See, for example, the story of "Victoria" (pseud.) in Barna Group, *Porn Phenomenon*, 102–3.

124. Jersey states: "You get ripped. Your insides can come out of you. It's never ending. You're viewed as an object and not as a human with a spirit. People don't care. People do drugs because they can't deal with the way they are being treated." Cited in Haley Halverson, "Report: The Gender-Based Torture Found in the Pornography Industry."

125. Cited in Haley Halverson, "Report: The Gender-Based Torture Found in the Pornography Industry."

126. Cited in Haley Halverson, "Report: The Gender-Based Torture Found in the Pornography Industry." For some additional testimonies, see Fight the New Drug, "10 Ex-Porn Performers Reveal the Brutal Truth behind Their Most Popular Scenes," Fight the New Drug website, September 3, 2019, accessed December 14, 2019, https://fightthenewdrug.org/10-porn-stars-speak-openly-about-their-most-popular-scenes/.

"and not in mere seeming."[127] After the catechumens die with Christ and are reborn in the waters of baptism, the entire congregation renews their baptismal vows, voicing words that engage us as participants in this public liturgical action.

The pornographic gaze also beholds persons who have allowed their human vulnerability to be made public. However, as a viewer of pornography, I am not a participant in this vulnerability but a voyeur. I behold the vulnerability of other human beings from a protected and private vantage-point. On the viewer's side of the screen, philosopher Roger Scruton reflects, there is no personal subject who could extend love to another "since there is nothing ventured of the self." Pornography is a depersonalizing habit that can harm, as psychologists and psychotherapists are discovering, not only relationships and marriages but even "the very capacity to engage in them."[128] From my side of a computer screen, I can neither give nor receive love. Iconic vision, in contrast, Jean-Luc Marion elucidates, is not only a manner of seeing but also the grace of being mercifully seen. In Nicholas of Cusa's *De visione Dei sive de Icona*, Marion explains, *visio Dei* means both "to see God" *and* "God sees."[129] Cusa prays: "Your face is turned to all faces which look on you. . . . Whoever looks on you with a loving face will find only your face looking on oneself with love."[130]

The sacraments of baptism and Eucharist anticipate that day-beyond-days when we "will obtain the freedom of the glory of the children of God" (Rom 8:21). Pornography, in contrast, can impair the capacity for free moral action that is one dimension of our creation in the divine image and likeness (Gn 1:26–27) and one of the characteristics that distinguish humans from other animals. As chapters 2 and 3 explain, pornographic images are supranormal stimuli that affect the brain in a manner similar to the way substances create chemical depen-

127. Cyril of Jerusalem, "The Mystagogical Lectures," lecture 2, para. 7, p. 167.

128. Roger Scruton, "The Abuse of Sex," in *The Social Costs of Pornography*, ed. James R. Stoner Jr. and Donna M. Hughes (Princeton, N.J.: The Witherspoon Institute, 2010), 124.

129. Jean-Luc Marion, "Seeing, or Seeing Oneself Seen: Nicholas of Cusa's Contribution in *De visione Dei*," trans. Stephen E. Lewis, *Journal of Religion* 96, no. 3 (2016): 313–16.

130. Nicholas of Cusa, *De visione Dei*, VI: 19, 21. Cited in Marion, "Seeing, or Seeing Oneself Seen," 316.

dencies; viewing pornography thus may be not only habit-forming but can also become impulsive, compulsive, or addictive.[131] The sacramental life also forms habitual patterns of action but in a fundamentally different way. Sacramental life requires *askesis*—a discipline and training—that strengthens the will to cooperate freely with the grace of the Holy Spirit in virtuous action. *Askesis* practiced in the context of the sacramental life does not repress eros but purifies and intensifies desire in the fire of God's love through a *via purgative* that shapes human desires in conformity with the desire of God.[132] "Or," writes Anglican theologian Sarah Coakley, "to put it in the language of Pauline theology, it is the same Spirit that inflames the heart with love (Rom 5:5), who also imparts the (much neglected) 'gift' of 'self-control' (Gal 5:23). Here lies the crucial difference between authentic, Spirit-endowed union

131. There is discussion as to whether or not habitual internet pornography viewing is one of the behaviors that can be medically classified as an addiction. The American Psychiatric Association's 2013 edition of the Diagnostic and Statistical Manual (DSM) renamed the prior edition's chapter on "Substance Related Disorders" with the title "Substance Use and Addictive Disorders" and added a subsection on gambling behavior. The DSM also called for further study of Internet Gaming Disorder (IGD), noting that internet gaming "prompts a neurological response that influences feelings of pleasure and reward," which, in the extreme, results in addictive behavior. The DSM, however, states that other internet practices such as excessive use of social media or pornography are not analogous to IGD and called for additional research on internet-related behaviors. In a 2014 "Current Controversies" section of the journal *Current Sexual Health Reports*, David Ley, Nicole Prause, and Peter Finn note the exclusion of internet pornography from the DSM's discussion of addictive behavior and conclude that the extant empirical evidence does not support the use of an addiction model to describe high-frequency use of visual sexual stimuli. In contrast, Todd Love, Christian Laier, Matthais Brand, Linda Hatch, and Raju Hajela conclude after their review of a large body of literature on internet pornography and impulsive, compulsive, out of control, and hypersexual behavior that the evidence does indeed support the classification of internet pornography consumption as a potentially addictive behavior that should be recognized as such in future editions of the DSM. Their review of the literature engages and critiques the position of Ley et al. and other studies that do not support an addiction model. See American Psychiatric Association, *Diagnostic and Statistical Manual of Mental Disorders*, 5th ed. (Arlington, Va.: American Psychiatric Publishing, 2013); David Ley, Nicole Prause, and Peter Finn, "The Emperor Has No Clothes: A Review of the 'Pornography Addiction' Model," *Current Sexual Health Reports* 6 (February 2014): 94–105; Todd Love et al., "Neuroscience of Internet Pornography Addiction: A Review and Update," *Behavioral Sciences* 5, no. 3 (2015): 389, 390, 394, and 412–13.

132. For a theological alternative to cultural assumptions that one must respond to sexual desire with either libertinism or repression, see Sarah Coakley, *The New Asceticism: Sexuality, Gender and the Quest for God* (London: Bloomsbury Continuum, an imprint of Bloomsbury Publishing, 2015), 12.

(with Christ and each other), and abuse, in which sin and blindness pervert the workings of desire from their Godward direction."[133]

God's love is given eternally in the procession of the Word and the Holy Spirit: *bonum est diffusivum sui*. Yet despite our creation in the image of the trinitarian God, the self-conscious human being with predator eyes has a proclivity to a self-centeredness that Augustine described as a state of being *incurvatus in se* (turned-in-on-oneself). The pornographic gaze feeds this self-ward turn. A person viewing pornography typically does so in isolation from others, and the pornographic gaze often leads to a state of sexual arousal that finds release in a self-pleasuring act. Sacramental vision, in contrast, draws us out of ourselves by the power of the attraction of divine glory in a *sortie de soi* (ecstasis of the self) that is a threshold of the knowledge of God. When one steps inside the doors of Notre-Dame Cathedral in Amiens, France (Fig. 1-9), writes Bishop Robert Barron, one is first plunged into darkness, and, then, as eyes adjust to the new surroundings, "heads are wrenched almost automatically up, because every major line in the building is vertical, shooting skyward like an arrow. I have seen [this happen] numerous times.... The building forces the visitors out of themselves, inviting them to transcendence."[134]

I have never been to Notre-Dame Cathedral in Amiens, but I have inhabited a temple of human self-curvature in which major lines of my consciousness were focused intently on myself. And I have also stood with others in the dark night of Holy Saturday around an urn of paschal fire. The churches upon whose thresholds I have stood on this holy night were far less grand than Notre-Dame Cathedral. Nonetheless, my heart leapt beyond itself like the tongues of fire that were dancing toward the stars, and the light of Christ, symbolized by the paschal flame and passed from person to person on pure white candles, gradually extinguished the darkness and invited me to transcendence and to joy.

133. Sarah Coakley, *God, Sexuality, and the Self: An Essay "On the Trinity"* (Cambridge: Cambridge University Press, 2013), 15.

134. Robert Barron, *Heaven in Stone and Glass: Experiencing the Spirituality of the Great Cathedrals* (New York: Crossroad, 2000), 79.

PART 1

An Age of Pornography

JILL MANNING

2 ⇷ The Influence of Pornography on Women

You may recall the scene near the end of the classic 1939 film, *The Wizard of Oz*, in which Dorothy and her loyal companions finally arrive at the wizard's palace. Once inside, they encounter an impressive façade of fire, lights, and towering pillars. As they nervously prepare to ask the wizard if he will grant their most fervent wishes, the green curtain gets pulled back, and the friends *see* for the first time that the wizard is nothing more than an insecure man struggling to be something he isn't. In this moment, the friends also realize that the gifts that they had journeyed so far to claim—heart, courage, intellect, and the means to get Dorothy and Toto home to Kansas—had been theirs all along.

Similarly, pornography's seductive façade fools many into thinking it is a healthy form of expression and a beneficial pastime, but when we pull back the curtain of fantasy and take an honest look at what a growing body of scientific research and clinical observations reveal about the systematic impact of pornography, we realize it is actually a very dark subject that is directly associated with the exploitation of human persons. Conversely, a careful examination of lives free of pornography reveals that we really do have all that we need to live and to love in wholehearted, authentic ways. *God gives us this grace.*

Through the process of mainstreaming pornography, we have collectively forgotten that pornography is *dispensable*; that its effects are *preventable*; and that it is *unnecessary* for human development, sexual maturation, happiness, or relational success. In fact, both empirical research and my clinical experience indicate pornography is an impediment to these goals.[1] The interdisciplinary collaboration *Seeing*

1. For an overview of research studies, see Eric W. Owens et al., "The Impact of Internet Pornography on Adolescents: A Review of the Research," *Sexual Addiction &*

with the Eyes of the Heart (Eph 1:18) gives us the opportunity to take advantage of the gift a dark topic offers when handled carefully and viewed through a spiritual lens—this gift being that dark topics allow us to discern and recognize important truths more quickly precisely because they stand in sharp contrast to the darkness. Just as heavenly stars are best seen in a pitch-black sky, so can a discussion about pornography help us achieve a laser-like focus on those things that are true and that help us increase our resilience to pornography's influence and our empathy for those suffering in silence.[2] I will contrast pornography's dark lies to the truths I have learned as a researcher, therapist, wife, and mother with particular attention to pornography's impact on women.

Females of all ages, socio-economic backgrounds, and stages of life are impacted by the pornography that has become pervasive in our society today. Who are the women who come to mind for you when you think of pornography's influence on women? I am sure if we discussed our answers openly, we would learn that women from all walks of life are affected and that their experience is overwhelmingly negative. When I think of the impact on women, I think of:

- The barely adult woman in the pornographic film who numbs herself with illicit drugs while engaging in sexual acts that are eerily similar to the abuse she faced as a young girl;
- The eleven-year-old girl who was sold into a Cambodian brothel by her desperately poor parents and is raped daily by foreign tourists whose deviant appetites are shaped by pornography consumption;
- The woman who attempts to fix the family computer and discovers a trove of explicit websites and images downloaded by her husband, along with links to ads for escort and erotic massage services, the titles and names make her nauseous as the sting of betrayal sets in;

Compulsivity 19, no. 1/2 (2012): 99–122; Jill C. Manning, "The Impact of Internet Pornography on Marriage and the Family: A Review of the Research," *Sexual Addiction & Compulsivity* 13, no. 2/3 (2006): 131–65.

2. I develop some of the points in this chapter in a book written for youth entitled *What's the Big Deal about Pornography? A Guide for the Internet Generation* (Salt Lake City, Utah: Shadow Mountain, 2008).

- The college student who is trying to navigate a dating scene and social landscape made significantly more complex and arguably less safe because of the pervasive internet pornography use by her male peers and the increasing acceptance of it by her female peers;
- The teenager who sends a semi-nude photo of herself to a boy she likes (as 20 percent of American girls her age have done) and then quickly finds out it has been forwarded to her entire freshman class;[3]
- The twenty-seven-year-old woman who learns her father has been addicted to pornography for years. Suddenly countless interactions and memories now make sense and are painful to think about.

While these females differ from one another, they are bound by common experiences of isolation, trauma, disconnection, exploitation, shame, fear, and jeopardized well-being. This chapter will focus on some of the effects experienced by young single adult women and married women that are widely noted in research and that I have personally witnessed in my clinical work, including: sexual miseducation, objectification, complexified social and dating relations, negative body image, increased tolerance for physical and sexual abuse, and marital distress.

Sexual Miseducation

Although men are roughly 6.5 times more likely to use internet pornography than women, research indicates a growing number of women are consuming pornography.[4] In a 2008 study of college-age students, 31 percent of the women surveyed reported using pornography (compared with 87 percent of the men) and almost half agreed that viewing pornography is acceptable (compared with 67 percent of the

3. Power to Decide (formerly, The National Campaign to Prevent Teen and Unplanned Pregnancy), *Sex and Tech: Results from a Survey of Teens and Young Adults* (Washington, D.C.: The National Campaign to Prevent Teen and Unplanned Pregnancy, 2008), accessed September 20, 2018, https:// powertodecide.org/sites/default/files/resources/primary-download/sex-and-tech.pdf.

4. Steven Stack, Ira Wasserman, and Roger Kern, "Adult Social Bonds and Use of Internet Pornography," *Social Science Quarterly* 85, no. 1 (2004): 85.

men).[5] To put this in context, the women surveyed were more accepting of pornography than their fathers were just one generation ago.[6] A key finding in this same study was that the intellectual acceptance of pornography is as strongly correlated to women's attitudes and behaviors as is their actual consumption.[7]

In my research and clinical practice, I have learned that pornography is a major socializing agent and the primary sexual educator for the internet generations. If, through pornography, a person stood a decent chance of acquiring accurate, respectful, and helpful information about sexuality and was able to decipher and avoid illegal, demeaning, fraudulent or violent material, I still wouldn't like it, but I would be less concerned. However, my clinical observations have taught me that internet pornography is handicapping people from being able to develop a healthy sexual self and is impacting their attitudes and behaviors on multiple levels. Pornography influences everything from how singles speak of and frame sexuality, to why and how they pierce certain body parts, to what they expect to give and receive in romantic relationships.

We also know that regular exposure to pornography is associated with desensitization to offensive material, which is significant because research also shows that when most people are first exposed to pornography they tend to have a negative reaction. This is especially true of females. An Australian survey of youth aged eleven to seventeen found that they commonly used the words "sick," "yuck," "disgusted," "repulsed," and "upset" to describe their initial reaction to pornography.[8] As desensitization increases, we see an increased tolerance toward sexually explicit material, and a growing need for more novel or bizarre material to achieve the same level of interest or response. We also see this happening on a larger cultural scale with coarsening media standards and ratings creep.

5. Jason S. Carroll et al., "Generation XXX: Pornography Acceptance and Use among Emerging Adults," *Journal of Adolescent Research* 23, no. 1 (2008): 16–18.

6. Carroll, "Generation XXX," 25.

7. Carroll, "Generation XXX," 24.

8. Michael Flood and Clive Hamilton, *Youth and Pornography in Australia: Evidence on the Extent of Exposure and Likely Effects*, Discussion Paper Number 52 (Canberra: The Australia Institute, 2003).

Research indicates that youth whose sexual education has been influenced by pornography:

- Have misperceptions about the extent of sexual activity in the general populace and the prevalence of less common sexual practices;
- Have a decreased desire to be monogamous and a greater acceptance of promiscuity as a normal state of interaction;
- Assume that abstinence constitutes a health risk;
- Begin to view love in a cynical manner;
- Believe that marriage is sexually confining.[9]

Exactly how these beliefs and dynamics will play out in the lives of women is unclear, but it is reasonable to assume that they will not bear good fruit for them or society at large. As a woman, a mother, and a clinician, it concerns me that an increasing number of young females have come to view sexual relations as a spectator sport and as a form of recreation totally detached from consequences, relationships, or a procreative and sacred role. Pornography promotes the notion that sexual education requires a lot of practice with a wide range of people if sexuality is to be enjoyed to the fullest later in life. When we look at the research, however, we learn that people who reserve sexual relations for marriage: (1) are *more* satisfied with their future sexual experiences; (2) have little to no risk of sexually transmitted disease and unwanted pregnancies; and (3) end up having stronger marriages than people who were promiscuous prior to marriage.

Objectification

Pornography discourages sensitivity and respect toward others because it treats people like objects who simply exist to satisfy sexual urges or desires. As one female noted after her male partner began using pornography: "I am no longer a sexual *person* or partner to him, but a sexual *object*. He is not really with *me*. . . . He seems to be thinking about something or someone else—likely these porn women. . . .

9. Dolf Zillman, "Influence of Unrestrained Access to Erotica on Adolescents' and Young Adults' Dispositions toward Sexuality," *Journal of Adolescent Health* 27, no. 2/1 (2000): 42.

He is just using me as a warm body."[10] The act of treating a person like an object is called *objectification.* Objectification takes away human qualities and adds the qualities of an object—something that doesn't speak, doesn't have feelings, and can't make choices—so that people are less likely to relate to, understand, or be sensitive toward the person.

In pornography, objectification takes place in many ways, including when pornography covers the face or mouth of a person; shows only parts of a person's body; does not give a person a name; calls a person derogatory or sexually suggestive names; extracts a person's physicality from their personhood, including their family relationships and life history; hides or misrepresents the true emotions of a person; and shows a person in a disrespectful, degrading, or inhumane light. Amsterdam School of Communications Research Professor Jochen Peter and University of Amsterdam Distinguished Professor of Communication Patti M. Valkenburg's study of Dutch adolescents found that increased exposure to sexually explicit material increased the likelihood that both male *and* female adolescents would view females as sexual objects.[11] Exposure to sexually explicit materials was "both a cause and a consequence" of this perception.[12] In stark contrast, the Bible teaches that the human person is created in the very image of God (Gn 1:26) and that the body is a temple of the Holy Spirit (1 Cor 3:16). When we objectify one another, we diminish our humanity and diminish our God-given ability to love and care for others.

10. Raymond M. Bergner and Ana J. Bridges, "The Significance of Heavy Pornography Involvement for Romantic Partners: Research and Clinical Implications," *Journal of Sex & Marital Therapy* 28, no. 3 (2002): 197.

11. Jochen Peter and Patti M. Valkenburg, "Adolescents' Exposure to a Sexualized Media Environment and Their Notions of Women as Sex Objects," *Sex Roles* 56, no. 5/6 (2007): 381–95; "Adolescents' Exposure to Sexually Explicit Internet Material and Notions of Women as Sex Objects. Assessing Causality and Underlying Processes," *Journal of Communication* 59, no. 3 (2009): 407–33.

12. Peter and Valkenburg, "Adolescents' Exposure to Sexually Explicit Internet Material," 425.

Complexified Social and Dating Relations

Young women are facing increasingly complex interactions with young men as the result of the pornographic undercurrents in social and dating relations. Many of the young women I have worked with dislike the fact that young men consume pornography, but they are conflicted about how to reject this behavior while at the same time garnering and competing for their romantic attention. Young women once had allure and mystery on their side. Today, young men are inundated with photo-shopped images of naked, surgically altered, and sexually engaged females, which dramatically alters the flirtatious dance between the sexes.

When a supranormal stimulus is introduced into a social system, it sparks radical changes. The concept of a supranormal stimulus was developed by animal biologists and refers to the idea that *exaggerated imitation can exert a stronger pull than the real thing.* The term, which so aptly applies to pornography, was originally coined by Nobel laureate Niko Tinbergen who discovered that male butterflies were more attracted to dummy, cardboard female torsos with elongated and brighter stripes than to a live, receptive female butterfly! Ponder for a moment how this would impact a kaleidoscope of butterflies in which 87 percent of the young males are chasing cardboard and half of the young adult females thought this was acceptable. One does not need to be a biologist to realize the short and long-term effects would be devastating to the collective well-being of the system.

Sadly, it is not uncommon for women to tell me that they have become insecure about themselves after learning about a boyfriend's or husband's pursuit of "cardboard." They have fallen prey to toxic comparisons between themselves and the women portrayed in pornography and are convinced they do not measure up.

Negative Body Image

Pornography contributes to increased risk of developing a negative body image. This is a logical effect for many reasons, but one reason is that the pornified body is treated as a commodity that can be bought, sold, exploited, and abused with seemingly no consequences. The pornified body is often surgically altered, presented as one-dimensional, and referred to using the basest language and jargon. Because women are the focal point of pornographic images, females take the biggest hit both in what they expect of themselves and in what is expected of them. As one young woman explained, sexually explicit materials leave her feeling "very unattractive ... you can say that you aren't influenced by this, but no one can resist. You do want to have these ideal bodies."[13]

I recall working with a young woman who was particularly plagued with feelings of inadequacy in comparison to the women her boyfriend sought online. She and I did an interesting exercise together. We divided a piece of paper into two columns. On the left side, I helped her come up with various qualities exhibited by the women in pornography, and in the right-hand column, we listed characteristics of women who are spiritually grounded in who they *really are*. After a couple of weeks, she realized there was ultimately no comparison and that the women in pornography needed empathy, compassion, and help rather than our ill-guided comparisons. It was a turning point for her.

Increased Abuse and Its Tolerance

As a clinician, I am witnessing more females tolerating emotional, physical, and sexual abuse in dating relationships because they see the same acts eroticized in pornography and mass media. After all, how bad can abusive or demeaning treatment be when this is what we are collectively entertained by so frequently?

Pornography is indeed a factor in the epidemic of sexual violence in our society. Evidence of this includes the study by Michele Ybarra, associate professor at Johns Hopkins Bloomberg School of Public Health, and Kimberly J. Mitchell of the Crimes against Children Research Center at the University of New Hampshire. Their research found that males who frequently consume pornography and who have predisposing risk levels toward sexually aggressive behavior manifest levels of

13. Lotta Löfgren-Mårtenson and Sven-Axel Månsson, "Lust, Love and Life: A Qualitative Study of Swedish Adolescents' Perceptions and Experiences with Pornography," *The Journal of Sex Research* 47, no. 6 (2010): 574.

sexual aggression four times greater than peers who view pornography infrequently.[14] A more recent longitudinal study conducted by Ybarra and her Bloomberg School of Public Health colleagues found that adolescents exposed to sexually explicit material were six times more likely to be sexually aggressive than those who were not exposed.[15] Significantly, this sixfold increase was manifest not only after exposure to sexually explicit material that included violent acts but also after exposure to sexually explicit material that did not. A meta-analytic study by psychology professor Neil M. Malamuth (UCLA), Tamara Addison of McMaster University, and Mary Koss, Regents' Professor in the Mel and Enid Zuckerman College of Public Health at the University of Arizona, found a reliable association between frequent pornography use and sexually aggressive behavior,[16] and a meta-analysis by Associate Professor of Communication Mike Allen (University of Wisconsin-Milwaukee) and doctoral students Tara Emmers, Lisa Gebhardt, and Mary A. Giery found a positive correlation between exposure to pornography and the acceptance of rape myths (such as the belief that rape is not a serious crime, or that rape is the fault of the victim.)[17]

Distressed Marriages

Turning our attention to married women, it is important to realize that the majority of people struggling with internet-related sexual addictions and compulsions are married, heterosexual males—typically in their late thirties.[18] Therefore, examining the impact of pornography on wives of pornography users is a legitimate focal point.

14. Among male participants without predisposing risk levels, pornography consumption did not correlate with increased sexual aggression. Michele L. Ybarra and Kimberly J. Mitchell, "Exposure to Internet Pornography among Children and Adolescents: A National Survey," *CyberPsychology & Behavior* 8, no. 5 (2005): 473–86.

15. Michele L. Ybarra et al., "X-Rated Material and Perpetration of Sexually Aggressive Behavior among Children and Adolescents: Is There a Link?" *Aggressive Behavior* 37, no. 1 (2011): 1–18.

16. Neil M. Malamuth, Tamara Addison, and Mary Koss, "Pornography and Sexual Aggression: Are There Reliable Effects and Can We Understand Them?" *Annual Review of Sex Research* 11, no. 1 (2000): 26–94.

17. Mike Allen et al., "Exposure to Pornography and Acceptance of Rape Myths," *Journal of Communication* 45, no. 1 (1995): 5–26.

18. Al Cooper, David L. Delmonico, and Ron Burg, "Cybersex Users, Abusers, and Compulsives: New Findings and Implications," *Sexual Addiction & Compulsivity* 7 (2000): 5–29.

To provide an overview of pornography's impact on married women and marriage generally, this table compares research findings on key factors associated with strong, stable and satisfying marriages with empirical findings on the effects of pornography:[19]

Characteristics of Stable & Healthy Marriages	*Common Effects of Pornography*
Mutual belief in the institution of marriage	Decreased desire to marry and have children
Fidelity (body, mind, heart)	Infidelity (users are three times more likely to commit adultery and four times more likely to hire a prostitute)
Mutual respect	Decreased sensitivity of men toward women and a decreased likelihood that gender relations are approached with an ideal of mutual respect
Trust	Decreased trust
Sexual relations that strengthen the marital bond	Increased risk of sexual dysfunction and dissatisfaction
Spiritual foundation and reverence for sacred aspects of life	Diminished spirituality and respect for sacred aspects of life
An assumption of permanence regarding the marital relationship	Increased risk of separation and divorce

Although women in various kinds of relationships can experience intense and adverse reactions to a romantic partner's pornography use, there is a significant difference between the reactions of women who are dating or cohabitating and the reactions of women who are married. According to research findings, married women are significantly more distressed by a partner's online pornography consumption than women in dating or cohabitating relationships.[20] Married

19. Manning, "Impact of Internet Pornography on Marriage and the Family," 131–65.
20. Ana J. Bridges, Raymond M. Bergner, and Matthew Hesson-McInnis, "Romantic

women typically view internet pornography consumption as a significant threat to the marital bond and to family safety. As would be expected, the distress that married women report increases according to the perceived frequency of their husband's online sexual activities, and it occurs without correlation to their religious beliefs.

One reason married women are deeply impacted by a husband's pornography use is that North American women are generally socialized to seek and to expect marital relationships that are founded upon mutual respect, trust, honesty, shared decisionmaking, equality, and romantic love. In stark contrast to these relational and marital ideals, pornography promotes and eroticizes the antithesis: power imbalances, discrimination, disrespect, abuse, violence, voyeurism, objectification, and detachment. Consequently, when a North American, married woman discovers that her husband has been secretly consuming pornography, the discovery not only devastates her sense of safety and trust, but it also threatens the foundation upon which she has constructed her relational world. She no longer experiences being the chosen or beloved woman in her husband's world. Moreover, she is suddenly confronted with how psychologically, spiritually, and sexually split her supposedly "modern man" really is.[21]

It is not uncommon for women who discover they have been sexually betrayed to say things like, "I have no idea who he is anymore," "I feel like I have lived a lie the entire time I have been married," or "I thought we had a good marriage until this was revealed." As one woman lamented, "I have been excluded, isolated, barred from intimacy with him. I have lost someone whom I thought was my best friend and most intimate companion in life. He now has a whole secret life from which I am completely excluded and about which he continually lies to me."[22]

To add insult to injury, many wives are directly blamed for their husband's pornography use by the husband himself, family members,

---

Partners' Use of Pornography: Its Significance for Women," *Journal of Sex & Marital Therapy* 29, no. 1 (2003): 13.

21. Jill C. Manning, "The Impact of Pornography on Women: Social Science Findings and Clinical Observations," in *The Social Costs of Pornography: A Collection of Papers*, eds. James R. Stoner Jr. and Donna M. Hughes (Princeton, N.J.: The Witherspoon Institute, 2010), 69–87.

22. Manning, "Impact of Internet Pornography on Marriage and the Family," 144.

friends, and even clergy. Blame of any kind only compounds the trauma of discovery or disclosure. Many women I have worked with clinically describe stinging insinuations that the marriage must be unsatisfying, that she has "let herself go," that she is sexually closed-minded, or that she is overly focused on her children and is not giving her husband enough attention. Too often, those seeking to blame the woman dismiss both her experience of the marital relationship and the historical context of her husband's pornography habit. Consequently, pornography use is justified and its effects are left unchallenged. Unfortunately, when wives are scapegoated in this way, pornography problems (including pornography addictions) are enabled and the cultural chime of boys-will-be-boys is reinforced and everyone loses.

Many researchers have found that women feel betrayal, loss, mistrust, devastation, disorientation, and anger upon the discovery of a husband's pornography use or online sexual activity.[23] Some researchers have even shown that individuals who discover that their partner is engaged in compulsive pornography use or other sexually addictive behaviors can manifest symptoms of post-traumatic stress disorder (PTSD). A 2006 study of wives who discovered a husband's pornography use, by Barbara A. Steffens of Cincinnati Christian University and Child and Family Counselor Robyn L. Rennie, found that 69 percent of these women met all but one of the criteria for PTSD and almost half of those had moderate to severe symptoms.[24] Additionally, many women experience physiological effects such as fatigue, fluctuations in appetite or libido, and other signs and symptoms of anxiety and depression, including suicidal tendencies in some cases.[25]

It is also common for women to report dramatic changes in personal conduct in the wake of this kind of marital and personal crisis. For instance, I have worked with women who, upon learning of their husband's pornography use, began viewing pornography themselves,

23. Bridges, Bergner, and Hesson-McInnis, "Romantic Partners' Use of Pornography"; Manning, "Impact of Internet Pornography on Marriage and the Family"; Jennifer P. Schneider, "Effects of Cybersex Addiction on the Family: Results of a Survey," *Sexual Addiction & Compulsivity* 7, no. 1/2 (2000): 31–58.

24. Barbara A. Steffens and Robyn L. Rennie, "The Traumatic Nature of Disclosure for Wives of Sexual Addicts," *Sexual Addiction & Compulsivity* 13, no. 2/3 (2006): 247–67.

25. Manning, "Impact of Internet Pornography on Marriage and the Family."

started drinking or using drugs, engaged in revenge affairs, or participated in sexual acts they previously found degrading or contrary to personal or religious values. These abrupt changes in behavior usually represent maladaptive attempts to cope with the sense of threat and competition evoked by a spouse's betrayal, as well as desperate efforts to reclaim a sense of control and stability.

Over and above their intense emotional distress and upheaval, these women also experience increased risk of marital distress, domestic violence, separation, and divorce. Internet pornography and online infidelity are now two of the leading causes of divorce. At a 2002 meeting of the American Academy of Matrimonial Lawyers, an organization of the nation's foremost divorce and matrimonial law attorneys, 62 percent of the 350 lawyers in attendance said that the internet had played a role in the divorces they had handled in the past year and that 56 percent of these cases involved internet pornography.[26]

Conclusion

Pornography represents a highly deceptive portrayal of the human body. Moreover, it promotes a façade and censors the truth about the consequences of the behavior it depicts. It also censors the joys of authentic relationships, as well as the beauty, light, and power of real women—while simultaneously insulting the best in men. We can help counter this deceptive form of censorship by pulling back the curtain of fantasy, choosing to be informed, remaining steadfast in our focus on God's light and truth, and actively healing the shame in our own lives that makes us prone to forgetting who we really are. Combatting and healing the effects of pornography is a task for men and women alike; with awareness, honesty, and moral courage it can be done.

26. See Manning, "Impact of Internet Pornography on Marriage and the Family," 141.

WILLIAM M. STRUTHERS AND
KYLER MULHAUSER

3 ⇻ The Effects of Pornography on Men

A Neurological Perspective

This image broke the internet.[1] In February 2015, a blogger posted a photo of a dress and asked a simple question: "What color is it? Is it white-and-gold or blue-and-black?" You can show this same image to any two people and one might always see the blue-and-black dress, while the other might always see the white-and-gold dress. And this is true regardless of the conditions under which the image is viewed. Sometimes, two people will see the same object in remarkably different and incompatible ways because each person has been conditioned in how they perceive the object.

How can the same object, under the same lighting conditions, be perceived in such different ways? Psychologists will suggest that this is an issue of color constancy. We naturally assume that the color is constant from one context to another—a green shirt will be green whether we wear it inside or outside, or whether we wear it in the morning or in the evening. A green shirt is always a green shirt. But on closer inspection, we may realize that we are actually using perceptual cues to help us interpret what we see. For example, items off to the side or in the background of the figure may help us to understand and interpret what we are viewing. How do these peripheral objects relate to the primary object? Texture, shape, color, tone, saturation, and relative proximity of objects in space all contribute to our understanding of what we are viewing—including its color. We see things differently in the middle of the night than we do at noon.

1. Adam Rogers, "The Science of Why No One Agrees on the Color of this Dress," *Wired* (February 26, 2015), accessed July 1, 2017, https://www.wired.com/2015/02/science-one-agrees-color-dress/.

Additionally, there is the influence of reproduction. A real dress made of different fabrics, textures, patterns, and colors is not quite the same as a digitized reproduction. The real dress has been transformed into a different medium, which further influences our perception and understanding of what we are viewing. Yet the visual qualities of the object and the medium through which they are translated are not the only variables that affect how we perceive visual information. Context is also extremely important. Even under highly controlled conditions, with all else being equal, one person will see the dress as white and gold and another will see the dress as blue and black. How the dress is perceived has as much to do with the person viewing it.

So, what does this internet meme have to do with pornography? Pornography has everything to do with perception and production. Using pornography shapes how men view sexuality, how men view women, and how men view themselves. Men often experience pornography differently than women do, in part because men are neurologically wired to experience sexually explicit visual information differently than women. When we talk about the effect of pornography on men, we find that it influences the way men see and think about sexuality. A person's perception of an object—this controversial dress, for example—may be informed by other objects that this person views.

What is pornography? Clearly defining pornography for a content analysis study can be a difficult task. Supreme Court Justice Potter Stewart famously concluded about the definition of pornography in 1964, "I know it when I see it." As people of faith, we see the human body as a creation of beauty and power. The nude form is simply the body in a state of undress. Michelangelo's sculpture of David is not pornography; a medical textbook with photographs of a naked body is not pornography. Either by intention or use, pornography relies on being sexually arousing. The line between non-pornographic and pornographic can be subtle: a change of facial expression, the inclusion of seductive lingerie, and the tells of pornography become apparent. There was a time when access to these kinds of images was limited. Today, pornography producers have used cable television and the internet to disperse widely their photographs and films. What are the consequences for American men? We explore this question from the perspective of our expertise in biopsychology and neuroscience and our Christian faith.

The Male Brain: Hardwired for Intimacy

Men are neurologically driven to seek sexual intimacy. From a biblical perspective, we understand this relational drive as a means to serve our sanctification. Sanctification is the process by which we become the holy men and women God created us to be: fully mature and good persons living in the image of God. The sexual longings that we feel are part of our vocation to intimacy—to know and be known, to love and be loved. Just as God is relational (as Father, Son, and Holy Spirit), human beings, created in the image of God, are relational, created for rich forms of intimacy: parent-child relationships, brotherhood, sisterhood, friendships, and marriage.[2] Our relational desires, including our sexual drive, propel us toward each other and toward God. In connecting with each other and knowing one another, we are called beyond our individual finitude into the transcendent love of God. Whether that transcendence is found in sexual union with a spouse or in the selfless giving of our time and affection to others, we discover something outside of ourselves and experience the love, holiness, and goodness of the Creator as we give selflessly to another.[3]

Because we are hardwired for intimacy, we are receptive to sexual imagery. Our brains respond differently to viewing sexual images than they do to images of a chair, a beautiful landscape, or religious iconography (although there are interesting similarities in the ways that sexual and religious experiences are processed neurologically). Our brains operate in such a way that some categories of information receive more attention than do others. For example, we are quick to notice and remember faces. We are also quick to notice nudity. Sexually solicitous cues naturally receive more attention than do other objects. Our brains give certain visual information priority over other visual

2. For more on our vocation to intimacy, see William M. Struthers, "Living in a Hyper-Sexualized Culture" (Wheaton College Chapel Message, Wheaton, Ill., March 28, 2011), accessed November 12, 2017, https://www.youtube.com/watch?v=uQq3-YPEmQM.

3. William M. Struthers, *Wired for Intimacy: How Pornography Hijacks the Male Brain* (Downers Grove, Ill.: Intervarsity Press, 2009), 157–59.

information. Men, more so than women, enjoy *looking* at the naked body—and this is true across cultures. The relationship between a man's brain and sexually explicit imagery is very complex. Scientific findings seem to suggest that a man's brain may be changed by exposure to sexually explicit material, but it also appears to be the case that a man's brain is hardwired to be attracted to sexually explicit images. Males, on average, tend to be more sensitive than females to visual cues: men first look at the body, then the face, and then the context.

Hijacked on the Flight to Intimacy: The Effects of Pornography on the Male Brain

The hard-wiring of the male brain to receive and respond to visual sexual images makes men vulnerable to the pornography that is so readily accessible in our culture. The wiring in the male brain developed in order to enable reproduction with a mate—not in order to view hundreds of nude female bodies on a computer or a smart phone. Several researchers have investigated the impact that sexually arousing images have on men and women to determine if the brain responds differently to pornography than other images. They report that sexually explicit images activate the brain in a unique way for both men and women.[4] And, what is more, they found important differences in the ways that males and females processed pornographic imagery.

Neuroimaging studies found multiple differences in brain activation patterns of male and female participants viewing sexually arousing photographs. The ventral tegmental area (VTA) and amygdala are regions involved in sexual anxiety and arousal. Views from a functional MRI (fMRI) show differences in activation for men and women. We see bilateral activation of these areas in men, but only partial activation in women.[5] Additionally, the activation is more intense in men than it is in women, as is evident in the bright yellow coloring in the

4. Heather A. Rupp and Kim Wallen, "Sex Differences in Response to Visual Sexual Stimuli: A Review," *Archives of Sexual Behavior* 37, no. 2 (2008): 206–18; Martin Walter et al., "Distinguishing Specific Sexual and General Emotional Effects in fMRI—Subcortical and Cortical Arousal during Erotic Picture Viewing," *Neuroimage* 40, no. 4 (2008): 1482–94; Stephan Hamann, "Sex Differences in the Responses of the Human Amygdala," *The Neuroscientist* 11, no. 4 (2005): 288–93.

5. Hamann, "Sex Differences," 292.

brain images.[6] The pathway from the VTA to higher brain regions is part of the brain's dopamine-containing reward circuit. This is the same brain circuitry that is activated by addictive substances like cocaine and amphetamines. Also visible in the fMRI is activation of the occipital lobe, the area of the brain that processes visual information. Here too we see slightly more activation for men than women.

Neuroimaging studies have shown that spiritual experiences are partially processed in the temporal lobe. Research demonstrates that people who are religious find that viewing pornography creates shame and significant amounts of spiritual conflict.[7] Our lab is currently researching the effects that viewing pornography has on a person's conscience and sense of spirituality, as well as the role of the mirror neuron system in the reception of pornographic images. This research, in its early stages, is already a very interesting area of study for our lab.

We do know from our research, and multiple studies that have been completed elsewhere, that pornographic images can have a hypnotic effect on the brain, potentially impairing a man's capacity for decision-making and good judgment.[8] Like the hijacker who veers an aircraft away from its intended destination, pornography can pull the male brain off course and the effects on lives and relationships can be long lasting. The consequences of pornography usage include miseducation, impulsivity and increased inclination to risk-taking, the development of compulsions and addictions, dependency on a supranormal stimulus, the objectification and dehumanization of both women and men, and social isolation and dysfunction.

Miseducation

There is broad agreement that sexually explicit material influences the way that people—especially young people—learn about sexuality. Children are being exposed to pornography at earlier and earlier ages and they are learning about sex from their peers and from viewing pornography. Numerous studies have found that pornography func-

6. Hamann, "Sex Differences," 292.

7. See, for example, Joshua B. Grubbs and Samuel L. Perry, "Moral Incongruence and Pornography Use: A Critical Review and Integration," *Journal of Sex Research* 56 (2019): 29–37.

8. Struthers, *Wired for Intimacy*, 11.

tions in the lives of youth today as a form of "Sex Ed."[9] Young people begin to form ideas about what is expected of them sexually and what to demand from a partner. Their thinking about sex is informed by a pornographic culture where sex is a recreational commodity. Furthermore, early exposure to pornography is associated with more risky sexual behaviors, earlier age of first intercourse, and increased use of alcohol and drugs.[10] Pornography is sometimes referred to as an "accelerant" for sexual experimentation and it leads to a host of negative outcomes—especially for young people. Pornography is not true "Sex Ed" but sexual miseducation.

Risk-Taking and Impulsivity

One focus of our research concerns risk-taking and impulsivity as it relates to pornography use and hypersexual behaviors. We found that individuals who were being treated for hypersexuality made riskier decisions and were less responsive to aversive feedback in a simulated reward-based game called the Iowa Gambling Task.[11] This task measures risk-taking and decision-making behavior. The participant is presented with four decks of cards and is asked to select a card from each deck. Two of the decks contain frequent loss penalties (i.e., losing play money), while two of the decks contain infrequent loss penalties. The men with hypersexuality selected from the frequent penalty decks just as often as they did from the infrequent penalty decks. On the other hand, the men without hypersexuality selected from the frequent penalty deck much less often and showed a preference for the decks with only infrequent penalties. We interpreted these results to suggest that individuals whose pornography use has developed into

9. Chyng Sun and colleagues write, for example, "that online pornography is a significant source of sex education for young people, that it is lacking in information about the consequences of risky sexual choices, and that it portrays inaccurate and unrealistic expectations about sexual encounters." Chyng Sun et al., "Pornography and the Male Sexual Script: An Analysis of Consumption and Sexual Relations," *Archives of Sexual Behavior* 45 (2016): 984. In support, they cite numerous research studies published between 2005 and 2010 and conducted in several different countries.

10. Eric W. Owens et al., "The Impact of Internet Pornography on Adolescents: A Review of the Research," *Sexual Addiction & Compulsivity* 19, no. 1/2 (2012): 99–122.

11. Kyler R. W. Mulhauser and Willliam M. Struthers et al., "Performance on the Iowa Gambling Task in a Sample of Hypersexual Men," *Sexual Addiction & Compulsivity* 21, no. 2 (2014): 170–83.

a condition of hypersexuality demonstrate an impaired ability to recognize and respond to aversive feedback, such as monetary penalties. While people in the control group changed their strategy in order to avoid the penalizing decks, the hypersexual group seemed to either not to notice the frequent penalties or they failed to implement a new strategy in order to avoid the penalties. These findings are consistent with executive dysfunctions resulting in higher risk tolerance and poorer decision making.

In other research, the brain regions activated in men while viewing pornography correspond to an area called the mirror neuron system. The mirror neuron system in the brain of the viewer neurologically mimics the actions of the people being observed even though the body does not actually execute the behavior itself. For example, if you were to view someone swinging a tennis racket, the motor cortex in your brain, which is the area that controls your arm muscles, would also be activated in a similar pattern—even though your arm would not move. It is as if your brain, with the mirror neuron system, is rehearsing the actions and activities of the people you view without your full physical engagement in those activities. When a man views pornography (and this is the case for both men and women, though it seems to be especially true for men), he is vicariously engaging in the same behaviors as the performers. Part of his brain is responding in sync with the pornographic material he is viewing.

This may be a factor underlying the results of a study published in 2014 that evaluated the brain structure and function of sixty-four healthy men relative to the amount of pornography they viewed.[12] The study found that the men who view more pornography engaged in more compulsive sexual behaviors and had notable differences in their brain circuitry. This association is both significant and important, though the causality of the relationship has not yet been established. It is not yet clear if pornography is actually shrinking parts of the brain (e.g., the right caudate nucleus) or if individuals with certain neurological features are more susceptible to the allure of pornography. It

12. Simone Kühn and Jürgen Gallinat, "Brain Structure and Functional Connectivity Associated with Pornography Consumption: The Brain on Porn," *JAMA Psychiatry* 71, no. 7 (2014): 827–34.

may be that both, in fact, are part of the problem. It may be that having certain brain characteristics may make a person more susceptible to being attracted to pornography and that heavy use of pornography contributes to significant changes in the brain.

Release . . . and Compulsion

The effects of pornography in our society can be compared to the effects of second-hand smoke in the era when smoking was commonplace. Cigarette smoke filled homes and public places to such an extent that even non-smokers were exposed. The non-smoker could choose to try to avoid the cigarette smoke (which was not always possible) or to become a smoker. Pornography today, like second-hand smoke, enters our minds uninvited via pop-up ads on computer screens, email solicitations, and the soft-porn that pervades advertising, television, and film.

As we have explained, our brains are wired to notice nudity. If our attention lingers upon a sexually stimulating nude image, prolonged exposure can stimulate the brain to produce norepinephrine, a pharmacological switch-hitter that can act as a hormone or a neurotransmitter that plays an important role in sexual arousal and sexual memory.[13] If a man viewing pornography acts on his arousal, typically through masturbation, this action produces a neurochemical release of dopamine and serotonin, among other hormones, that contribute to a feeling of pleasure and relaxation. Such sensations may help to counteract stressful experiences associated with a difficult day at school or work or interpersonal tension. It is not hard to imagine how a cycle of stress and pornography use can quickly develop. Higher levels of chronic stress will demand higher levels of reliable relaxation. For some men, pornography becomes that reliable stress reliever. The neurochemicals that pornography viewing stimulates may also provide temporary relief from feelings of deprivation, isolation, or insecurity.

A man who uses pornography to relieve tension or insecurities, however, may soon find that he has been hijacked. Pornography acts

13. For a more detailed explanation of the neurological effect of pornography on the brain, see Struthers, *Wired for Intimacy*, 83–111.

on the brain's reward system in the same way as do addictive drugs like cocaine or amphetamines. And if pornography is like cocaine, internet pornography is like crack cocaine. The neurological mechanisms for pleasure associated with eating, drinking, and sex all operate on the same reward circuit. In their proper and healthy contexts, we find eating, drinking, and having sex to be pleasurable and this is good—these are survival mechanisms and part of the way God designed us. But pornography exploits the brain's reward system, causing it to function beyond its own natural capacity. Our brains were never intended to view hundreds of nude women in succession at the click of a button or swipe of a phone screen. This supranormal stimulus activates neurochemicals in the brain that result in insatiable cravings and compulsions.

Dependency on a Supranormal Stimulus

Pornographic images combined with masturbation can produce a remarkably robust sexual experience from a chemical and neurological perspective: norepinephrine produces a feeling of excitement and anticipation; dopamine produces a feeling of euphoria or ecstasy; serotonin provides a sense of relaxation and peace; and oxytocin, the "cuddle drug," enables mate bonding to occur. An important question, however, is with whom or what is one bonding? Pornography is sex on steroids—a supranormal stimulus. It is highly unlikely that we would regularly be in the presence of thousands of naked, copulating people in the real world. But with internet pornography, watching multiple sexual partners engaged in a large number of sexual encounters is quite easy; in fact, it can be a daily occurrence in the privacy of our own homes. Pornography takes our sexual drive for communion—and redirects it in an addictive, isolating activity in which we "bond" with pixels on a screen.

Pornography is sinister in that it uses something designed for good (sex as a pleasurable experience), removes it from its intended context (the intimate love of a marital relationship), and amplifies it with unrestricted access to sexual images. Removing sex from the protected context of marriage is how the progression to sexual addiction begins. Pornography will always demand a newer experience—something more risqué, something more edgy—to achieve the same feeling of excitement. Most pornography users don't look at the same centerfold year after year or the same internet image day after day. Tolerance demands a new experience. Over time, dependency on newer and newer experiences starts to develop.

Not only does this fuel addiction, but many men are unable to perform sexually with a woman because they have become so dependent on the unrealistic images and scenarios available through pornography that a real human person simply cannot compete. There is mounting evidence of this problem. For example, a 2016 review of studies and reports from multiple domains (biological, psychological, and clinical) found a sharp rise in sexual difficulties and dysfunction in men under forty that cannot be explained by factors already known to cause dysfunction, such as obesity, substance abuse, and smoking. The evidence indicates that these elevated rates of dysfunction may be explained by the sharp rise in pornography consumption and warrants further study of this relationship.[14]

Objectification and Dehumanization

The brain is a remarkable organ that modifies itself. As it responds to signals in the environment to meet a need, it builds circuits that form the basis of the response that will enable these needs to be met readily in the future. Just as a daily walk through the same area of a forest eventually creates a path that becomes the normal route of passage through the woods, so too habitual pornography usage can carve a path that becomes our default mode of response to sexual stimuli. The more we activate this neurological pathway, the more deeply it is worn into our brains. When one views pornography, and particularly when one acts out sexually while viewing, hormones and peptides bind and consolidate specific neural pathways. Once these pathways are established, it will be easier and easier to travel them and they can shape our mode of perceiving and relating to other persons. What form of perception and relationship is pornography wiring into our brains? Pornography diminishes the female "performer's" humanity by re-

14. Brian Y. Park et al., "Is Internet Pornography Causing Sexual Dysfunctions? A Review with Clinical Reports," *Behavioral Sciences* 6, no. 3 (2016): 1–25.

moving her sense of agency, limiting her human power and dignity, and casting her as an object to be exploited. Pornography's objectification of both women and men is dehumanizing. Pornography is not harmless for those involved in its creation nor those involved in its consumption—pornography destroys at both ends of the transaction.

Mirror neurons amplify the violation of human dignity that is inherent in the production of pornography. When we watch something repeatedly, like a favorite baseball player at bat, our mirror neurons mentally enact the player's skilled swing and posture and map this pattern onto our brains in a way that will shape our future behavior. Pornographic images and films do not just bounce off our eyes without effect. They prime us to mirror the relationships and actions we see on our screens. When we view pornography, our neurons are mirroring the actions of the pornography actors, and when we actually engage in a sexual act we are primed to do the things that we have seen. This can include things that it would otherwise never have occurred to us to do, such as engaging in forms of sexual aggression.

Pornography also contributes to cultural narratives that commodify sexuality. Pornography is produced for optimal marketability and profitability. And because it exploits the brain's reward system, like all addictive products, pornography is a block-buster industry. Producers of pornography change the white balance, so to speak, of how we view other human beings—dialing down the signs of personhood and dialing up the cues of exploitation. The pornography industry has created a narrative, one that has altered the way that we think about sexuality and that has trained many men to see only the blue and the black of humanity, ignoring the white and the gold. The full array of human intimacy—with nuance, dimensionality, vulnerability, and interdependency—is lost to a dimming of the light. Even when we bring that dress that broke the internet into the full spectrum of the sunlight at midday, it is still seen as only blue and black.

Social Isolation and Dysfunction

A study conducted in Israel found that youth who use the internet for pornography are less socially integrated than those who do not. They have weaker attachments and commitments to their families and schools.[15] A study in Greece found a significant association between social maladjustment and frequent internet pornography use among adolescents.[16] And research in the United States found that youth who manifest behaviors characteristic of clinical depression are more likely to use internet pornography than those who do not.[17]

Not only is social isolation or maladjustment correlated with the likelihood that youth will seek out internet pornography, but the use of pornography can contribute to further isolation and social dysfunction. In a 2011 article entitled, "He's Just Not That Into Anyone," Davy Rothbart explores the effects that viewing pornography has on a man's ability to engage romantically with women in our American culture.[18] Many of the young men he interviewed did not feel a need for a romantic partner because pornography had satiated their sexual drives. They could return home after work and access whatever pornography they wanted, masturbate, and have their sexual urges met with minimal complication. A pornography user without a compulsive or addictive habit is in total control of the images he consumes: how many, which ones, when to start, when to stop. And he will never have to deal with the complications, the messiness, that is inherent in real human intimacy. He will also not experience the joy of true love and intimacy.

Reclaiming Our God-Given Dignity and the Joy of Authentic Love

How can something so clearly destructive as pornography be so powerful? The answer, as we have seen, has everything to do with brain function. Neuroscience can help us to understand not only how pornography can hijack our brains but also what we can do to counteract

15. Gustavo S. Mesch, "Social Bonds and Internet Pornographic Exposure among Adolescents," *Journal of Adolescence* 32, no. 3 (2009): 601–18.

16. Artemis Tsitsika et al., "Adolescent Pornographic Internet Site Use: A Multivariate Regression Analysis of the Predictive Factors of Use and Psychosocial Implications," *CyberPsychology & Behavior* 12, no. 5 (2009): 545–50.

17. Michele L. Ybarra and Kimberly J. Mitchell, "Exposure to Internet Pornography among Children and Adolescents: A National Survey," *Cyberpsychology & Behavior* 8, no. 5 (2005): 473–86.

18. Davy Rothbart, "He's Just Not That Into Anyone," *New York Magazine* 44, no. 4 (January 30, 2011), accessed September 30, 2018, http://nymag.com/news/features/70976/.

it. Viewing pornography changes the circuitry of the brain. Turning our attention away from pornography can also change our circuitry. Each time we make a decision not to view pornography, each time we shield our brains from its images, the brain is modified. Praying, recalling passages from Scripture, or focusing our attention on something truly beautiful are all practices that can help us to fortify this mental shield. Over time, we can build a neuropharmalogical stronghold that says "no" to pornography's dehumanization of ourselves, our sisters and brothers in Christ, and our children. By intentionally redirecting the neurochemical flow, the path toward right thinking becomes the preferred path and is established as the mental habit. The path to recovery relies on the very rules that govern how the wounds were initially created. By deepening the "holiness" pathways, habitually doing what is right and good becomes part of our embodied nature.[19]

If one is a compulsive pornography viewer, ending this compulsion will not be easy. Neuroscience helps us to understand why. A brain that has become accustomed to the neurochemical "high" that pornography produces will go through withdrawal without the pornographic stimulus. A difficult detox period will be necessary. Research on breaking addictions indicates that two keys to success are a desire to end the compulsion and social support. Pornography usage is typically characterized by secrecy and feelings of shame, and users who desire to break their compulsion often attempt to do so alone so that their secrecy can be maintained. This, however, is almost always a recipe for failure. Social support is necessary, and the Christian community as the Body of Christ can play an essential role in sustaining people in recovery. If my brother in Christ is suffering from a pornography compulsion, I must accompany him. When, for example, he feels the urge to view pornography, he should know that he has the option of calling me instead, and I will take him out for coffee and be with him as long as necessary until that urge is gone. An hour later, I will call and follow-up to make sure that he is okay. We need each other. This is not a journey that men can walk alone.[20]

19. Struthers, *Wired for Intimacy*, 106–107.

20. William M. Struthers, "Wired for Intimacy" (Pure Passion Media Presentation, 2012), accessed September 20, 2018, https://www.youtube.com/watch?v=sWXqSFuIXSc.

If someone who is in recovery has a relapse, the shame that he experiences can result in an escalation of pornography usage, as the neurochemical high of pornography becomes a way to temporarily block the feelings of shame. This is a vicious cycle. Another way that Christian communities can support people in recovery is to ensure that they have a confidant or a confessor who can meet their shame with the grace and forgiveness of God.

Another practice that Christians can employ to counteract pornography's distortion of our vision is to behold one another with the eyes of the heart (Eph 1:18). If a pornographic image is thrust upon you, look directly into the eyes of the woman who is being exploited by the pornography industry. You will find that it is much more difficult to consume another human being when your eyes meet. And if your brain has been rewired such that the pornographic gaze has become your default mode of perceiving all women, look every woman you encounter in the eye. Behold one another and remember that each of you is created in the image and likeness of God (Gn 1:26–27).[21]

The church as the Body of Christ can cultivate practices that can help us all to behold one another's God-given dignity. In addition, the Christian community can advance a narrative of sexuality that is an alternative to the narrative of the pornographic culture that exploits the male brain and dehumanizes us all with apparent effortlessness. The psychological, sociological, and domestic burdens brought on by pornography are not helped by an emaciated theology of human sexuality. In many Protestant Christian communities, the only explicit guidance about pornography is "Don't look at it—it's bad" and the only explicit guidance about sex is "Don't do it—wait until you're married." The even more persuasive, implicit message is the message of silence: "It's not safe to have questions about sex—don't talk, don't feel." We have moved to a hermeneutic of legalism. And legalism leads to one of two extremes: repression of sexuality or limitless license of sexuality.

The antidote to the sex-as-commodity narrative proclaimed by pornography begins with proactive engagement by parents, pastors, and Christians in open dialogue about the full meaning of sexuality. Adolescents and parents too often collude in avoiding important con-

21. Struthers, "Living in a Hyper-Sexualized Culture."

versations about sex. Parents are often uncomfortable talking about sexuality with their kids—and so many don't. Children learn through observation and experience that sexuality must be something bad, something we don't discuss openly. So, they are left to discover what sexuality is on their own—or from a culture of exploitation ready to play the role of educator. The single best antidote to the amplified sexuality of our culture comes through trusting relationships, open and accepting dialogue, and a robust theological understanding of sexuality. Parents must cultivate these opportunities with their children. Pastors must open the dialogue with their congregations. And Christian men and women must embrace a fuller appreciation of the inalienable dignity of all men, women, and children.

What does the Gospel have to say to our pornographic culture? The Gospel maintains the dignity of every human being and stands in opposition to the dehumanization required for pornography's effectiveness. The Gospel also honors sacrifice and faithfulness—bulwarks that protect the vulnerability of true intimacy. A rich theology of human sexuality—informed by neuroscience, psychology, and other disciplines—can offer a robust counter narrative to the sex-as-commodity story our culture has come to embrace. While pornography seeks to limit and exploit human sexuality, the Gospel restores it as a gift of intimacy, communion, authentic love, and joy.

1-1. REPLICA OF THE INTERIOR OF THE SECOND SYNAGOGUE OF DURA-EUROPOS

1-2. CHURCH BAPTISTERY WALL PAINTING, PROCESSION OF WOMEN

1-3. *CURING THE CRIPPLED AND THE RAISING OF TABITHA*,

TOMMASO MASOLINO DA PANICALE

1-4. LEFT WALL OF THE BRANCACCI CHAPEL, MASACCIO

1-5. INTERIOR OF THE BRANCACCI CHAPEL, MASACCIO

1-6. SAINT PETER BAPTIZING THE NEW CONVERTS, MASACCIO

1-7. SANCTUARY OF HOLY TRINITY CATHEDRAL, HAITIAN ARTISTS

1-8. WEDDING FEAST AT CANA, MURAL, HAITIAN ARTISTS

1-9. INTERSECTION OF NAVE AND APSIS, NOTRE-DAME D'AMIENS

4-1. THE TRANSFIGURATION, CATHEDRAL OF THE TRANSFIGURATION OF THE SAVIOR

4-2. SAINT MARIA SKOBTSOVA, PHOTOGRAPH

4-3. *SAINT MARIA OF PARIS*, ICON BY THE HAND OF RANDI SIDER-ROSE

4-4–4-7. *THEOTOKOS OF TENDERNESS* (PROGRESSIVE STAGES), ICON BY THE HAND OF RANDI SIDER-ROSE

4-8 *CRUCIFIXION WITH VIRGIN MARY AND JOHN THE EVANGELIST*

4-9. *THE VIRGIN OF VLADIMIR*

4-10. *THE HOLY FACE* OR *ACHEIROPOLETOS*

4-11. GEOMETRY OF *THE HOLY FACE*

4-12. *THE NATIVITY* WITH GEOMETRY

4-13. *OLD TESTAMENT TRINITY*, ICON BY THE HAND OF ANDREI RUBLEV

5-1. *THEOTOKOS ENTHRONED*

5-2. *THEOTOKOS ENTHRONED*, CLOSE-UP

5-3. *PANAGIA*

5-4. *MADONNA OF HUMILITY*, GIOVANNI DI PAOLO

5-5. *VIERGE OUVRANTE* (CLOSED STATE)

5-6. *VIERGE OUVRANTE* (OPEN STATE)

5-7. FACING PAGE: *RAVENSBURGER SCHUTZMANTELMADONNA*, MICHEL ERHART OR FRIEDRICH SCHRAMM

5-8. *AFRICAN MADONNA*, LISA FRACICA

5-9. *BALTIMORE HOLY FAMILY*, BROTHER MICHAEL O'NEILL MCGRATH

5-10. *GUATEMALAN ANNUNCIATION*, REV. JOHN B. GIULIANI

5-11. *GUATEMALAN MOTHER AND CHILD*, REV. JOHN B. GIULIANI

5-12. *JAPANESE MADONNA*, UNKNOWN ARTIST

5-13. *MADONNA AND CHILD*, IN (CLARA) JEONG-OK

5-14. *OUR LADY OF CHAMINADE*, STUDIO OF FR. DAMIEN HIGGENS

5-15. *THE VIRGIN HODEGETRIA*

5-16. *MARY, UNTIER OF KNOTS*, JOHANN GEORG MELCHIOR SCHMITTNER

6-1. *THE TRIUMPH OF SAINT THOMAS AQUINAS*, SIENESE ARTIST

6-2. *THE ECSTASY OF SAINT TERESA OF AVILA*, GIAN LORENZO BERNINI

6-3. "INITIAL O" FROM THE SONG OF SONGS, *ALARDUS BIBLE*

6-4. CHRIST AND THE SPONSA, *ROTHSCHILD CANTICLES,* FOL. 18V

6-5. CHRIST AT THE COLUMN AND THE CROSS,
ROTHSCHILD CANTICLES, FOL. 19R

6-6. THE ANNUNCIATION, *MEDITATIONS ON THE LIFE OF CHRIST*

6-7. *THE ANNUNCIATION*, ROGIER VAN DER WEYDEN

6-8. *MADONNA AND CHILD*, LIPPO MEMMI, AND *PIETÀ OF CHRIST*, SIMONE MARTINI

6-9. *CUPID AND PSYCHE*

6-10. *THE VIRGIN AND CHILD IN AN INTERIOR*, WORKSHOP OF ROBERT CAMPIN

6-11. *THE HOLY FAMILY WITH SAINTS ELIZABETH AND JOHN THE BAPTIST*, PETER PAUL RUBENS

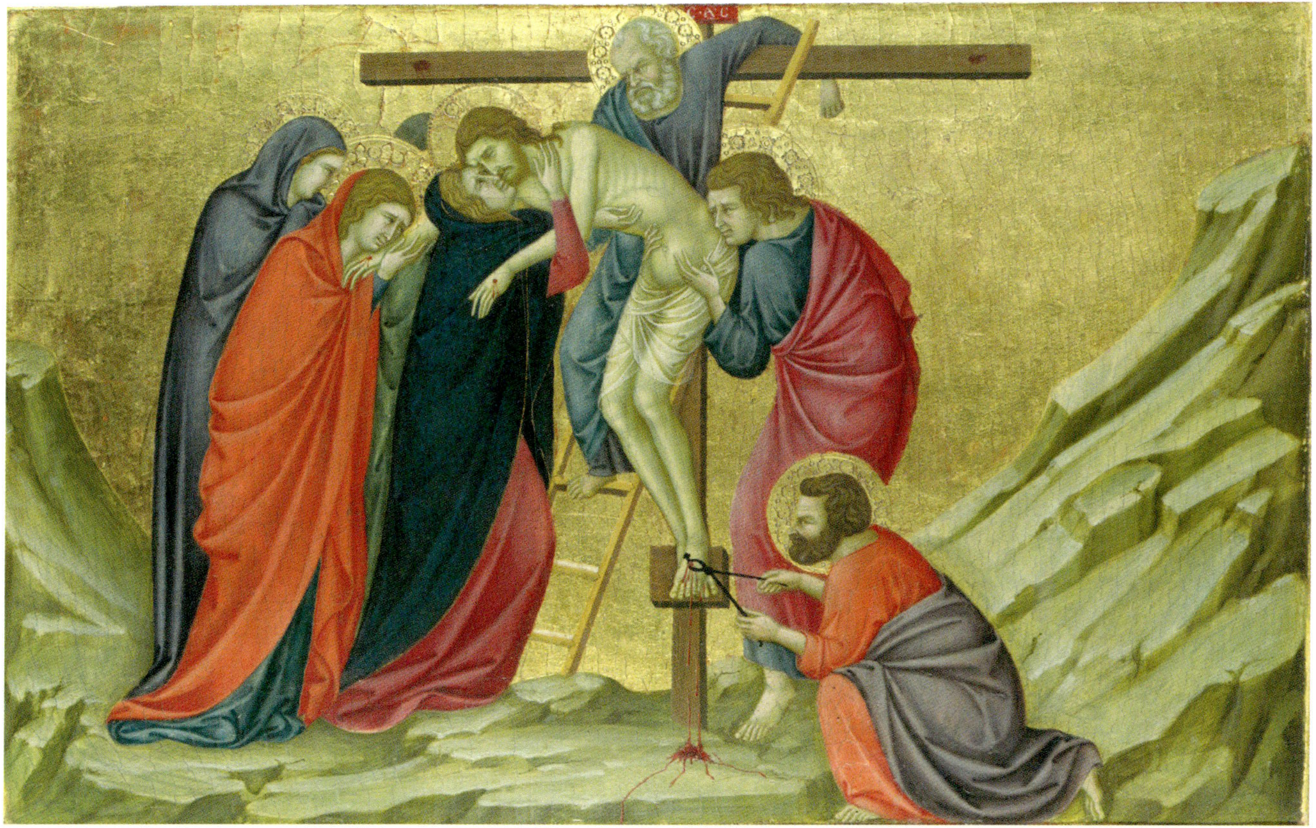

6-12. *THE DEPOSITION*, UGOLINO DI NERIO

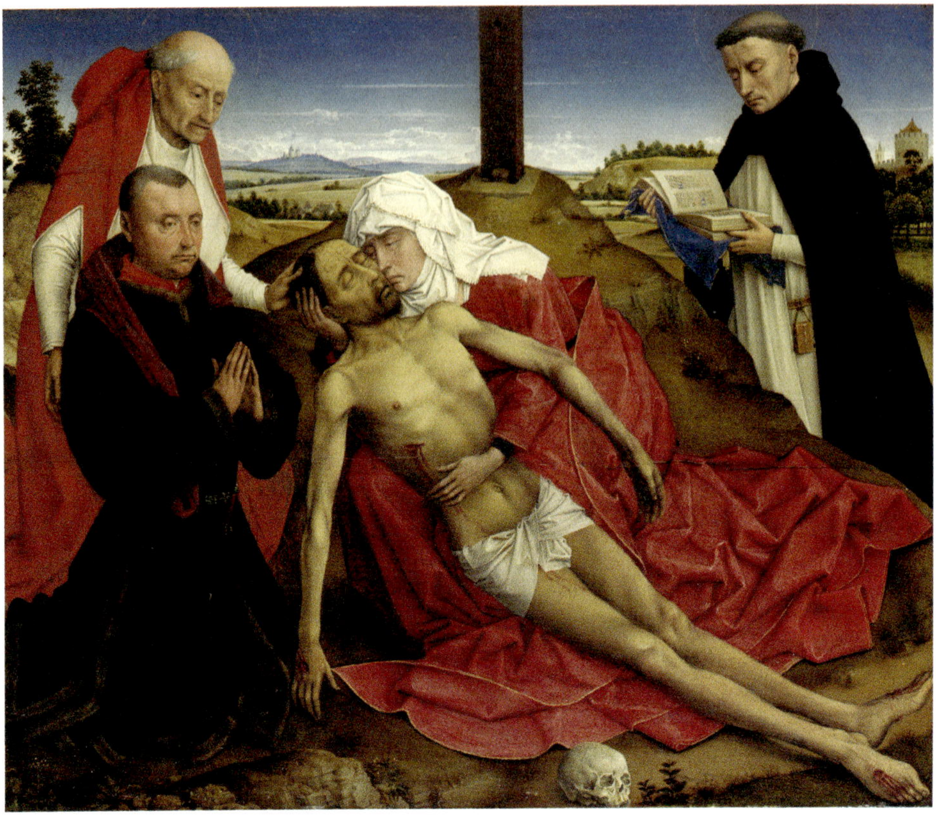

6-13. *PIETÀ*, WORKSHOP OF ROGIER VAN DER WEYDEN

6-14. *IMAGO PIETATIS*, ADRIATIC SCHOOL

6-15. *POLYPTYCH OF THE PRESENTATION IN THE TEMPLE*, PSEUDO-JACOPINO DI FRANCESCO

6-16. *IMAGO PIETATIS*, MICHELE GIAMBONO

6-17. *LAMENTATION OVER THE DEAD CHRIST*, CARLO CRIVELLI

6-18. *NOLI ME TANGERE*, TITIAN

6-19. *CHRIST AND SAINT JOHN*

6-20. *SAINT FRANCIS EMBRACES THE CRUCIFIED CHRIST,*

FRANCISCO RIBALTA

6-21. *SAINT FRANCIS OF ASSISI IN ECSTASY*, CARAVAGGIO

6-22. *THE YOUNG HOLY FAMILY*, DANIEL BONNELL

6-23. *THE HOLY FAMILY*, NEILSON CARLIN

8-1. *MADONNA DEL LATTE*, AMBROGIO LORENZETTI

8-2. *THE LUCCA MADONNA*, JAN VAN EYCK

8-3. *VIRGIN AND CHILD*, HANS MEMLING

8-4. *HOLY FAMILY WITH MUSIC-MAKING ANGELS*, MASTER OF FRANKFURT

8-5. FACING PAGE: ADAM AND THE OFFERINGS OF CAIN AND ABEL, JAN AND HUBERT VAN EYCK

8-6. FACING PAGE: EVE AND THE MURDER OF ABEL BY CAIN, JAN AND HUBERT VAN EYCK

ADAM
EVA
ADAM NOS Ī MORTE PCIPITAT
EVA OCCIDENDO OBVIT

8-7. *GHENT ALTARPIECE*, JAN AND HUBERT VAN EYCK

8-8. *LAST JUDGMENT ALTARPIECE*, ROGIER VAN DER WEYDEN

8-9. *ALTARPIECE OF THE VIRGIN*, ROGIER VAN DER WEYDEN

10-1. *CHRIST PANTOCRATOR*

12-1. *THE SEVEN WORKS OF CHARITY*, MASTER OF ALKMAAR

NOTE: THE ILLUSTRATION IS SHOWN IN TWO SECTIONS TO ALLOW MAXIMUM SIZE FOR THIS PAGE.

12-2. "FEED THE HUNGRY," MASTER OF ALKMAAR

12-3. "GIVE DRINK TO THE THIRSTY," MASTER OF ALKMAAR

12-4. "CLOTHE THE NAKED," MASTER OF ALKMAAR

12-5. "CARE FOR THE SICK," MASTER OF ALKMAAR

13-1. *CALLING OF SAINT MATTHEW*, CARAVAGGIO

15-1. *THE ANASTASIS*, FRESCO IN THE PARECCLESION OF THE CHORA CHURCH OF THE HOLY SAVIOR

16-1. *OUR LADY OF RECOVERY*, SUZANN MIRIELLO

16-2. NORTH TRANSEPT ROSE WINDOW, NOTRE-DAME, PARIS

PART 2

The Visual Culture of Christianity

RANDI SIDER-ROSE

4 ⇇ Learning to See

The Sacralized Vision of Byzantine Iconography

Around the year AD 727, in Constantinople, a crowd composed mostly of women rioted when the emperor removed an icon of Christ from the palace gates. The three-dimensional, golden image of Christ, originally erected by iconophile emperor Justinian and empress Theodora, had come to represent the whole of religious art, and its removal signaled the beginning of what we now call the first iconoclastic controversy. As mobs raged against each other and icons were burned, John of Damascus helped to clarify the theology of the iconophiles. In contrast to the iconoclastic insistence that matter is "worthless and dead,"[1] Saint John reminds us that the doctrine of the Incarnation affirms that we must honor (though not worship) the material world:

> I do not worship matter; I worship the Creator of matter who became matter for my sake, who willed to take His abode in matter; who worked out my salvation through matter. Never will I cease honoring the matter which wrought my salvation! I honor it, but not as God.[2]

The Seventh Ecumenical Council further articulated the Damascene's theology by making the distinction between worship (*latreia*) and veneration (*proskynesis*). We venerate the icon but we worship only the Holy Trinity.

As iconophiles continued to hone their theology, they realized it was important to affirm not only matter and material symbols but also representational images, with a likeness to the person they represent.

1. Daniel J. Sahas, ed., *Icon and Logos: Sources in Eighth Century Iconoclasm* (Toronto: University of Toronto Press, 1986), 277D.

2. John of Damascus, *On the Divine Images: Three Apologies against Those Who Attack the Divine Images* (Crestwood, N.Y.: St. Vladimir's Seminary Press, 2000), 23.

Iconoclasts thought the symbols of the Eucharist and the cross were sufficient for Christians, who should otherwise be worshipping only "in spirit and in truth."[3] Instead, iconophiles argued that the Word of God assumed a human nature and could be seen as an incarnate person and therefore could be "imaged." It is an integral part of honoring a person, whether Christ or his saints, to honor that person's particular visage (*prosopon*) in an icon, not just the idea or symbol of that person. As Patriarch Nikephoros put it, the greater the similarity between the image and the prototype, the greater the glory given to the prototype.[4] Because of this two-fold purpose, honoring matter and honoring particular, visible images, the still-united Christian Church affirmed icons as not just possible but indispensable.

In an uncanny way, the iconoclasm of the eighth century revisits us in the twenty-first century. In today's secular world, matter is often seen as nothing but an inert resource—"worthless and dead"—for our use or abuse. The images we choose to put before ourselves can reflect and reify this worldview, even though people sometimes insist they are not affected by what they choose to see or watch. We pretend that the act of seeing is just a physical function of the eyes, not related to our soul. Pornography, for example, is only possible when one pretends that the humanity of both the viewer and the viewed is not body and spirit but "mere flesh" to be acted upon and used at whim.

By contrast, if we believe in the Incarnation, in the sacred potential of matter, including bodies, we should put images before us that reflect and symbolize this belief. Scripture affirms the spiritual practice of choosing what we see: "I will set no worthless thing before my eye" (Ps 101:3). Furthermore, implicit in "seeing with the eyes of the heart" (Eph 1:18) is the belief that we should be seeing from the core of our personhood, body and soul, created in the divine image (Gn 1:26–27). This type of seeing allows us to see more accurately because in seeing with our whole selves—body, heart, and soul—we are better able to affirm the wholeness of others.

The spiritual practices of iconography, now in the twentieth cen-

3. Jn 4:24.

4. Nikephoros, *Antirr.* 1.22, as translated and quoted by John Travis, *In Defense of Faith: The Theology of Patriarch Nikephoros of Constantinople* (Brookline, Mass.: Hellenic College Press, 1984), 44.

tury no less than during the eighth-century iconoclastic controversy, help form the faithful to be able to see with the eyes of the heart. Iconographic practices involve not only prayer in front of icons, but also the practice of painting icons, which is both a devotional practice and an aesthetic technique. Taken together, the spirituality and aesthetics of iconography counter the kind of dualistic anthropology that leads to pornography.

Devotional Practices

Devotional practices around iconography reflect and shape beliefs about the respect due to the image of God found in both icons and every human being. Orthodox Christians keep at least one icon corner, or devotional area, in their home, itself considered to be a "little church." When praying as a family or individually, we face the icons, even when our eyes are closed. We light candles before them, we chant and prostrate before them, and we kiss them. These forms of veneration pass to the person represented, just as kissing the photograph of someone we love expresses love for the person represented.

Out of love and respect, the Orthodox faithful kiss icons (and Bibles) if they are accidentally dropped, try not to stack or carry them in a cavalier fashion, and hesitate to poke or touch the icons' surfaces unnecessarily. Similarly, many Orthodox churches print black-and-white outlines of icons on bulletins rather than full-color reproductions, or at least dispose of the bulletins in a respectful annual burning by the priest. Within the church, icons commissioned by parishioners cover the walls, various stands, and the iconostasis at the front of the church. The great number of icons helps the Orthodox faithful viscerally sense and venerate the "great cloud of witnesses" (Heb 12:1) in both individual and corporate prayer.

As an iconographer, I am blessed to participate in the devotional practice of painting the icons. Iconography is a "prayer of the hands," and iconographers pray before sitting down to paint as well as during the various stages required to complete an icon. Indeed, iconographers' natural materials—selected from the animal, vegetable, and mineral realms—remind us that we are called to offer the whole world back to the Creator. First the wood is braced, cut and sanded; next, liquified rabbit skin and linen is applied, reminding us of Christ's shroud. This wood-plus-cloth provides a flexible base for the ten or more layers of gesso, a mix of chalk (calcium carbonate) and rabbit skin, in a process that takes about a day for a large icon. Finally, the board is sanded with increasingly fine sandpaper, ending with a marble-like white finish that symbolizes the iconographer's intent to present oneself as a "tabula rasa" for God to write his will for us. Where gold will go, such as the halo and background, red clay mixed with animal skin is traditionally applied and burnished, the iconographer's breath providing the final adhesive to make the gold leaf stick. Finally, the board is painted in a long—even months-long—process in which each stroke can be envisioned as a prayer.

As you can see, the devotional practices of iconography counter the mentality that matter, and by extension flesh, is "worthless and dead." Aesthetic traditions of iconography—how icons look in terms of what we now call their "style"—also developed to counteract pernicious spirit-body dualisms. In response to iconoclasm, while theologians labored to clarify how a material image did (and did not) depict divinity, iconographers were addressing exactly these questions wordlessly through their religious art. Compelled to express symbolically God's presence in embodied existence through their limited, material craft, they refined artistic techniques that facilitated a sacralized vision of creation and the human person. These techniques include the transfiguration of light, the stylization of anatomy, geometric ordering, and the use of inverse distance perspective.

Transfigured Light

The icon of the Transfiguration (Fig. 4-1) invites us into a sacralized vision of the world. At one time, every iconographer in the Orthodox tradition began his or her practice of this divine art by painting this icon,[5] though the practice should be questioned from the perspective of technical difficulty! Nevertheless, the theology of the icon of the Transfiguration should be closely studied by all students of the icon.

The icon depicts the event recounted in Matthew 17. Like all of

5. Paul Evdokimov, *The Art of the Icon: A Theology of Beauty*, trans. Steven Bigham (Redondo Beach, Calif.: Oakwood, 1990), 299.

us, the disciples needed to have their spiritual eyes opened, so Jesus took Peter, James, and John up to a high mountain, Mount Tabor. On the mountain, the divine glory that had been veiled within the humanity of Jesus Christ was revealed, "and he was transfigured before them; his face shone like the sun and his clothes became white as light" (Mt 17:2). On Christ's right and left appeared Moses and Elijah, symbolic of the law and the prophets. These men who had beheld the presence of God on Mount Horeb (Ex 3) and Mount Carmel (1 Kgs 19) now experienced with the disciples an expressly trinitarian theophany. "This is my beloved Son," the divine voice testified, and the disciples fell prostrate to the ground. Tradition holds that all of creation participates in this moment, just as we pray at vespers on the Feast of the Transfiguration: "All rejoice today, for in the divine light all of nature shines. This is why nature cries out with joy."[6]

The icon of the Transfiguration does not depict light coming from the sun or from any other identifiable source that would cause shadows. Rather, Christ—and to some extent, the whole scene—seems more generally illumined, as if from within. Contributing to this effect, iconographers layer transparent pigments, letting the light of the colors below and even the gesso shine through. Final white highlights are painted as shards of light. And the gold leaf used for the haloes, details, and sometimes entire backgrounds also contributes symbolically to the expression of uncreated Light.

The icon is painted in this way, without shadows and with the paint and gold communicating light, because in the Transfiguration the Divine Light of God became visible as a special grace granted to the disciples at this moment. As St. Gregory of Palamas articulated in his famous debate with Barlaam of Calabria, the disciples were able to see the uncreated Light of God, because even though we cannot know God in his essence, we can know his energies when he reveals himself.

Though the Transfiguration is the quintessential iconographic expression of uncreated Light, all icons symbolically portray Divine Light, regardless of the subject matter. After all, this kind of revelation was not limited to Mount Tabor, but has happened throughout history. One thinks of the light seen by St. Paul during his conversion,

6. Evdokimov, *Art of the Icon*, 306.

or accounts of the occasional illumination of the saints, such as St. Seraphim of Sarov. Indeed, each of us hope for our bodily resurrection in transformed, illumined flesh. Thus, icons of saints, no matter what physical trials they went through, are portrayed as physically restored.

Somehow this aesthetic technique of portraying illumined flesh must be balanced with knowledge of what the person looked like, insofar as this is known. We remember Nikephoros' maxim, that the greater the similarity, the greater the glory given to the prototype. This provides a particular challenge to iconographers in the modern day, when we actually have photographs of recent saints, such as the twentieth-century Saint Maria of Paris. I attempted to paint her according to photographs, so that she would be recognizable. But I was also careful to use the iconographic tradition of portraying illumined flesh (Figs. 4-2 and 4-3).

We achieve this depiction of illumined, resurrected flesh on a technical level by a progression from dark tones to light. In distinction from other styles of painting, we start with a dark flesh-tone and gradually build up the highlights, always letting what is below shine through. You can see this permeation of light in the progressive stages of the icon I wrote, based on the fifteenth-century Virgin *Eleousa* icon currently found at the Cleveland Museum of Art (Figs. 4-4, 4-5, 4-6, and 4-7). The process of building up an icon in this manner, each stage taking several hours, gives ample time for prayerful reflection about illumined flesh.

Stylized Anatomy

Another iconographic technique that developed to illustrate the transformation of matter is the "stylization" of anatomy, or so we would call it from our post-Renaissance perspective. In other words, certain anatomical features and characteristics are portrayed differently than they would be in a post-Renaissance artistic style, or differently from what we in the West would consider "realistic." The figure of Christ in this icon of the Crucifixion, for example, is at least nine "heads" tall (in the measuring unit of life drawing), in contrast to the typical six to eight (Fig. 4-8). These exaggerated proportions accentuate both Christ's divine nature as well as the reality of his death on the cross.

Other aspects of the painting echo this emphasis on divine nature. His eyes are closed, signifying death, but his face does not betray the pain of his torture and crucifixion. His body, though sagging and pierced, remains incorruptible. To the left of the cross stands the Virgin Mary. "The fingers of her left hand," Evdokimov comments, "are near her throat, as though she is trying to loosen the tightness caused by an unspeakable pain.... Mary cannot move; she is frozen in suffering."[7] And yet, she is not collapsing at the horror of her son's disfigured flesh. She, too, knows the hope of the Resurrection, even at her moment of greatest suffering.

This icon emphasizes that it is not just the moment of Christ's substitutionary atonement in death that is necessary for our salvation, but every event in Christ's life, from birth to ascension. The glory of the Resurrection, therefore, plays a role in the representation of all the events preceding it, including this most agonizing moment of death. Christ crucified is portrayed through a sacralized vision in which we behold the soteriological meaning of the cross as a triumph over sin and death through the flesh. The vertical trunk of the cross expresses the *descensus* and *ascensus* of the Word of God in the mystery of the Incarnation and glorification, and the foot of the cross extends down into a cavern in which we can see the skull of Adam, symbolic of the entire human race. This icon communicates in one image the doctrine of *theosis*: God became human, that humans might become divine.[8]

The icon of the Virgin of Vladimir is another instance of the use of stylized anatomy to express symbolically the union of matter and spirit in the flesh (Fig. 4-9). This Byzantine icon was painted by a Greek artist in Constantinople and brought to Russia in the twelfth century. Over the course of history, it has survived fires and Tartar attacks. The Virgin's nose is thinned and her ears and mouth minimized, symbolizing the final transfiguration of the senses. Her eyes, however, are

7. Evdokimov, *Art of the Icon*, 315.

8. Irenaeus, *Adversus haereses*, 5, preface, in Patrologiae cursus completus, series graeca [hereafter PG], ed. Jacques Paul Migne (Paris: Migne, 1857–66), 7:1120; Athanasius, *De incarnatione verbi*, 54, in PG 25:192B; Gregory of Nazianzus, *Poema dogmatica*, 10, 5–9, in PG 37:465; Gregory of Nyssa, *Oratio catechetica magna*, 25, in PG 45:65D. Cited in Vladimir Lossky, *In the Image and Likeness of God*, ed. John H. Erickson and Thomas E. Bird (Oxford: A. R. Mowbray, 1974), 97.

enlarged, and they engage us directly and contemplatively. The head of Christ is out of proportion to his infant body and has mature features. This is not due to a lack of understanding of the anatomy of children on the part of the iconographer. Rather, the portrayal of the child-man symbolically represents the eternal wisdom of the Word of God, who has existed since before the creation of the world, even though he came into the world as an infant who placed his cheek affectionately against his mother's in a quintessentially human gesture. In fact, since children and babies are always portrayed with small heads, an icon such as "Christ Blessing the Children" arguably affirms the status of children as just as important as adults, in a manner parallel to the story the icon represents.

Contemporary viewers—especially those who grew up without icons—often object to icons' stylized anatomy, while responding positively to their more realistic aspects. Raised in the Protestant tradition, I initially found the small-headed Christ child foreign and jarring. However, as I learned that this was part of the symbolic language of the icon, itself a form of theology akin to written texts, I began to appreciate the icon's stylized anatomy. One virtue of the symbolic language of iconography is that it frees the beholder from a closed relationship with an object that must be interpreted as the singular vision of a particular artist and opens the possibility of communion with the prototype beyond. Wood and paint can then become impregnated with the *prosopon*, or countenance, of the eternal.

Many people over the years have asked me whether, because I start with such a dark skin base (described above as integral to the method of "building up" light from dark), my icons are based on an African tradition. In fact, the opposite is true. I have been trained in the Russian tradition, which begins with a darker skin-base, while icons from Africa and Egypt—Coptic icons—historically begin with a notably light skin-base. I had not previously thought of skin color as a symbolic convention. However, I have come to realize that iconography is part of a long and widespread tradition of portraying the Divine as the other, rather than as our own mirror image. In this, iconography is distinct from much contemporary religious imagery, which portrays Christ as similar and relatable to the artist's own community. If early

Christians struggled to grasp that the Divine became *human*, perhaps today we have the hardest time remembering that the *Divine*—in all his mystery and otherness—became human, and that we lose sight of this miracle if we attempt to make God in our own image.

Geometric Order and Harmony

Iconographers also symbolize the communion of the material and spiritual worlds through the harmonious geometrical order of their icons. As did ancient Greek and Egyptian artists, the iconographer prepares a surface for painting by sketching lines and arcs that provide a structure for the images. Orthodox iconographers follow a specific geometric pattern for each particular icon in our tradition. For example, the underlying geometry of the icon of the Holy Face dates back to antiquity, and iconographers always follow this same basic structure for every icon of this type. Regardless of the size and proportion of the board, the same geometric lines and arcs almost always underlie the Holy Face (Figs. 4-10 and 4-11). This creates an aesthetic sense of interconnected harmony, even if the viewer is unaware of the complexity below the surface of the pigments.

Another good example of the interconnected harmony of iconographic composition is the more complex, festal icon of the Nativity of Christ. This icon depicts the effect that the Incarnation of the Divine Logos has on all of creation (Fig. 4-12).[9] The event of God become human, called the "festival of re-creation" by St. Gregory the Theologian,[10] transformed the earthly existence of not only all humans but also all plants and animals. The icon's geometric structure represents this recreation, encompassing the rock and tree formations that branch out from the tomb-like cave wherein Christ lies. The icon also emphasizes Jesus' full humanity and real birth. In the lower right corner of the icon, servants bathe the naked Christ child, whose needs

9. Moreover, the doctrine of the Incarnation gives the justification for the creation of icons themselves. As the Second Council of Nicaea articulated: since the Son of God has come into the world of visible realities, his humanity builds a bridge between the visible and the invisible. By analogy, visible created materials can be used within the logic of symbols to represent and evoke the mystery of the Incarnation.

10. St. Gregory the Theologian, *Discourse* 38, in PG 36:316B. Cited in Leonid Ouspensky and Vladimir Lossky, *The Meaning of Icons*, trans. G. E. H. Palmer and E. Kadloubovsky (Boston, Mass.: Boston Book and Art Shop, 1969), 157.

were the same as those of any other human infant. And Mary's exhausted pose attests to Jesus' literal birth. Joseph, too, is shown with very human emotions. He is thoughtful and perhaps conflicted, as the devil, in the guise of an old man, tempts him with doubts while Mary, representing the Church, looks upon him with compassion.

The icon of the Nativity of Christ trains our eye to see the interconnected order of creation, harmonized not only within itself but also with God. A single ray extends from the top of the icon, but the star light divides into three beams, symbolizing the action of the triune God in the economy of creation and redemption. "In music," Evdokimov writes in a commentary on the symbols, structure, and colors of the icon of the Nativity, "certain harmonies evoke a feeling of beatitude; pictorial beauty at its highest degree also attains pure beauty. It directly expresses the divine, without any didactic teaching."[11] Some people say that the purpose of art is to give an unblinking view of the starkness of reality, though by this they may mean a grim or even grotesque vision. Iconographers do portray reality, but as Christians, we believe that reality is an interconnected and beautiful whole that reveals the divine.

Inverse Perspective

A fourth technique that shows the interpenetration of the human and divine is the use of an apparent distortion of perspective. In a realist painting, the artist recreates our natural field of vision in which objects appear to become smaller as they recede into the distance. Inverse or isometric perspective emphasizes the foreground so that figures seem to come out from the icon.

The fifteenth-century icon of the Holy Trinity by Andrei Rublev is a classic example of the iconographer's use of inverse perspective (Fig. 4-13).[12] Because neither the Trinity nor God the Father can be pictorially represented, the symbolism of the icon of the Trinity is based on the story in Genesis 18 of the hospitality that Abraham and Sarah extended to three strangers, who ultimately were revealed to be

11. Evdokimov, *Art of the Icon*, 272.

12. On Rublev's icon, see Gabriel Bunge, *The Rublev Trinity: The Icon of the Trinity by the Monk-Painter Andrei Rublev*, trans. Andrew Louth (Crestwood, N.Y.: St. Vladimir's Seminary Press, 2007).

angels. Abraham and Sarah invited the wayfarers to rest while they prepared a special meal for their guests. In Rublev's version of this icon, the pedestals beneath the feet of the angels seated at the table are depicted using inverse perspective. Rather than narrowing as they recede into the distance, the parts of the pedestals that are farthest from the viewer are the widest. Similarly, the table legs that are farthest from the viewer have the same proportions as those that are nearest.

Inverse perspective contributes to the capacity of the icon to teach us to see. When we venerate an icon, we do not look *at* the icon with an objectifying gaze but rather respond to an iconic presence coming towards us. Rublev's icon of the Trinity is a superb example of how icons teach us to see. Other versions of this icon portray Abraham and sometimes also Sarah, laughing in the door of her home at the idea that she might give birth in her elder years. In Rublev's adaptation, however, we see only the angels at the table, which opens out to us, giving us, the viewers, the opportunity to exhibit the hospitality that Abraham and Sarah extended towards the three guests. Whether we accept or reject this opportunity, the offer has been made.

Conclusion

Aesthetic techniques—such as inverse perspective—do not magically force a response in the viewer. Much less do they bring about a compulsive reaction as a grotesque picture might evoke disgust or a pornographic image feelings of lust. On the contrary, iconography is not only an aesthetic form of theology but also an ascetic tradition and devotional practice. The Christian ascetic traditions—the fasting calendar, a rule of prayer, practices of iconography—free us from enslavement to human passions. Though the contemporary, secular assumption of "freedom" is often "the absence of rules," the much longer tradition of the Church recognizes that the right rules set you free from passions such as involuntary responses.

Why limit what you put before you? Why practice an asceticism of the eyes? Why might we avoid or limit what we see on the screen? One reason is that these images may evoke involuntary responses, which are not free. Some responses can be willfully resisted, but it is better not to "set a worthless thing before your eyes," to quote the psalmist again. Freedom lies *not* in having involuntary responses of shock or lust, but in choosing to take steps towards God in response to his love. The rules of the Christian tradition enable us to become more human, and to be human is not to be shackled with involuntary impulses, but to be able to see the beauty and interconnectedness of creation and the glory of the image of God in every human being.

Icons depict the transfiguration of the world and, in so doing, help us to see and even to bring about this transfiguration. Iconographers bring their "first fruits" to the craft, while remaining acutely aware that all of their materials come from the Creator and that their skills fall short of the glory of God. As with our participation in the liturgy, and as with our corporal service to our fellow humans, we hope that iconography is one humble step towards allowing ourselves to be written on and formed as the humans we were meant to be before God. The resulting artifact is one that "says," like the offertory during the liturgical service, that a human created in the image of God is one who freely returns the whole world to God in thanksgiving, sacrifice, and praise.

DANIELLE M. PETERS

5 ⇷ A Transformative Encounter

A Historical and Theological Reflection on the Contribution of Marian Imagery to the Capacity for Sacramental Vision

When he was archbishop of Buenos Aires, Jorge Bergoglio—now Pope Francis—admitted in an interview: "I discovered ... Our Lady [as someone who] stirs consciences ... like a mother who places things in order."[1] In another context, the pontiff explained that this discovery became strongly evident to him when hearing confessions in the Basilica of Luján, Argentina. Describing the internal layout of the basilica and the location of the confessionals, he observed that Our Lady of Luján is placed in the center of the basilica in such a way that persons entering the confessionals on the left side of the altar will not necessarily see the image, whereas those who use the confessionals on the right side always do. "I have had experiences hearing confessions on the left and right [side of the main altar]," he said.[2] And, to his surprise, he noticed a big difference. When penitents approached the confessional on the left side of the basilica, theirs were "normal confessions.... But in the right [confessional], there appeared the whales, the big fish!"[3] Why this disparity? Then the cardinal realized: "Because they had seen her!"[4] Of course, in referring to "her," he meant Our Lady, whose image of grace the pilgrims about to enter the confessional had just encountered. They saw her seeing them and were transformed by her maternal glance and unassuming integrity.

1. Alexandre Awi Mello, *Ela é minha Mãe! Encontros do Papa Francisco com Maria* (São Paulo: Edições Loyola Jesuitas, 2014), 55. Unofficial translation.
2. Awi Mello, *Ela é minha Mãe!* 56.
3. Awi Mello, *Ela é minha Mãe!* 59.
4. Awi Mello, *Ela é minha Mãe!* 53.

Likewise, Pope Francis's predecessor, Pope Saint John Paul II, understood the silent power of the created likenesses of Our Lady: "Images, icons, and statues of Our Lady, present in houses, public places, and countless churches and chapels, help the faithful to invoke her constant presence and her merciful patronage in the various circumstances of life. By making the Blessed Virgin's motherly tenderness concrete and almost tangible, they [the images, icons, statues] invite us to turn to her trustfully and to imitate her."[5] The late Polish pontiff made great efforts to include a pilgrimage to a Marian shrine during each of his 102 pastoral visits across the globe, thereby highlighting the local importance of these places of grace and the charism inherent in Marian icons.

Catholic culture has always been identified by the practice of enshrining images of Mary in churches and homes. Representations of Our Lady in popular piety respond to the thirst for the sacred and open up to the divine. Icons and statues of the Blessed Virgin offer solace in moments of difficulty and serve as a reminder of a life pleasing to God. In our time, visual imagery has increased exponentially due to digital technologies; inversely, the use of religious imagery in many Catholic homes and even in Catholic churches has decreased. No doubt, this striking fact weakens Catholic visual culture and the resulting void is often filled by a continual stream of media imagery, including pornographic images that are deforming to the soul.

This chapter presents a historical and theological reflection about Our Lady's pictures of grace as they have impacted the individual, the Church, and society.[6] These considerations will leave us with more insights—and perhaps also with more questions—as to how a renewal of Marian imagery might both protect our imagination from the intrusion of pornography and purify the hearts of women and men who have been exposed or addicted to pornography. The chapter be-

5. John Paul II, *Theotókos: Woman, Mother, Disciple: A Catechesis on Mary, Mother of God* (Boston, Mass.: Pauline Books & Media, 2000), 252. See also John Paul II, Encyclical Letter *Redemptoris Mater* (March 25, 1987), 36.

6. For an in-depth study of both historical developments and theological reflections, see Karl Kolb, "Typologie der Gnadenbilder," in *Handbuch der Marienkunde*, ed. Wolfgang Beinert and Heinrich Petri, 449–81 (Regensburg: Friedrich Pustet, 1997), 2:449–81; Walter Pötzl, "Marianisches Brauchtum an Wallfahrtsorten," *Handbuch der Marienkunde*, 2:483–553.

gins with a historical survey of developments in Marian iconography over the course of two millennia, continues with a theological account of iconography in both the Eastern and Western traditions, and concludes with a reflection on the transformative grace that Marian imagery makes visible.

Marian Iconography in Christian History

Unique among comparable forms of religious and popular art, Marian iconography mirrors the history of theological and anthropological development of more than eighteen hundred years of Christian iconographic traditions. Since the early beginnings of the Church, painters and sculptors were supported by preachers and poets who praised Our Lady in vivid metaphors. It is impossible to systematize all of the images of *Polynomous*—the woman of many names—since the local cult and time-bound representations of Mary through the centuries are innumerable.[7] Christian art through the ages has presented Mary in all kinds of settings, costumes, and attitudes through which the devout imagination can glimpse her reality. Artistic renderings include images taken from the Gospel narratives that portray Mary as Madonna, untouched maiden, nursing mother, and mourning mother of the Pietà tradition. She has also been rendered as majestic queen, Byzantine noblewoman, Flemish housewife, and African mother. This rich diversity of representations reflects the breadth of Christian experience over the course of history.

Early Stages

The very first icon portraying the Mother of God is attributed to St. Luke.[8] In the years before the Council of Ephesus in AD 431, which proclaimed Mary as *Theotokos* (God Bearer), Our Lady became a central figure in iconography and was portrayed most frequently as

7. The term *Polynomous* originates from Pseudo-John Damascene, *Homilie 2 "in Annuntiationem,"* Patrologiae cursus completus, series graeca, ed. Jacques Paul Migne (Paris: Migne, 1928–36), 96:648 C1.

8. To view an icon in this tradition, see "Vladimir Icon Origins," "All About Mary" website, International Marian Research Institute, University of Dayton, accessed October 20, 2018, https https://udayton.edu/imri/mary/v/vladimir-icon-origins.php.

Virgin, Mother of God, and Mother of the Church.[9] Of these images, the Enthroned *Theotokos* became the most disseminated and revered image of Mary.[10] This icon shows Our Lady seated on a golden throne either with the Christ child on her lap (Fig. 5-1 and 5-2) or, later, next to her son in a heavenly setting. Both variations emphasize her royalty and mediating power. Art portraying *Maria lactans* (Nursing Mary),[11] or *Galaktotrophusa* (Suckling Mother), was popular in Egypt as early as the late fourth century and is often erroneously associated with the pagan gods of Egyptian origins (based on the Isis-Horus legends).[12] The earliest known depiction of the Nursing Mother is painted in the Priscilla Catacombs, ca. AD 250.[13]

Another prominent representation of Mary within the early Church is the praying Mary—*Maria Orans* (in the Latin tradition) or *Blacherniotissa* (in the Greek tradition). In these images, Mary is portrayed with both of her arms lifted up, which stresses her powerful intercession with her son.[14] Sometimes, her uplifted arms are

9. Before the first iconoclasm (roughly from the sixth through the eighth century), thirty-two churches and cloisters had been named after Mary.

10. The Vatican Museums exhibit sarcophagi, pectoral crosses, royal seals, reliquaries, and religious jewelry from that time depicting the enthroned *Theotokos*.

11. For images of *Maria lactans*, see Kimberly Hope Belcher's chapter 8, in this volume, and "An Early Coptic Nursing Mary," in "Gallery of Maria Lactans," Fish Eaters website, accessed October 20, 2018, https://www.fisheaters.com/images/marialactans2.jpg.

12. Authentic art seeks to communicate truth and beauty that leads the viewer to contemplation. When it depicts the human body or a relationship of love, it may include nudity, but not in an exaggerated way so as to obscure the subject as a whole. Pornography, in contrast, reduces the persons portrayed to their sexual attributes, with the purpose of provoking sensuous craving in the viewer. See Karol Wojtyła, *Love and Responsibility* (Boston, Mass.: Pauline Books and Media, 2013), 192–93. For an explanation of sacred art, see *Catechism of the Catholic Church*, 2nd ed. (Washington, D.C.: United States Conference of Catholic Bishops, 2000), 2501; John Paul II, *Letter to Artists* (April 4, 1999); Benedict XVI, *Address to Artists* (November 21, 2009).

13. To view the image from the Catacombs, see "Our Lady as painted in the Priscilla Catacombs, ca. AD 250," in "Gallery of Maria Lactans," Fish Eaters website, accessed October 20, 2018, https://www.fisheaters.com/images/marialactans1.jpg. Parenthetically, the very first Marian shrine in the U.S. is dedicated to *Nuestra Señora de Leche y Buen Parto* (Our Lady of Milk and Good Birth). This statue (ca. AD 1600–1620) is kept in the shrine of St. Augustine, Florida. To view an image, see "*Nuestra Señora de Leche y Buen Parto* (Our Lady of Milk and Good Birth)," in "Gallery of Maria Lactans," Fish Eaters website, accessed October 20, 2018, https://www.fisheaters.com/images/marialactans160020.jpg.

14. To view *Maria Orans* images, see "Orans of Kiev. Mosaic. XI c." Wikipedia, created September 28, 2005, https://en.wikipedia.org/wiki/Orans#/media/File:Oranta_Kiev.jpg.

supported by her son, who is exposed in a medallion on her chest, as in the wall painting above a doorway from the narthex to the nave in the Church of our Lady of the Pastures in Cyprus (Fig. 5-3). In these representations, called *Panagia*, Mary appears also as a type of Ecclesia, the Church.[15]

After the Iconoclasm

The Seventh General Council in Nicaea in AD 787 solemnly defined the principles for the practice of venerating religious images and pointed out the abuses and distortions created by idolatry. Immediately, the cult relative to religious images became reestablished as an integral part of the faith. As a result, there was an increase of churches dedicated to the Blessed Virgin Mary. In addition, her image appeared on coins and royal seals; thus, Our Lady continued to be a vital part of religious culture. Yet, this era did not bring many new forms of Marian representation. The two most venerated images of Our Lady were the enthroned Mary with the Christ child and the standing Madonna, hands lifted in prayer. The former is depicted in two classical images known as *Hodegetria* (She Who Shows the Way) (Fig. 5-15) and *Eleousa* (Our Lady of Tenderness). (See Fig. 4-7 for a contemporary icon in this tradition).[16] The *Orante* image developed into the tradition of the Life-Giving Spring or Fountain, which shows Mary as the one who receives and distributes God's living waters to humanity, in need of both spiritual and physical healing.

We can observe distinct developments in Marian iconography in both the Eastern and Western traditions. In the East, Russia integrated Byzantine icons and named them after the monastery or city where the icon had been venerated and where possible miracles had occurred. Thus, the *Hodegetria* became the *Mother of God of Smolensk*, and the *Eleousa* was called a *Vladimirskaja* (Fig. 4-9).[17] In the

15. View additional *Panagia* images at Orama World: World's Oldest Orthodox Christian Online Store, "Panagia: Platytera-of-the-heavens," image uploaded July 6, 2014, https://www.oramaworld.com/images/byzantine_icons/aged/panagia-%22platytera-of-the-heavens%22-aged-byzantine-icon-th39_300.jpg.

16. View another image of the *Eleousa* at "Mother of God Icon Eleousa (Oumilenie)," *Cleansing Fire* (blog), created August 4, 2010, http://www.cleansingfire.org/wp-content/uploads/2010/08/Eleousa-icon.jpg.

17. To view an image of the Mother of God of Smolensk, see: "Mother of God at

West, icons were often adapted to liturgical practices and local religious traditions. Thus, new forms and expressions of Mary's role in salvation history reflected the religious mentality prevailing at the time. Old Testament metaphors were attributed to Mary, such as that of the enclosed garden (Song 4:12) (Fig. 5-4). In this scene, Mary sits with her child in a paradise meadow surrounded by a natural hedge or a fence. These portrayals depict Mary's immaculate purity, as well as her humility and election as bride and mother of God. In the fourteenth century, small devotional pictures (holy cards) and the home altar first began to appear in Italy and then spread to the neighboring countries. Devout pilgrims would obtain small pictures of Our Lady at pilgrimage places and keep them in their prayer books or homes, thereby strengthening personal and family devotional practices.[18]

Around 1450, a sentimental style began to break through all over Europe; holy cards portrayed idyllic images with allegorical meaning. Mary was shown playing with her child and offering him a symbolic "toy." Flowers and angels pointed heavenward, teaching the child to read, write, and sing. Images of the Christ child offering an apple or grapes to his mother directed attention to Mary as the new Eve, or to the Eucharist, while a lamb recalled Christ's title as Lamb of God.[19] Sometimes virgin saints were depicted as playmates of the child Jesus or Mary. Other images within this genre show the events of Mary's life: the child Mary with St. Anne, the birth of Jesus, the flight to Egypt, the sorrowful mother, and the Assumption of Mary into heaven. These holy cards evoked piety in the imagination of young and old.

Smolensky," *Assist Icon-Painting Shop*, accessed October 20, 2018, http://accist.ru/images/CIMG7937.jpg.

18. A curious practice emerged in Germany throughout the eighteenth to twentieth centuries. Small images with portrayals of Our Lady were ingested as folk medicine. Devout believers of that time believed that Mary was the ultimate physician and that by swallowing the *Schluckbildchen*, they partook of her curative powers.

19. To view an image of an offering of apples and grapes, see Joos van Cleve, "Virgin and Child," The Met Museum website, accessed October 20, 2018, https://www.metmuseum.org/toah/images/hb/hb_1982.60.47.jpg. To view an image of Mary as the New Eve, see ChurchPOP Editor, "7 Church Fathers on that Profound Insight of Mary as the New Eve," ChurchPOP website, September 11, 2014, https://churchpop.com/2014/09/11/7-church-fathers-mary-new-eve/.

After the Council of Trent (1545–63)

One of the most important ecumenical councils, the Council of Trent, convened in 1545 to respond to the Protestant Reformation. The council confirmed Mary's unique position among the saints and issued guidelines concerning the appropriate manner of her veneration. After the council, large numbers of Marian images were created to support doctrinal and catechetical teaching. The French School, for example, focused on Christocentric and theocentric Mariology. Artists often portrayed Mary as a young woman, hovering over the waning moon, and surrounded by angels bearing attributes of the Litany of Loreto to indicate her immaculate conception.[20] A popular image of the Counter-Reformation period (1545–1648) shows Mary stepping on the dragon to symbolize her victory over the devil (Gn 3:15). This image of Mary defeating the devil led to portrayals of Our Lady as the Victorious Empress and Queen of Heaven.[21] Sculptors created pillars topped with a statue of Our Lady of Victory as a way to point to her exalted position. One of the earliest columns stands erected in front of Santa Maria Maggiore in Rome. By the end of the seventeenth century, most European cities had erected a Marian column in their market places to honor Our Lady and to implore for her intercession in times of war, famine, and epidemics. The Marian pillars were pilgrim destinations as well as rallying points for politics and patriotism.[22]

In France, West Prussia, Sweden, Spain, and Portugal, we find the Shrine Madonna, which is a statue of Our Lady that can be opened. Hidden within the statue are scenes of the Incarnation and Passion of Christ or representations of the Trinity, as in the *Vierge Ouvrante* (Figs. 5-5 and 5-6).[23] The sublime representation of Mary as a dwelling

20. To view an image, see "Queenship of Mary," *Di Meliora* (blog), accessed October 20, 2018, https://dimeliora.files.wordpress.com/2010/12/queenshipofmary.jpg.

21. To view an image, see "Queen of Heaven," *Michael Angell* (blog), accessed October 20, 2018, http://michaelangell.com/wp-content/uploads/2010/07/QueenofHeaven.jpg.

22. Perhaps better known, yet more recent, is the Column of the Immaculate Conception erected in central Rome near the Spanish Steps in the nineteenth century. Since December 8, 1953, popes have come there annually to offer a bouquet of flowers to Our Lady commemorating the Feast of the Immaculate Conception.

23. This Madonna type originated in women's monasteries and was inspired by medieval mysticism and Cistercian spirituality. Trent did not explicitly condemn the

place of the triune God irresistibly attracts the faithful to her. A variety of images focusing on Mary's compassion and mercy were created during the fourteenth through sixteenth centuries. In Italy she was venerated as *Madonna della Misericordia* (Madonna of Compassion), in Germany as *Schutzmantelmadonna* (Sheltering-Mantle Madonna) (Fig. 5-7), in Spain as *Nuestra Señora de las Mercedes* (Our Lady of Mercy), and in France as *Vièrge au Manteau* (Virgin with a Cloak or Cape).[24] The group of people huddled beneath Mary's protective mantle in these images were often members of the hierarchy, of a religious order, or of a region in urgent need.

With the beginning of the Baroque period, in the seventeenth century, the faithful expressed their affection for Mary by dressing statues of Mother and child according to liturgical feasts and seasons. Dresses, capes, and royal insignia were the usual donations from the aristocracy and the thanksgiving offerings from individuals who had received help in times of great need. In order to accommodate this pious practice, artists created sculptures based on the original icons. Among the most famous are Our Lady of Loreto, Our Lady of Altötting, and Our Lady of Einsiedeln. These three images have an added dimension; they also belong to the category of the famous Black Madonnas.[25]

---

creation and veneration of the Shrine Madonnas. Its decree on sacred images of December 3, 1563 was generic by design, entrusting local bishops with the right to accept or reject specific images. See Gudrun Radler, *Die Schreinmadonna "Vierge ouvrante": von den bernhardinischen Anfängen bis zur Frauenmystik im Deutschordensland: mit beschreibendem Katalog* (Frankfurt am Main: Kunstgeschichtliches Institut der Johann Wolfgang Goethe-Universität, 1990), 51–123. For more on this tradition, see Johann G. Roten, "Vierge Ouvrante or Shrine Madonna," "All About Mary" website, International Marian Research Institute, University of Dayton, accessed October 20, 2018, https://udayton.edu/imri/mary/v/vierge-ourvante-what-is.php.

24. For images of the *Schutzmantelmadonna* in addition to that included in the inset, see Piero della Francesca, "Polyptych of Misericordia," Wikimedia, uploaded October 8, 2009, https://upload.wikimedia.org/wikipedia/commons/0/0c/Piero,_Pala_della_misericordia,_madonna_della_misericordia.jpg.

25. For an image of one exemplar, see Runoko Rashidi, "The Black Madonnas of Europe: Miracle Workers and Holy Icons," *Atlanta Black Star* website, March 26, 2014, https://atlantablackstar.com/2014/03/26/black-madonnas-europe-miracle-workers-holy-icons/. Two theories are connected with these images. The first maintains that their black coloring—caused by candles, incense smoke, and dust—illustrates a verse from the Song of Songs: *nigra sum, sed formosa* ("I am black but beautiful") (Song 1:4). This theory was strengthened by the numerous commentaries on the *Canticles* of St. Bernard of Clairvaux comparing the soul to the bride, most authentically personalized in Our Lady. The second, less religious theory, argues that Black Madonnas were

Marian images of grace of the Baroque period were venerated especially under the titles of Mother of Good Counsel, Our Lady of Prompt Succor, Our Lady of Mercy, and Our Lady of Victory. Devotion to Mary under these titles spread to mission countries as well and inspired varieties of Marian art, which highlighted Mary's succor or a particular miracle that she had mediated. Marian images also constituted a powerful rebuke to the Counter-Reformation's exclusion of Mary, especially north of the Alps. Marian devotion permeated Catholic Europe so deeply that Marian images were even brought into battle as spiritual weapons during wars such as the Great Siege of Malta (1565), the Battle of Lepanto (1571), and the Battle of Vienna (1683), where victory over the Turks was attributed to the intercession of Our Lady and the rosary prayer.

The Baroque era also produced books vividly depicting the lives of Jesus Christ and of Mary. This, in turn, exponentially influenced popular piety and art. In particular, the poignant hymn, the *Stabat Mater*, composed in the thirteenth century, contributed to the devotion to the Sorrowful Mother and to the Seven Joys and Sorrows of Mary. Two major kinds of Marian images celebrated a comeback at that time: the Pietà (fourteenth century) and the Heart of Mary pierced by seven swords (fifteenth century). Often, religious communities promoted devotion to Mary as Mediatrix of Grace as they disseminated the scapular or rosary.

Marian Images of Grace in the Sixteenth through the Twenty-first Centuries

Influenced by the Italian Renaissance, Raphael (1483–1520) gained prominence for painting ordinary women as models for the Immaculate Conception and the Mother with the Christ child. Over the past centuries, artists have created images to commemorate apparitions,

ancient pagan goddesses subsumed by Christianity. This theory supports the idea that the Virgin Mary is indeed the most inculturated woman of all ages and cultures. Black Madonnas should not be confused with inculturated dark-skinned Madonnas, meaning artwork by African or African American artists of our time. For more information, see Michael Duricy and Vincenzina Krymow, "The Black Madonna: Past and Present," *Marian Studies* 57, Article 10 (2006): 190–241, accessed October 20, 2018, https://ecommons.udayton.edu/cgi/viewcontent.cgi?article=1024&context=marian_studies.

such as Our Lady of Guadalupe (1531), Our Lady of Lourdes (1858), and Our Lady of Fatima (1917). Sacred art of the last century often portrays the artist's personal experience, be it his suffering of wars or his longing for a mother figure. Recent Marian imagery often focuses on the humanness of the Christ child encountering his mother, or on the suffering of Mary cradling her son in the Pietà. And contemporary artists continue to signal Mary's universal character by portraying Our Lady in diverse ethnicities—such as the *African Madonna* by Lisa Fracica (Fig. 5-8), the African American Mother in the *Baltimore Holy Family* by Brother Michael O'Neill McGrath (Fig. 5-9), the *Guatemalan Annunciation* and *Mother and Child* by Father John B. Giuliani (Fig. 5-10 and 5-11), the *Japanese Madonna* (Fig. 5-12), the Korean *Madonna and Child* (Fig. 5-13), and the Polynesian *Our Lady of Chaminade* (Fig. 5-14).

Theological Reflection

The history of Marian art testifies to the enduring prophetic mystery of a young woman whose undivided surrender to God generated "Jesus who gave to the world the Life that renews all things."[26] Every sacred image portraying Mary proclaims that her name and memory will continue to be a blessing "from generation to generation" (Lk 1: 48). Authentic Marian art always originates in sacred Scripture and takes its bearing from the traditions of the Church. Its origin and subsequent veneration occur in an atmosphere of contemplation and prayer, which lift the faithful to an encounter with the supernatural reality of the Incarnation, the central event in human history. The internationally known mariologist, Johann G. Roten, SM, argues that religious art should follow three principles: (1) it should have an emotional impact on the soul; (2) it should be theologically sound; (3) it should express the artistic sensibility and understanding of its time and culture.[27] In the East, strict rules of iconographic subject matter and technique convey the timeless and universal quality of the mys-

26. Vatican Council II, *Lumen Gentium* (November 21, 1964), 56.

27. Johann G. Roten, "Popular Religion and Marian Images," *Marian Studies* 45, Article 9 (1994), 72n9, accessed October 20, 2018, http://ecommons.udayton.edu/marian_studies/vol45/iss1/9.

teries conveyed through the icon. The artists of the West, on the other hand, endeavor to portray "how changing cultures grappled with the Incarnation."[28]

Eastern Iconography

For Eastern Christians, the icon is a "divine representation," a visible gospel, revealing the Blessed Trinity's beauty and order. Every human person, created in the image and likeness of God, is an icon of the first icon, Jesus Christ, who is the Incarnation of God's Logos, uniting in one person the uncreated divine nature and a created human nature. Thus, each iconographer aims to establish a personal encounter between the divine, the representation of the image, and the person venerating the icon. Pondering an icon in silence and awe opens the person to an ever-increasing transformation of life with and in God. While icons are used to enhance the beauty of a church, they are most important as a catechetical tool within both churches and Christian homes. They resemble doors to God's mystery and thus have the character of an epiphany, a manifestation of God, made visible not only in Jesus Christ but also in the lives of Mary the Mother of God and all the saints.

As noted in the historical survey, the very first icon portraying the Mother of God is attributed to St. Luke. From this blueprint, three principle classical versions of Marian icons developed in the East: the *Hodegetria*, the *Eleousa*, and the *Platytera*. The *Hodegetria* (Greek: Ὁδηγήτρια, Russian: *Одигитрия*), means, literally, "She who shows the Way" (Fig. 5-15). Mary, looking at us, points to her divine child, portrayed as a small man with grown up features, who, like his mother, directs his gaze at us. He often holds a scroll in his left hand; with his right hand, he either reaches out for his mother, or else extends it in blessing. Mary's gesture towards her son recalls her words at the wedding feast of Cana (Fig. 1-8), when she directed the servants: "Do whatever he tells you" (Jn 2:5). The *Hodegetria* icon is meant to teach us that Mary is the virginal *Theotokos* whose life and mission is wholly

28. Johann G. Roten, "From Epinal to Plateau D'Assy: Religious Art and the Marian Century," in *Mary on the Eve of the Second Vatican Council*, ed. John C. Cavadini and Danielle M. Peters, 79–110 (Notre Dame, Ind.: University of Notre Dame Press, 2017).

Christ-centered and that devotion to her will always lead to a more vital relationship with her son.[29]

The second classical Marian icon, the *Eleousa* (Greek: *Ἐλεούσα*), literally means "showing tenderness or mercy." It depicts Our Lady inclining her head toward Jesus and touching his cheek (Fig. 4-7; see also Fig. 6-8).[30] Jesus, in return, focuses his attention on his mother, embracing her with one arm and sometimes holding a scroll in his other hand. The icon focuses on the intimate mother and child relationship and draws the faithful into this loving exchange, which is a symbol for the soul in prayer, contemplation, and adoration.

The third principle icon from the East is the *Platytera,* which means "Greater than the Heavens" and portrays the Virgin with arms raised in prayer. This icon, also referred to as *Orante* (the praying one), is found behind the main altar in every Orthodox church. Mary's outstretched arms signal her receptivity and availability for God's service while her total spiritual transparency evokes the fullness of God's grace.[31] The icon is a visual interpretation of the prophecy of Isaiah: "The virgin shall be with child, and bear a son, and shall name him Immanuel" (Is 7:14). From these three basic types of Marian icons developed a large variety of exemplars, which, today, can be found in Orthodox churches, Catholic churches in the West, as well as in many homes (domestic churches).[32]

Marian icons and the variety of exemplars draw our attention first and foremost to Our Lady's soteriological role. They point to the vo-

29. The three stars on Mary's veil symbolize her virginity before, during, and after the birth of the Christ child. See Pius X, Encyclical Letter on the 50th Anniversary of the Definition of the Immaculate Conception *Ad Diem Illum Laetissimum* (February 2, 1904), 5.

30. A variant of the "Virgin of Tenderness" is the *Galaktotrophusa* or "Holy Milk-Giver," a pendant to the *Virgo lactans.*

31. A later variation, Life-giving Spring or Life-giving Font (Greek: *Ζωοδόχος Πηγή, Zoodochos Pigi,* Russian: *Живоносный Источник*) shows Mary hovering over a fountain as receiver of God's Life who then distributes these waters of both spiritual and physical healing to humanity. This portrayal alludes to the Blessed Virgin Mary as mediatrix and intercessor.

32. For example, in the *Kyriotissa,* the enthroned Mother of God, Mary is seated with the holy child on her lap, appearing solemn and majestic. Often archangels are pictured, either as her guardians or in positions of veneration. The *Nikopeia* shows Mary either standing or sitting, stern and regal, holding the Christ child before her with both hands.

cation and mission of the *Theotokos* whose entire existence is to be *Ancilla Domini*, the handmaid of the Lord. Thus, Mary is never an obstacle in our quest for God; rather she leads us to him and teaches us how to live in loving communion with him and his will. Seen as a pedagogical tool for the religious and moral life, Marian icons "symbolize the three steps of Christian and Marian existence: our quest for God (*Orante*), our life in Christ (*Eleousa*), and our existence for others leading them to Christ (*Hodegetria*)."[33] This *triplex mariana* permits us to become the beneficiaries of Mary's "ability to confront and disarm the polarities that so often bring human endeavors to impasse: the subjective and objective, the expansive and the parochial, the affective and the intellectual."[34] Mary's visible presence in iconography is exemplary, insofar as her maternal solicitude welcomes and articulates the deeply personal plea of her children to be freed from the chains of slavery, distorted love, and the leading of a double life.

Western Iconography

Sacred art in the West attempts to convey a theological message or give cultural expression to divine revelation. This is true, in a particular way, of specific Marian representations, since the mission of the Blessed Virgin is essentially one of mediating and bridge building.[35] In fact, the more salient traits of Mary in our present culture, according to authors such as E. M. Toniolo, are power and mercy, both of which are bridges between God and humanity.[36] G. Agostino and other authors hold that the recurrent image of the "popular Mary" conveys her "living presence—maternal, mediating, and sharing in human suf-

33. Johann G. Roten, "How Can Spirituality Be Marian?" *Marian Studies* 52, Article 5 (2001): 7–52, accessed October 20, 2018, http://ecommons.udayton.edu/marian_studies/vol52/iss1/5.

34. Diane Schoemperlen, *Our Lady of the Lost and Found: A Novel* (New York: Viking, 2001), 315.

35. Important means for spreading and developing Marian popular art in our age are religious films and animated children's movies. The influence of these media in the formation of the faithful is largely underestimated. See, for example, the careful study of Michael Duricy, "The Life of Mary in Film: Marian Films in the Twentieth Century," *Marian Studies* 60, Article 14 (2009): 275–86, accessed October 20, 2018, http://ecommons.udayton.edu/marian_studies/vol60/iss1/14.

36. E. M. Toniolo, "La figura di Maria nei canti popolari," *La Madonna* 26 (1978): 32–60.

fering."[37] Within the Western tradition, theological themes of Mary as powerful mediator and consoling mother have been expressed in three major Marian icons: Mary as Queen of Heaven, Mary as mother and model of the Church, and Mary in the mournful Pietà.[38]

The most popular of these Marian icons has been the Queen of Heaven image, which originated during the Counter-Reformation and was reinforced by the Miraculous Medal and the great apparitions of the nineteenth and twentieth centuries. Mary's queenship is one of love and service, not of domination and prestige. She is often portrayed standing above the clouds, crowned with twelve stars (Rev 12:5), and holding a scepter in her hand. Mary's queenship is a gift of her son inviting her as Queen Mother to channel graces to her spiritual children in abundance. More recently, pilgrimages to Medjugorje further contributed to the popularity of this image.[39] The distance between Our Lady "above the clouds" and the beholder on earth is not felt as separation or estrangement. Rather, the knowledge of Mary's intercession for the world before the throne of God reassures the faithful of her victory and power. At the same time, her image as the Queen of Heaven signals the Christian universal call to holiness.

A second popular representation in the West shows Mary as mother and model of the Church. One of its best-known exemplars is the *Mater Ecclesiae*, a mosaic commissioned by John Paul II and prominently displayed at the northwest corner of St. Peter's square. In addition to the power of Mary's intercession before God on our behalf, this image underscores her mediation within the Church, her son's Mystical Body. Theological attention to Mary, model of Christian life, owes a debt of thanks in part to Pope Saint Paul VI's humanism and John Paul II's personalism. The former's new humanism advocates Christian values of love, friendship, prayer, and contemplation as essential to true human progress and fulfillment.[40] The latter's personalism is a

37. G. Agostino, "Chi e Maria per il popolo?" *La Madonna* 32 (1984): 6.

38. Roten, "Popular Religion," 73. See also, W. Beinert, *Maria-eine ökumenische Herausforderung* (Regensburg: Friedrich Pustet, 1984), 75–116.

39. See Donald Calloway, *No Turning Back* (Stockbridge, Mass.: Marian Press, 2010). The author attributes his conversion to Catholicism and deliverance from pornography to Our Lady of Medjugorje.

40. See Paul VI, Encyclical Letter *Populorum Progressio* (March 26, 1967).

response to the dehumanizing philosophical and political agenda that Karol Wojtyła had experienced behind the Iron Curtain. For the late Slavic pope John Paul II, culture is the medium through which the person becomes more fully what he or she is called to become. For this reason, we can better appreciate his fierce condemnation of the culture of death imminent in the Western world, which he opposed with an appeal to a vision of a civilization of love.[41]

Contemporary depictions of Mary as mother and model of the Church emphasize Mary as not only a caring wife and mother, but also as a strong and free woman who was tried by many challenges, as the Gospels attest. These different emphases on Mary's attributes are not contradictory. Freedom that is liberation from sin is freedom, indeed! Immaculately conceived, Mary was wholly free to assent completely and without restraint to God and his will. Images of Mary as mother and model of the Church accentuate her feminine genius, thereby mediating courage and hope in challenging times.[42]

A third major image of Mary in the West is the Pietà—the mourning mother cradling her crucified son. In the aftermath of terrorism, world wars, and unprecedented cultural transformations, popular culture in the West has been urgently seeking the meaning of life and theological responses to suffering and death. The Pietà corresponds to this essential need and is therefore one of the most sought Marian representations of our time.[43]

Each of these three popular Marian representations—the Queen of Heaven, the *Mater Ecclesiae*, and the Pietà—conveys a theological message visually and simply. The images, when contemplated, awaken longing, invite us to prayer, and often begin the process of conversion. For example, Catholics believe in the intercessory power of Our Lady. This belief, however, remains disembodied and abstract until we gaze

41. See John Paul II, Encyclical Letter *Evangelium Vitae* (March 25, 1995).

42. John Paul II, *Redemptoris Mater*, 25, and Apostolic Letter *Mulieris dignitatem* (August 15, 1988), 9–11.

43. See Roten, "Popular Religion," 77. A popular, albeit controversial example, is Mark Balma's rendering of John F. Kennedy's dying moments, capturing the grieving Jacqueline Kennedy cradling the mortally wounded president in her lap. See Johann G. Roten, "Pietà of Mark Balma," "All About Mary" website, International Marian Research Institute, University of Dayton, accessed October 20, 2018, https://udayton.edu/imri/mary/p/pieta-of-mark-balma.php.

upon the image of Our Lady of Perpetual Help, an image that "is literally charged and permeated with the ardent prayers and bold expectations of innumerable faithful, past and present."[44] This phenomenon can be observed at countless pilgrimage places and churches.

Since images of Our Lady represent common beliefs, they also create community and cultural identity. In the representation of Our Lady of Guadalupe, for example, "the traditional motif of the *Orante*, of the Immaculate Conception, and of an expecting Lady are merged with the features and the attire of an Indian Woman."[45] Suddenly, in this iconic constellation of features, the Mexican faithful identify with the Lady herself and, implicitly, assent to her message. "You cannot truly be considered a Mexican," writes Mexican novelist Carlos Fuentes, "unless you believe in the Virgin of Guadalupe."[46]

Our historical survey of Marian iconography has shown how Marian imagery engages, reflects, and forms human beings' faith, culture, and self-awareness.[47] Hence, the crucial importance of the presence of statues and images in homes and churches cannot be stressed enough: "By their mere presence they may shape the religious imagination of many generations . . . in times of intense psychological development and explicit religious education."[48] Likewise, religious images in books, missalettes, parish bulletins, classroom materials, and greeting cards stimulate and form the faithful's imagination. "Because they are varied in style and theme, they allow for a broader selection and, potentially, for a more personalized identification with a specific motif or type of Marian image."[49]

"In Looking At Your Image, We Are Transformed Into Your Image"

These words from a popular German religious song addressed to Our Lady express Mary's transformative power: "*Im Anschauen deines*

44. Roten, "Popular Religion," 67.

45. Roten, "Popular Religion," 66.

46. Quoted in Donald Demarest, "Guadalupe Cult in the Lives of Mexicans," in *A Handbook on Guadalupe*, ed. Franciscan Friars of the Immaculate (Waite Park, Minn.: Park Press, 1996), 114.

47. This is true, of course, also of pornographic pictures.

48. Roten, "Popular Religion," 78.

49. Roten, "Popular Religion," 79.

Bildes, da werden wir verwandelt in dein Bild"—"In Looking At Your Image, We Are Transformed Into Your Image." This is especially true of Marian images that are venerated in churches and home shrines. The atmosphere at holy places, informed by countless prayers and sacrifices, helps us to experience Mary's maternal presence and our affiliation with her. Johann Roten emphasizes, "The Marian image, to be truly popular, should concern and touch the whole person—as child, adolescent, adult, and member of society . . . the Marian image should communicate affective security to the child in us, knowing (and, if possible, knowledgeable) admiration to the adolescent in us, active challenge (Mary as spiritual model) to the adult, and a sense of religious and cultural solidarity to the social being in us."[50] The life and example of Mary as the *eschatological icon* becomes the magnet uniting us to herself and awakening the soul's longing for assimilation.[51] The intensity and purity of her love attracts our brokenness and is an impulse to let go of anything that would disturb this relationship.[52] Father Joseph Kentenich (1885–1968), founder of the Schoenstatt Movement, draws attention to the fact that a genuine bond with Our Lady will gradually bring about a profound Marian likeness and attitude, since "the child will necessarily bear the features of the mother! . . . Hence, when we love the Mother of God, then we love what she loves."[53]

Mary's perfect beauty is a privilege she has received for a mission. Contemplating Mary's beauty, Paul VI observed: Mary as "the *tota pulchra* [all beautiful] signals the Way of Beauty that leads to Beauty."[54] Marc Ouellet notes that "the beauty of being Christians is transmitted from her to us by osmosis, less by imitation than by generation, since we are reproductions of her Christian beauty due to her effective mediation that is the work of the Holy Spirit."[55] Mary's living fiat to

50. Roten, "Popular Religion," 120.

51. *Catechism of the Catholic Church*, 972.

52. Cited in Jonathan Niehaus, *Schoenstatt's Covenant Spirituality* (Waukesha, Wis.: Schoenstatt Editions, 1992), 42.

53. Joseph Kentenich, *Aus dem Glauben leben* [Sermons at St. Michael's Parish, Milwaukee, Wis. between 1962–65.], vol. 14 (Vallendar-Schönstatt: Patris, 1986), 209–10.

54. Paul VI, *Discourse to the Mariological Congress* (May 16, 1975).

55. Marc Ouellet, "The Beauty of Being Christians," in *The Beauty of Being a Christian: Movements in the Church. Proceedings of the Second World Congress of the Ecclesial*

God both models and mediates our cooperation with grace that allows Christ's beauty to shine through us.[56] Mary's beauty typifies "the perfect expression for beauty in every person."[57] She embodies the complementarity and harmony of human and divine beauty.[58] Indeed, Mary as "*Tota Pulchra* assures us that the victory of love is possible . . . that grace is stronger than sin, and that redemption from any form of slavery, is therefore possible."[59]

As sensible beings, we need tangible signs to unite us with the divine. While a picture of itself does not magically effect this union, a sacramental image does have the power to channel graces into the receptive soul. Just so, certain sacred images and pilgrimage places are known for curing specific physical or spiritual needs. Since time immemorial, traditions and local customs have invoked Mary under her healing titles including "Physician of all physicians," "Miraculous Heavenly Physician," and "Consoler of the downcast." The healing power of Lourdes and its water are well known.[60]

One purpose of this volume is to draw forth resources from the Christian tradition that may contribute to the cultivation of a sacramental imagination within a culture in which pornography is pervasive.[61] In this context, three Marian images deserve special recognition because of their potential to mediate the healing of compulsive and distorted sexual behaviors: Our Lady of Luján, Mary Undoer of Knots, and Mother Thrice Admirable of Schoenstatt.

Pope Francis himself promotes the sacred image Our Lady of Lu-

---

Movements and New Communities, Rocca di Papa, 31 May–2 June 2006, ed. The Pontifical Council on the Laity (Rome: Libreria Editrice Vaticana, 2007), 49.

56. The notion of archetypal experience, developed amply by von Balthasar, implies the idea of model but also that of mediation. See Hans Urs von Balthasar, *Seeing the Form*, vol. 1 of *The Glory of the Lord: A Theological Aesthetics*, eds. Joseph Fessio and John Riches, trans. Erasmo Leiva-Merikakis (San Francisco, Calif.: Ignatius Press, 1982), 301ff.

57. Ouellet, "Beauty of Being Christians," 48.

58. Roten, "Popular Religion," 110.

59. Benedict XVI, Address *Homage to the Immaculate at the Spanish Steps* (December 8, 2008). This slavery, of course, includes the slavery of pornography.

60. The image communicates its sacredness to those who venerate it and to the soil, the wood, foliage, and branches of the tree where the image is hung.

61. See United States Conference of Catholic Bishops, *Create in Me a Clean Heart. A Pastoral Response to Pornography* (Washington, D.C.: United States Conference of Catholic Bishops, 2015), 13.

ján for catching "big fish" because he is convinced that Our Lady has a manner of touching people. In the metaphor of the fish, we may presume that he speaks of grave matters, either in the spiritual or moral realm. Marked by perfectionism and rationalism, our time has trained us to suppress our "fish" until they haunt us. Pope Francis offers a second example of Our Lady of Luján as the fishing rod that supplies the necessary heavy-duty tackle: "I remember one time, the first 'big fish' moment which affected me. He ... was a young man ... 22 or 23 years old. He was a big guy, with earrings, long hair which fell across his shoulders ... The guy was very 'post-modern.' ... He said: 'I have a very big problem! ... So, one day I couldn't take it anymore and told my mom everything and asked what I should do.' She told me: 'Go to Luján so that Our Lady will tell you what to do.' So, I asked the young man: 'Did you see her?' And he responded: 'Yes. And I think that I need to do this, this, this, and this.'"[62] With this example the Argentinian pontiff stresses the importance that we all, like the young man's mother, can be ambassadors of Our Lady. Like and with Mary, all of us are called to become "a bridge that connects God and the human person [with the message] of being loved forever despite our sinfulness."[63] It would be pastorally sensitive to accept Pope Francis's testimony and assign a prominent place to a beautiful image of Our Lady close to the confessional.

Mary, Undoer of Knots, also known as "Untier of Knots," our second healing image, is of German origin but has received international recognition through its promoter, Pope Francis. He discovered the painting in the Church of St. Peter in the Bavarian town Augsburg. It shows Our Lady untying the many knots in a long white ribbon (Fig. 5-16). The theological message comes to us from St. Irenaeus, bishop of Lyons (martyred in AD 203) who emphasized: "The knot of Eve's disobedience was loosed by the obedience of Mary. What the virgin Eve had bound in unbelief, the Virgin Mary loosed through faith."[64] The painting by Johann Georg Melchior Schmittner also con-

62. Awi Mello, *Ela é minha Mãe!* 59.

63. Francis, Bull of Indiction for the Extraordinary Holy Year of Mercy *Misericordiae Vultus* (April 11, 2015), 2.

64. Irenaeus, *Against Heresies*, III.22. Cited in Luigi Gambero, *Mary and the Fathers of the Church* (San Francisco, Calif.: Ignatius Press, 1999), 58.

tains a personal history. It was commissioned around 1700 by Msgr. H. Langenmantel as a gift of gratitude. When his grandfather was on the verge of separating from his wife, the couple sought help from Jakob Rem, SJ. The priest prayed to the Blessed Virgin Mary asking her to preserve the bond of this matrimony and to untie all knots that threatened the bond. As a result, peace was restored, and the couple did not separate. When he was archbishop, Pope Francis considered this episode so powerful that he disseminated replications of the picture in his homeland of Argentina. He was conscious of every family's anguish brought about through the knots of discord in relationships. Often these include addictions, which suffocate the soul, take away the heart's joy, and lead to separation from God. In recent years, novena prayer cards and booklets with the image of the Undoer of Knots have become popular in the United States where Our Lady seems to specialize in untying the twisted knots of compulsive behavior, including addiction to pornography.

Among the best-known Marian representations of the world is the Mother Thrice Admirable of Schoenstatt, an image of grace that has been the trademark of the International Schoenstatt Work since 1915.[65] The picture of Mary and Jesus is honored in the more than 200 Schoenstatt Shrines throughout the world under the title of "Mother Thrice Admirable, Queen, and Victress of Schoenstatt."[66] The image is

65. Peter Wolf, *Ein Bild geht um die Welt: 1915–2015* (Vallendar: Schönstatt, 2015). To view an image, see Charlene G. Becicka, "Happy Mother's Day" *Truly Alive* (blog), May 11, 2014, http://charleneslm.weebly.com.

66. A print of the painting by Luigi Crosio, originally entitled "Refuge of Sinners," was donated to the members of the Marian Sodality at Schoenstatt in 1915. The sodalists retitled the picture "Mother Thrice Admirable" in keeping with their goal for Schoenstatt to become a center for Catholic renewal in the twentieth century, as Ingolstadt in Bavaria had been during the sixteenth century. In Ingolstadt, Mary was venerated as the "Mother Thrice Admirable" (MTA) by Jakob Rem, SJ (1546–1618), a leader in the Catholic Counter-Reformation, and his followers. Father Jakob Rem, SJ, was also instrumental in preserving the marriage of the grandparents of Msgr. H. Langenmantel, which led to the painting of the image of Our Lady, Untier of Knots. The title Mother Thrice Admirable derives, in turn, from the Litany of Loreto, where Mary is invoked as "Mother most admirable." The title "Queen" was officially added to "Mother Thrice Admirable" in 1939, twenty-five years after Schoenstatt's foundation, during a coronation ceremony in the original Shrine, as an act of thanksgiving and self-surrender and in petition for Mary's protection against the dangers of National Socialism. The title "Victress" was officially added by Father Kentenich during a coronation on May 31, 1966, in acknowledgement of Mary's triumph in ending the fourteen-year separation (1951–65) of the founder from

enthroned in the home shrines of countless families and individuals, and approximately 300,000 pilgrim shrines reach more than 14 million families in 110 nations.[67] The history of the Mother Thrice Admirable's activity from her shrines attests to the countless moral miracles that have occurred through her intercession. The charism of Our Lady of Schoenstatt from her Schoenstatt Shrine is the formation and ordering of love in her spiritual children. The founder of Schoenstatt, Father Joseph Kentenich, observed that religious education of our time has little succeeded in addressing the emotional needs of children, adolescents, and adults. Consequently, this dimension of spiritual formation remains largely underdeveloped. He concluded: "When the emotional and irrational life is suppressed by the spiritual and religious demands of the ideal of perfection, the neglected and despised affectionate life emigrates from the Church and falls victim to the temptations of secularism."[68] By contrast, the education of Our Lady of Schoenstatt is directed to the whole person, including the emotional, rational, and supernatural life and love. The three graces received by all pilgrims to the Schoenstatt Shrines are the graces of feeling "at home" there, of being spiritually transformed, and of receiving apostolic zeal. They coincide in the most general terms with those graces traditionally experienced by pilgrims to holy places, as anthropologist Victor Turner's influential study of pilgrimage in Christian culture confirms.[69]

Conclusion

Even when the rift between the sacred and profane is wide, sacred art continues to build a bridge, leading to religious experiences. Marian icons, in particular, transmit a glimpse of God's mystery.[70] Mary teaches us that where Love becomes visible in a person, there beauty

---

his foundation, and allowing him, with the blessing of Pope Paul VI, to resume the task of Schoenstatt's leadership.

67. Peter Wolf, *A Picture Goes Around the World 1915–2015: Schoenstatt's Marian Image*, trans. Margaret Gründing (Waukesha, Wis.: Schoenstatt Editions USA, 2019).

68. Joseph Kentenich, *Reply to the Report on the Canonical Visitation of the Apostolic Movement of Schoenstatt from February 19–28, 1949* (Manuscript, May 31, 1949), 311.

69. Victor Turner, *Image and Pilgrimage in Christian Culture: Anthropological Perspectives* (New York: Columbia University Press, 1978), 6.

70. John Paul II, *Homily on Easter Sunday* (April 4, 1999).

and order shine forth. As Mother of Beauty, Our Lady points beyond herself to the One who has made her beautiful. Only in God is her—and our—existence meaningful and beautiful. Pope Benedict XVI touched upon this mystery: "Authentic beauty unlocks the yearning of the human heart … to reach for the Beyond. If we acknowledge that beauty touches us intimately, that it wounds us, that it opens our eyes, then we rediscover the joy of seeing, of being able to grasp the profound meaning of our existence."[71] Being wounded by love lends wings to the soul, lifting it upwards towards seeing with the eyes of God. This vision of infinite and true Beauty readily abandons all deceptive and dazzling distortions of beauty, to embrace, like Mary, Love itself. Indeed, this vision will transform the soul to become itself an icon of this love.

71. Benedict XVI, *Address to Artists* (November 21, 2009).

DIANNE PHILLIPS

6 ⯫ The Visual Culture of Catholicism

Defining Catholic visual culture in a single essay is a daunting task. This culture encompasses a wide range of imagery in a variety of media whose purposes are many and varied, as exemplified by the juxtaposition of a fourteenth-century panel painting of St. Thomas Aquinas (Fig. 6-1) with Bernini's seventeenth-century sculpture of the ecstasy of St. Teresa of Avila (Fig. 6-2). The use of imagery was somewhat slow to be adopted in Christianity because of the marginal status of the first Christians, the Mosaic prohibition against idolatry, and the role of imagery in pagan cults. However, the central Christian teaching on the Incarnation ultimately provided the principal warrant for religious art: because God became human in the person of Jesus Christ and dwelt among us in the created world, depictions of him could represent the Word made flesh—the one who is both divine and human. Around AD 600, Pope Saint Gregory the Great articulated a threefold justification for religious art that has been held by the Church ever since: religious art teaches about the life of Christ to people who cannot read scripture; it aids the memory of the believer in retaining Christian teaching because it is easier to remember that which is seen rather than simply heard; and it stimulates devotion to Christ and the saints in the Christian viewer because images of their love and suffering more effectively arouse our empathy than do texts.

Even a twenty-first-century viewer can readily recognize that the fourteenth-century panel painting of St. Thomas Aquinas (Fig. 6-1) has a didactic function. The Sienese artist who painted this image shortly after Thomas Aquinas's canonization in 1323 created a carefully ordered composition depicting the transmission of knowledge. From the Logos at the apex, knowledge flows down through the prophets, evangelists, and apostles, then through Thomas Aquinas before descending to the people of the world, thereby instructing the viewer about the hierarchy of teaching authority. Bernini's seventeenth-century sculpture of St. Teresa of Avila also instructs its viewer, but in a different way. The sensuous figure of St. Teresa rapt in mystical ecstasy (Fig. 6-2) as she is pierced by divine love, is obviously designed to elicit an affective response. While the images discussed in this chapter tilt strongly toward the more affective, Bernini end of the spectrum, great Catholic art does not compartmentalize the intellectual from the emotional. Though the systematic and hieratic composition of the St. Thomas Aquinas panel clearly celebrates his wisdom and knowledge, the open books piled on Thomas's lap also allude to the fecundity of his learning and gesture to the "Seat of Wisdom" motif associated with the image of the Virgin Mary holding the Christ child in her lap. Moreover, this magnetic figure of St. Thomas became the focus of a popular cult, with many wax *ex votos* presented by the laity who regarded it as a source of miracles.[1] Conversely, the St. Teresa in Ecstasy sculptural group, set within the Cornaro Chapel in Santa Maria della Vittoria in Rome, is a work of consummate intellectual and technical sophistication, directly informed by Baroque ideas about theater and the spiritual.

Given the topic of this volume, this chapter will focus on how Catholic imagery enlists the sensual dimensions of human bodily existence to visualize the passionate love God has for his creatures and the human yearning for fulfillment in life with God. The series of pictures selected for discussion demonstrate how marital and erotic motifs are employed to express and inspire that mutual love. Hunger (and thirst) and sexual desire are probably the two most fundamental features of human bodily existence. Christian faith, especially as lived in the Catholic tradition, employs both as a way to think and speak about human relationship to God: about how God loves and desires us, how we respond to that love, and how we find completion in it. Religious art of the high medieval through early modern periods especially explored this theme, which meshed so perfectly with the emergence and

1. Joanna Cannon, *Religious Poverty, Visual Riches: Art in the Dominican Churches of Central Italy in the Thirteenth and Fourteenth Centuries* (New Haven, Conn.: Yale University Press, 2013), 150.

development of an artistic style that prized the naturalistic representation of the human figure as the most potent pictorial vehicle for the expression of meaning.

The scriptural impetus for this kind of Catholic imagery stemmed from the medieval interpretation of the Song of Songs, the explicitly erotic poem in the Old Testament that recounts the passion of unnamed lovers. In the twelfth century, exegetes interpreted this love between a man and woman as an apt symbol of God's love for humankind: they read the Song of Songs allegorically with the bride of the Song representing the soul and the bridegroom representing Christ who woos her. [2] In an historiated initial from a late eleventh-century Bible (Fig. 6-3), within the confines of the "O" that begins the first word ("*Osculetur*") of the Song of Songs, the artist represented the two figures in a loving embrace about to kiss. Chapter one begins, "Let him kiss me with the kiss of his mouth: for thy breasts are better than wine."[3] The two figures are encircled by the rings of the cosmos, their heads surrounded by a single cruciform halo. The male figure on the left is further identified with the inscription "Christ," the female figure wearing her bridal veil is identified as "Ecclesia." Thus, in addition to symbolizing the union of God and the soul, the bridegroom and bride of the Song were understood as personifications of Christ and his Church, and the "kiss of the mouth" in the first verse assimilated to reception of the Eucharist when, by consuming the consecrated bread and wine—the Body and Blood of Christ—the believer is drawn up into the life of God.[4]

The theme of the amorous encounter of the soul and God is elab-

2. There is a vast scholarly literature on the interpretation of the Song of Songs. For studies relevant to its understanding during the Middle Ages, see Ann W. Astell, *The Song of Songs in the Middle Ages* (Ithaca, N.Y.: Cornell University Press, 1990), and E. Ann Matter, *The Voice of My Beloved: The Song of Songs in Western Medieval Christianity* (Philadelphia, Pa.: University of Pennsylvania Press, 1990). For its impact on art, see Marilyn Aronberg Lavin and Irving Lavin, *The Liturgy of Love: Images from the Song of Songs in the Art of Cimabue, Michelangelo, and Rembrandt* (Lawrence, Kans.: Spencer Museum of Art, University of Kansas, 2001).

3. Biblical passages are quoted from the 1899 American edition of the Douay-Rheims translation of the Latin Vulgate.

4. The interpretation originated with Ambrose. See, Karl Shuve, *The Song of Songs and the Fashioning of Christian Identity in Early Latin Christianity* (Oxford: Oxford University Press, 2016), 154.

orated and placed in relation to the Incarnation and Passion of Christ in an early fourteenth-century manuscript known as the *Rothschild Canticles* (Figs. 6-4 and 6-5), the subject of a masterful monograph by Jeffrey Hamburger.[5] Likely made for women religious, the *Rothschild Canticles* is a theological miscellany that includes a double-page spread with an intriguing suite of pictures following a folio with a series of short excerpts paraphrased from scripture and from Gregory the Great's *Moralia in Job*: "Let him kiss me with the kiss of his mouth: for thy breasts are better than wine" (Song 1:1); "The righteous love thee" (Song 1:3); "His left hand is under my head, and his right hand shall embrace me" (Song 2:6); "Behold, I stand at the gate, and knock. If any [will come] to me, I will come into him and will sup with him and he with me" (Rv 3:20); "Thou has wounded my heart my sister, my spouse; thou has wounded my heart with one of thy eyes and one hair of thy neck" (Song 4:9); "The omnipotent Father deceived the devil, the old serpent, with a hook when in his mercy he sent to death his only incarnate son, in whom the devil was able to see the suffering flesh, but was unable to see the unsuffering divinity" (Gregory the Great, *Moralia in Job, XXXIII, ix*).[6] Pondering these passages, the reader would turn the folio to confront an opening with a full-page illustration on each facing page.

On the upper register of the left leaf, the lovers embrace and then the woman (the sponsa/bride) knocks at the door of her beloved, who draws her into the dark opening of his shelter (Fig. 6-4). Below, she wears the bridal veil and wields the lance directed toward Christ who is poised between the column of the Flagellation and the cross of the Crucifixion on the facing page (Fig. 6-5). She simultaneously points to her eye, thus wounding his heart with one glance of her eyes, in accord with Song of Songs 4:9. This is an image of the soul's "wounding love" that releases the effusion of Caritas (self-giving love) from Christ's side, referring to the lance wound inflicted at the Crucifixion whence the water and blood gushed from Christ's side—an image that links the two meanings of "passio"/passion: both suffering and ecstatic

5. Jeffrey F. Hamburger, *The Rothschild Canticles: Art and Mysticism in Flanders and the Rhineland circa 1300* (New Haven, Conn.: Yale University Press, 1990), 72–77.

6. See Hamburger, *Rothschild Canticles*, 175, for the transcription of these texts on fol. 17v and translations on 72–77.

love. It was connected to the medieval theory of vision that conceived the act of seeing as a reciprocal exchange between the eye and the object. The object of her gaze is the nude Christ, one foot (symbol of his humanity) bound to the column, which was a symbol of divine Wisdom, and the other affixed to the cross, but his hands freely wielding the instruments of the Passion and pointing to his side wound, whose shape relates to the dark opening of the beloved's shelter on the facing page. This extraordinary representation of the naked Christ is a pictorial meditation on Gregory the Great's observation that the devil was only able to see the suffering and defeated human figure of Christ but failed to recognize his unsuffering divinity, an idea derived from the scriptural verses about how God's wisdom appears as foolishness to the world (1 Cor 1:18–25).

So, although at first glance these images in the *Rothschild Canticles* appear to be a simple set of pictures, it is clear that the female viewer would bring to them a sophisticated understanding and could appreciate at once both the theological subtleties and the appealing image of the beautiful figure of Christ as the focus of her meditative prayer and object of her love, a figure into whose image she aspired to be assimilated. As Hamburger observes, Mechthild of Hackeborn, a thirteenth-century Benedictine nun, described the encounter with Christ on the cross in a way that parallels this image and invokes the language of amorous desire and its consummation: "'On this couch of love he is still waiting for thee with desire unutterable. But if thou desirest to be his bride, thou must utterly renounce all delight and approach him on his little bed of sorrow, on which the Lord has placed him, and join thyself to his side, which Love has wounded.'"[7]

The Incarnation as manifestation of God's loving desire for hu-

7. Hamburger, *Rothschild Canticles*, 76. Late medieval secular literature likewise expresses an appreciation for the erotic aura of the naked corpus upon the cross. Compiled in the fourteenth century, Franco Sacchetti's *Le Trecento Novelle*, ed. Michelangelo Zaccarello (Florence: SISMEL, 2014), Novella 84, tells a bawdy tale of the adulterous wife of a Sienese artist who specializes in monumental painted crucifixes on which the body of Christ is carved in relief. Surprised by the unexpected return of her husband while she is engaged with her lover, she hides him in her husband's adjoining workshop by instructing him to stretch out upon one of the unfinished crosses as though a faux corpus, which she covers with a linen cloth. The anecdote betrays at once an awareness of the carnal attraction of the naked male figure on the cross and also the notion that devotion to the suffering, crucified Christ had special appeal for late medieval women.

mankind informs even simpler imagery such as the illustration for the chapter on the Annunciation in a mid-fourteenth-century Italian manuscript of the *The Meditations on the Life of Christ* in the Snite Museum of Art at the University of Notre Dame (Fig. 6-6). While the artist's style is simple and direct, as is characteristic of Bolognese illumination, the image has been carefully calibrated to the text. In the lines immediately above the illumination, God in heaven speaks to the Angel Gabriel and tells him to go to Mary and announce to her that "my son has *desired* her beauty and chosen her for his mother [italics mine]." Visually that sentence of text elides into the blue ovoid shape that hovers just above the rear left corner of the Virgin Mary's room, from which red lines extend upon which the dove of the Holy Spirit descends: its flight path will cross the capital of the pink column (again, a symbol of Wisdom), the open book on her prie-dieu (assumed to be open at Isaiah 7:14, the prophecy of the virgin birth), and ultimately land on her womb.

The theme of mutual desire between the bride and bridegroom in the Song of Songs continued to inform Renaissance representations of scenes from the life of the Virgin Mary and the life of Christ, as subtly expressed in an Annunciation panel by Rogier van der Weyden (Fig. 6-7). It is obviously more technically sophisticated than the two previous examples, but the suave naturalism with which Rogier executes this very frequent subject serves complex theological meanings. The setting is an opulent fifteenth-century bedroom, presumably in a tower high above the city, as is indicated by the panoramic view from the rear window, the inaccessible location referring to Mary's virginity. The Virgin Mary is interrupted in prayer by the Angel Gabriel, who wears ecclesiastical dress; we should also recall that the Virgin Mary was the type of Ecclesia. Kneeling before a prominent and luxurious bed covered with deep red draperies (a color associated with the Passion)—hers is a crucified love, as is also symbolized by the cross of the window frame—she awaits the heavenly bridegroom. The golden medallion hanging at the head of the bed represents Christ as the Sun of Justice, a scriptural appellation integral to the nativity story. The bedchamber as a site of mystical union of the soul with God again derives from the Song of Songs; the bed refers to the bed of Solomon in Song of Songs 3:7—Wisdom is made incarnate at the Annunciation. The cushioned bench before the empty fireplace (devoid of the fire of lust) has lion finials, another Solomonic reference to the throne of Wisdom. Light floods in through the window at the right, illuminating both the open book and also the Virgin's front torso, as she turns and tilts her head (likely a reference to Ps 45[44]:11). Rays of (divine) light penetrating glass were understood as a metaphor for the preservation of her virginity in the conception of Christ. The painting is comprised of motifs that on the surface register as completely natural, albeit romantic, but that, upon reflection, cast the Annunciation as a marital union between God and humankind that will be consummated upon the bed of the Passion.

As Leo Steinberg convincingly demonstrated in his *The Sexuality of Christ in Renaissance Art and in Modern Oblivion*,[8] nuptial motifs were even assimilated into non-narrative pictures; for example, the left panel of a fourteenth-century Sienese diptych represents the Madonna and child opposite Christ upright in the tomb, depicted to the right (Fig. 6-8). Art historians have typically described the loving gestures shared by the Christ child and his mother that crop up in late medieval religious painting simply in terms of a new appreciation for the emotional experience of ordinary family life, but their meaning is deeper than that. The "chin- chuck" that the Christ child gives his mother in the Florentine panel is not simply the playful grasping of an infant, but an erotic gesture appropriated from the art of antiquity, as in the Cupid and Psyche sculpture group (Fig. 6-9).[9] In conjunction with the Virgin's carefully rendered translucent veil and the child's arm that embraces her shoulders, the Virgin Mary is represented both as the Mother of God and the sponsa/bride of the Song of Songs, completely consistent with her role as figure of the Church. The bond between mother and son is especially apparent in the intense exchange of gazes between them, at once characteristic of maternal behavior with a newborn yet also alluding to the "look of (wounding) love" in Song of Songs 4:9.

8. Leo Steinberg, *The Sexuality of Christ in Renaissance Art and in Modern Oblivion*, 2nd rev. ed. (Chicago, Ill.: University of Chicago Press, 1996). For a summary of Steinberg's thesis, which deserves to be better known among theologians, see Dianne Phillips, "Leo Steinberg's Artistic Vision," *First Things* 218 (December 2011): 35–39.

9. On the chin-chuck gesture, see Steinberg, *Sexuality of Christ*, 3–7.

The expression of loving desire between the Virgin Mother and the Christ child is even more explicit in a small fifteenth-century panel from Robert Campin's workshop (Fig. 6-10) in which the infant Jesus not only chucks his mother's chin but also puckers up to kiss her—the kiss of the mouth from the Song of Songs. Though the Virgin Mary is in luxurious blue garments, the Christ child is naked, and daintily fondles his genitals. As Steinberg has so brilliantly demonstrated, this gesture that is so typical of infant boys was deliberately introduced into images of the infant Christ in the late medieval period to proclaim the truth of the Incarnation: that in the birth of Jesus, God did indeed condescend to become fully human.[10] As the new Adam who humbly submitted to the human condition and suffered death on a cross for the sins of humankind although he was sinless, Christ "undid" the original sin of the old Adam. It is noteworthy how the body of the infant Christ in the National Gallery panel aligns directly with the cross of the window frame to which the viewer's eyes are insistently directed by the orthogonals of the ceiling and wall in the right half of the painting. The humility that Christ demonstrated in becoming a human infant is further underscored by the basin of water warming before the fire on the floor for his bath (even though his perfect purity obviated the need for cleansing) and by the basket of diapers and swaddling cloths at the lower right corner. The Virgin Mary likewise does not sit on the luxuriously cushioned bench behind her, but rather, humbly upon the floor. Her lavish blue draperies—a heavenly color—whose folds spread out from her lap to the floor, form a sort of human altar table at whose center is the white napkin just beneath the body of the Christ child. It deliberately evokes the visual memory of the consecration of the Host (the Body of Christ) above the corporal spread upon the altar.

The exploitation of the sensual for religious purposes reached its apex in the Baroque period, as a painting of the Holy Family by Peter Paul Rubens makes clear (Fig. 6-11).[11] It includes nuptial, sapiential,

10. Steinberg, *Sexuality of Christ*, 8–79, considers the incarnational theology motivating the display of Christ's genitals in late medieval and Renaissance representations of infancy scenes. For Steinberg's discussion of the Campin panel, see 257–61.

11. See Marcia B. Hall and Tracey E. Cooper, eds., *The Sensuous in the Counter-Reformation Church* (New York: Cambridge University Press, 2013), for some illuminating recent studies.

and Eucharistic allusions: the chin-chuck that the infant Christ bestows upon his mother; the Virgin's regal profile pose upon a wooden seat of Wisdom; and the breadth of her lap and white cloth upon it on which Jesus sits as if on an altar. The beauty and voluptuousness of the Virgin Mary is typical of Rubens's women, but it is not simply a matter of his own personal aesthetic. The exposure of her breast in readiness to nurse the infant Christ was another sign both of Jesus' true humanity, nourished at the breast like a normal human infant, and of the Virgin's mercy and charity in her gift of self, thereby guaranteeing her intercessory efficacy. In this period, an aristocratic woman, as the Virgin Mary is depicted, typically would send her child to a wet nurse for the first two years of life. Attention to the details of this painting makes clear that the Catholic sacramental imagination readily understood that things of this world point to God. For example, the Moses basket of the cradle upon which the aged St. Elizabeth leans as she gazes intently upon the Mother and child refers to Christ as the new Moses, the long-awaited fulfillment of the law and the prophets. The careful display of the Christ child's feet reminds the viewer that they will be pierced at the Crucifixion. The lamb behind the toddler John the Baptist who lifts its leg and is petted by St. Joseph refers to Christ as the Lamb of God. In short, all the formal elements of the painting, which modern viewers may regard as merely characteristic of Rubens's sensuous and tactile style and his delight in the visible world, serve a sophisticated theological understanding.

"Seeing with the eyes of the heart" is easy when the subject of the picture is a captivating baby and his mother but it becomes more difficult—and necessary—when the subject is a human being tortured upon a cross. From the later middle ages on, one of the tasks of religious artists was to create Passion images that emphasized the humanity of Christ and the reality of his suffering and, at the same time, elicited love and compassion rather than revulsion from the viewer. Artists responded to this challenge not only by developing a style that carefully balanced increasing naturalism with the idealization of the human figure but also by transposing the spousal motifs from Madonna and child imagery to Passion images. In a panel painting of the deposition of the dead Christ from the cross by Ugolino di Nerio, the loving embrace that was characteristic of mother and child persists even in his death (Fig. 6-12). Although the image does not strike the viewer as at all bizarre, upon reflection one realizes that a corpse is not able to embrace or kiss. In Ugolino's *Deposition*, Jesus shares the "kiss of the mouth" from the Song of Songs with his mother, as his pale beautiful body—whose near-nudity contrasts sharply with the intensely colored and voluminous clothing of his faithful disciples—is lowered carefully from the cross. This picture was part of the predella of an altarpiece made for the high altar of the Franciscan church of Santa Croce in Florence. The narrative scene of the removal of Christ's luminous body from the cross is related to the celebration of the Eucharist upon the altar, where Christ's body, soul, and divinity are made present in the consecrated Host, the "living bread which came down from heaven" (Jn 6:51), that is elevated by the priest.

In a Northern Renaissance Pietà from the workshop of Rogier van der Weyden (Fig. 6-13) the nuptial union of the Virgin Mary, type of the Church and of the Christian soul, with her son and bridegroom is further developed. The scene of the Virgin Mary's lamentation over the dead Christ is imagined—vividly and realistically rendered by the artist for the adoration of the fifteenth-century donor kneeling at the left, presented by his patron St. Jerome. The Virgin Mary is seated humbly on the rocky ground of Golgotha. She holds the nearly-naked body of her son across the opulent crimson drapery of her lap so that we recall that he is the fruit of her womb. The proximity of her left hand to Christ's side wound reminds us that the birth of the Church occurs with the flow of water and blood that issued from it when he was pierced by the centurion's lance at the Crucifixion.[12] In fact, the Virgin's hand that wraps around Christ's waist extends over the trickle of blood that flows from the side wound toward his groin, the site of his first wounding in his circumcision as an infant.[13] Mary's veil signifies her bridal state and she tenderly supports Christ's head to

12. On the representation of the theme of the Virgin Mary's maternity at Calvary in late medieval art, see Amy Neff, "The Pain of *Compassio*: Mary's Labor at the Foot of the Cross," *Art Bulletin* 80, no. 2 (1998): 254–73.

13. Steinberg characterizes this trajectory of blood from side wound to groin as the "blood hyphen" linking the initiation of Christ's wounding in his circumcision with its consummation. Steinberg, *Sexuality of Christ*, 58.

kiss his mouth as he extends his left arm across her body as though responding to the embrace. Behind the rock upon which the cross stands, St. Dominic reads contemplatively in an open book, its splayed shape echoing the angle of Christ's body—the Word made flesh whose death redeems the original sin of Adam (cf. the skull at the base of the painting aligned with Christ's loincloth and the Virgin's veil). We can see how brilliantly the artist has fused the themes of the crucified Christ as the Wisdom of God, Mary as the seat of Wisdom, and the fulfillment of the soul's longing in her embrace of divine love and mercy. Apposite to this conjunction of the crucified Christ and St. Dominic reading, it is fruitful to recall a passage from a letter written by Jordan of Saxony, a thirteenth-century Dominican friar, to a Bolognese Dominican nun, Diana d'Andolò. Blessed Jordan movingly characterizes Christ crucified on the cross in terms of an illuminated manuscript; for Dominicans, scriptural study was a kind of prayer. He writes, "That law which is perfect because it takes away all imperfections, is charity, and you find it written with strange beauty when you gaze at Jesus your Savior stretched out like a sheet of parchment on the cross, inscribed with wounds, illustrated in his own loving blood. Where else, I ask you, my dearest, is there a comparable book of love to read from?"[14]

Although the use of sensual and erotic elements flourished especially in religious art of the Renaissance and Baroque periods, a significant source of the motifs of the intense love between Christ and the Virgin Mother was Byzantine art, which had a major impact on Italian artists in the late medieval period, especially in the regions dominated by Venice.[15] For example, a fourteenth-century Italo-Byzantine devotional panel (Fig. 6-14) of a type known in the West as the *Imago Pietatis* (the image of pity/piety), whose origins stem from a miraculous Byzantine icon in Santa Croce in Gerusalemme in Rome, represents the half-length figure of Christ, upright in the tomb as though "alive

14. Simon Tugwell, ed., *Early Dominicans: Selected Writings*, The Classics of Western Spirituality (New York: Paulist Press, 1982), 405.

15. On Byzantine representations of the Virgin Mary and Christ, see the essays in Maria Vassilaki, ed., *Mother of God: Representations of the Virgin in Byzantine Art* (Milan: Skira, 2000). For the appropriation of Byzantine iconographic motifs in Italian art, see Anne Derbes, *Picturing the Passion in Late Medieval Italy: Narrative Painting, Franciscan Ideologies, and the Levant* (New York: Cambridge University Press, 1996).

in death," as is typical of these images. The *Imago Pietatis*, or Christ as the Man of Sorrows, as it is also called, carried distinct Eucharistic meaning and came to serve as a pictorial emblem of the doctrine of the real presence of Christ in the consecrated Eucharistic elements. The inclusion in the panel in Florence of the figure of the Virgin Mary, drawing close to her Son to embrace and kiss him (the "kiss of the mouth"), provides an exemplar of the passionate and compassionate response that contemplation of the suffering Christ ought to elicit in the believer, preparing her or him for fruitful reception of the Eucharist.

In the gable of the central panel of an altarpiece made for a Dominican women's convent in Bologna (Fig. 6-15), we can see the progressive elaboration of the *Imago Pietatis* type so that it becomes a dramatic representation of the Virgin Mary embracing Christ in the tomb. Here Christ's corpse becomes almost animated as he props his right elbow on the edge of the tomb and now he, not his mother, wraps his left arm around her shoulders. His pose facilitates the detailed representation of his ribcage, a reference to Psalm 22(21):18, "they have numbered all my bones." It also allows for the direct display of the wounds of the Passion in his hands and, especially, in his side. It is no accident that the side wound is directly aligned with the infant Christ being presented over the altar by the Virgin Mary to the High Priest, Simeon, who receives the baby with veiled hands in the main panel below. Simeon's prophecy addressed to the Virgin Mary at the Presentation, that the child is "set for the fall ... of many in Israel ... and thy own soul, a sword shall pierce" (Lk 2:34–35), is actually inscribed upon the altar in the scene. The artist shows the fulfillment of Simeon's prophecy by placing the Virgin Mary directly *behind* Christ in the tomb in the gable, so that one can readily imagine the lance that pierced his side also transfixing her. The artful rendering of the two figures in the gable exemplifies the relation of *passio* and *compassio* in a powerful image that fuses the sensual and the spiritual.

The pictorial potential of the body of Christ and its exploitation as a focus of ocular desire that would properly arouse the love of the viewer came to full fruition in the Italian Renaissance, when the naturalistically represented human figure became the dominant vehicle for meaning in art. Two paintings, one by Michele Giambono (Fig. 6-16), the other by Carlo Crivelli (Fig. 6-17), exemplify the unabashed eroticism with which Italian artists imbued the devotional subject of the "dead" Christ. Giambono represents the *Imago Pietatis*, the Man of Sorrows, upright in the tomb, carefully and deliberately displaying the wounds of the Passion: the streams of blood from his side wound are created in gesso, raised as though in relief from the surface of the painting. The decorated shroud drapes over the edge of the tomb, transforming it into a kind of altar, with the elaborate gold motif embroidered on the cloth adroitly concealing Jesus' genitals, and thus alerting the viewer to this sign of his humanity. It is appropriate that this image of the suffering, human, Eucharistic body of Christ is adored by a small figure of St. Francis kneeling in the background: the incarnational emphasis of Franciscan spirituality was a significant stimulus to the proliferation of naturalistic religious imagery with emphatic affective appeal in the late middle ages.

Carlo Crivelli creates a hybrid image that combines elements of the *Imago Pietatis* type, the lamentation over the dead Christ, and the entombment of Christ (Fig. 6-17). Again, the figure of Christ is rendered at once active and passive, artfully conveying his dual nature.[16] He is lowered into the tomb by his grief-stricken disciples and at the same time he actively embraces his mother and seems to gaze deeply into her eyes. Her eyes searching his face, she tenderly measures the breadth of the side wound with her fingers: Mary as figure of the Church directs our attention to the site of the institution of the Church and her gesture also serves to prompt our recollection of Simeon's prophecy of the "piercing" she will suffer with her son. Her love for Christ is obviously intense, but she is portrayed with the wrinkled face and sharp profile characteristic of an older mother. Suspended above the cloth of honor behind the figure of Christ is a lavish garland of fruits: he is the fruit of the Virgin's womb, and, as St. Paul writes, in the Resurrection, he will be "the firstfruits of them that sleep" (1 Cor 15:20). As in Giambono's painting, Crivelli draws attention to Christ's

16. On Renaissance artists' deliberate employment of contradictory gestures when representing the dead Christ as a means to convey his concurrent divine and human natures, see Steinberg, *Sexuality of Christ*, 202.

groin by the white loincloth that slips provocatively low about his hips and that aligns with the central vertical axis of the composition. He also charges Christ's exposed lower leg and foot with meaning: the projection of the leg hints at the future animation of Christ's body that will "power" the Harrowing of Hell and the Resurrection (1 Cor 15:25–27). It also carries retrospective meaning, referring to the nail wounds in Christ's feet at the Crucifixion and even further back to the typical pose of the infant Christ in the Presentation in the Temple scenes, where he is often shown extending a bare leg as he is passed between the Virgin Mary and the High Priest, Simeon.[17]

The physical longing shared between Mother and child that characterizes so many infancy and Passion images of the late medieval and early modern periods also becomes a feature of representations of Mary Magdalene and Christ, as exemplified by Titian's painting of their encounter just after the Resurrection, the *Noli me tangere* (Fig. 6-18). Sensuality was readily enlisted in the depiction of the Magdalene, both because of her reputation as a reformed prostitute, which became traditional after Gregory the Great conflated the identities of various women in the Gospels into one, and because of the connection between the immoderate sexual conduct associated with her past and its conversion into an equally extravagant desire for God, as manifested in her lavish and intimate acts of washing Christ's feet with tears of contrition and wiping them with her flowing hair, the sign of her sexuality. Mary Magdalene became the consummate exemplar of penitence, attractive because of her physical beauty that was linked to her past reputation; the sexual nature of her sins may, in part, have contributed to her appeal to male clerics.[18]

Titian works in this vein: he represents Mary Magdalene as a beautiful young woman who has fallen to her knees upon realizing that

17. On the symbolism of Christ's bare leg as referring to the sacrificial Eucharistic lamb, see Matthew J. Milliner, "The Sexuality of Christ in Byzantine Art and in Hypermodern Oblivion" (Religion and Culture Web Forum, The Martin Marty Center for the Advanced Study of Religion, University of Chicago Divinity School, January 2014), accessed August 15, 2018, http://docplayer.net/26299398-The-sexuality-of-christ-in-byzantine-art-and-in-hypermodern-oblivion.html.

18. On the cult of Mary Magdalene, see Katherine Ludwig Jansen, *The Making of the Magdalene: Preaching and Popular Devotion in the Later Middle Ages* (Princeton, N.J.: Princeton University Press, 2000).

the man holding a garden hoe, whom she thought was the gardener, is actually the risen Christ.[19] She wears a deep red mantle—the color of passion—over filmy white garments, and her long blonde hair falls loose over her shoulders. Her pose and raised right hand convey her longing to touch her Lord, which he deflects by drawing up his shroud to cover his body and curving his torso away from her touch: we don't need a title to know that this is the moment when Christ tells Mary, whom he had earlier allowed to perform such an intimate act of loving service in washing his feet, "do not touch me" (Jn 20:17). Titian underscores the balletic motion between these two figures, with the tree and bushes in the middle distance just behind Christ and the Magdalene. Christ's resurrected body is beautiful and luminous, the wounds of the Passion barely visible—just the nail wound in his foot. The coloration of his smooth skin contrasts with the earth tones of the landscape but is related to the light of the morning sun that warms the horizon and illuminates the left side of his body. Nearly nude, his hips are wrapped with a filmy loincloth. The knotting of the loincloth and flourish of the shroud at the level of his groin again reminds us that he suffered death as a fully human male. Moreover, the function of the shroud as a veil between his risen body and the touch of Mary Magdalene is a brilliant pictorial allusion to the believer's loving encounter with Christ under the veil of the sacrament of the Eucharist.

In the pictures discussed thus far, the roles of the male and female figures are largely congruent with their gender: Christ as the bridegroom/lover and the Virgin Mary as the bride (and mother, and Ecclesia) or Mary Magdalene as the adoring penitent soul. But the feminine and subordinate role—because it was understood in relation to Christ as Lord—was quite readily transferred to male figures, as a late medieval sculpture group of Christ and St. John makes clear (Fig. 6-19). The subject of Christ's beloved disciple resting upon his master's breast was extracted from representations of the Last Supper. St. John is depicted as a beautiful, youthful, almost feminine figure with a smooth beardless face and curly hair. He is the bridal soul united to Christ the bridegroom, signified by their tenderly joined right hands. Jeffrey

19. The attribute of the hoe signifies Christ's role as the gardener of the soul and, further, as the New Adam in the garden of paradise.

Hamburger has explained how images such as these conveyed the idea that John's virginity facilitated his visionary insight into divine Wisdom, which suffuses his Gospel and the book of Revelation.[20] This particular sculpture was probably made for a women's convent, so that the nuns would understand their lives in terms of complete surrender to God and ultimate union with him, following the example of St. John.

The assumption of the feminine role by a male figure to express his spiritual relation to Christ continued to appear in Baroque art, as in an unusual Spanish painting by Ribalta of St. Francis embracing the crucified Christ and trampling upon the leopard-like beast of Revelation 13:2 (Fig. 6-20).[21] As though in response to St. Francis's ardor—note that he is about to kiss the side wound to drink the blood that issues from it—the dead yet animated Christ bestows the "wedding" crown of thorns upon Francis's head as the angel at the left reaches to replace Christ's crown of suffering with a crown of flowers. Although this is not a representation of the stigmatization of St. Francis, it clearly refers to that event by conveying that Francis's mystical union with Christ was accomplished by his bodily embrace of the wounding of the Passion. The painting was made for a Franciscan Capuchin house in Valencia. The sensuality of the painting combines passionate, erotic gestures with figures that are clearly masculine; the body of Christ in fact is quite muscular. The longstanding interpretation of the bride of the Song of Songs as representing the Christian soul facilitated male clerics' and monastics' identification with her spousal role.

In the same period as Ribalta's painting, Caravaggio represented St. Francis swooning in ecstasy as a beautiful youthful male angel supports his body (Fig. 6-21). The homoerotic charge of these images likely was a legacy of Platonic ideas about the beautiful male form as the consummate figure whose initial sensual appeal ultimately draws the mind upward to contemplation of the invisible divine beauty.[22]

20. Jeffrey F. Hamburger, *St. John the Divine: The Deified Evangelist in Medieval Art and Theology* (Berkeley, Calif.: University of California Press, 2002).

21. Wendy Hower Livingston, "The Mystery of the Leopard" (Blogpost, August 1, 2008, Nasher Museum of Art at Duke University), accessed March 21, 2017, http://nasher.duke.edu/2008/08/the-mystery-of-the-leopard/, (post removed by January 2020).

22. For a consideration of the theological significance of the beautiful youthful male in Renaissance religious art, see Maya Corry, "The Alluring Beauty of a Leonardesque

While the intertwining of sexuality and spirituality in the premodern eras was commonplace, modern discomfort with these pictures is not unjustified, and, likewise, was voiced by earlier moralists. The overt sensuality of Baroque style and its theatricality can easily overwhelm the theological meaning of these paintings, tipping the balance toward the explicitly carnal and even lascivious. Even though the "ravished" figure in this painting is male, it is obvious that these images depend upon a gendered pictorial vocabulary that marks the feminine as subordinate, languishing here before the invisible male lover.[23]

This is where we come up sharply against the limitations of pictures. Because God became human in the person of a man, Jesus of Nazareth, once his body becomes the focus of religious art rendered in a naturalistic style, a cascade of other implications rushes in. When referred to Christ and translated into pictorial form, the marital metaphors drawn from scripture, which so powerfully express God's relation to God's people and God's relation to the human soul, are not readily comprehensible if Christ's identity as bridegroom is not visibly congruent with the physical body of Jesus of Nazareth. At the same time, it is essential to note that the male Christ of the pictures examined in this paper is almost always represented as either a vulnerable infant or a man dying on the cross: they are not images of worldly aggressive power.

Nevertheless, the viability of this imagery in the contemporary world is tenuous. In the United States, the residue of Protestant antipathy to the sensuality of Catholic imagery, which was associated with the unwelcome waves of European immigration in the nineteenth-century, was internalized as Catholics moved into the American mainstream in the twentieth-century.[24] With the rise of secular modernity, not only did religious art practically disappear as a legitimate

---

Ideal: Masculinity and Spirituality in Renaissance Milan," *Gender and History* 25, no. 3 (2013): 565–89.

23. Their stylistic offspring in the secular realm are the sexually suggestive covers typical of mid-twentieth-century popular romance novels.

24. For a discussion of the conflicted nature of nineteenth-century American Protestant responses to the sensory "excess" of Catholic liturgical and visual culture, see John Davis, "Catholic Envy: The Visual Culture of Protestant Desire," in *The Visual Culture of American Religions*, ed. David Morgan and Sally Promey, 105–28 (Berkeley, Calif.: University of California Press, 2001).

genre for talented artists but also the human figure receded as a subject of interest.[25] Since the later twentieth-century, feminist theory has exposed the ways that a visual vocabulary that marks the feminine as weak and passive and the masculine as powerful and active far too readily buttresses oppressive social and political regimes. And, most recently, the clerical sexual abuse scandal has made deeply problematic for contemporary artists the representation of the adorable but nearly nude infant Christ or the suffering but beautiful adult body of Christ as suitable subjects for devout contemplation.

Two recent paintings show how contemporary American artists have responded to the challenges of the current moment and the place of sensuality in religious images. The first is a painting by Daniel Bonnell of *The Young Holy Family* (Fig. 6-22). It is obvious that he was profoundly affected by the famous early twentieth-century symbolist painting by Gustav Klimt of two lovers, *The Kiss (Lovers)*, in Vienna's Belvedere Museum. As Joseph and Mary had a virginal marriage, Bonnell tones down the eroticism of Klimt's painting while trying to retain its emotional intensity: Joseph does not kiss the Virgin Mary but holds her and the child tenderly, the fusion of their bodies conveying the loving unity of the Holy Family, not the ecstatic sexual union of Klimt's couple. Bonnell has said this of his art: "My painting reflects on the ultimate human need to fulfill an intrinsic longing that extends from birth to death. Simply put, it is a need to be held."[26] He retains traces of religious symbolism in the white bird—the dove of the Holy Spirit—on the window sill and the white apron falling over the Virgin Mary's lap just below the tiny infant whom she cradles in her arms, drawing him to her breast.

Neilson Carlin, the artist of the Holy Family icon commissioned for the World Meeting of Families held in Philadelphia in 2015 (Fig. 6-23), has taken a completely different approach, eschewing modernism for a return to the more traditional, academic style that prevailed in

25. On the aversion to religious subject matter in the contemporary art world, see Daniel Grant, "'I Don't Want That Crap in My Gallery': Why the Art World Frowns on Expressions of Faith," *Commonweal Magazine* (March 6, 2017), accessed August 15, 2018, https://www.commonwealmagazine.org/i-dont-want-crap-my-gallery.

26. Daniel Bonnell, "Artist Statement," website of artist Daniel Bonnell, accessed August 15, 2018, http://www.bonnellart.com/artist-statement.html, (statement removed by January 2020).

nineteenth-century religious art. In Carlin's *Holy Family*, the religious symbolism is explicit and the reverential mood clear. He has, however, chosen to depict the Virgin Mary, St. Joseph, and Jesus as people of ordinary average looks: their costume and setting is of the distant past, but their faces are contemporary. The toddler Jesus—not naked, but fully clothed in a baptismal shift—is very serious and his blessing gesture solemn and deliberate. The teaching message is much clearer and the dignity of the Holy Family emphasized, but it comes at the cost of human warmth.

I am afraid that my conclusion is disappointing. I am not an artist and so cannot imagine how or if it is possible in the twenty-first century to create Christian religious imagery that preserves Jesus Christ as its primary subject and represents him in a way that unifies the intellectual and emotional dimensions of Christian response. It is probably obvious that I think that late medieval and Renaissance artists created some of the most visually compelling and theologically sophisticated images that not only teach but also move the viewer and are captivating to look at. At this current historical moment, when human bodies are so degraded and commodified in contemporary imagery, I think that it is imperative that religious art manifest the human figure in a way that is both believable and lovable. How to do that within the parameters of the story of Christ and the teaching of the Church—while avoiding sexism and racism, yet not abandoning the power of the erotic metaphors from scripture whose visualization so profoundly shaped the religious art of the twelfth through seventeenth centuries—is a critical challenge for the Catholic Church in the West.[27] I hope that there are some young artists among our readers who will be eager to embrace it.

27. For an interesting attempt to fuse the traditional and contemporary in a religious painting, see Matthew J. Milliner, "A New Madonna della Misericordia in Orvieto," website of the Studio for Art, Faith and History, accessed August 15, 2018, https://www.artfaithhistory.org/arts-in-the-academy-essays/#itemId=5d3eaca1f9125d00018e9ae4. Milliner recounts the creation of a new painting of the venerable Madonna of Mercy type by students and faculty in the summer program at Orvieto sponsored by Gordon College, an evangelical Protestant college. As Milliner explains, the iconography of the painting was informed by ecumenical ideals. Interestingly, the heroic nearly-nude body of Christ that occupies the center of the otherwise brilliantly colored painting is represented in grisaille. "Quoted" from a drawing of the Pietà by Michelangelo, the monochromatic figure of the dead Christ is imbued with a spectral quality.

PART 3

The Sacramental Imagination

DAVID W. FAGERBERG

7 ↞ "Seeing with the Eyes of the Heart" and the Sacramental Imagination

The reflections in this volume have a scriptural anchor from Ephesians 1:18—"seeing with the eyes of the heart"—but we will understand that passage more fully if we put it in its context. In his letter to the Church at Ephesus, Paul is giving his big overview of salvation history. The book of Ephesians isn't a study guide for a quiz; it's a study guide for the final exam. Maximus the Confessor said, "Seek the reason why God created, this is knowledge,"[1] which I've always thought would make a great final exam question for one of my courses: "Why did God create? Please be complete in your answer." Ephesians is Paul's blue book essay. If the Trinity is perfect—perfectly happy, perfectly complete—why did God create? And if he went so far as to create an angelic realm, why go beyond that spiritual creation to make a material one? And why raise up one special creature in that material world as a microcosm who overlaps both the angelic and the animal? Why men and women with sensual bodies and spiritual souls?

Paul gives his answer in three parts. First, he says this is an eternal plan that has always existed in the mind of the Father. "He chose us before the foundation of the world to be holy and without blemish" (1:4) and "he destined us for adoption" (1:5). So that's what God is up to! His purpose is to adopt us into the circulation of love that flows between the three persons of the Trinity.

Second, the Father brought his will to pass through Jesus Christ, in whose blood we have been redeemed (1:7), and who accomplished the Father's "plan for the fullness of times, to sum up all things in Christ,

1. Maximus the Confessor, "The Four Hundred Chapters on Love," in *Maximus Confessor: Selected Writings*, trans. George C. Berthold, The Classics of Western Spirituality (New York: Paulist Press, 1985), 76.

in heaven and on earth" (1:9–10). Redemption is the fulfillment of creation, and creation was the beginning of redemption. It is important to say this because otherwise religious people are tempted to think that they are redeemed *from* the world, instead of participating in Christ's redemption *of* the world. Redemption is not Plan B, a retraction of Plan A. God has no regrets about creating men and women with material bodies. In fact, his plan for the fullness of times can be seen in a body walking the shores of Galilee. The Son's Incarnation makes known the Father's mystery the way a carpenter makes known the architect's blueprint. Michelangelo brought forth his ideas in stone; the Father brought forth his Word in flesh. We do not know the mystery *despite* the body (that was the error in dualism, which supposed spirit and body were opposed one to the other) but *through* the body. It is sacramental knowledge.

Third, St. Paul explains that this mystery also involves us. "In him we were also chosen, destined in accord with the purpose of the One who accomplishes all things according to the intention of his will" (1:11). In the promise of the Holy Spirit, we received "a first installment of our inheritance toward redemption as God's possession" (1:13–14). This is deep calling to deep. Even the pagans understood that eating, drinking, and being merry because tomorrow we die comes up short as a philosophy for life: see the honor they gave to their ancestors and how they prepared bodies for burial. They had the suspicion that we are made for something more than could be attained in this world.

And now we finally reach verse eighteen, from which this volume of essays takes its title. You will not understand the mystery that Paul has been trying to explain unless "the eyes of *your hearts* be enlightened, that you may know what is the hope that belongs to his call" (1:18). What could the eyes of the human heart see, if they were opened? Something from *God's own heart*, says John Chrysostom in his blue book essays called his homilies on Ephesians. He exclaims:

> Strange! What Friendship! For [God] tells us His secrets; the mysteries ... of his will, as if one should say, He has made known to us *the things that are in His heart*. For here is indeed the mystery which is full of all wisdom and prudence.... [T]his He desired, this He travailed for, as one might say, that

He might be able to reveal to us the mystery. What mystery? *That He would have man seated up on high.* And this has come to pass.[2]

We are created in the image of God to grow into the likeness of God and be seated up on high. If we had enlightened eyes, we could see God's plan in action: persons deified, minds uplifted, bodies transfigured, imaginations spiritualized. In the phrase by Athanasius about the activity of the Word of God, commonly repeated by all the Church fathers, "He, indeed, assumed humanity that we might become God."[3]

Of all bodily creatures, men and women are the only ones capable of seeing with their heart. The eye of the heart can be attuned to the wavelength of the mystery of God and show up the sacramentality of things that are not seen by bodily eyes alone. The fathers of the Church said a sacrament is when one thing is seen, but another is understood.[4] In the sacramental imagination, we see one thing with our eyes and understand more deeply with our heart. But the pornographic imagination goes blind in one eye, and the full range of reality is no longer evident to its perception. We only see a part of the world, sometimes producing a false view of the true world. The world pornography offers up is illusion, delusion, fantasy, and fanciful. We do not meet people as they really are in this illusory video world.

The philosopher Ludwig Wittgenstein wrote that "the world of the happy man is a different one from that of the unhappy man."[5] For there are two worlds: the world we are given and the world we create. On the one hand, "world" can be used to refer to the objective state of affairs beyond me, which is the world I am given. It refers to the facts of my existence, my family, my genetic makeup, my social environment, indeed, being itself. This world-cosmos is good, as being is good, and it is given by God and accompanied by certain natural laws.

2. John Chrysostom, "Homily I on Ephesians 1:1–2," in vol. 13 of *Nicene and Post-Nicene Fathers: Series 1*, ed. Phillip Schaff, Oxford translation revised by Gross Alexander (Peabody, Mass.: Hendrickson, 1994), 53–54. Emphases added.

3. Athanasius, *On the Incarnation* (Crestwood, N.Y.: St. Vladimir's Orthodox Theological Seminary, 1982), 93.

4. Augustine, "Sermon 272," in *Sermons on the Liturgical Season* (New Rochelle, N.Y.: New City Press, 1993), 300.

5. Ludwig Wittgenstein, *Tractatus Logico-Philosophicus*, trans. D. F. Pears and B. F. McGuinness (London: Routledge & Kegan Paul, 1961), 6.43 (p. 72).

On the other hand, "world" can be used to refer to what I do with that raw material, what I construct as my subjective world. This is a product, a spiritual artifact, one's life accomplishment. This is not finished in a day or a decade, but only upon the death bed. And we do not have a choice as to whether to construct this second, subjective world, we only have a choice as to whether to do so intentionally. Are we attentive and deliberate as we construct this interior world? Are we alert to what components we bring into it? When constructing the world of the subject we can include things (stories, images, and actions) that will make us cowardly or brave, generous or miserly, responsible or negligent, and, in the case of sexual chastity, the stories, images, and activities we include can bring us into the light or into the shadows.

I submit that the subjective world of the sacramental person is completely different from the subjective world of the idolatrous person. The sacramental person sees the world through the prism of God's "plan for the fullness of times, to sum up all things in Christ, in heaven and on earth" (Eph 1:9–10), but the idolatrous person sinks deeper into his own passions and uses creation only for self-gratification. Augustine defined sin as a state of being *incurvatus in se*: being curved in upon oneself, being self-absorbed. Do objects in the world serve us sacramentally by seating us up on high, or do they turn us back upon ourselves? That is not a choice the world makes about itself, it is a choice we make about the world. There is nothing wrong with money, sex, or beer; the problem is with avarice, lust, and gluttony. Christian doctrine insists that the fall was a spiritual one, not a material one. Though two persons may see the same things, they may see them differently, with different imaginations.

The sacramental person is drawn further up and further in, until he or she reaches the gracious love of the Creator. Do not think this sacramental viewpoint is less real because it is spiritual, or because it concerns an understanding that comes from the heart, or because it is something that must be constructed over time. In fact, this view has more reality, and not less—a point that C. S. Lewis took pains to explain in his book *The Great Divorce*. He portrays a visit by "ghosts" from a gray town to a bright, sunlit land, and the ghosts find heaven so real, so substantial, that they are uncomfortable in it. It hurts their feet to walk on the grass, they cannot break a daisy stalk, they fear the rain falling on them. "It was the light, the grass, the trees that were different; made of some different substance, so much solider than things in our country that men were ghosts by comparison."[6] The narrator sees a ghost who had on his shoulder a little red lizard, twitching its tail and whispering things in his ear. We learn by the end that the lizard is lust, and all along the ghost had the suspicion that the lizard would not fit in. "I told this little chap that he'd have to be quiet if he came along—which he insisted on doing. Of course his stuff won't do here: I realize that. But he won't stop. I shall just have to go home."[7]

A flaming Spirit—an angel—asks the ghost-man if he would like the lizard to be quieted, and he says "of course." But then the angel surprises him by asking if he may kill the lizard. In Lewis's text, the angel must ask permission eight or nine times, while the ghost protests that they can discuss that later, or that he only wanted it silenced, or that it will soon go to sleep, or that it would kill him, too. Finally, he relents and the Burning One breaks the back of the lizard and flings it on the ground. I will let Lewis finish the account in the words of the narrator who witnessed this. The ghost was becoming solider by every moment.

> And if my attention had not wavered I should have seen the actual completing of a man—an immense man, naked, not much smaller than the Angel. What distracted me was the fact that at the same moment something seemed to be happening to the Lizard.... What stood before me was the greatest stallion I'd ever seen....
>
> Horse and master breathed each into the other's nostrils.... In joyous haste the young man leaped upon the horse's back.... They were off before I well knew what was happening. There was riding if you like![8]

The mystery is explained to the narrator by the Teacher he has met.

> "Nothing, not even the best and noblest, can go on as it now is. Nothing, not even what is lowest and most bestial, will not be raised again if it submits to death. It is sown a natural body, it is raised a spiritual body. Flesh and blood cannot come to the Mountains. Not because they are too rank, but because

6. C. S. Lewis, *The Great Divorce*, in *The Complete C.S. Lewis Signature Classics* (San Francisco: Harper, 2002), 476.

7. Lewis, *The Great Divorce*, 522.

8. Lewis, *The Great Divorce*, 525.

they are too weak. What is a lizard compared with a stallion? Lust is a poor, weak, whimpering whispering thing compared with that richness and energy of desire which will arise when lust has been killed."[9]

The spiritual world is more real, more substantial, more solid than the world of shadows, and, if it is mastered, sex has the good and fruitful power it was meant to have.

Let me turn back to play with the metaphor of sight a little more. Most often, we use the metaphor of the camera in order to describe the act of seeing. We understand light to bounce off objects in the room and enter our eye to print an image there, the way light enters through the lens of a camera to write on the film—literally *photo-graphe*. The Greek philosophers understood this metaphor, but they had a second one, as well, and I am interested in how it also describes our experience of seeing. Plato said that sight was accomplished by rays that the eye cast upon things. Aristotle called them eye-beams, and the idea is still present in certain phrases of our speech: we speak of someone with "a fire in his eye," or someone "whose eyes grew dim." "Did you see the light in his eye?" We can still understand Charles Dickens when he wrote, "With affection beaming in one eye." Affection beamed forth, like from a lighthouse.

I am not proposing that we should restore this as a theory of optics, but I am proposing that it still describes, in a way, what happens when we see. We "train our eye" upon objects in the objective world and take in their images to construct our subjective world. Our eye is constantly ranging, searching, exploring, passing over things, like Sauron's great eye in *Lord of the Rings*. This is why the ancient Greeks considered sight to be the most aggressive of all the senses. The other four must wait for an object to come within range of the body, but sight can seize an object that is far away. It extends forth to grasp an image of the thing and take it into the mind. When this is done without permission, it gives sight a kind of violent character, and this is what makes voyeurism creepy. An example is when unscrupulous people push pornography into the vision of others against their wills, sometimes in the so-called "soft porn" of advertising and film.

Now, about this kind of looking, I think there are two questions

9. Lewis, *The Great Divorce*, 526.

to ask. The first question would seem to be: what do we seize with our eyes? With what images do we construct our subjective world? Should we exercise any caution about what we take in? Dag Hammarskjold wrote, "You cannot play with the animal in you without becoming wholly animal, play with falsehood without forfeiting your right to truth, play with cruelty without losing your sensitivity of mind. He who wants to keep his garden tidy does not reserve a plot for weeds."[10] We might wish that we could forget the weeds we just stared at, but we cannot "unsee" anything. A sight is neither fully expunged nor diluted by the influx of additional images. An unexpected reminder, a certain train of consciousness, can bring the image back unbidden. Studies have shown that porn is literally addictive, because it has an impact on the body, rewiring the brain, so to speak. And even when the image is not in our consciousness, it is in our unconsciousness and still influencing us, so complex is our psychology. We are generally careful about what we allow children to see because we know the power of images, and yet the average age of a boy's first exposure to internet porn is by some accounts only eleven years, and there are reports that children as young as three are being exposed.[11] It's a pity that we are not more cautious over what we allow ourselves to see. We do not fill a room with horrid paintings if we want it to be beautiful, and if we want a beautiful mind we cannot hang its walls with pornographic images that will never stay in the attic where you think you have banished them, but will return, uninvited.

That is the first question: what do we seize with our eyes? There are some images that have no business being in our mind and we cannot make an excuse for harboring them. But there seems to be a second question, as well: do we play any role in creating the images that we possess? As Wittgenstein hinted at, the world of one person can be completely different from the world of another person, even though both live on the same planet. Two people may see the same thing by

10. Dag Hammarskjold, *Markings* (New York: Alfred A. Knopf, 1964), 15. Hammarskjold was the second secretary-general of the United Nations until his death in 1961, and only one of three people to have been awarded the Nobel Prize posthumously. President Kennedy called him the greatest statesman of our century.

11. Fight the New Drug, "What's the Average Age of a Child's First Exposure to Porn?" Fight the New Drug website, August 20, 2019, accessed December 16, 2019, https://fightthenewdrug.org/real-average-age-of-first-exposure/.

different lights, and these lights comes from our souls and characters, the inner place where grace works. The same object can become pornographic in the wrong imagination. If we saw with the eyes of the heart, we would see a different world. If we were pure, we would see with purity.

So, this second question asks how we look at the world—with what sort of eye beam? All objects in the world stand ready and waiting to lift us up on high, but we might be unwilling to see them sacramentally. Like Esau who sold his birthright for a bowl of porridge, we sell short the world around us. Indeed, the word "pornography" comes from *porneia*, which derives from *pernao*, which means "to sell off." *Porneuo* means "I prostitute." No thing is impure, because it comes from the hand of God; but we might sell off our purity. We are looking at God's creation; it is God's creation as far as the eye can see; and all of God's creation is good, including men, women, bodies, and sex. Yet one person becomes chaste, the other lascivious. How is that? Because the world looks entirely different through sacramental eyes than it looks through pornographic eyes. Things look different because we look at them differently.

The ascetics of the early Church experimented with what it took to retrieve the heart from the passions and so orient it to God that everything in the world would direct their sight to God, and nothing in the world wouldn't direct their sight to God. Here is a story from the *Lives of the Desert Fathers* about Bishop Nonnus, an abbot who was made Archbishop of Antioch. To his pure eyes, everything was sacramental:

> Our holy bishop began to tell [the other bishops] something for the instruction and salvation of all who were listening. As we were all listening with enjoyment to his holy teaching, suddenly there passed by in front of us the foremost actress of Antioch, the star of the local theatre. She was seated on a donkey and accompanied by a great and fanciful procession. She seemed to be clothed in nothing but gold and pearls and other precious stones. Even her feet were covered with gold and pearls. The male and female slaves accompanying her were extravagantly clothed in costly garments, and the collars round their necks were all of gold....
>
> The worldly crowd could not get enough of their beauty and attractiveness. As they passed by us the air was filled with the scent of musk and other most delicious perfumes, but when the bishops saw her passing by so immodestly, with her head bare, and the outlines of her body clearly visible,

nothing over her shoulders as well as her head, and yet the object of such adulation, they all fell silent, groaned and sighed, and averted their eyes as if being forced to witness some grave sin.

The most blessed Nonnus, however, looked at her long and hard, and even after she had passed by he looked after her for as long as she remained in sight. Not till then did he turn round and speak to the other bishops.

"Weren't you delighted to see such beauty as hers?"

They answered nothing. He leant his head down on to his knees and shed tears into the handkerchief which he held on his lap between his holy hands. He sighed deeply and turned again to the bishops.

"Weren't you delighted to see such beauty as hers?"

Again, they answered nothing.

"Truly, I was extremely delighted. Her beauty pleased me very much, for God has preordained to bring her here into the presence of this worthy and eminent bishop of Antioch as a judgment on us all.... Think, my beloved brothers. How many hours did this woman spend in her dressing room, washing herself and dressing herself and decorating herself with the utmost care and attention, so that there might be nothing lacking in the beauty of her ornamentation, simply so that she would not disappoint all her various admirers, who are here today and gone tomorrow? But for us there is an almighty father in heaven, an immortal spouse who makes promises to those who serve him, who offers heavenly riches and eternal rewards which are beyond estimation....We have his promise that we shall see the great and splendid and inestimable face of our bride, which Cherubim dare not gaze upon, but we do not take care to adorn ourselves, or purge ourselves of all the filthy thoughts of our wretched souls. We just let them lie there."[12]

Now there is a sacramental imagination! Nonnus had a stronger eyebeam than ours, so he could see everything in the world with purity. But I feel like I should add, "Kids, don't try this at home." An alcoholic does not leave open bottles around the house, and someone addicted to pornography should not leave certain browser windows open on his computer screen. Indeed, one of the suggestions I have heard is to let another person look over your browser history: if you have sites on it you are embarrassed to let another person see, why were you there in the first place? St. Paul says he gave milk instead of solid food to the Corinthians because there are different levels of maturity, and for the time when we are on our milk diet we must take caution about what

12. Jacob the Deacon, "The Life of St. Pelagia the Harlot," in *Vitae Patrum*, trans. Benedict Baker, online publication, last updated July 12, 2004, accessed October 20, 2018, http://www.vitae-patrum.org.uk/page46.html.

images we let in. Avoid images that would corrupt your imagination; take custody of your eyes. This was a phrase the ascetical tradition used to indicate that we must be careful with what we look at. We fill ourselves with what we look at; indeed, we become what we look at. The old joke goes, "'Doc, it hurts when I do this.' 'Don't do that.'" Similarly, if something corrupts you when you look at it, don't look at it. Be attentive and thoughtful about the objects on which your light-beam falls, because you are never going to unsee the thing.

If your eye causes you to sin, pluck it out; better for you to enter into the kingdom of God without your computer than to be thrown into Gehenna with it (Mk 9:47). But better still is to redeem your imagination and heal your eye so that it can see by the spiritual sun. The saints show us that there is also a diet of solid food by which we can see everything in the world purely, sacramentally, as specifically designed to lift us up on high. The Christian reaction to the world need not be one of living in constant dread of human sensuality. Human sensuality is potentially beautiful, which is precisely what pornography fails to see. Purity prevails when something is seen in the right way, at the right time, in the right measure, and for the right reason. This is why the Catholic tradition does not define chastity as a weak, timid, puritanical aversion to pleasure. Rather, it defines *chastity as power*. In his exhortation on the Christian family, Saint Pope John Paul II wrote, "In the Christian view, chastity by no means signifies rejection of human sexuality or lack of esteem for it: rather it signifies spiritual energy capable of defending love from the perils of selfishness and aggressiveness, and able to advance it towards its full realization."[13] In the world we can see truth, goodness, and beauty. A true artist paints a nude, not a naked lady. Good literature can describe sensual themes without becoming obscene. The beauty of the world is not made up of fifty shades of gray, but a hundred thousand shades of glory. Not only is the Carmelite nun Therese of Lisieux canonized a saint, but so are her parents, Louis and Marie-Azelie Guerin, the first husband and wife in the Church's history to be canonized as a couple. The same Church that honors celibacy as an eschatological witness honors marriage as a sacrament of holiness.

13. John Paul II, Apostolic Exhortation *Familiaris Consortio* (November 22, 1981), 33.

There is a difference between purity and prudishness, a point Chesterton made to his contemporaries when they accused the Victorians of suffering the latter in their attitude toward sex. Chesterton responded, "What disgusted [the Victorian], and very justly, was not the presence of a clear realism, but the absence of a clear idealism. Strong and genuine religious sentiment has never had any objection to realism; on the contrary, religion was the realistic thing, the brutal thing, the thing that called names."[14] Religion should be calling names now more than ever. Christian theology has no objection to realism. Pornography is not realistic; it is projected fantasy, and Christian theology is not disgusted with it for having erotic themes; Christian theology is disgusted with it because the absence of a clear idealism means the erotic themes are not dealt with realistically. Pornography overlooks the dignity of the human person who is instead objectified as only a body; it ignores the capacity of a married sexual relationship to sacramentalize Christ's relationship with the Church. It fails to appreciate the upward draw that eros can exercise on us. What is harmful about pornography is that it blinds us in one eye and coarsens us, concealing the sacramental character of the world from our sight, obscuring the true, the good, and the beautiful. It ignores the true end of human beings. The end of an acorn is an oak, and the end of a human being is a redeemed person, sanctified and reborn, who becomes by grace what Christ is by nature in order to enter into the divine love that flows between Father, Son, and Holy Spirit, thereby being seated up on high to join in the liturgy described in the book of Revelation. Jan and Hubert van Eyck's *Ghent Altarpiece* gives us one image of this liturgy of divine love (Fig. 8-7). That's what a sacramental imagination is capable of seeing. That's the mystery Paul was describing. That is the Father's intent, the Son's accomplishment, the Holy Spirit's task, the Church's mission, and our call.

14. G. K. Chesterton, *Heretics*, in vol. 1 of *G. K. Chesterton Collected Works*, ed. David Dooley (San Francisco, Calif.: Ignatius Press, 1986), 49.

KIMBERLY HOPE BELCHER

8 ↠ Sacramental Exposure

Pornography trains the human eye in a destructive anthropology, but its opposite, a sacramental gaze, aims not for purity but for revelation—or, in a word, exposure. Pornography reduces the human person to a body image, doing violence to a person in order to commodify sexual pleasure. And the prophetic witnesses against this violence are not necessarily theological voices, nor are their utterances always in the form of theological arguments: sometimes they come in the form of R&B music videos. I want to nurture here a kind of sacramental gaze that can recognize in so-called secular music a provocation to a more incarnational anthropology of the body. Christian art, liturgy, and preaching have been and can be subversively pro-body and pro-eros. Practices, visual or verbal, that evoke empathy and refuse to control another's body reveal love, intimacy, and the ineradicable mystery of a human person. That eros, in the end, is *more* alluring than a pornographic body.[1]

Dance and the Challenge of Embodied Spirituality

Liturgical discussions in North America occasionally attend to, and are almost always stymied by, the question of whether dance can be permissible in the liturgy. In African liturgy, dance is essential;[2] in

1. I would like to thank the Division for Mission at Saint Mary's College, conference attendees, and students in my doctoral seminar at Notre Dame, as well as Elizabeth Groppe and Lauren L. Murphy for their valuable feedback on this essay and assistance with editing.

2. See E. Elochukwu Uzukwu, *Worship as Body Language: Introduction to Christian Worship: An African Orientation* (Collegeville, Minn.: Liturgical Press, 1997); Kariamu Welsh-Asante, ed., *African Dance: An Artistic, Historical, and Philosophical Inquiry* (Trenton, N.J.: Africa World Press, 1996); Laurenti Magesa, *Anatomy of Inculturation: Transforming the Church in Africa* (Maryknoll, N.Y.: Orbis, 2004); Charles E. Farhadian,

African American worship, too, it is uncontroversial.[3] In "Western" environments, however, it is deemed problematic.[4] The movement of the body is here associated with either aesthetic entertainment or sexual stimulation rather than religious eros. Yet, I argue in this essay that there is a movement in popular dance that aims to heal the erotic gaze, to reclaim the black female dancer's twerking body for a sacramental encounter.[5]

In the North American context, the distinction between artistic dance and popular dance can show us more about a vision not only of embodied movement but also of human nature. Ballet is "high art," which means that even when its costumes are just as revealing as those of pop musicians, it raises no eyebrows. It also has a reputation as being "feminine" and "white," even when performed by black or male artists. It is mostly performed by professionals.[6] Workout dance, while being more accessible to nonprofessionals, subjects aesthetic considerations to the utilitarian demands of health. Popular dance, which is strongly associated with sexual desire, has marked male and female moves, dress, and roles. Many of the moves, along with the music that accompanies them, originate in black culture. This style of dance is widely emulated by youth culture, so while it is performed by professionals it is imitated in many other contexts. Popular dance includes many black cultural elements that are mass produced for a largely white audience; it is permeated by heterosexual and stereotyped gender relationships; and it is interpreted as highly erotic.

---

ed., *Christian Worship Worldwide: Expanding Horizons, Deepening Practices*, Calvin Institute of Christian Worship Liturgical Studies Series (Grand Rapids, Mich.: Eerdmans, 2007); Guido Oliana, "African Language, Drum, and Dance," in vol. 2 of *God and Popular Culture*, ed. Stephen Butler Murray and Aimée Upjohn Light, 225–44 (Santa Barbara, Calif.: ABC-CLIO, 2015).

3. See, e.g., Mary E. McGann, *A Precious Fountain: Music in the Worship of an African American Catholic Community*, Virgil Michel Series (Collegeville, Minn.: Liturgical Press, 2004).

4. In Western cultures, "dancing is tied with love, with diversion, with profaneness, with unbridling of the senses.... For that reason it cannot be introduced into liturgical celebrations of any kind whatever: that would be to inject into liturgy one of the most desacralized and desacralizing elements." Congregation for Divine Worship, *Saltatio Religiosa* [On Dance in the Liturgy], *Notitiae* 11 (1975): 202–05.

5. In this chapter, I do not intend to argue for liturgical dance but rather to argue for a Western move to reclaim dance from its desacralized and desacralizing status.

6. Ballet is rejected in *Saltatio Religiosa* for being inadequately participative.

In many ways, popular dance commodifies African American culture for white eyes, female bodies for heterosexual male gazes, and erotic desire for economic gain.[7] Given this, it may seem impossible to see the exposed bodies of popular dancers with an antipornographic gaze, as a site of grace.

The emergence of these categories of dance in the United States neatly parallels the evolution of nudity in art imagery over the early modern period. In *A Complex Delight: The Secularization of the Breast, 1350–1750*, Margaret Miles observes that the depiction of the naked female form diverged into three genres: art, anatomical drawings, and pornography. Art, like artistic dance, was an expression of aesthetic beauty, closely associated with the "cultured" upper class.[8] Anatomical drawings, like workout dance, reflect a medical approach to health isolated from the understanding of the human subject as a holistic intellectual, emotional, moral, and spiritual being. Pornography, like contemporary popular dance, was a mass commercialization of erotic imagery. Each of these three genres of art and dance—the aesthetic, the health-conscious, and the erotic—separate one aspect of embodiment from the full human experience. In contrast, early Christian imagery sought to unite the aesthetic, the moral, the erotic, along with the spiritual dimension of human experience.

Christians continue to draw strength from the sacramental imagination of the premodern period. At the same time, it is wise to study the sacramental gaze of cultures that preserve an understanding of the dancing human body as in touch with the divine. Many contemporary voices challenge the division of the erotic and the spiritual in artistic media and images of the human body, along with the racial and social hierarchies that often accompany this division. One of the most lyrical protests to the separation of the erotic from the spiritual may be that of Janelle Monáe. Monáe's 2013 album *The Electric Lady* subverts the hierarchies between high and low culture, between black and white

7. On the racialized and gendered gaze of pop music videos, see Jacob Turner, "Sex and the Spectacle of Music Videos: An Examination of the Portrayal of Race and Sexuality in Music Videos," *Sex Roles* 64 (2011): 173–91. In brief, African American and female performers are far more likely to be dressed and portrayed in sexualized ways.

8. Margaret R. Miles, *A Complex Delight: The Secularization of the Breast, 1350–1750* (Berkeley, Calif.: University of California Press, 2008).

culture. Rather than telegraphing dancers' sexuality as sexual availability, the album and its associated audiovisual media shows us the female body as belonging to the woman herself, seeking a spiritual and somatic anthropology. Monáe often reflects on the body and uses dance as a symbol of the full experience of humanity. In the video for her 2010 song "Tightrope," she wears her signature tuxedo and explores a fictional world in which dancing, which has been forbidden, explodes in the margins. The irrepressible dance is a proof of the irrepressible humanity of the oppressed. One might say that Monáe espouses a "liberation theology of dance" in her work. Dance is key to the experience of being a human and to African American resistance to oppression. In Monáe's work, dance speaks of the irreplaceability of the human body as well as its integration with spirituality.

In the video for the 2013 single "Q.U.E.E.N.," Monáe explicitly challenges the idea that dance—including the controversial twerking—can be reduced to sexual titillation. "Is it peculiar that she twerks in the mirror? And am I weird to dance alone late at night?" the lyrics ask. "What's the price of fame? Am I a sinner with my skirt on the ground?" The first pair of rhetorical questions suggests the dancer herself is the primary spectator for black dance, and the second demands a space for renown within the sphere of (black) musical artistry that does not depend on pornographic exposure. Moreover, by addressing these questions to the viewer, Monáe challenges the viewer to reject the link between black femininity, fame, and the pornographic gaze.

Closely related to these questions are Monáe's more explicitly religious questions in the same song, which include: "Hey sister, am I good enough for your heaven? Say, will your God accept me in my black and white? Will he approve the way I'm made?" Here, Monáe challenges the viewer both to reject the merely sexual lens and to appreciate the dancing black, female bodies as an expression of spirituality and human dignity. The visual backdrop to Monáe's challenging questions is a very white museum. Into this "high culture" environment, Monáe, Erykah Badu, and the rest of the band bring R&B and hip hop music, black dance, black dialect, and a defense of black culture;[9] Monáe sings: "They be like 'oooh, let them eat cake,' but we eat

9. Janelle Monáe, "Q.U.E.E.N." official music video featuring singer Erykah Badu,

wings and throw them bones on the ground." Among its complex set of messages, the video questions the exclusion of black dance from white culture's assumptions about the expression of religious values.[10]

In order to better understand the questions posed by Monáe in "Q.U.E.E.N." and their importance for the recovery of a sacramental vision of the body and its sexuality, I will offer a few points of context. First, Monáe's albums address gender, sexuality, and race in contemporary America indirectly, by constructing a fictional sentient android race oppressed by humans. The leader of these androids is "the ArchAndroid," "The Electric Lady," or "Cindi Mayweather"—played by Monáe herself.[11] Monáe is clearly in conversation with science fiction, but unlike most fictional robots, Monáe's androids are full of passion, sensual sensitivity of every kind, and drive. In her videos, the androids are portrayed by black artists, but the reserve of fiction deflects the viewer or listener from applying themes simplistically to the contemporary American situation.

Second, *The Electric Lady* is an album addressing the experience of women, specifically black women who are marginalized and oppressed. It is especially directed to a female audience, which can be seen in several lyrical addresses to "ladies" as well as the ubiquity of women in the foreground of the videos for the singles on the album. A little over two minutes into the Q.U.E.E.N. video, there is a shot with two audience members—a significant exposure in Monáe's oeuvre, which often reflects the experience of being seen.[12] The women in this

---

directed by Alan Ferguson (May 1, 2013), 1:45, accessed October 20, 2018, https://www.youtube.com/watch?v=tEddixS-UoU.

10. See Monáe, "Q.U.E.E.N." 1:45. This scene features members of Wondaland singing the frequently repeated line, "Don't judge me!"

11. *ArchAndroid* was the title of Monáe's second album. This fictional world is most clearly expressed in the transitions between songs on the albums, as well as in the videos.

12. See, for example, the video "Many Moons," in which Cindi Mayweather performs on stage during an android auction, which resembles, in different ways, both a slave auction and a fashion show. Monáe plays both Mayweather and the androids being shown for sale, and the video makes much of Mayweather's fans and the android buyers. "Dance Apocalyptic," part of *The Electric Lady*, also explores these themes, but like "Q.U.E.E.N." the audience in this video is composed of women. The composition of the shot at the conclusion of the line "Is it peculiar that she twerk in the mirror?" shows the woman who is twerking in a striped dress in front of a mirror on a small screen, emphasizing her self-expression while also demonstrating her communication with the female viewers. Monáe, "Q.U.E.E.N." 2:01.

shot are portrayed very differently than the adoring fans that become problematic in other videos—they are not only watching Monáe dance but are also dancing themselves. Moreover, they are liberators; they were the characters, who, in the video's prologue, had freed the band from the museum prison. In constructing a female, active, and liberating audience, the album seems to subvert the commonly presumed heterosexual male audience that will find the sexualized portrayal of the female artist attractive. This is another kind of displacement, one that attempts to deflect the possibility that Monáe's sexuality will be commodified and merchandized. Third, in "Q.U.E.E.N.," remarkably, there are no camera shots that highlight the hips or rear of the dancers. Rather, when the camera gaze moves in for a more intimate view, it moves to their faces.[13]

Monáe's questions about the dancing body and its spirituality critique the commodification of the black female dancing body in contemporary music.[14] The objectifying gaze within contemporary music represents a departure from the African and African American experience of the dancing body as a connection to the divine. Monáe's critique provokes her viewers, and especially Christians, to reclaim the exposed body not as pornography but in solidarity. In the remainder of this essay, I will use the image of *Maria lactans* and the work of Jean-Luc Marion to heal the pornographic gaze and to construct a hermeneutic lens that can empathetically enjoy the dancer's pleasure in her own embodied and moving *imago Dei* rather than attempt to possess the body with the eyes.

Maria Lactans and the Sacramental Gaze

The sacramental imagination and Christian art suggest that sacramental exposure to a vision of the disrobed human body can reveal the grace of God offered to humanity. In 1350, as Miles argues, the

13. For more information on the genre characteristics of music videos, see Carol Vernallis, *Experiencing Music Video: Aesthetics and Cultural Context* (New York: Columbia University Press, 2004).

14. "Hey sister, am I good enough for your heaven? Say, will your God accept me in my black and white? Will he approve the way I'm made? Or should I reprogram, deprogram and get down?" Monáe, "Q.U.E.E.N." 6:03.

exposed breast of Mary nursing the infant Jesus was a symbol of the grace by which God nourishes humanity. In some examples of the genre, such as Ambrogio Lorenzetti's *Suckling Madonna* (ca. 1325–48), the baby Jesus makes eye contact with the viewer, inviting him or her to share his nourishment (Fig. 8-1). Such images existed in a culture with an iconic worldview that included the idea that Jesus "nursed" the Church by feeding it with his Body and Blood in the Eucharist, and that Mary was a symbol of Christ's humanity, since he "assumed flesh from the Virgin." The divine spiritual nourishment embodied in the Eucharist could be glimpsed in the image of the bared breast of Our Lady. In contrast, by 1750, Miles writes, "the breast was eroticized and medicalized, no longer usable, or used, as a religious symbol."[15]

The way we envision the human body shapes the way we envision human nature. The bare human body, especially, tells us what we think the human person is capable of, and if the bared human body speaks to us only of careless sexual contact or sexual violence, then our anthropology has no room for divinization. We need to reclaim portrayals of the human body in which the viewer is invited to participate with, to feel together with, and perhaps to emulate the naked humanity of the person being depicted, rather than to judge, desire, or possess her or his body. In Catholic art of the fourteenth and fifteenth centuries, the aesthetic, the erotic, and the real combine, not so much to express the human longing for God (though it does that), but to express God's erotic longing for and ecstatic invitation to humanity, as Dianne Phillip's essay in this volume elucidates.

Like the black female dancers of "Q.U.E.E.N.," Jesus and Mary are humanized through embodied movement in Christian art. Henry Maguire, in *The Icons of Their Bodies*, argues that the humanity of the Blessed Virgin Mary and of Jesus is emphasized by their more dynamic poses, suffused with emotion, which contrast with the stillness that characterizes icons of other saints.[16] A new emphasis on Christ's humanity sprang out of the mendicant orders and late medieval mystical and devotional texts. In the fourteenth and fifteenth centuries, this

15. Miles, *Complex Delight*, ix.

16. Henry Maguire, *The Icons of Their Bodies: Saints and Their Images in Byzantium* (Princeton, N.J.: Princeton University Press, 1996), 84.

humanism came to be reflected in a new use of nudity to portray the humanity, vulnerability, and tenderness of Mary and Jesus.

One characteristic of this imagery is the multiple layers of meaning and referents available in the interpretation of various elements of the image; in fact, the same image can generate seemingly contradictory interpretations of the human body. This is, perhaps, most clearly and emphatically the case in regard to the portrayal of nakedness. Take for instance the 1437 *Lucca Madonna* by Jan van Eyck (Fig. 8-2). Van Eyck is well known for his combination of realism, especially in the depiction of the human subject, and symbolism derived from iconography and scriptural typology. In this image, Mary feeds the nude infant Jesus from her exposed breast. Jesus holds a fruit in his left hand and touches Mary's wrist with his right. Many earlier images show the infant making eye contact with the viewer, suggesting an invitation to participate in the spiritual nourishment symbolized by Mary's milk, but the *Lucca Madonna* adds another layer of meaning. While the intimacy of the images of the nursing Madonna naturally evoke a domestic setting, the vessels on the right side could exist either in a kitchen or a sacristy. Taken together with the architectural elements, like the decorative window and columns, the image suggests both a bedroom and a small chapel, and Mary's squared and draped lap is at the same time an altar. The infant's naked body, lying on that altar, evokes Eucharistic associations through which the viewer is invited to participate in the image. It is obvious here that neither Mary's exposure nor Jesus' nudity is expected to be interpreted sexually by the viewer. On the contrary, the exposed breast and nude infant are signs of the humanity of Christ, accepted from the Virgin at the Incarnation. To the late medieval sacramental imagination, the erotic image recalled the compassion and love of the Trinity in the Incarnation and the institution of the Eucharist. The other dimension of eros, caught up in fallen humanity's experience of sexual desire, is also recalled by the fruit in Christ's left hand at the very center of the frame, echoed by the two fruits on the windowsill.

Fruits are a common motif in images of the Madonna and the Christ child. Sometimes, they clearly suggest the nourishing roundness of Mary's breast, as in this Hans Memling image painted between

1485 and 1490 (Fig. 8-3). Other images of the nursing mother make the parallel between the fruit and the breast yet more explicit, such as *Holy Family with Music-Making Angels* attributed to the Master of Frankfurt (Fig. 8-4). But, of course, the fruit also evokes the story of the Fall, and nakedness as a motif further focuses that allusion, as evident in the Adam and Eve paintings from Jan and his brother Hubert van Eyck's *Ghent Altarpiece* (Figs. 8-5 and 8-6). The nudity of Adam and Eve generates complex responses, for the figures are beautiful and sensual, but not alluring; their faces and postures recall their shame but seem to express peace and contemplation, and their visual focus is on the central figure of God enthroned at the center of the upper register of the altarpiece (Fig. 8-7). These images, unlike contemporary imagery of the human body, are aesthetic, erotic, realist, and contemplative all at once. They reflect the entirety of the whole human story, from its creation at the upper outsides to its destiny in the lower center (where the Eucharist would have been visible at its elevation in the Mass).[17]

Our culture offers us very limited alternatives for understanding and enacting our humanity: artistic beauty; purely physical definitions of wellness; sexuality commodified and offered to the male gaze; or a spirituality that must maintain itself free of performative aesthetics, eroticism, and physicality. Such a spirituality has little left to offer to an integrative human vision. The sacramental gaze, in contrast, holds in tension the ambiguities of human life: God's loving creation, the shame of human sin, and the redemption of humanity that restores the dignity and power of the body.

In the Rogier van der Weyden altarpiece of the Last Judgment, nakedness characterizes the vulnerable and pathetic crowd stumbling toward hell, but equally the redeemed bodies of those gratefully moving toward heaven and contemplating the enthroned Christ (Fig. 8-8). The risen Christ is wrapped only in a cope that reveals his upper body, reminding viewers of the nakedness of the crucified Christ (Mt 27:35; Jn 19:23–24). In another van der Weyden altarpiece, we can see the nakedness of Christ at his nativity, at his burial, and finally wrapped in the cope as he appears to Mary Magdalene at the Resurrection

17. For more on the history of salvation, see David W. Fagerberg's preceding chapter in this volume.

(Fig. 8-9). In these images, the nakedness of the human body is not an isolated symbol of beauty, still less an invitation to be consumed by lust, but rather a sign of the whole trajectory of salvation history: a depiction of humanity created by God, burdened by sin, and redeemed by the death and resurrection of Jesus. What understanding of the human being can underpin such an integrative sacramental vision?

The Exposed Human Body as Icon, Not Idol

Jesuit Karl Rahner, in his essay "The Theology of the Symbol," draws on the classic theology of the sacraments to explore the human body as a necessary realization of the soul.[18] The sacraments produce their supernatural effects by exercising the natural function of the elements (water cleanses by washing, bread nourishes spiritually by nourishing physically). Similarly, the human body represents the human person because the person *is* body and yet includes an interiority, the soul, which is exactly what the physical body really *means*. Creation, in the Christian perspective, was always intended to communicate to embodied spiritual creatures the presence of God, not through mental exercises making us aware of God as something represented outside creation, but because creation provides the place for every real encounter that human beings have with God.

For Rahner, the visible body is a symbol, not primarily because of how it is seen by others, but because of how, by the body, I dwell in the world and make myself visible to (that is, give myself to) others. Of course, the human person is more than he or she can ever communicate to another person, but any knowledge of who I truly am that I impart to another comes through my body, either directly through my words and actions, or indirectly through the products of my actions, like works of art or words on a page.

Rahner enlarges this idea of symbols by including within it the ancient Christian notion that the world, and each thing in it, exists by participating in God. A symbol, he argues, exists first and foremost because each thing, in order to be in the world at all, exists "by really

18. Karl Rahner, "Theology of the Symbol," in *More Recent Writings*, vol. 4 of *Theological Investigations*, trans. Kevin Smyth, 221–52 (Baltimore, Md.: Helicon, 1966). This is only one of a number of important themes in this seminal essay.

projecting its visible figure outside itself as its—symbol, its appearance, which allows it to be there, which brings it out to existence in the world."[19] One of his paradigmatic examples is the human body, which is the symbol of the human person. Of course, the human body does not represent the person as one thing represents a thing that is other than itself (like the stop sign and the idea of stopping, or the letters on the page and the idea conveyed by the word). Rather, the human body is a symbol that imparts to the receiver, as much as he or she can receive, the reality it symbolizes. Rahner calls this kind of symbol a "real symbol" to distinguish it from the merely conventional kind. This symbol shares important characteristics with the sacraments, which are modes by which God reaches out to humanity, communicating the divine nature to the extent that humans are able to receive it. God is reaching out to give God's self to us throughout creation, but the sacraments are a privileged place where that grace becomes visible: first, because sacraments are perfectly suited to human beings' ability to receive grace; and, second, because they are a link between the created order we live in and the humanity of Jesus Christ in whom we are saved. The Eucharist is the paradigm of sacramental communication because in it the Body of Christ becomes our nourishment. The sacramental Body and Blood of Christ are, then, the real symbol of the saving Incarnation of the Word, because they impart to us (as far as we are able to receive it) the fullness of the risen Christ, who is the image of the Father.

We can see the root of this retrieved understanding of humanity and salvation in the early Christian understanding of baptism. Fourth-century baptismal rites were converging toward a shared structure from a variety of local traditions: generally, they consisted of a period of public catechesis and exorcism, a repudiation of Satan and adherence to Christ, a pre-baptismal anointing, a water bath with a trinitarian confession of faith, one or more post-baptismal anointings, and the reception of the Eucharist.[20] Many modern commentators

19. Rahner, "Theology of the Symbol," 231.

20. For a useful collection of primary sources on these rites, see Edward Yarnold, *The Awe-Inspiring Rites of Initiation: The Origins of the R.C.I.A.* (Collegeville, Minn.: Liturgical Press, 1994). For a more thorough treatment of the variations in practice during this period, as well as in preceding and following centuries, see Maxwell E. Johnson, *The*

have been surprised by the paradox in fourth-century Christianity that Christians disapproved of public nudity (including mixed-gender public bathing) but practiced naked baptism.[21] It is true that in many regions female deacons were commissioned for the most scandalous moments of the rite: the full-body anointing with oil before the bath and the descent into the bath itself.[22] Nevertheless, it is significant that the moment of stripping is given significant theological weight in the homilies given to the newly baptized by their bishops, while the moment of receiving a new garment (which is emphasized in the modern rite) is scarcely treated at all. It is hard not to conclude that stripping deserved and received theological attention precisely because it was shocking and potentially scandalous; because it was dangerous and yet obligatory, it could be liberative and powerful.

The sacramental imagination is intrinsically transgressive; the baptismal stripping challenged late imperial Roman culture, which like our own late modern culture, broadcast the power and status of a person by means of his or her clothing. Against this context, the baptismal rite recalls (from the Genesis narrative of Adam and Eve) the concept that the clothed body originates in a garment given after the consumption of the forbidden fruit. Clothing is a symbol of human sin, while the naked body, vulnerable and erotic, is identified with Christ's humanity. The significance of nakedness is such that female initiands were to loosen their hair, according to *Apostolic Tradition*, so that "no one . . . take any alien object down into the water."[23] In the fourth century, homilies were given by bishops to inspire and educate

---

Rites of Christian Initiation: Their Evolution and Interpretation, revised and expanded edition (Collegeville, Minn.: Liturgical Press, 2007).

21. Some modern scholars have speculated that public nudity in Christian initiation seemed unproblematic in its proper historical context because, for example, there were Roman baths in which both sexes bathed together. But this seems to have been already an archaic practice, at least among the upper classes, by the fourth century, and additionally, the same bishops who preach about initiatory stripping are often critical of public nudity in other contexts. Contemporary texts like the *Didascalia Apostolorum* dictated that women should always be anointed by female deacons in order to avoid the impropriety of the bishop doing the full-body anointing, so there was some anxiety about the practice.

22. Johnson, *The Rites of Christian Initiation*, chapters 4–5.

23. Johnson, *The Rites of Christian Initiation*, 99–106. *Apostolic Tradition* contains a number of later additions to an early core; this instruction regarding the hair is identified as likely part of the earlier core.

candidates whose motives for conversion to newly legalized Christianity might be as much political as personal. We might expect, then, that they would express concern about the male gaze falling on nude female bodies, or prohibit the loose hair often associated with promiscuity, or defend the whole-body anointing that in some rites followed the stripping. But the "gaze" of the homilies is defined neither by what the bishop saw nor by what the bishop does not see. Instead, the homilies narrate the events using "you" to focus on—and thereby share—the body experience of the initiands. The gaze enshrined in the homilies is an empathetic gaze, which attempts to share the feeling flesh of those who have been baptized.

In his *Mystagogical Catecheses*, or homilies to the newly baptized, Cyril of Jerusalem reminds the assembly of the stripping rite, investing it with drama: "Immediately, then, having entered, you stripped off your clothing."[24] Cyril interprets the tunic that is removed as "the old man with his deeds." Nakedness here connotes a renewed innocence, a return to the pre-Fall condition of humanity, so that the candidates bear the image of "the first-formed Adam, who was himself naked in paradise and not ashamed."[25] At the same time, the person being stripped is also interpreted as a type of the crucifixion. Christ's triumph on the cross is interpreted as a disrobing through an interpretation of Colossians 2:15: Jesus "in his nakedness 'disarmed the principalities and powers, and openly triumphed over them on the tree.'"[26] The naked initiand's iconic representation of Jesus' Crucifixion is intensified by the practice of baptizing in the Constantinian Basilica of the Holy Sepulchre, built on the geographical site of Christ's burial: after the full-body anointing, the homilist says, the naked initiand is "led to the holy and divine pool of baptism, just as Christ was taken from the cross to the tomb that stands before you."[27]

There is a power in these images that derives from the unusual in-

24. Cyril of Jerusalem, *Lectures on the Christian Sacraments*, ed. Maxwell E. Johnson, (Yonkers, N.Y.: St. Vladimir's Seminary, 2017), 97–99. Some scholars believe that these homilies were written by Cyril's successor, John, but the authorship does not affect the interpretation I offer here.

25. Cyril, *Lectures on the Christian Sacraments*, 99.

26. Cyril, *Lectures on the Christian Sacraments*, 97.

27. Cyril, *Lectures on the Christian Sacraments*, 99.

timacy and shocking vulnerability of nudity and skin-to-skin contact in this historic setting. The intimacy is displaced from an intimacy between the baptizing clergy and the newly baptized to an intimacy between Christ and the baptized through the homilist's use of the bride's quotation in the erotic Song of Songs to encourage the new initiands to continually pursue a holy life: "I have taken off my clothing; how shall I put it on?"[28]

The erotic element and the emphasis on renewed creation is even stronger in John Chrysostom's interpretation of the stripping in one of his postbaptismal homilies:

> At the appointed hour of the night, [the bishop] strips you of all your clothes, and as if he were about to lead you into heaven itself by means of these rites, he prepares to anoint your whole body with this spiritual oil.... After this anointing he takes you down into the sacred waters, at the same time burying the old nature and raising "the new creature, which is being renewed after the image of the creator." Then by the words of the priest and by his hand the presence of the Holy Spirit flies down upon you and another man comes up out of the font, one washed from all the stain of his sins, who has put off the old garment of sin and is clothed in the royal robe.[29]

Like the Flemish paintings, the naked body in these homilies represents a humanity already structured by the narrative of creation, sin, and redemption. In this case, though, these meanings are not merely symbolically represented but are experienced in the flesh.[30] The shared flesh-experience of baptism provides the basis for a narrative empathy with the bodies of the new initiates. Moreover, this flesh-intimacy is directed ultimately toward the unity of the candidate with the Trinity; the anointing all over is interpreted by Theodore of Mopsuestia in terms of a new, but by no means modest, garment: "Unlike clothes, which only come in contact with part of the body, and even if they touched the whole surface of the body would still not come in contact with the internal organs, our whole nature will 'put on the im-

28. Cyril, *Lectures on the Christian Sacraments*, 97–99.

29. John Chrysostom, "Baptismal Homily II," trans. Edward Yarnold, in Yarnold, *The Awe-Inspiring Rites of Initiation*, 160–61.

30. See M. L. Lyon and J. M. Barbalet, "Society's Body: Emotion and the 'Somatization' of Social Theory," in vol. 2 of *Embodiment and Experience: The Existential Ground of Culture and Self*, ed. Thomas Csordas, 48–66 (New York: Cambridge University Press, 1994).

perishable' at the moment of the resurrection, by virtue of the working of the Holy Spirit within us."[31] This invisible garment of oil that anoints the whole body, even the most intimate organs veiled by the skin, implies that the naked Christian is at all times "clothed" with the Holy Spirit. In these baptisms, the naked human flesh is experienced first by those baptized, then "heard" and shared by all those listening to the homily. The intimacy that the baptizands experience with the risen Christ through the stripping, anointing, and immersion is given to all those listening to the Easter sermons. It is a way of returning to the flesh experience for those who were baptized long ago.

Like the naked flesh of the baptizands, Mary's breast and Jesus' genitals in early Renaissance art symbolized the human nature of all people. Rahner says, "Each part [of the body] bears ... within itself the symbolic force and function of the whole, by contributing its part to the whole of the symbol.... A word used to designate part of the human body (head, heart, breast, hand) in a symbolic sense, does not signify only the part as such, that is, as a quantitative, material part of the whole body: it always signifies the one whole, composed of the symbol-generating origin and the material piece."[32] At the same time, not all parts of the body are created equal: naked flesh and the organs associated with procreation bear the burden of theological anthropology in a special way. In the fourth-century sacramental imagination, the intimacy generated in the flesh by nude baptism was, ultimately, a participation in the intimacy of the Trinity and could be shared among believers.

Is it possible to reclaim the multivalence and ambiguity of the human body, to make a little room for the sacramental communication of God to be visible to us in the way it was to Cyril of Jerusalem, Theodore of Mopsuestia, and the van Eycks? David Gibson thinks it is not. After lamenting the loss of the images of Mary breastfeeding, he concludes sadly, "But I have to think it's impossible to 'unsee' something as sexual and sensual, or to 're-consecrate' the breast—even the Virgin Mary's."[33] Perhaps it would be ill-advised to return to nude adult

31. Theodore of Mopsuestia, "Baptismal Homily II," trans. Edward Yarnold based on the French translation of R. Tonneau, in Yarnold, *The Awe-Inspiring Rites*, 185.

32. Rahner, "Theology of the Symbol," 248–49.

33. David Gibson, "Jesus Was Not a Bottle Baby: What Happened to Maria Lactans?"

public baptisms, but the public witness of Janelle Monáe says, I think, that it is not only possible but morally necessary to re-consecrate our gaze on human beings' exposed flesh. The sacramental imagination is, often quite explicitly, the ability to consecrate the sensual, not to de-sexualize but to re-spiritualize or en-spiritualize the body, to allow us to see beyond the surface of things, to permit a glimpse, if only through contemplation, of the unimaginable depth beneath ordinary reality.

The Flesh and the Erotic Gaze

To retrieve a sacramental erotic vision, I turn to Catholic philosopher Jean-Luc Marion. In place of a distinction between idols and icons, Marion distinguishes between two different ways of seeing: the idolatrous and the iconic gaze. There is a complicated relationship in Marion's work between the character of the image gazed upon and the intention of the viewer; it is enough here to say that the character of the gaze is determined by both, and it is the gaze itself that is the primary concern in my essay. For Marion, to look idolatrously is to project one's own idealized image on the thing one sees. One does not see the whole thing for itself but reduces the thing to what it means for the viewer.[34]

Marion calls the alternate kind of gaze iconic, because it does not reduce the thing seen to the image the viewer wants to see. The pornographic gaze reduces women to those women, parts, and poses that the male viewer finds most sexually stimulating; an iconic gaze, on the contrary, recognizes that the true beauty of the body is its faithful expression of its own interiority (per Rahner's soul-body relationship). This gaze re-personalizes the one who is seen: the *excess* or *more* that the viewer desires is mutuality in human relationship. For Marion, as for Emmanuel Levinas, the iconic enfleshment of the person is most clearly seen in the face, where life accumulates. The iconic gaze depends on seeing an *excess* in the other that is akin to the excess of my own experience—in other words, to see in the other's flesh a self like my own self. For Marion, the experience of feeling my own flesh, its

Commonweal Magazine (December 11, 2012): https://www.commonwealmagazine.org/jesus-was-not-bottle-baby-what-happened-maria-lactans, accessed October 20, 2018.

34. Jean-Luc Marion, *God without Being: Hors-Texte*, trans. Thomas A. Carlson (Chicago, Ill.: University of Chicago Press, 1991), chapters 1–3.

pain and pleasure, not only comes up in our daily experience but is actually the basis for experience itself.[35] The difference between my flesh and yours is that I feel using my flesh and that I cannot feel without my flesh. I feel pain and pleasure in my own flesh, and I cannot feel the pain and pleasure in your flesh. This is the grounds for my identity as a person—I feel the materiality of my flesh as I feel no other materiality in the world. It is also, however, the grounds for empathy: because I am confronted with the mystery of my own ability to experience, to not only use a body like a machine but to be that body, I am able to recognize in you another feeling flesh, another self. The iconic gaze, then, arouses solidarity—a desire to feel what the flesh of the other feels—not a desire to possess the flesh of another.

For Marion, love is the desire, ingrained in humanity, to share the feeling flesh with another.[36] This, for Marion, is an experience of transcendence: one longs both to give one's whole experience over to another, to be fully heard, and to feel together with another, to feel another's feeling flesh. This is the heart of the human desire for relationality. But then it becomes obvious why sexual love—which carries the potential for an ecstasy in which two participants momentarily seem to feel one another's flesh—serves as a paradigm not only for human relationship but also for the human-divine relationship. Through the work of Jesus Christ, human beings are offered the experience of sharing, not only with God, but with one another, the one divine and human feeling-flesh of the Word Incarnate. Our erotic longing for this outcome may be exemplified by, but goes far beyond, our sexual longings for union with another human being. Moreover, these sexual longings, in Marion's view, are always a desire for intimacy and relationality, the mutual ecstatic belonging to one flesh, rather than about simple physical pleasure. We can see, in this light, why the fourth-century homilies on initiation present the embodied experience of the initiands as one shared with the preachers themselves and with the whole community. The erotic dimension of the baptismal stripping and anointing does not point to sex but beyond it to the ultimate

35. Jean-Luc Marion, *In Excess: Studies of Saturated Phenomena* (New York: Fordham University Press, 2002), chapter 4.

36. Jean-Luc Marion, *The Erotic Phenomenon* (Chicago, Ill.: University of Chicago Press, 2007).

union of humanity in its origin (symbolized in Adam and Eve) and in its destiny (in the risen Christ).

We can think about an iconic gaze in the sacraments that sees in the "communion line" a joyous procession of the baptized streaming toward heaven. But marriage is also a lifetime of developing the iconic gaze, which comes to see in the exposed flesh of the lover the revelation of God the lover of the world. If the commercialization of popular music is selling the experience of a pornographic or idolatrous gaze, which reduces artists to their saleable exposure, to change the gaze is to challenge the idea that these bodies can be commodified and to commit instead to seeing them as icons of the humanity of Christ.

The Christian erotic gaze, then, neither elevates nor evades sexuality but sees in the human body the gift of the ineradicable desire and capacity for love. This love, ultimately, in its real communication of the self and its seeking to share the flesh with another, is a participation in the trinitarian perichoretic dance, which is shared with human beings through creation and redemption. And this iconic, erotic gaze is not limited to sexuality, or, in fact, to things we consider beautiful. The ultimate visibility of God's love in the world is the image of the condemned, abandoned, dying man on the cross, a visibility that becomes visible, paradoxically, only when the risen body disappears from the grave (Mk 20) and the risen Christ is seen in the marginalized, judged, and humiliated among us (Mt 25:31–46).[37]

I think we can dismantle the wall that divides embodiment from spirituality because we already see some cultural phenomena in our society that approach the human body not in terms of its ability to provoke pleasure (especially in men) but in terms of its humanity, its dignity, and its capacities that, ultimately, for Christians, point to God. I think especially of the "body positivity" movement that combats shame about the human shape. Another movement seeks to reclaim a mother's birthing and breastfeeding of a child as a beautiful, as well as functional, intimate human relationship and a true purpose of the female body. I think also of the female and black artists who speak of their own embodied experiences supported by media and allies. Of

37. Jean-Luc Marion, *Prolegomena to Charity* (New York: Fordham University Press, 2002), chapters 5–6.

course, these movements are not exclusively Christian, but the conviction that the human body represents the unity and dignity of the human race is a feature of the Christian sacramental imagination.

A baptismal anthropology should be careful to avoid a simplistic vision that Christian bodies are "modest" and nude bodies are "pornographic." Instead, a baptismal anthropology points to a more complex world within which vulnerable bodies are redeemed and human sexual desire is a precious sacramental sign of the erotic and all-consuming love for humanity of the crucified and risen Christ. This sign should not be squandered on pornography, but neither should it be thrown out with the baptismal water. Instead, we should cultivate an empathetic gaze to replace the "possessive gaze" of commercial depictions of the human body (especially the female body), and we should seek out art that evokes such an empathetic gaze.

To return to Janelle Monáe and her questions, we can see the music video for "Q.U.E.E.N." as an invitation to refuse the objectifying lenses normally applied to popular dance, those that construe the dancer as an object, either for possession or for comparison. Instead, the viewer is invited into an intimacy in which he or she imaginatively participates in the feeling flesh of the dancers. One can enjoy their moving bodies by seeing (indeed, empathetically feeling, and perhaps echoing in one's own dance) the joy they express in their movement. The viewer is asked to step in, on behalf of the Creator God, to "approve the way [they're] made."[38]

Near the end of the "Q.U.E.E.N." video, the listener overhears one side of a conversation Monáe has with an unheard voice. "Yeah," she calls out. "Yeah. Let's flip it. I don't think they understand what I'm trying to say." She laughs, slightly, and adds again, "Yeah."[39] After this conversation, the video cuts to Monáe dressed in her classic tuxedo (her "working uniform") rapping about her vocation. This segment is overflowing with allusions to race and American cultural history, but I will focus on her "theology of the booty," in which Monáe re-

38. See Monáe, "Q.U.E.E.N." 3:17. In this segment, Monáe asks "Will your God accept me in my black and white?"

39. If this represents a vocational call from God, it is echoed by the following video, which calls "The Electric Lady" (a fictional icon that both is and isn't Monáe herself) "a modern day Joan of Arc."

purposes and reinterprets the ubiquitous "booty" of popular music to express her commitment to her vocation. "Even when you edit me, the booty don't lie. I'm-a keep singing, I'm-a keep writing songs.... March through the streets, 'cause I'm willing and I'm able, categorize me, I defy every label!" Here Monáe once again refuses the ubiquitous oversexualization of musicians ("even if you edit me") but makes the release of the body in dance part of her mission to preach the truth, to "march through the streets," and to "keep selling hope." Her flesh is shared, through her art, not to evoke a possessive gaze in the viewer (that ultimately asks the viewer for cash), but to invite the viewer to empathize, to become an activist, and, ultimately, to preach likewise: "While you selling dope, we gon' keep selling hope. We rising up now, you gotta deal, you gotta cope. Will you be electric sheep—electric ladies, will you sleep? Or will you preach?"[40] This invitation, as Marion shows, requires more vulnerability: the "booty" does not reflect sexual availability, promised but never actually delivered, but rather offers up the whole person, especially the invisible part, hoping for a relationship of love rather than the reduction to an object. There is no guarantee: even if "the booty don't lie," there is still an uphill battle, for each viewer, to interpret its eroticism with empathy and compassion rather than judging it, desiring to possess it, or seizing it.

Art, like liturgy, changes culture, not (directly) institutions. Monáe's "Q.U.E.E.N." works not by promoting a particular political agenda through reason but by seducing the viewer into an alternate world. The sacramental imagination enables the viewer to hear both Jesus and the world speaking together an invitation. In the words of Janelle Monáe's "Tightrope," one can find a Eucharistic invitation: "Some calling me a sinner, Some calling me a winner, I'm calling you to dinner. You can rock or you can leave." But it also finds, in Jan van Eyck's punning inscription "*Als Ik Kan*" ("As best I can"), an invitation to see the humanity of the artist who has tried to share his eyes with us through his hands. Ultimately, it asks us to adopt a lens of love and see, as much as possible, in our shared humanity the potential for participation in the transfigured humanity of the crucified and risen Christ.

40. See Monáe, "Q.U.E.E.N." 6:00.

PART 4

Cultivating a Sacramental Imagination in an Age of Pornography

ANN W. ASTELL

9 ⇜ Memory, the Sacrament of Marriage, and the Song of Songs

About three years ago, "Nina," a friend of mine, discovered that "George"—her husband of many years and the father of their five children—had secretly become a frequent user of internet pornography. When confronted, he at first denied the charge. When denial was no longer possible given evidence to the contrary, he refused to accept counsel and treatment for his addiction. Shocked to know that their marital relations were experienced, from his side, through the lens of pornography and that he had been regularly having sex in his imagination with other women, Nina felt deceived, abused, and betrayed. A generous and pious Catholic, a catechist in her parish, exemplary in good works, Nina had entered into their marriage with a sacramental understanding. Unwilling to live with George under the condition of his continued, compulsive use of pornography, she moved out and initiated divorce proceedings. The notice in the local newspaper caught the attention of another woman, who contacted Nina to inform her that she had had a child by George after they had met on the internet.

Studies show that the domestic tragedy of Nina and George, played out in a small town in Indiana, is far from uncommon. Sixty-two percent of the 350 attendees at the November 2003 meeting of the American Academy of Matrimonial Lawyers reported that the internet had played a role in the divorces they had handled during that year; fifty-six percent of the divorce cases, moreover, "involved one party having an obsessive interest in pornographic websites."[1] Mary Eberstadt and Mary Anne Layden point to one nationally representative

1. Study cited in Pamela Paul, "The Porn Factor," *TIME Magazine* 163, no. 3 (January 19, 2004): 99, 101. See also Mary Eberstadt and Mary Anne Layden, *The Social Costs of Pornography: A Statement of Findings and Recommendations* (Princeton, N.J.: The Witherspoon Institute, 2010), 24.

2004 study of 531 internet users, which found "that those who had had an extramarital affair were more than three times more likely to have used internet pornography than were users who had not had an affair."[2] Husbands and wives alike suffer a sense of betrayal by spouses who use pornography.[3] By its very definition, after all, pornography "perverts the conjugal act, the intimate giving of spouses to each other," by "removing real or simulated sexual acts from the intimacy of the partners, in order to display them deliberately to third parties."[4] Many studies bear witness to the "betrayal, loss, mistrust, devastation, and anger" felt especially by wives at the discovery of a husband's "pornography use and/or online sexual activity."[5] This "unique distress and harm" is due, Eberstadt and Layden opine, to the sharp contrast between the marital relationships women typically seek, which are "founded upon mutual respect, honesty, shared power, and romantic love," and the sexual encounters afforded men by internet pornography, which "enshrine the opposite: relationships based on disrespect, detachment, promiscuity, and often abuse."[6]

The contrast is even greater if the marriage sought is not only a civil union, but also a sacrament, believed to communicate Christ's grace to the couple and, through them, to the Church. *Gaudium et Spes*, Vatican Council II's *Pastoral Constitution on the Church in the Modern World*, describes conjugal love as follows: "Authentic married love is caught up into divine love and is governed and enriched by Christ's redeeming power and the saving activity of the Church.... Sealed by mutual faithfulness and hallowed above all by Christ's sacrament, this love remains steadfastly true in body and in mind, ... radiate[s] from

2. Steven Stack, Ira Wasserman, and Roger Kern, "Adult Social Bonds and Use of Internet Pornography," *Social Science Quarterly* 85, no.1 (March 2004): 75–88, cited in Eberstadt and Layden, *Social Costs of Pornography*, 24.

3. Monica Therese Whitty, "Pushing the Wrong Buttons: Men's and Women's Attitudes toward Online and Offline Infidelity," *CyberPsychology & Behavior* 6, no. 6 (December 2003): 569–79.

4. *Catechism of the Catholic Church*, 2nd ed. (Washington, D.C.: United States Conference of Catholic Bishops, 2000), 2354.

5. Eberstadt and Layden, *Social Costs of Pornography*, 23.

6. Eberstadt and Layden, *Social Costs of Pornography*, 23. See also Jill C. Manning, "The Impact of Internet Pornography on Marriage and the Family: A Review of the Research," *Sexual Addiction & Compulsivity* 13, no. 2/3 (September 2006): 131–65, esp. 139–41, 145–46.

the equal personal dignity of wife and husband . . . [and] cooperate[s] with the love of the Creator and the Savior" in begetting and educating children.[7] Pornography, by contrast, separates sex from marriage and from its three-fold good, as classically defined by Saint Augustine: *proles* (children), *fides* (mutual fidelity and support), and *sacramentum* (the grace given the couple to participate in, and to be an efficacious sign of, the love between Christ and the Church).[8] Quoting Genesis 2:24 in his Letter to the Ephesians, Saint Paul describes the fleshly union of man and woman in marriage as "a great mystery," a *magnum sacramentum*, referring "to Christ and the Church" (Eph 5:32), and he exhorts husbands and wives to pattern their relationship after that divine-human espousal. Augustine follows Paul in his sacramental understanding of marriage, and Augustine and Paul alike follow Jesus, who taught that "what therefore God has joined together, let no man put asunder" (Mt 19:6). Moses, Jesus explained, had only permitted divorce because of hard-heartedness, but "from the beginning it was not so" (Mt 19:8).[9]

Referring to Genesis, Jesus asks his listeners to remember the creation of humanity as male and female and to remember marriage itself as a sacrament "from the beginning." Pornography, which assaults the memory by flooding it with sexual images, works to bury and deface precisely this deep memory of the sacramental meaning of sexual relations and of erotic love. Clinically proven to cause short-term memory loss,[10] pornography's most pernicious effect is actually the apparent loss or deep burial of memories held "from the beginning." An under-

7. Vatican Council II, *Gaudium et Spes* (December 7, 1965), 48–50.

8. See Saint Augustine, *The Good of Marriage*, in *Treatises on Marriage and Other Subjects*, trans. Charles T. Wilcox (Washington, D.C.: The Catholic University of America Press, 1999), 48; Pius XI, Encyclical Letter *Casti Connubii* (December 31, 1930), 10. In the words of the Second Vatican Council: "As a mutual gift of two persons, this intimate union, as well as the good of the children, imposes total fidelity on the spouses." *Gaudium et Spes* (December 7, 1965), 48.

9. I use *The Holy Bible*, Revised Standard Version, Catholic Edition (San Francisco, Calif.: Ignatius, 1966). Jesus' teaching on divorce is close to that of the rabbinic House of Shammai, which allowed divorce only in the case of very serious transgressions. The House of Hillel was more lenient. See *The Jewish Annotated New Testament*, 2nd ed., ed. Amy-Jill Levine and Marc Zvi Brettler (New York: Oxford, 2017), 46.

10. Christian Laier, Frank P. Schulte, and Matthais Brand, "Pornographic Picture Processing Interferes with Working Memory Performance," *Journal of Sex Research* 50, no. 7 (October 2013): 642–52.

graduate student who attended the "Seeing with the Eyes of the Heart" conference shared the haunting testimony that the first pornographic image he ever saw is still stronger in his memory than the memory of his mother's face.[11]

Modern purveyors of pornography downplay its deleterious effects upon the memory, even as they supply the steady stream of visual and auditory impressions that make it increasingly impossible for users to remember anything else. Pornography sites become a diabolic "book of experience" for them,[12] perhaps their only experience of sex, which has been reduced to sensations of sexual pleasure and abstracted from the reality of any personal relationships. Pornography use makes people less capable of falling in love, less inclined toward marriage, and less desirous of intercourse with their husband or wife;[13] it disturbs existing marital relationships at every level and frequently leads to divorce.

Is there, then, a memory cure for pornography users, whose memory, over-crowded with high-resolution impressions, incurs forgetfulness—not only the forgetting of daily appointments and duties, as occurs among persons with compulsive pornography addictions—but also of the divine and human mysteries? Is there anything powerful enough in the memory of the Church and in her communal imagination to cast out these pornographic images, replacing them with sensory images that are erotic, powerful, and poetic enough to anchor a deep remembrance of marriage as a sacrament of divine love?

The Song of Songs—sometimes called Canticles or the Song of Solomon—is, I argue, a biblical and liturgical remedy for the problem of pornography. Called "the book of our experience" by Saint Bernard of Clairvaux,[14] the Song of Songs offers a preventive medicine, as

11. I thank Elizabeth Groppe for sharing this anecdote with me.

12. My ironic allusion here is to Saint Bernard of Clairvaux, famous for describing the Song of Songs to his fellow monks as "the book of our own experience." See St. Bernard of Clairvaux, "Sermon 3" in *On the Song of Songs 1*, trans. Kilian Walsh (Kalamazoo, Mich.: Cistercian Publications, 1971), 16.

13. Jenny Riddell, "Desire and Memory: The Impact of Internet Pornography on the Couple Relationship, and Processing of Early Trauma in Therapy," in *Love in the Age of the Internet: Attachment in the Digital Era*, ed. Linda Cundy, 81–97 (London: Karnac Books, 2015); Manning, "Impact of Internet Pornography on Marriage and the Family," 142–45.

14. St. Bernard of Clairvaux, "Sermon 3," 16.

well as an imaginative cure, for the damage inflicted upon memory by pornography's diabolic "book." Regarded by the early Church as a prophecy of the sacraments of Christian initiation,[15] the Song lushly celebrates the soul's bridal incorporation into Christ's Mystical Body, the Church, whose resplendent beauty is that of "a bride adorned for her husband" (Rv 21:2). As the Song's liturgical use attests, pornography's strong opponent in the life of the Church is not only a Christian asceticism, which wisely guards the doors of the senses by which impressions enter the memory, but also a Christian sacramental imagination that strengthens the remembrance of God's love through a rich memorial culture inclusive of the erotic.

On December 21, during the Advent days of the "O Antiphons" sung before Christmas, Song 2:8–14 is the first reading for Holy Mass. It announces the eager coming of the beloved, who leaps over the hills and who rejoices at the change of seasons, winter giving way to an abundance of springtime blossoms. Heard in its liturgical context, the reading points to Christ, soon to appear in the flesh (see Jn 1:14) at the start of a "new creation" (2 Cor 5:17). Evocative of the Annunciation to Mary, hailed in Nazareth by the angel (Lk 1:26–38), and of the pregnant Mary's own travel in haste into the hill country to visit her cousin Elizabeth (Lk 1:39–56), that same passage from the Song (2:8–14) is used in the liturgy both for the Consecration of Virgins and Religious Profession and for the Conferral of the Sacrament of Marriage (Song 2:8–10, 14, 16a; 8:6–7). Praising a "love strong as death," unable to be quenched by "many waters" (Song 8:6–7), the Song is read on the feast of Saint Scholastica.[16] Chronicling the bride's ardent search for her

15. See Jean Daniélou, "The Canticle: A Song of Sacraments," *Orate Fratres* 25, nos. 3–4 (1951): 97–103, 161–65. See also in this volume Kimberly Hope Belcher's chapter, "Sacramental Exposure," in which she refers to the use of the Song of Songs in the early Christian ritual for baptism.

16. The passage from Song 8:6–7 can be interpreted as a lyrical rendering of a famous episode in Gregory the Great's Life of Saint Benedict (*Dialogues*, 2.33). Visiting his sister Scholastica, Benedict is determined to leave in order to return to the monastery before nightfall, as the *Rule* prescribes. Prompted by the law of charity and perhaps aware of her own approaching death, Scholastica begs him to stay. Her tears and prayers are answered by the "flashes" of lightning and the "many waters" of a rainstorm that prevent Benedict's departure. Like Monica and Augustine at Ostia (*Confessions*, 9.10.23), Scholastica and Benedict spend the night in heavenly conversation. See Gregory the Great, *Life and Miracles of St. Benedict: Book Two of the Dialogues*, trans. Odo J. Zimmermann and Benedict R. Avery, 67–70 (Collegeville, Minn.: St. John's Abbey Press, 1949).

beloved, Song 3:1–4b belongs to the lectionary for the feast of Saint Mary Magdalene, who encountered the risen Christ in the garden and, overcome with joy, clung to him (Jn 20:11–18).[17]

The present-day liturgy, then, secures the sacramental interpretation of the Song as a symbolic and figural representation of Christ's love for the Church and for the individual soul. Saints like Scholastica, Mary Magdalene, and—above all—the Virgin Mary play the bride's part in the drama of salvation, welcoming Christ as the soul's bridegroom and giving figural expression to the Church's love for him.

In comparison to earlier versions of the liturgy, however, that of the present gives relatively little place to the Song of Songs, even in liturgies for Marian feasts such as the Assumption, where the Song was traditionally used.[18] Edmée Kingsmil recalls, "When I joined the Community of the Sisters of the Love of God in 1966, the *Monastic Diurnal*, which we then used, was rich in verses from the Song of Songs, notably the 'Common of Feasts of the Blessed Virgin,' in which all the antiphons came from the Song.... Over the next ten years or so, all trace of the Song would be eliminated from our worship."[19] In Kingsmil's analysis, this loss reflects and tragically reinforces a modern inability to understand the Song's literal eroticism within the context of Scripture as a whole. Mistaking the Song of Songs for a titillating text, included by some historical accident in the biblical canon, or worried that it might be construed as such, liturgical reform has allowed to fall into disuse the very love-song that, understood in context, has the power to immunize its readers against pornography.

To be sure, patristic and medieval commentators acknowledged the problem of the Song as a possible stumbling-block, but also (and above all) its divine inspiration and its liberating and curative potential. Although present-day internet pornography is more available, graphic, and psychologically addictive than pornographies of the past, pornography has a long history and includes all writings and visual

17. See Jack R. Lundbom, "Mary Magdalene and Song of Songs 3:1–4," *Interpretation* 49, no. 2 (1995): 172–75. See also Dianne Phillips's discussion of paintings of Mary Magdalene in her essay "The Visual Culture of Catholicism," chapter 6 of this volume.

18. See Rachel Fulton, *From Judgment to Passion: Devotion to Christ and the Virgin Mary, 800–1200* (New York: Columbia University Press, 2002), 248–51, 267–75, 290.

19. Edmée Kingsmil, *The Song of Songs and the Eros of God: A Study in Biblical Intertextuality* (Oxford: Oxford University Press, 2009).

images—ancient, medieval, and modern—intended to cause sexual excitement, to titillate. To misread the Song of Songs—that is, to read it carnally—is possibly to mistake it for pornography. To read it correctly, sacramentally, is to find a cure for sensual lust and to rediscover the meaning and joy of marriage.

In support of this thesis, I draw on a long Christian tradition that begins with Origen, Ambrose, and Augustine. Following a hint from Augustine's *Confessions*, Saint Bernard of Clairvaux interpreted the Song allegorically to help his monks, vowed to celibacy, to deal with the memories of their former sexual experiences.[20] Most recently, Paul Griffiths has written a figural commentary on the Song, aimed at helping all Christians, especially married couples, to recover a sacramental and ecclesial understanding of eros, of the love that languishes, that desires another's love in return, that invites incarnation. Commenting on the Song's sensuous description of the beloved's body, Griffiths writes, "This is not pornography."[21] Understanding the difference is already to have remembered what pornography wants to be forgotten.

A collection of love-lyrics remarkable for their erotic physicality, the Song is attributed to King Solomon, famous for his wisdom, his building of the Temple, and his many wives.[22] Resembling the love-poems of ancient Egypt, a version of the Song may originally have been composed to celebrate Solomon's marriage with the daughter of Pharaoh,[23] but the language of the Song, transmitted as one of the holy books of the Hebrew scriptures, seems to reflect its much later composition in Aramaic and its use as an allegorical expression of Israel in its Babylonian exile (sixth century BC) longing for her Lord, whom the prophet Hosea (eighth century BC) depicts as a faithful, desirous, and forgiving Spouse. The Song itself makes no direct mention of God. It focuses instead on the desirous love of the unnamed, lyrical

20. See Jean Leclercq, *Monks and Love in Twelfth-Century France: Psycho-historical Essays* (Oxford: Clarendon Press, 1979).

21. Paul J. Griffiths, *Song of Songs: Brazos Theological Commentary on the Bible* (Grand Rapids, Mich.: Brazos Press, 2011), 90.

22. According to 1 Kgs 11:1–8, Solomon had seven hundred wives and three hundred concubines.

23. See Michael V. Fox, *The Song of Songs and the Ancient Egyptian Love Songs* (Madison, Wis.: University of Wisconsin Press, 1985).

speakers. Discussing the sacrament of matrimony, the *Catechism of the Catholic Church* observes: "Tradition has always seen in the *Song of Solomon* a unique expression of human love, insofar as it is a reflection of God's love—a love 'strong as death' that 'many waters cannot quench' (Song 8:6–7)."[24]

Recognizing the erotic power of the text, an ancient Christian tradition restricts its readership, as far as possible, to clerics at least thirty years old who are knowledgeable enough of the Scriptures to read the Song in the interpretive context of the Bible as a whole, that is, sacramentally.[25] The *Glossa ordinaria* warns that "only a man of perfect knowledge and oaken faith should read the *Canticum*, lest anyone be stirred to merely fleshly desires by its carnal images."[26] In "The Merchant's Tale," the poet Geoffrey Chaucer provides an example of an old lecher named January who lewdly paraphrases the Song of Songs in speaking to his young wife May, whom he uses as a sex object. Chaucer's narrative, replete with irony, makes it clear that January is sadly mistaking the Song of Songs for pornography ("olde lewed wordes") and marriage itself for legalized fornication.[27]

Mystics beginning with Origen, however, saw the Song as a divinely intended means, a *machina* or lever, to direct human desire to a divine object, the Incarnate Word, and thus to integrate, in Christ's love, the ascending powers of the human soul—its memory, sensory imagination, affects, will, reason, and intelligence. Secure in a Christological allegory, which identifies Christ with the lover of the Song, they dared the danger and the peril of the Song's literal meaning in order to gain for God something precious: the warmth of the human soul's bridal love. Inspired by Origen's allegorical interpretation of the Song, Saint Ambrose used its verses when he preached to consecrated virgins and to newly baptized Christians, joined to Christ's body, the Church.[28]

24. *Catechism of the Catholic Church*, 1611.

25. See Saint Jerome, *Prologus in Hiezechielem*, Corpus Christianorum Series Latina 75, ed. Francis Glorie (Turnhout: Brepols, 1964), 3–4.

26. Quoted in Ann W. Astell, *The Song of Songs in the Middle Ages* (Ithaca, N.Y.: Cornell University Press, 1990), 27.

27. Geoffrey Chaucer, "The Merchant's Tale," in *The Riverside Chaucer*, 3rd ed., ed. Larry D. Benson (Boston, Mass.: Houghton Mifflin, 1987), *CT* IV.2149.

28. F. B. A. Asiedu, "The Song of Songs and the Ascent of Soul: Ambrose, Augustine, and the Language of Mysticism," *Vigiliae Christianae* 55, no. 3 (2001): 299–317, esp. 301.

Saint Augustine—unlike his teacher, Saint Ambrose—quotes relatively rarely from the Song of Songs, preferring to turn, again and again, to the Psalms.[29] In one of the most famous passages in *Confessions,* however, Augustine fuses together imagery from Solomon's Canticle and from Plato's *Phaedrus* and *Symposium* to recap the whole course of his spiritual journey as a divine romance leading to a spiritual consummation:

> Late have I love you, beauty so old and so new.... You called and cried out and shattered my deafness. You were radiant and resplendent; you put to flight my blindness. You were fragrant and I drew in my breath and now pant after you. I tasted you, and I feel but hunger and thirst for you. You touched me, and I am set on fire to attain the peace which is yours.[30]

Augustine thus participates in the tradition, stemming from Origen, which interprets the biblical love-song of King Solomon as an expression of the soul's mystical union with God, the soul's spiritual senses corresponding to those of the body.[31] The bride in the Song of Songs praises her lover's cheeks as "beds of spices, yielding fragrance" (Song 5:13); she hears his calling voice, "most sweet" (Song 2:8, 5:16); she sees him "radiant and ruddy" (Song 5:10); she describes herself, "sick with love," being fed with his fruit, apples, and raisins, "sweet to [her] taste" (Song 2:3, 5); she recalls her heart thrilling from within at the touch of his hand (Song 5: 4), which moved her to "open" her chamber to him (Song 5:6) at night—a poetically coded reference to sexual climax, but also a symbol of the soul's innermost surrender to Christ.

For Augustine, the soul's union with God and the palpable delight of the spiritual senses in that union works to free him, upon his conversion, from what he calls his "sexual habit"—long exercised with his concubine of many years, the mother of his son Adeodatus, then with another woman, and planned to be continued at a later date with a still-underage fiancée. Strengthened by Christ's grace, Augustine re-

29. Asiedu, "The Song of Songs," 312–17.

30. Saint Augustine, *Confessions*, trans. Henry Chadwick (Oxford: Oxford University Press, 2008), 10.27.38.

31. See Karl Rahner, "The Doctrine of the 'Spiritual Senses' in the Middle Ages," in *Experience of the Spirit: Source of Theology*, vol. 16 of *Theological Investigations*, trans. David Moreland, 109–28 (New York: Crossroad, 1979). See also the essay by Boyd Taylor Coolman in this volume.

ports that he was finally able to heed God's command "to abstain from sleeping with a girl-friend," to forgo marriage, and to choose celibacy.[32] In his waking consciousness, the convert Augustine is reasonably free from temptation due to sensual lust. In his dreams, however, the "images of acts which were fixed there [in his memory] by [his] sexual habit . . . attack [him],"[33] disturbing his sleep. "When I am awake they have no force," Augustine writes, "but in sleep they not only arouse pleasure, but even elicit consent, and are very like the actual act."[34] He returns to "peace in [his] conscience" only when he awakens after a wet dream and realizes "that we did not actively do what, to our regret, has somehow been done in us."[35] Still imperfect, haunted by the past still present to his memory, Augustine nonetheless hopes for God's complete victory in the "perfect peace" of his soul.[36]

Augustine confesses these continued temptations in Book 10 of *Confessions* shortly after the passage suffused with images from the Song of Songs, which begins: "Late have I love you" (quoted above). The proximity of these passages in *Confessions* may have inspired Saint Bernard of Clairvaux to preach his famous eighty-six sermons on the Song of Songs to his fellow Cistercians. As Jean Leclercq points out, the Cistercians admitted to their newly founded order adult vocations—men who were widowers or who had had sex outside of marriage as youths—unlike the older Benedictines, who relied for their vocations upon child oblates.[37] Responding to the pastoral needs of his monks, therefore, Saint Bernard used the love-language of the Song to evoke and gather up their memories, recorded in the "book of [their] experience,"[38] and to transform them by fusing them together with their memory of Christ and their genuine experience of him, present in their souls, in the community, and in the sacraments.

In order to accomplish this, Bernard in sermon after sermon first engages the imagination of his listeners, asking them to picture

32. Augustine, *Confessions*, 10.30.41.

33. Augustine, *Confessions*, 10.30.41.

34. Augustine, *Confessions*, 10.30.41.

35. Augustine, *Confessions*, 10.30.41.

36. Augustine, *Confessions*, 10.30.42.

37. See Leclercq, *Monks and Love in Twelfth-Century France*, 8–26.

38. Bernard of Clairvaux, "Sermon 3," 16. See also the many references to personal experience in the concluding paragraphs of "Sermon 1."

the scene, to feel the emotion, conveyed by each verse of the Song. He proceeds slowly, often devoting several sermons to a single verse. He invites his monks to identify themselves with the bridegroom who passionately desires the bride, but also with the bride who yearns for her beloved's kiss and embrace. After capturing their interest and emotional engagement, he transfers and transforms that interest—often abruptly—by associating the literal imagery of the love-lyrics, verse by verse, with the sacramental signs of the life of the Church, lived out in the daily work and prayer of the monastery. After imagining the Song's lovers performing the "business of love" in the vineyards, for example, he tells his listeners, "Let us not dally outside, lest we seem preoccupied with the allurements of lust, but listen with modest ears to the sermon on love that is at hand. And when you consider the lovers themselves, think not of a man and a woman but of the Word and the soul."[39]

The sermons seamlessly weave together scriptural phrases drawn from the whole of the Bible—a feat of memory, enabled by the practice of *lectio divina*, which is designed to heal memories, purify the imagination, and lead to contemplation. As Mary Carruthers has emphasized, the meditation of medieval monks was a "craft of thought."[40] Practicing *lectio divina* both signified and effected a monk's conversion of life. Memorizing Scripture in order to be able to understand and to recall it in prayer, to make its vocabulary one's own, effectively reprogrammed one's memory and affected one's experience of everything else by building up a biblical pattern of associations, wherein personal experience, past and present, found its meaning.

Whereas Augustine and, above all, Bernard used the divinely inspired Song of Songs as a means to help sexually experienced men to perceive and to live out their celibacy as a spiritual marriage, the modern theologian Paul Griffiths, a married layman, argues that the multi-layered sort of biblical exegesis used by premodern interpreters of the Song can be adapted to help married couples to grasp the sacramental nature of their relationship and its physical expressions and

39. Bernard of Clairvaux, "Sermon 61," in *On the Song of Songs 3*, trans. Kilian Walsh and Irene M. Edmonds (Kalamazoo, Mich.: Cistercian Publications, 1979), 141.

40. Mary J. Carruthers, *The Craft of Thought: Meditation, Rhetoric, and the Making of Images, 400–1200*, Cambridge Studies in Medieval Literature 34 (Cambridge: Cambridge University Press, 2000).

(I would add) to resist and to refuse a pornographic definition of it. Similar to the three-fold exegesis of medieval commentators (literal/historical, allegorical, and tropological), Griffiths's interpretation of the Song, stanza by stanza, considers (1) its surface features (lexicon, syntax, verb tense, etc.), (2) its theological significance, often with reference to biblical types or figures, and (3) its ethical and moral application to the life of the reader, whom Griffiths addresses in the second person. After spelling out the "import" of the Song's verses "for the ordering of your loves—loves, that is, of yourself, of the Lord, of other people, and of the world and what is in it,"[41] Griffiths typically concludes each sectional exposition with reference to Mary, the bride of God par excellence, the Mother of God's Son and of the Church, and the perfect model for an intimate love of God.

"This text [the Song] wants to seduce you," Griffiths insists, adding, "it is, in part, my task to return its kiss in such a way as to make it easier for it to have you and for you to be had by it."[42] Casting himself, the Song's interpreter, as a go-between, Griffiths steadfastly insists that the Song, no matter how seductive, is not pornography, even when it speaks indirectly, poetically, about sexual intercourse. Language about sex, he explains, typically falls on a spectrum between that found in dry, physiology textbooks, at one extreme, and that found in "quotidian physical pornography," such as *Playboy* centerfolds and advertisements, at the other.[43] "The Song does not belong on this spectrum," Griffiths explains, because "it is reticent, leaving an opening for imagination and memory"—the memory of God's love for his people, abiding from generation to generation and witnessed in the Scriptures.[44] "The human desire to love and to be loved, to caress and be caressed, exceeds its own fulfillment and indicates its own insufficiency," writes Griffiths. "It begs for a story and for the memories and hopes that enframe stories. Every act of human physical love is therefore already and inevitably figural. The only question is: what does it figure?"[45]

The Song of Songs is full of exotic and arresting comparisons that

41. Griffiths, *Song of Songs*, lvi.
42. Griffiths, *Song of Songs*, lvi.
43. Griffiths, *Song of Songs*, 115.
44. Griffiths, *Song of Songs*, 115.
45. Griffiths, *Song of Songs*, 24.

make the reader think, recalling what he or she can from the treasure-hoard of memory in order to try to understand such things as how the bridegroom's lips are "lilies" (Song 5:13), how the bride's neck can be like a tower hung with shields (Song 4:4), her hair like "a flock of goats" (Song 4:1), her teeth compared to "a flock of shorn ewes that have come up from the washing, all of which bear twins" (Song 4:2). (Thinking long and hard about the last-mentioned comparison brought great pleasure to Saint Augustine!)[46] Because lyrical, the Song is also full of gaps, abrupt changes in mood and voice, that challenge the reader, again, to remember what has previously been said, to imagine what might have occurred between the lines to prompt an utterance, to wonder who is speaking and why. The Song literally poses questions, which elicit wonderment: "Who is that coming up from the wilderness, leaning upon her beloved" (Song 8:5)? "What is your beloved more than another beloved" (Song 5:9)? "Whither has your beloved gone" (Song 6:1)? Remembering the bride's dreams, the Song is also literally about memory and about the hope that springs from the memory of what is good and beloved: "I slept, but my heart was awake" (Song 5:2).

Evocative of sex and of the languishing for love, the Song of Songs outclasses pornography by awakening the very remembrance that pornography seeks to stifle: the memory of a deeply personal love, mutually shared and capable of surviving periods of absence and seasonal change; of that love's propensity toward fruitfulness; and, ultimately, of God, the source of all love, especially of a love "strong as death" (Song 8:6). Set, in part, in a garden, a vineyard, and a pasture, the Song helps us to remember marriage "from the beginning," as it was first established in a figural Eden and as it is promised for the end of time in Revelation, where the visionary apostle sees "the holy city, new Jerusalem, coming out of heaven from God, prepared as a bride adorned for her husband" (Rv 21:2).

Writing about Saint Bernard of Clairvaux's doctrine of love, expounded in his sermons on the Song of Songs, Julia Kristeva—the well-known French linguist, psychoanalyst, and feminist theorist—

46. See Saint Augustine, *On Christian Doctrine*, trans. D. W. Robertson Jr. (Indianapolis, Ind.: Bobbs-Merrill Educational Publishing, 1958), 2.6.7 (pp. 37–38).

closes her essay with the observation that "we are secularly ignorant" of the "alchemy of idealization" that enabled a premodern saint like Bernard to discover God, the ultimate object of human longing, in and through the signs and symbols of the Song.[47] She wonders, however, about what light Bernard's writings might throw, even now, "on the lay experience of love—the daily human experience, the humdrum and the singular one."[48] She concludes: "If we have difficulty loving, it is because we have difficulty idealizing," whereas "when we succeed in loving," it is because "someone, man or woman or child, or a word, a flower ... was able to withstand our unflagging power of distrust, hatred, and fear," our refusal to give of ourselves.[49] Bernard and the other readers of the Song can teach us, Kristeva suggests, not to "get love, pleasure, and desire mixed up."[50] Marriage, understood as a sacrament, teaches the same distinction. Married love, "merging the human with the divine, ... pervades the whole of [the spouses'] lives," according to *Gaudium et Spes*; "it far exceeds mere erotic inclination, which, selfishly pursued, soon enough fades wretchedly away."[51] What an invaluable lesson for people to learn in an age of pornography!

Two friends of mine, professors of philosophy, enjoyed a romantic, mutually faithful partnership for almost two decades, without the legality of marriage. They then experienced a religious awakening that moved them both to turn their attention to the spiritual resources of the Church, its monastic traditions, its Jewish roots, and its sacraments. They decided to request the sacrament of marriage and, with the glad assistance of a Jesuit friend, they prepared for the sacrament and planned the celebration of their wedding Mass.

For one of the readings, they chose a passage from the Song of Songs, which they elected to read themselves, alternating voices to give a lyrical, public expression to the dialogue between the biblical lovers, whom tradition identifies as bride and bridegroom. In preparation for this reading, they familiarized themselves with the Church's

47. Julia Kristeva, *Tales of Love*, trans. Leon S. Roudiez (New York: Columbia University Press, 1987), 169.

48. Kristeva, *Tales of Love*, 168.

49. Kristeva, *Tales of Love*, 169.

50. Kristeva, *Tales of Love*, 168.

51. Vatican Council II, *Gaudium et Spes* (December 7, 1965), 49.

ancient and medieval commentaries on the Song. With the aid of practice and grace, they managed to read aloud the Song's exotic poetry at the liturgy without dissolving into the utter embarrassment of blushes and giggles. They made themselves vulnerable, to be sure, but the Eucharistic context of the reading by the bride and groom made its performance on that joyful day an unforgettable witness to Christian marriage as the "great sign" (*sacramentum magnum*) of Christ's love for the Church (Eph 5:32) and a means of Christ's grace.[52]

Appropriating the Song's words as their own, the wedding couple on that day in Chicago joined the ranks of countless couples who have found their love and their desire mysteriously figured in Solomon's prophetic Canticle. In a prologue to his commentary on the Song of Songs, the twelfth-century exegete known as Honorius Augustodunensis finds the story of God's love for humankind to include a series of historical human courtships and marriages: those of Abraham and Sarah, Isaac and Rebekah, Jacob and Rachel, Solomon and Pharaoh's daughter.[53] These love-relationships, Honorius observes, announce the Incarnation of God's own Son in the womb of the Virgin Mary and Christ's enduring union with the Church, his bride.

The Song of Songs thus remembers a great genealogy of divine and human love that has its beginning "in the beginning" (Gn 1:1), in the Word (Jn 1:1), and its end in Christ, who is Alpha and Omega (Rv 1:8; 21:6, 22:13). Ultimately, it envisions a love so real, so beyond any merely human expression, that it exposes pornography for the counterfeit it is and enables its forgetting. The excess of pornography feeds on its own unreality, which leads its desensitized users, in a desperate quest for fulfillment, increasingly to up the ante, to view "depictions they themselves would have once regarded as taboo or off-limits."[54] The ecstasy of the Song is a vastly different kind of excess: "Eye has not seen, ear has not heard, nor the heart of man conceived, what God has prepared for those who love him" (1 Cor 2:9).

52. See Nathaniel Peters's essay "Vision, Memory, and the Eucharist's Reformation of the Mind," chapter 10 of this volume.

53. Honorius Augustodunensis, *Expositio in Cantica Canticorum*, Patrologiae cursus completus, series latina, ed. Jacques Paul Migne (Paris: Migne, 1857–66), 172:353–58.

54. Eberstadt and Layden, *Social Costs of Pornography*, 20.

NATHANIEL PETERS

10 ⇸ Vision, Memory, and the Eucharist's Reformation of the Mind

Today we often think of memory not as part of who we are, but as a tool that we can use. By contrast, medieval authors saw memory not just as a matter of storing information in a place but as an important dimension of human personhood and community. The formation of memory was an essential part of a person's moral and intellectual development, and memory was a means of recalling and connecting truths. In this chapter, I offer a brief account of the medieval understanding of memory and vision. I then turn to one particular medieval thinker, the twelfth-century Cistercian William of Saint-Thierry, who elucidates the ways in which the Eucharist forms our minds in the image of Christ and the triune God. Finally, I conclude with reflections on some of the ways in which we can apply William's insights in our own times, particularly with respect to the malformation of memory that pornographic culture effects.

Vision, Memory, and the Medieval Mind

We should begin with a consideration of how someone in the twelfth-century would have understood the activity of vision. We assume that sight is a largely passive phenomenon. For example, when I ponder the experience of seeing a tree, I think about light reflecting off the tree, entering my eyes, and hitting the rods and cones. By contrast, medieval thinkers understood sight to be an active phenomenon. Saint Augustine (AD 354–430) had great influence on twelfth-century theories of vision, and he, in turn, received his understanding of vision—the so-called extramission theory—from Plato.[1] Augustine believed that

1. David Chidester, *Word and Light: Seeing, Hearing, and Religious Discourse* (Urbana, Ill.: University of Illinois Press, 1992), 3–4. See also Book XI of "The Trinity," in

vision originates with the internal fire that animates and warms the body. This fire collects and glows behind the eyes, which then project it in the form of a ray that is focused on the object, rather like Cyclops from the X-Men. Unlike Cyclops, however, the ray touches the object and doubles-back to the eye. The image of the object is then imprinted on the soul—like a shape being pushed into clay—and retained in the memory.[2] As historical theologian Margaret R. Miles puts it, Augustine thought that the object does not so much catch the eye as the eye catches the object. Unlike other, more passive senses such as hearing, sight involves interacting with things and incorporating images of these things into oneself.[3] The images that the ray brings into the mind leave their imprint on the intellect and are then stored in the memory so that they can be recalled. They become a part of the soul.

In her noted work *The Book of Memory,* Mary Carruthers explains that for medieval authors, memory is not the mere retention and regurgitation of facts, but the skill of moving information instantly, directly, and securely. Memory is to be used creatively, not simply for the sake of exact recall.[4] Medieval thinkers see memory as a *thesaurus,* a store-room or treasury, or a dovecote, a structure with distinct compartments for each of many doves from which they can go forth and fly about.[5] For example, in the preface to his *Chronicle,* Hugh of St. Victor instructs his novices on methods for memorization of the psalms. He knows that they have already memorized the psalter for the liturgy and can chant it in choir. But he wants to teach them how to store and retrieve specific verses without having to recite entire psalms. His goal is quick recollection and retrieval for teaching, preaching, and debate. He wants to help the novices build a dove-

The Works of Saint Augustine: A Translation for the 21st Century (Hyde Park, N.Y.: New City Press, 1991), for Augustine's understanding of vision as an analogy of the Trinity and Kari Kloos's *Christ, Creation, and the Vision of God* (Leiden: Brill, 2011) for more on the sacramental character of sight, especially in theophanies.

2. Margaret R. Miles, *Image as Insight: Visual Understanding in Western Christianity and Secular Culture* (Boston, Mass.: Beacon Press, 1985), 7; Chidester, *Word and Light,* 3–4.

3. Miles, *Image as Insight,* 45.

4. Mary J. Carruthers, *The Book of Memory: A Study of Memory in Medieval Culture* (New York: Cambridge University Press, 2008), 9, 21, 23, 40–42.

5. Carruthers, *The Book of Memory,* 40–42.

cote so that particular doves can come and go when they are needed.[6]

One final point about the medieval memory from Carruthers: an excellent memory was associated with exemplary holiness. St. Anthony of Egypt learned the whole Bible by hearing it read aloud. His companions were astonished that he never saw the words written out. St. Francis was reputed by his followers to have "a remarkably exact and copious memory." And at the canonization trial of St. Thomas Aquinas, people heaped praise on his memory.[7] With good reason, Carruthers writes, for "contemporary sources suggest strongly that the entire *Summa Theologica* was composed mentally and dictated from memory, with the aid at most of a few written notes, and there is no reason to disbelieve them."[8] This indicates, Carruthers argues, the great value that medieval culture placed on memory. The training of memory was not a matter of convenience or even merely of necessity; it was a matter of ethics and character. A person without memory would be not just a person with inadequate intellectual ability, but someone without moral and spiritual formation.[9] If a person wanted to become holy, he or she needed to fill the storehouse of memory with holy things.

William of Saint-Thierry on the Eucharistic Formation of the Mind in the Triune Love of God

With this understanding of vision and memory in mind, we now turn to William of Saint-Thierry. William was born around AD 1080 in the French city of Liège, which was a center of new Eucharistic piety and theological speculation.[10] He served as abbot of the Benedictine monastery of Saint-Thierry before becoming a Cistercian monk, and he remained a Cistercian until his death in 1148. While he is most known for his works on the monastic life and on trinitarian theology—such as *The Mirror of Faith*, *The Enigma of Faith*, *The Golden Epistle*, and *The*

6. Carruthers, *The Book of Memory*, 103.

7. Carruthers, *The Book of Memory*, 14.

8. Carruthers, *The Book of Memory*, 8.

9. Carruthers, *The Book of Memory*, 14.

10. Bernard McGinn, *The Growth of Mysticism* (New York: Crossroad, 1994), 225–26; Paul Verdeyen, *La théologie mystique de Guillaume de Saint-Thierry* (Paris: FAC-éditions, 1990), 121.

Nature and Dignity of Love—Matthieu Rougé notes that his Eucharistic theology is like a subterranean river, which, though largely invisible, surges forth at particular points in the progression of his thought.[11]

William's treatment of Eucharistic reception in his treatise *On the Sacrament of the Altar* begins by asking an important question: What makes the Eucharist necessary food for eternal life? He answers by distinguishing between bodily reception, or the mere ingestion of the Eucharistic elements, and spiritual reception, in which Christ's presence is received in the soul with love. It cannot be that bodily reception alone is enough for salvation, he explains, because Scripture warns against such presumption and gives examples of those who have received badly, to a bad end.[12] Moreover, the Eucharist is not for the nourishment of the body—as most meals are—but of the soul. The one who receives it seeks more of the life of the soul. As the life of the body is the soul, so God is the life of the soul. Since God is love, the life of the soul is the love of God. The Eucharist therefore exists to increase our love for God, "who is his love itself and who is possessed where he is loved."[13]

William describes our growth in the love of God using metaphors of food and eating. Christ heaps up a great mound of love for him in his flesh by suffering and dying out of love for us. This love is "the wonderful nourishment of life for our souls," which we then "take in with greedy mouths, when we recognize it sweetly and put away in the stomach of memory whatever things Christ did or suffered for us. And this is the banquet from the flesh and blood of Jesus; for the one who receives, has life abiding in him."[14] Receiving the flesh of Christ

11. Matthieu Rougé, *Doctrine et experience de l'eucharistie chez Guillaume de Saint-Thierry* (Paris: Beauchesne, 1999), 110.

12. See, for example, 1 Cor 11:29 and the contrast between the Eucharistic receptions of Judas and Peter in Jn 13. In a similar vein, those who use pornography should avail themselves of the sacrament of confession to repair the bond of charity broken by their sin before receiving the sacrament that signifies and strengthens that bond.

13. "Vt igitur ille ametur, qui est ipse amor suus et qui habetur ubi amatur, ad hoc enutrire nos debet cibus iste. Quicquid enim Redemptor noster in carne fecit, ob hoc utique fecit, ut amaretur a nobis; non quod egeret ipse nostro amore, qui bonorum nostrorum non eget, per omnia sufficiens ipse sibi, sed quia, quos beatos facere susceperat, nisi eum amando non poterant esse beati." *De sacramento altaris*, VI.15–20, in *Guillelmi a Sancto Theodorico omnia opera pars III: Opera didactica et spiritualia*, ed. Stanislaus Ceglar and Paul Verdeyen (Turnhout: Brepols, 2003). The English translations of *De sacramento altaris* are my own.

14. "Quam tunc auidis faucibus sumimus, cum dulciter recolligimus et in uentre

in the Eucharist stores in our memory the deeds of that flesh on our behalf, and this brings as its fruit an increase in our affection or bond of love with him. This, in turn, moves us to offer ourselves to the one who offered himself to us. By works of faith and charity, one who has eaten the Eucharist spiritually returns to the Lord's table the food that was received.[15] He "abides in Christ by the banquet of Christ through the affect of pious love, and he has Christ abiding in him through the effect of this holy work."[16] The more he loves, the more he eats, and the more he is built into a greater mound of the love of which he has but a pledge now, with the promise of fulfillment in the life to come. This exchange of love, William concludes, is what Jesus meant when he said, "Whoever eats my flesh abides in me and I in him" (Jn 6:56).[17]

These themes from *The Sacrament of the Altar* appear again in *Meditation* X, where William writes that picturing the passion of Christ teaches us to love God, the highest good.[18] Our love for the Father comes through the way and door of the Son. According to the precepts of the law, the one who seeks to ascend to God and desires to offer gifts and sacrifices should

> walk calmly and smoothly over the level of his own likeness, to a Man like himself, who tells him on the very threshold: "I and the Father are one." And he is forthwith gathered up to God in love through the Holy Spirit and receives God coming to him and making his abode with him, not spiritually only but corporally too, in the mystery of the holy and life-giving body and blood of our Lord Jesus Christ.[19]

memoriae recondimus, quaecumque pro nobis fecit uel passus est Christus. Et hoc est conuiuium de carne Iesu et sanguine; cui qui communicat, habet uitam in se manentem" (*Sac alt*, VI.66–70).

15. William of Saint-Thierry, *Sac alt*, VI.70–74.

16. "Sicque in Christo manet bonus conuiua Christi per piae dilectionis affectum, habetque Christum in se manentem per sanctae operationis effectum" (*Sac alt*, VI.78–80). See also, Rougé, *Doctrine et experience*, 50.

17. William of Saint-Thierry, *Sac alt*, VI.87–88.

18. As Rougé puts it, "C'est bien le Christ, et non l'eucharistie, qui constitue notre trésor. Mais c'est grâce à l'eucharistie que ce trésor peut, en toute vérité, être en notre possession" (*Doctrine et Experience*, 69).

19. "Quid enim melius praeparatum, quid suauius potuit esse dispositum, quam quod ascensuro homini ad Deum suum offerre dona et sacrificia secundum praeceptum legis, non sit ei ascendendum per gradus ad altare eius, sed per planum similitudinis, placide et pede inoffenso, eat homo ad hominem similem sibi, in primo ingressus limine dicentem sibi: Ego et Pater unum sumus. Statim que per Spiritum sanctum affectus assumptus in Deum, et ipse Deum in semetipsum excipiat uenientem et mansionem apud

It is in receiving and loving Christ in our sacramental reception of the Eucharist and meditation on his passion that we receive his Spirit. This reception of the Spirit binds us to Christ, uniting our loving sacrifices and works to his self-offering to the Father. In this spatial language, William is outlining to his monastic community the trinitarian way in which the Eucharist forms our souls and joins us to God. The one who receives the Eucharist has the Holy Spirit operating in him and is able to offer back Christ-like works to the Father. By the Spirit he is joined to Christ, and his offering can be joined to Christ's because he acts with the love of the Spirit, which is Christ's love.

In *Meditation* VIII, William explains that meditation on the memory of the Eucharist can serve as a form of spiritual Eucharistic reception. In this meditation, he asks God to receive his own spirit, which he offers, and then asks that the Holy Spirit may infuse and permeate him. This happens, he explains:

> when we eat and drink the deathless banquet of your body and your blood. As your clean beasts, we there regurgitate the sweet things stored within our memory, and chew them in our mouths like cud for the renewed and ceaseless work of our salvation. That done, we put away again in that same memory what you have done, what you have suffered for our sake. When you say to the longing soul: "Open your mouth wide and I will fill it," and she tastes and sees your sweetness in the great Sacrament that surpasses understanding, then she is made that which she eats, bone of your bone and flesh of your own flesh. Thus is fulfilled the prayer that you made to your Father on the threshold of your passion. The Holy Spirit effects in us here by grace that unity which is between the Father and yourself, his Son, from all eternity by nature; so that, as you are one, so likewise we may be made one in you. This, O Lord, is the face with which you meet the face of him who longs for you. This is the kiss of your mouth on the lips of your lover; and this is your love's answering embrace to your yearning bride who says: "My beloved is mine, and I am his; he shall abide between my breasts." And again, "My heart has said 'My face has sought you.'"[20]

---

eum facientem, non tantum spiritualiter sed etiam corporaliter per mysterium sancti et uiuifici corporis et sanguinis Domini nostri Iesu Christi." *Meditatio*, X.X.94–104, in *Guillelmi a Sancto Theodorico omnia opera pars IV: Meditationes devotissimae (Meditativae orationes)*, ed. Paul Verdeyen (Turnhout: Brepols, 2005); *Meditations*, in *On Contemplating God, Prayer, Meditations*, trans. Penelope Lawson (Kalamazoo, Mich.: Cistercian Publications, 1970), 154–55.

20. "Hoc est quod agitur cum facimus quod in tui commemorationem nos facere praecepisti, quo in salutem filiorum tuorum nil dulcius, nil potuit prouideri potenti-

Here we see many themes from *On the Sacrament of the Altar* echoed in a more explicitly trinitarian reflection. The Eucharist holds the memory of Christ's saving work, and meditation on these memories increases our love for Christ. This spiritual reception, in turn, further conforms the communicant to Christ. The assimilation to Christ takes place through the gift of the Holy Spirit, who graces the recipient with participation in the unity between the Father and the Son, thereby binding those who receive worthily to one another in Christ and the Father. William's meditation on the memory of Eucharistic reception evokes the erotic language of the Song of Songs (Song 1:2), and, as Matthieu Rougé notes, William compares communion in the triune God to the nuptial bond, speaking of Eucharistic conformity to Christ with the words that Adam spoke upon encountering the newly created Eve: "This is bone of my bone, and flesh of my flesh" (Gn 2:23).[21]

William's most significant writing on spiritual reception of the Eucharist through meditation occurs in his celebrated letter to the Carthusians of Mont-Dieu, in which he offers counsel on the basics of living the monastic life. In his discussion of reading, prayer, and meditation, he writes that it is beneficial and important to devote at least one hour of the day "to an attentive passing in review of the benefits conferred by [Christ's] Passion and the redemption he wrought, in order to savor them in spirit and store them away faithfully in the memory. This is spiritually to eat the Body of the Lord and drink his Blood in remembrance of him who gave to all who believe in him the commandment: 'Do this in remembrance of me.'"[22] Here, meditation and

---

us, cum manducantes et bibentes incorruptibile epulum corporis et sanguinis tui, sicut munda animalia tua, ab intestino memoriae cogitandi dulcedine, quasi ad os reducimus, et in nouum et perpetuum salutis nostrae officium, nouo semper pietatis affectu ruminantes, rursum suauiter in ipsa recondimus memoria quid pro nobis feceris, quid fueris passus. Vbi dicis animae desideranti: Dilata os tuum et ego adimplebo illud. Et illa gustans et uidens suauitatem tuam sacramento magno et incomprehensibili, hoc efficitur quod manducat, os ex ossibus tuis et caro de carne tua, ut sicut orasti Patrem iturus ad passionem, hoc Spiritus sanctus operetur in nobis per gratiam, quod in Patre et te, Filio eius, est ab aeterno per naturam, ut sicut uos unum estis, ita et nos in uobis unum simus. Haec est, Domine, facies tua ad faciem te desiderantis; hoc est osculum oris tui ad os te amantis; hic est amplexus dilectionis tuae ad amplexum sponsae tuae suspirantis tibi et dicentis: Dilectus meus mihi, et ego illi; in medio uberum meorum commorabitur. Et: Tibi dixit cor meum: Exquisiuit te facies mea." *MD*, VIII.VII.71–92; *Meditations*, 142–43.

21. Rougé, *Doctrine et experience*, 251.

22. "Scit etiam quicumque habet sensum Christi quantum christianae pietati ex-

spiritual reception of the Eucharist are effectively identical. Because meditation on the Passion allows a monk to grow in love of Christ and store that love in his memory, it produces the same spiritual fruit as receiving the Eucharist in the sacrament. William elaborates:

> Now if you wish, and if you truly desire it, this is at your disposal in your cell at all hours both of day and of night. As often as you stir up sentiments of piety and faith in recalling to mind what he did when he suffered for you, you eat his body and drink his blood. As long as you remain in him through love and he in you through the sanctity and justice he works in you, you are reckoned as belonging to his Body and counted as one of his members.[23]

The extent to which William equates meditation and Eucharistic reception seems shocking, and yet this is entirely consistent with his theology of spiritual reception. Upon receiving Christ physically and spiritually in the Eucharist, a person is reminded of Christ's saving work and grows in love by a gift of the Spirit. This memorial and increase of love are also possible by meditation, and hence the fruits of each are the same. This does not, however, negate the uniqueness and importance of the sacrament. In previous works, William wrote

---

pediat, quantum seruum Dei, seruum redemptionis Christi deceat, et utile ei sit una saltem aliqua diei hora passionis ipsius ac redemptionis attentius recolligere beneficia, ad fruendum suauiter in conscientia et recondendum fideliter in memoria; quod est spiritualiter manducare corpus Domini et bibere eius sanguinem, in memoriam eius qui omnibus in se credentibus praecepit dicens: Hoc facite in meam commemorationem." *Epistola ad Fratres de Monte Dei*, I.115, in *Guillelmi a Sancto Theodorico omnia opera pars III: Opera didactica et spiritualia*, ed. Stanislaus Ceglar and Paul Verdeyen (Turnhout: Brepols, 2003); *The Golden Epistle*, trans. Theodore Berkeley (Kalamazoo, Mich.: Cistercian Publications, 1971), 50.

23. "Siquidem sanctae huius ac reuerendae commemorationis mysterium, suo modo, suo loco, suo tempore celebrare licet paucis hominibus, quibus in hoc creditum est ministerium; rem uero mysterii in omni tempore et in omni loco dominationis Dei, modo quo traditum est, hoc est debitae pietatis affectu agere et tractare et sumere sibi in salutem, omnibus in promptu est, quibus dicitur: Vos autem genus electum, regale sacerdotium, gens sancta, populus adquisitionis, ut uirtutes adnuntietis eius qui de tenebris uos uocauit in admirabile lumen suum. Nam et sacramentum, sicut accipit ad uitam dignus, sic ad mortem suam et iudicium temerare potest indignus; rem uero sacramenti nemo percipit nisi dignus et idoneus. Sacramentum enim sine re sacramenti sumenti mors est; res uero sacramenti, etiam praeter sacramentum, sumenti uita aeterna est. "Si autem uis et uere uis, omnibus horis tam diei quam noctis, haec tibi in cella tua praesto est. Quotiens in commemorationem eius qui pro te passus est, huic facto eius pie ac fideliter fueris affectus, corpus eius manducas et sanguinem bibis; quamdiu in eo manes per amorem, ipse uero in te per sanctitatis et iustitiae operationem, in eius corpore et in membris eius computaris." *Ep frat*, I.117–119; *Golden Epistle*, 51.

of the necessity of the sacrament for the deification of the body and emphasized the importance of joining oneself to the sacrifice of Christ offered in the Mass. Meditation on the Eucharist is ultimately grounded in and enabled by reception of the Eucharist.[24]

Christ is the only-begotten Son of the Father who "silently manifests the nature and substance of the Deity to eyes which are worthy and fit for so great a revelation."[25] Citing Augustine, William explains that this is an invisible revelation of an invisible and incorruptible God whom we "see" in our soul to the degree that our soul has become like God through knowledge and love of him.[26] Our "seeing" in this life is obscured and far from the perfection of the land of the living (Ps 26:13; 114:9) where those taken up will see God "face to face" (1 Cor 13:12), and "seeing him as he is they will become like him." For "there, as in the Father and the Son, that which is vision is also unity" through the Holy Spirit.[27] In *The Nature and Dignity of Love*, William writes of memory generating from itself reason, and the two together generating love. He concludes: "So that the rational soul created in man may adhere to God, therefore, the Father claims the memory for himself, the Son the reason, and the Holy Spirit, who proceeds from both, claims the will proceeding from both."[28] Receiving Christ in the memorial of the

24. "Si donc Guillaume établit une distinction réelle entre la matérialité de la célébration extérieure et la participation intérieure à sa vertu, il n'en maintient pas moins que la grâce qu'il s'agit d'accueillir en soi, c'est la grâce de l'eucharistie. Si la discursivité du sacrement est en partie relativisée, ce n'est que pour mieux mettre en valeur la grâce du sacrement lui-même" (Rougé, *Doctrine et experience*, 104). William's theology of reception is also influenced by Origen's theology of the birth of the Word in the heart of the Christian. See Verdeyen, *La théologie mystique de Guillaume de Saint-Thierry*, 172ff.; Henri Crouzel, *Origen*, trans. A. S. Worrall (San Francisco, Calif.: Harper & Row, 1989), 70, 76, 125; and Hans Urs von Balthasar, *Parole et mystère chez Origène* (Paris: Les Éditions du Cerf, 1957), 105.

25. "Vnigenitus ergo Filius deitatis naturam atque substantiam insonabiliter narrans dignis idoneis que oculis tanto conspectui, etiam in hac uita inuisibiliter monstrat." *Aenigma fidei*, 5.68–69, in *Guillelmi a Sancto Theodorico omnia opera pars V: Opuscula adversus Petrum Abaelardum et de fidei*, ed. Paul Verdeyen (Turnhout: Brepols, 2007); *The Enigma of Faith*, trans. John D. Anderson (Washington, D.C.: Cistercian Publications, 1974), 38.

26. William of Saint-Thierry, *Aenig*, 5. He is citing Augustine, *Epistola* 147 and *Epistola* 92.

27. "Vbi etiam sicut in Patre et Filio, quae uisio, ipsa unitas est, sic in Deo et homine, quae uisio, ipsa et similitudo futura est." *Aenig*, 6; *Enigma*, 39.

28. "Memoria quippe habet et continet quo tendendum sit; ratio quod tendendum sit; uoluntas tendit. Et haec tria unum quiddam sunt, sed tres efficaciae; sicut in illa

Eucharist strengthens a person's memory, understanding, and love of God, conforming him or her to the Father, Son, and Holy Spirit according to the object of faith and the psychologically analogous way by which it is appropriated. Spiritual meditation is, therefore, an analogously trinitarian act in which the human intellect, memory, and will are conformed to Christ in the Spirit for the purpose of communion with the Father.

When we consider William's theology of Eucharistic reception and meditation in light of what he would have understood about vision and memory, we can imagine a monk gazing at a crucifix or participating in the celebration of the Eucharist. This monk sees the image of Jesus on the cross and draws it into himself with the ray of his eye, or perhaps he receives Christ's Body in the sacrament of the Eucharist. In both cases, he is imprinting this great sign of love on his memory and this is forming him in the love of Christ. He later meditates on this love, taking what he has seen and remembered and making it part of his personal experience.[29] Meditation and the Eucharistic reception of his beloved increase his love for Christ, which is to say that they increase the presence of the Holy Spirit in his soul. The Spirit binds him to Christ, who unites the monk's self-offering in the monastic life to Christ's self-offering to the Father. This is how the monk is incorporated into the Trinity in a manner that corresponds to the salvific economy of the Trinity which, in turn, corresponds to the Trinity's inner life of love.

Reforming Our Memories

In light of this exploration of the medieval understanding of memory and the Eucharistic practices of William of Saint-Thierry, let me

summa Trinitate una est substantia, tres personae. In qua trinitate sicut Pater genitor, Filius genitus, et ab utroque procedit Spiritus sanctus; sic ex memoria ratio gignitur, ex memoria et ratione uoluntas procedit. Vt ergo Deo inhaereret creata in homine rationalis anima, memoriam sibi uindicauit Pater, rationem Filius, uoluntatem ab utraque procedentem ab utroque procedens Spiritus sanctus." *De natura et dignitate amoris*, 3.120–28, in *Guillelmi a Sancto Theodorico omnia opera pars III: Opera didactica et spiritualia*, ed. Stanislaus Ceglar and Paul Verdeyen (Turnhout: Brepols, 2003); *The Nature and Dignity of Love*, trans. Thomas X. Davis (Kalamazoo, Mich.: Cistercian Publications, 1981), 55.

29. See Carruthers, *The Book of Memory*, 53.

now make some suggestions for further reflection and practice. First, vision is more active than we think. Even if we do not worry about someone shooting us with ocular rays from their evil eye, we should be careful of the posture of our hearts toward what we behold. Part of the problem of pornography is not just what we see but the voracity and rapacity with which we see it, which the subject matter of pornography only encourages. Could a beautiful depiction of the human body become pornographic for a person if that is how the person sees it? Yes. Pornography is a kind of image, but also a particular kind of disposition in the eye of the beholder. As Jesus said, "The eye is the lamp of the body. So, if your eye is sound, your whole body will be full of light; but if your eye is not sound, your whole body will be full of darkness. If then the light in you is darkness, how great is the darkness!" (Mt 6:22–23).

Second, as much as you are what you eat physically, you are what you eat mentally; you are what you remember. Twenty-first-century neuroscience and psychology support William's twelfth-century insight into the power of memory, as evident in chapter 3 of this volume by William M. Struthers and Kyler Mulhauser. How are we building our internal treasure houses or dovecotes? How are we training our children to construct their minds? We do not need to build an elaborate interior palace, but we should take stock of what it is that we remember and meditate on, and we should foster a memory of Christ in ourselves and those for whom we care. Praying with an icon can be especially helpful in this regard. One of the most famous, the *Christ Pantocrator* from the monastery of St. Catherine on Mount Sinai, depicts half of Christ's face in love, the other in judgment (Fig. 10-1). The eye of judgment opens your soul like a scalpel; the eye of mercy heals the cleansed wounds of sin.[30] Eucharistic adoration is an even more powerful form of reforming the memory. William wrote just before

30. The music of the Orthodox composer Arvo Pärt performs a similar function, as I have described elsewhere: "I heard the Tallis Scholars, the world's premiere polyphonic choral group, sing Pärt's setting of the O Antiphons two years ago. When they swelled to full volume, their voices were like a blinding light that filled every pore of the room (and wrung a sob from me). The words became a brilliant wave of prayer on which I was carried along." Nathaniel Peters, "The Composer of Silence," *The Catholic Herald* (October 5, 2017), accessed October 20, 2018, https://catholicherald.co.uk/magazine/the-composer-of-silence/.

the practice developed in the thirteenth century, but his understanding of meditation as a kind of spiritual reception fits perfectly with cultivating a love of and conformity to Christ by gazing on the sacrament that is truly his Body and Blood.

Third, we must remember that sight and memory contribute to our sanctity. William shows us that if what we remember is Christ's love for us, we can become more conformed to that love. Fourth, the sacraments, especially the sacrament of the Lord's Body and Blood, in which we receive the one whom we love and remember, are essential for transformation by the renewal of our minds (Rom 12:2). There we are presented with the love of our crucified and risen Lord, to whom we are physically and spiritually joined. In receiving the Son, we receive the Spirit who proceeds from him and binds us to him, thereby leading us in Christ to the Father, who has created us for participation in the divine nature (2 Pt 1:4). And that is our joy.

BOYD TAYLOR COOLMAN

11 ⇝ *Sensus Christi*

A Liturgico-Sacramental Therapy for a Pornographic Sensibility

The socio-cultural crisis aptly termed the "pornification" of American society shows no signs of abating.[1] The phenomenon goes well beyond the explicit consumption of pornographic images, though that is perhaps the foundation and core of it. It consists of a way of perceiving, not just human bodies, but all of reality, a way of perceiving that is so pervasive we may not be consciously aware of it; a particular overarching narrative of the way things are and how people are to be valued and treated; and a corresponding way of being in the world and of relating to others in it. Pornography's abstraction, commodification, and objectification of the human body are often seen as its most deleterious effects: "Pornography," writes Maria Morrow, "abstracts images of bodies from the people themselves, commodifying human body parts and human bodies, commodifying sexuality and the sex act itself."[2] Without denying or minimizing the cultural, economic, biological, and even neurological dimensions of pornography, it is helpful to insist that it is also a habit-forming practice, which occurs organically within a worldview that pornography also reinforces and ingrains.

Rightly, this volume attempts to resist this narrative, to combat this worldview, not merely by offering an alternative, not merely by setting down a different account over and against a pornographic one. It also tries to offer strategies for resistance and to imagine concretely

1. Pamela Paul, *Pornified: How Pornography Is Transforming Our Lives, Our Relationships, and Our Families* (New York: Times Books, an imprint of Henry Holt, 2005).

2. Maria C. Morrow, "Pornography and Penance," in *Leaving and Coming Home: New Wineskins for Catholic Sexual Ethics*, ed. David Cloutier (Eugene, Ore.: Cascade Books, an imprint of Wipf and Stock, 2010), 69.

and practically how to facilitate a reorientation, to catalyze a conversion, and to foster an immigration, so to speak, from a pornographic to a sacramental worldview.

The present essay offers a modest contribution to that larger project, one possibly useful tool among the many that will surely be needed, for escaping the world of pornography. Its utility will not likely be universal; some may find it minimally helpful or not at all. When implemented, it will certainly need to be used in conjunction with other tools, in a supplementary and, it is hoped, complementary way. It is addressed primarily to persons in their moral agency and responsibility, though it is integrally situated within larger communal and corporate contexts. More precisely, the tool described here is offered to those who count themselves intentional followers of Jesus Christ; it presumes, that is, implementation by a believing Christian in an ecclesial context. It will also most likely be most relevant to Christian men, who are still the predominant (though not exclusive) consumers of pornography. Its greater utility to men is also due to its heavy focus on the sense of sight (seeing, gazing, visualizing), which is of course the primary sense implicated by pornography, but which also seems to work differently for men than for women.[3] The perspective adopted here, finally, is explicitly theological and, one could say, spiritual, as distinct from (though not in opposition to or competition with) neurological, psychological, socio-cultural, and economic perspectives.

Sensus Christi

In the Latin Vulgate, the apostle Paul's First Letter to the Corinthians harbors an intriguing expression regarding the relationship between Jesus and his followers. In many modern English translations, Paul says that believers have "the mind of Christ" (1 Cor 2:16). But the Vulgate translates the Greek, *nous Christou*, as *sensus Christi*.[4] For most mod-

3. Struthers and Mulhauser state in chapter 3: "Men, more so than women, enjoy *looking* at the naked body—and this is true across cultures. The relationship between a man's brain and sexually explicit imagery is very complex. Scientific findings seem to suggest that a man's brain may be changed by exposure to sexually explicit material; but it also appears to be the case that a man's brain is hardwired to be attracted to sexually explicit images. Males, on average, tend to be more sensitive than females to visual cues: men first look at the body, then the face, and then the context," 71.

4. Though *nous* is typically translated into English as "mind" or "understanding,"

ern English speakers, the word "mind" has a rather narrow intellectual connotation, suggesting that in some way believers can (or should) think like Jesus. In Latin, by contrast, *sensus* has a deep and wide range of meanings, encompassing many of the different ways that humans encounter extra-mental reality, from the activity of the five physical senses, to the more interior dimensions of perception and experience, to the more typically intellectual or cognitive dimensions. Indeed, the list of English equivalents found in Latin dictionaries includes: perceive, feel, experience, think, realize, see, and understand. So, a helpful paraphrase of *sensus Christi* might be: "Christ's way of perceiving, experiencing, and knowing" or perhaps even "the sensibility of Christ." Given this broad definition, the term *sensus* encompasses all aspects of human experience, including those implicated in pornography.

The claim here advanced is that one useful tool in overcoming a pornographic sensibility among Christian believers is the acquisition, maintenance, and cultivation of the *sensus Christi*. Indeed, Paul's phrase provides a rich, multivalent notion for reflecting on what that might mean and how it might best occur, going well beyond a simplistic sort of WWJT—"what would Jesus think?" In particular, the above-noted semantic plenitude of the Latin term "*sensus*" allows it to be a versatile analytic tool for conceiving of a sacramental, as opposed to a pornographic, mode of experience. The grammatical ambiguity in the genitive phrase "of Christ," moreover, enables it to describe Christ as both remedial subject and object of a pornographic sensibility in need of healing transformation. Most significantly, it will be here argued that the possession of the *sensus Christi* is most properly understood within an *ecclesial* context, wherein it is acquired and maintained *sacramentally* and cultivated *liturgically*. In this way, the *sensus Christi* emerges as an antidote for what could be called the "pornographic sensibility" of the culture.

Bauer's New Testament dictionary indicates that the term "denotes the faculty of physical and intellectual perception, then also the power to arrive at moral judgments." It appears mostly in Pauline literature and was translated in the Vulgate sometimes as *sensus*, sometimes as *mens*. As Brian Dunkle, SJ, has observed in private conversation: "The Latin *sensus* carries a few more 'sensual' connotations than *mens*, although *nous* is more 'sensual' than 'mind.'" Walter Bauer, *A Greek-English Lexicon of the New Testament and Other Early Christian Literature*, 3rd ed. (Chicago, Ill.: University of Chicago Press, 2001).

Re-Situating the Pornographic Struggle

In the Christian therapeutic literature on the topic, the attention of those struggling with pornography is often directed to the Crucifixion of Christ, with an emphasis on such New Testament passages as: "I have been crucified with Christ" (Gal 2:20); "those who belong to Christ Jesus have crucified the flesh with its passions and desires" (Gal 5:24); "put on the Lord Jesus Christ, and make no provision for the flesh, to gratify its desires" (Rom 13:14). These texts are frequently depicted as helpful information, or even as the basis of a kind of cognitive therapy or meditational exercise, and then presented rhetorically as an admonition or exhortation to the believer struggling with pornography both to appropriate this connection to Christ, to his cross and passion specifically, and then to imitate Christ's Crucifixion in regard to one's own pornographic inclinations. The one who struggles with pornography must also "put to death ... whatever ... is earthly: fornication, impurity, passion, evil desire" (Col 3:5).

This approach is also often linked to certain underlying theological assumptions, specifically, soteriological frameworks, associated with classical Protestant views of justification by faith—understood as fully accomplished at the moment of conversion. This seems to prompt a rhetorical stance toward one who struggles with pornography in which he is reminded that, because of his faith in Christ, he *already* has all the grace needed for overcoming pornography use.[5] Continued failure can only be explained either by ignorance of this fact or by a mysterious inability to "tap" into that grace (i.e., to appropriate it

5. For example, Jon Snyder writes: "The truth of our identity in Christ is that we HAVE been made a new creation, we ARE now the righteousness of Christ, we HAVE been set free from the power of the enemy, we HAVE EVERY spiritual blessing already in Christ, our old man HAS been killed and crucified with Christ, we ALWAYS are victorious in Christ. When we get the grace to actually believe these truths from the Bible, it changes everything. As you read this book, God will establish these things in your heart more and more and heal you of many heart wounds. But through grace we don't have to wait until "some day" to walk in freedom—we are free today and in the Spirit we have access to everything we need to win every battle." Jon Snyder, *The Mighty Man Manual: Victory and Freedom over Lust, Pornographic, and Sexual Addictions* (Edgemont, Pa.: Jon Snyder and Mighty Man Ministries, 2009), 22. See: http://sharedhope.org/wp-content/uploads/2014/03/Mighty-Man-Manual-by-Jon-Snyder-SAMPLE.pdf.

effectively in the battle with pornography). But one senses that, on this model, the gap between the "already" of complete justification and the "not yet" of incomplete sanctification, and of the concomitant continued indulgence in pornography, remains exasperatingly inexplicable: If I am *already* crucified with Christ, if I have *already* died with Christ, if I have *already* crucified the flesh with its sinful desires, why the continued struggle with pornography?

The present proposal endorses this recourse to Christ crucified, but conceives of it in significantly different ways. From this perspective, a more Catholic soteriological framework that emphasizes liturgical practice, sacramental reception, and ecclesial community, may well offer a useful alternative paradigm, both in theory and in practice.

A striking feature of the theological renewal of Vatican II was that it negotiated the above-noted diastema between the "all ready" and the "not yet" of Christian experience both *liturgically* and *sacramentally*. That is, it conceived of believers "working out their salvation"—a salvation that God has already accomplished in Christ's paschal mystery—through sacramental participation in Christ in the liturgy, which then flows forth into ecclesial life. "In Christ," on the one hand, states *Sacrosanctum Concilium*, "'the perfect achievement of our reconciliation came forth,'" which he "achieved ... principally by the paschal mystery of his blessed passion, resurrection from the dead, and the glorious ascension, whereby '*dying, he destroyed our death and, rising, he restored our life*.'"[6] On the other hand, Christ sent the apostles (and their successors) to preach the message regarding what he had accomplished, so that these apostolic emissaries "might accomplish the work of salvation which they had proclaimed, by means of sacrifice and sacraments, around which the entire liturgical life revolves."[7] Yet this work is not different than the work already accomplished by Christ himself; rather, it is its "out-working" in the lives of persons who live in ecclesial communion: "To accomplish so great a work, Christ is always present in His Church, especially in her liturgical celebrations."[8] Thus, "the liturgy" is that "through which the work of our redemption

6. Vatican Council II, *Sacrosanctum Concilium* (December 4, 1963), 5.
7. Vatican Council II, *Sacrosanctum Concilium*, 6.
8. Vatican Council II, *Sacrosanctum Concilium*, 7.

is accomplished," which "daily builds up those who are within into a holy temple of the Lord, into a dwelling place for God in the Spirit (Eph 2:21), to the mature measure of the fullness of Christ (Eph 4:13)."[9] This liturgical out-working of salvation is the means by which believers "are sanctified," a "sanctification ... signified by signs perceptible to the senses" and "effected in a way which corresponds with each of these signs."[10] Within this liturgical context, which makes Christ present in his paschal mystery in a uniquely powerful and effective mode, the grace of Christ crucified and risen is offered to human persons, and it is received initially in the sacrament of baptism. Here, baptismal justification is understood as the real communication or infusion of the grace of Christ to the believer, by which the believer is "in-grafted" into Christ.[11] United thus to Christ as body to head, as branches to vine,[12] believers have a real, life-giving communion with their living Lord, a link, however, that needs—indeed requires—ongoing maintenance, cultivation, and intensification, which is always an increase of participation in Christ.[13]

The present proposal, accordingly, wishes to "locate" the believer struggling with pornography within this particular liturgical and soteriological framework and to ground all subsequent remedial strategies upon this foundation of sacramental *participation* in Christ's saving paschal mystery. As noted above, what follows will consider this sac-

9. Vatican Council II, *Sacrosanctum Concilium*, 2.

10. Vatican Council II, *Sacrosanctum Concilium*, 7.

11. "But though He died for all, yet all do not receive the benefit of His death, but those only to whom the merit of His passion is communicated." For "though no one can be just except he to whom the merits of the passion of our Lord Jesus Christ are communicated, yet this takes place in that justification of the sinner, when by the merit of the most holy passion, the charity of God is poured forth by the Holy Ghost in the hearts of those who are justified and inheres in them; whence man through Jesus Christ, in whom he is ingrafted, receives in that justification, together with the remission of sins, all these infused at the same time, namely, faith, hope and charity." See Council of Trent, *Decree on Justification* (January 13, 1547), 7.

12. "For since Christ Jesus Himself, as the head into the members and the vine into the branches, continually infuses strength into those justified, which strength always precedes, accompanies and follows their good works." Council of Trent, *Decree on Justification*, 16.

13. "Faith cooperating with good works, [they] increase in that justice received through the grace of Christ and are further justified"; "[they] proceed onward through Jesus Christ, by whom they have access unto this grace." See Council of Trent, *Decree on Justification*, 11 and 10.

ramental participation from the perspective of the different, though complimentary, ways in which the phrase "*sensus Christi*" can be understood.

Sensus Christi 1: Sensing *with* the Body of Christ

To begin, this sharing in the paschal mystery may be expressed helpfully in terms of a genuine participation in the *sensus Christi*, taking the phrase as a *subjective* genitive; that is, from the perspective of sharing in Christ's own *sensus*, or sensing *with* Christ.

Baptismal Reception of the Sensus Christi

As is well known, baptismal union with Christ has been perennially understood in the Christian tradition as a sharing in Christ's death and resurrection, a mystery articulated originally by the apostle Paul and reaffirmed recently by Vatican II: "By baptism [believers] are plunged into the paschal mystery of Christ: they die with Him, are buried with Him, and rise with Him."[14] Approaching this notion from the perspective of "sensing with Christ," it seems fitting to draw on the ancient Christian notion of "capital grace," namely, of the grace of Christ the head, which flows down into those united to him as to his body: "[Christ] is called head, since all the senses flow from the head to the members of the Church."[15] Just as all the *physical* senses are located principally in the head, while the rest of the body is able to sense by being joined to the head, so too all *spiritual* sensibility resides principally in Christ, while through baptism individual believers receive a capacity for spiritual perception by being joined to him: "they are made sensate by their head" (*sensificentur a capite*).[16] At least three implications flow from this.

First, for the man who struggles with pornography, it would follow

14. Vatican Council II, *Sacrosanctum Concilium*, 6. See also Rom 6:4; Eph 2:6; Col 3:1; and 2 Tim 2:11.

15. Alexander of Hales, *Glossa in quator libros Sententiarum Petri Lombardi*, Bibliotheca Franciscana scholastica medii aevi 12–15 (Quaracchi, Florence: Collegium S. Bonaventurae, 1951–57), *III Sent*, d. 19, n. 41.

16. Hugh of St. Victor, *De scripturis et scriptoribus*, Patrologiae cursus completus, series latina, ed. Jacques Paul Migne (Paris: Migne, 1857–66), 175:10A.

quite logically that baptismal union with Christ crucified would be the appropriate framework in which to situate his own attempts to mortify pornographic desires and practices, to put to death his own pornographic *sensus*. Here, having the *sensus Christi* is the personal appropriation *of*, by real sharing *in*, Christ's own act and experience (*sensus*) of self-denial and mortification.

Second, since sharing in the paschal mystery is not only sharing in Christ's death, but also sharing in his resurrected life, at least inchoately and proleptically, the baptized seek and appropriate a share in Christ's own resurrected human nature, a human nature that has conquered the devastating ravage of sin on the human *sensus*. As depicted in the *Anastasis* icon on the cover of this volume, "in the human nature united to Himself the Son of God, by overcoming death through His own death and resurrection, redeemed man and re-molded him into a new creation."[17]

Third, baptismally united to Christ, the believer shares in the *sensus* that Jesus himself possessed in his own human nature. The traditional assumption that Jesus himself possessed a rightly ordered sexuality,[18] as part of his complete human nature, means that, in principle, baptismally-mediated union with him is also a participation in his rightly ordered sexual sensibility (*sensus*).[19] In this light, the Gospel depictions of Jesus' direct and even physical interactions with women presumed to be prostitutes—table fellowship, even allowing his feet

17. Vatican Council II, *Lumen Gentium* (November 21, 1964), 7. See also Gal 6:15 and 2 Cor 5:17.

18. "In many hundreds of pious, religious works, from before 1400 to past the mid-16th century, the ostensive unveiling of the Child's sex, or the touching, protecting or presentation of it, is the main action. And the emphasis recurs in images of the dead Christ, or of the mystical Man of Sorrows." Leo Steinberg, *The Sexuality of Christ in Renaissance Art and in Modern Oblivion*, 2nd rev. ed. (Chicago, Ill.: University of Chicago Press, 1996), 3.

19. See Lee Siegel: "Steinberg relies on St. Augustine . . . to argue that Christ's erection was a singular way to demonstrate Christ's chastity. Without the capacity to yield to lust, Christ's triumph over carnal desire would have no human meaning. Unlike men after the fall of Adam, who fell victim to lust, Christ willed his erection; it was not an involuntary physiological event. By both willing and resisting it, he declared his victory over the stain of sin bequeathed to humanity by Adam and Eve, and over the death that their carnal weakness brought into the world. That, after all, is the significance of the resurrection." Lee Siegel, "Pope Francis and the Naked Christ," *The New Yorker* (December 17, 2013), accessed October 30, 2018, https://www.newyorker.com/books/page-turner/pope-francis-and-the-naked-christ.

to be washed by the hair of a sinful woman who may well have been a prostitute—appear strikingly germane. The Gospels depict not a Jesus who flees any contact with sexually available women or who simply shuns all potentially sexually laden interaction with the bodies of other people, but rather a Jesus whose physical relations and indeed sexual inclinations are rightly ordered and properly integrated.

Baptized into Christ, the believer shares in Christ's death, his resurrection, and his integrated relation to other women. In these three ways, to "have the *sensus Christi*" is not just to imitate the "mind of Christ" in some vague fashion. Rather, to have the *sensus Christi* is quite actually, to be members of Christ's Body, to share in his *sensus*—his own self-denial, the reality of his own restored human nature, his own rightly-ordered human eros.

Penance and Reconciliation

Begun in baptism, sacramental participation in the *sensus Christi* can be maintained or recovered, even cultivated and increased, through the sacrament of penance and reconciliation.[20] Rightly understood and practiced, this sacrament would seem to offer a powerful resource for believers struggling with pornography. Indeed, it has recently been described as a "counter-practice to pornography and pornification" that resists the objectification and commodification of the human body.[21]

In the current climate, this proposal may seem counter-intuitive for two different reasons, depending on one's demographic location. Catholics formed by pre-Vatican II's manualist, overly juridical approach to the sacrament of reconciliation, may well have psychological barriers that make the confessional an unwelcome place to seek and find forgiveness and healing from pornography use.[22] Conversely, the post-Vatican II "sea change" toward a more therapeutic model that psychologized the sacrament as little more than a "psychological

20. See Morrow, "Pornography and Penance," 62–83. As she notes (65n6), various terms for this sacrament are in circulation: "sacrament of reconciliation," "sacrament of confession," "sacrament of penance," and "sacrament of conversion."

21. Morrow, "Pornography and Penance," 65.

22. Servais Pinckaers, *The Sources of Christian Ethics* (Washington, D.C.: The Catholic University of America Press, 1995), 273. Cited in Morrow, "Pornography and Penance," 80.

back-pat" has perhaps evacuated the sacrament of its potential for effecting real and lasting repentance.[23] A via media between these overly legalistic and overly psychological paradigms might emerge from a deeper sense of sacramental participation in the *sensus Christi*. Such a via media may be able to incorporate both pre-modern, pre-manualist insights with modern psychological and therapeutic insights in order to offer a more inter-personal and personalist understanding of the sacrament of reconciliation.

The traditional Catholic conception of this sacrament consistently construes its grace as restoring the power of Christ's paschal mystery to the sinner. In his discussion, for example, Thomas Aquinas repeatedly stresses that this sacrament links the penitent to the "power of Christ's Passion,"[24] and the Council of Trent calls it that "by which the benefit of the death of Christ is applied to those who have fallen after baptism."[25] Frequent participation therein is a kind of "spiritual medicine,"[26] which has the power both to remove past sins, thus effecting reconciliation with God, and also to preserve the penitent "from future sins."[27] While these notions can be (and have been) understood impersonally and abstractly, they may be construed much more personally on the *sensus Christi* model.

Perhaps surprisingly, the Council of Trent's concluding summary of the sacrament of penance points strongly in this direction. It merits quotation in full:

23. See James M. O'Toole, "In the Court of Conscience: American Catholics and Confession," in *Habits of Devotion*, ed. James M. O'Toole, 174–77 (Ithaca, N.Y.: Cornell University Press, 2004). Cited in Morrow, "Pornography and Penance," 480.

24. "Consequently it is necessary for the sinner's salvation that sin be taken away from him; which cannot be done without the sacrament of Penance, wherein the power of Christ's Passion operates through the priest's absolution and the acts of the penitent." Thomas Aquinas, *Summa Theologiae*, trans. Fathers of the English Dominican Province, 5 vols. (Westminster, Md.: Christian Classics, 1948), III q. 84, a. 5 c.

25. Council of Trent, *Decree on the Most Holy Sacraments of Penance and Extreme Unction* (November 25, 1551), 1.

26. Aquinas explains that "Penance derives its power from Christ's Passion, as a spiritual medicine, which can be repeated frequently" (*ST*, III q. 84, a. 10 ad 5).

27. "True penance not only removes past sins, but also preserves man from future sins. Consequently, although a man receives forgiveness of past sins in the first instant of his true penance, nevertheless he must persevere in his penance, lest he fall again into sin" (*ST*, III q. 84, a. 8 ad 1).

While we thus, by making satisfaction, suffer for our sins, *we are made conformable to Jesus Christ*, who satisfied for our sins, from whom is all our sufficiency; having also thereby a most sure pledge, that if we suffer with him, we shall also be glorified with him. But neither is this satisfaction, which we discharge for our sins, so our own, as not to be *through Jesus Christ*. For we, who can do nothing of ourselves, as of ourselves, can do all things, he cooperating, who strengthens us. Thus, man has not wherein to glory, but all our glorying is in Christ: *in whom* we live; *in whom* we merit; *in whom* we satisfy; bringing forth fruits worthy of penance, which *from him* have their efficacy; *by him* are offered to the Father; and *through him* are accepted by the Father.[28]

At one level, repentance is the act of the penitent sinner himself, who voluntarily embraces its requirements.[29] Yet, Trent here directly and explicitly links the act of repentance to a real and profound *participation* in the passion and suffering of Christ. Quite clearly, the effect of the sacrament is to unite repenting believers to Christ crucified so fully that the entire act of repentance occurs within the ambient embrace of Jesus himself, is borne along by the power of his Passion, and is brought to fruitful fulfillment by his action. Here, Christ emerges less as the stern judge of the sinner and more as the one who offers himself to the penitent, who compassionately comes alongside, perhaps even as the exemplary penitent, offering himself as a resource for resistance.[30]

In Aquinas's view, there is also a place for "internal penance," a posture of continual and ongoing repentance, "outside" the formal sacrament of reconciliation, appropriate for one who, while not actually committing serious sin, is perhaps especially vulnerable to temp-

28. Council of Trent, *Penance and Extreme Unction*, 8. Emphases added.

29. "The sacrament of Penance, wherein the power of Christ's Passion operates through the priest's absolution and the acts of the penitent, who co-operates with grace unto the destruction of his sin" (*ST*, III q. 84, a. 5 c). Again: "In Penance, on the other hand, man shares in the power of Christ's Passion according to the measure of his own acts" (*ST*, III q. 86, a. 4 ad 3).

30. See Alexander of Hales: "In Christ . . . there was also sorrow for the sin (*dolor pro peccato*) of the human race, without which there would not be satisfaction, along with the other two, as is clear in true contrition. For even if he suffered punishment in his body, and co-suffered that punishment in his soul, unless there was also sorrow for sin (*dolor de peccato*), there would not be true satisfaction." See q. 16, disp. 4, mem. 5, n. 107, in *Quaestiones disputatae "antequam esset frater,"* Bibliotheca Franciscana scholastica medii aevi 19–21 (Quaracchi, Florence: Collegii S. Bonaventurae, 1960), p. 273.

tation and relapse.[31] This would seem to provide a powerful means of grace for one struggling with pornography, who, though not actually lapsing back into sin, continues to adopt the posture of ongoing repentance, thereby continuing to abide in the grace of reconciliation. From this perspective, it may also be possible more easily to assimilate into this sacrament the various and complex ways and means in which individuals are caught in the mire of pornography and the degrees of responsibility they might bear. Whether they are participating "with full knowledge and deliberate consent," or "with unintentional ignorance,"[32] or in full-scale addiction,[33] a person who is joined to and accompanied by Christ the compassionate Healer and Physician in this sacrament receives the grace appropriate to their condition, as in a "field hospital," which is not only a place of appropriate repentance, but also of compassionate care and healing.

On this account, then, the sacrament of penance and reconciliation stands squarely in the gap so often noted between the one wrestling with pornography and the resource of the cross of Christ and its healing, restorative grace. Situating this sacrament of reconciliation as a participation in Jesus' own suffering (*sensus Christi*) might allow it to be experienced as an effective means of recovery from and resistance to pornography.

Cultivated in the Eucharist

Above all, the Eucharist occupies the central place in this approach to pornographic sin. Vatican II not only affirms that the liturgy is that "through which the work of our redemption is accomplished" but fur-

31. Aquinas explains, "To do penance both internal and external belongs to the state of beginners, of those, to wit, who are making a fresh start from the state of sin. But there is room for internal penance even in the proficient and the perfect" (*ST*, III q. 84, a. 8 ad 2).

32. United States Conference of Catholic Bishops, "Create in Me a Clean Heart: A Pastoral Response to Pornography" (November, 2015), 5, with reference to the Catechism of the Catholic Church, especially no. 1860: "Unintentional ignorance and factors that compromise the voluntary and free character of the act can diminish a person's moral culpability."

33. "The moral culpability of an addicted person may be lessened depending on the circumstances, but the situation is particularly grave." See United States Conference of Catholic Bishops, "Create in Me a Clean Heart," 12.

ther specifies that our redemption is accomplished "most of all in the divine sacrifice of the Eucharist."[34] It is this sacrament "in which 'the victory and triumph of his death are again made present.'"[35] Here, in a unique way, Christ is personally present, "not only in the person of His minister, 'the same now offering, through the ministry of priests, who formerly offered himself on the cross,' but especially under the Eucharistic species."[36] For that reason, "no other action of the Church can equal its efficacy,"[37] because "from the Eucharist, as from a font, grace is poured forth upon us; and the sanctification of men and women in Christ ... is achieved in the most efficacious possible way."[38]

In the Eucharist, the reconciled believer who struggles with pornography (now forgiven through the sacrament of reconciliation) is, in a uniquely intense and efficacious way, united to Christ in his paschal mystery in its entirety, but especially to his suffering and death. Vatican II professes, "We must always bear about in our body the dying of Jesus, so that the life also of Jesus may be made manifest in our bodily frame."[39] Thus, the Eucharist is the primary means of cultivating (extending and deepening) our sacramental union with Christ, and indeed the *sensus Christi*, originating in baptism and maintained, recovered, cultivated in reconciliation.

In the Eucharist, especially, the notion of union with Christ offers the believer a sacramental means by which to offer himself, his own body and indeed his own *sensus*, through the self-offering of Christ himself. Vatican II explains, "We ask the Lord in the sacrifice of the Mass that, 'receiving the offering of the spiritual victim,' he may fashion us for himself 'as an eternal gift.'"[40] As Pope Benedict XVI wrote in *Deus Caritas Est*: "The Eucharist draws us into Jesus' act of self-oblation ... we enter into the very dynamic of his self-giving."[41] From this per-

34. Vatican Council II, *Sacrosanctum Concilium*, 2.

35. Vatican Council II, *Sacrosanctum Concilium*, 6, citing the Council of Trent, *Decree on the Holy Eucharist* (October 11, 1551), 5.

36. Vatican Council II, *Sacrosanctum Concilium*, 7, citing the Council of Trent, *Doctrine Touching the Sacrifice of the Mass* (September 17, 1562), 2.

37. Vatican Council II, *Sacrosanctum Concilium*, 7.

38. Vatican Council II, *Sacrosanctum Concilium*, 10.

39. Vatican Council II, *Sacrosanctum Concilium*, 12. See also 2 Cor 4:10–11.

40. Vatican Council II, *Sacrosanctum Concilium*, 12.

41. Benedict XVI, Encyclical Letter *Deus Caritas Est* (December 25, 2005), 13. My thanks to Fr. Robert Imbelli for drawing my attention to this text.

spective, the various Pauline statements noted above—being "crucified with Christ" (Gal 2:20); having "crucified the flesh with its passions and desires" (Gal 5:24); putting on "the Lord Jesus Christ, and make no provision for the flesh, to gratify its desires" (Rom 13:14)—find here their proper theological context, as grounded in, actualized by, and efficacious through, Eucharistic union with Christ. As Vatican II put it: "By offering the Immaculate Victim, not only through the hands of the priest, but also with him, [believers] should learn also to offer themselves."[42] The holiness and moral purity for which believers strive—to "offer their bodies as living sacrifices, holy and acceptable to God, which is spiritual service of worship" (Rom 12:1)—is enabled by the Eucharist. With this strategy the one struggling with pornography is offered, not merely a homiletical exhortation to imitate the Lord's cruciform example, but rather a real participation in the life-giving presence of his Passion, so that he "might become a Eucharist with Christ, and thus become acceptable and pleasing to God."[43]

In sum, the strategy offered here is to seek a remedial therapy for pornographic sin in an ecclesial context of liturgical activity and sacramental practice. More precisely, sacramental participation in the paschal mystery of the Lord, based in baptism, restored in reconciliation, expanded in Eucharist, cultivated in the communion of the Body of Christ, must be the foundation and framework—one might even fittingly say, the crucible—of the pursuit of and progress toward healing, wholeness, and holiness. Most precisely, this sacramental practice seeks to replace a pornographic sensibility with the *sensus Christi*, a participation in Christ's own sensibility—Christ's own restored human nature and rightly ordered sexuality, Christ's own self-mortification and suffering in the flesh, Christ's own sacrificial offering of his whole self, body and soul, to the Father.

Sensus Christi 2: Sensing the Body of Christ

As noted above, the phrase *sensus Christi* can also be taken as an objective genitive, where Christ is not the *subject* of a *sensus* in which

42. Vatican Council II, *Sacrosanctum Concilium*, 48.

43. Joseph Ratzinger, "Eucharist and Mission," in *Pilgrim Fellowship of Faith: The Church as Communion* (San Francisco, Calif.: Ignatius Press, 2005), 78.

the believer might therapeutically share (as treated above) but is the *object* of the pornography viewer's own *sensus*. Pondering a "sacramental imagination in an age of pornography" can evoke a kind of "Walker Percy moment" where something quite familiar and well-known reappears, as if for the first time. In this case, what reappears is this: since at least the early twelfth-century, most Western Catholics have worshiped God and celebrated the Eucharist, while gazing at a sensuous representation of Jesus' essentially naked body, which they have been encouraged to view while cultivating an affective response. But putting it this way "in an age of pornography" is rather unsettling. For, if we define "pornography" as the intentional cultivation of sexual affectedness or affectivity through a visual representation of a naked human body, then a rather eerie parallel seems to emerge between liturgy and pornography, at least at this point. And if we rush to suggest that the difference is whether or not the affective response is erotic or passionate or sensuous, Dianne Phillips's elucidation of Catholic art in "The Visual Culture of Catholicism" (chapter 6 in this volume) seems to occlude that strategy, at least for the medieval and early modern periods, in which liturgical meditational practices were often supported with quite erotic imagery and with the sensuous language of the Song of Songs.[44] And, even if we were to expunge the erotic dimension from our affective liturgical gaze, doesn't the nearly naked body of Christ still have a startling structural and formal parallel to pornography that seems problematic? So, what to do?

It may be tempting simply to get rid of such liturgical imagery altogether, to conclude that the sensuous nakedness of Christ is indeed a kind of "sacramental porn," which ought simply to be abandoned, especially "in an age of pornography." However understandable that impulse might be, however, I believe it to be misguided. Rather than running away from the sensuousness of the visual culture of the Cath-

44. Anyone familiar with medieval devotional practices around the Eucharist will know that this practice was central to many different spiritual and mystical traditions of the Middle Ages. Both men and women, such as Bernard of Clairvaux and Mechthild of Magdeburg, used erotic imagery and the sensuous language of the Song of Songs in their meditations. St. Bernard famously and provocatively spoke of and encouraged in his listeners a "carnal love of the carnal Christ" as the starting point for a transformative process by which desire and love were reoriented, reformed, and properly reordered so as produce both psychological health and spiritual well being.

olic liturgy, we ought to embrace it, for it may well contain the solution rather than exacerbate the problem. Perhaps, precisely in view of its structural parallel with pornography, liturgical gazing at the nearly naked body of Jesus may become a strategy for counteracting a pornographic sensibility.[45] But this is a complicated and delicate proposal, and so let me offer four tentative, experimental reflections on the matter.

First, there may be some utility in merely juxtaposing the image of Christ crucified over and against memories of pornographic images. Indeed, at one level this is what is often proposed to individuals struggling with pornography, as noted above. Therapists and counselors do sometimes recommend meditation on the Passion of Christ as a technique for dampening or diffusing pornographic temptation—like a douse of cold-water in the face.[46] While this may have some degree of effectiveness, it seems to offer merely a confrontation between two visual images, in which one is meant to neutralize the other, after which the visual exercise will have done its job, so to speak, and the erstwhile viewer of pornography will have avoided or reduced the offending activity. Yet, this seems fairly superficial: less a therapy for bringing about deep change and more a simple technique for avoiding a particular occasion for sin.

Might there be deeper resources here? For example, as a second point, does the fact that the stripped body of Jesus is not only sensuous and even attractive, but also suffering, vulnerable, victimized, degraded, and abused provide a more powerful image with which to "re-sensitize" the pornographic sensibility? Might one effectively overlay the suffering, naked flesh of Christ upon a "pornified" memory, in

45. "Our brains responds differently to viewing sexual images than they do to images of a chair, or a beautiful landscape, or religious iconography (*although there are interesting similarities in the ways that sexual and religious experiences are processed neurologically*)." See Struthers and Mulhauser in chapter 3, 70, emphasis added.

46. For example: "I would tell the person that while I understand how they feel, that it feels like an uncontrollable urge, that is the great deception of this sin. It isn't uncontrollable. If Jesus, freshly crucified, blood pouring down his agony riddled face, the crunch of bone as nail pierced his flesh, gasping for air on the cross, were physically present in your living room, would your urge still feel uncontrollable? Would you still click on to the filth that contributed to our Lord of Glory's suffering? I HIGHLY doubt it." See Tim Kimberley, "Elder Questions: Pornography," Credo House (blog), November 20, 2013, https://credohouse.org/blog/elder-questions-pornography.

such a way that would push the viewer of pornography to reframe his perspective and thus to see other people, especially other bodies, with compassion, sympathy, even identification with vulnerability and weakness? If pornographic images cannot be expunged from memory, might they at least be somehow healed by sensing this Body of Christ, that is, by this *sensus Christi*?[47] Might we re-vision "pornified" bodies through Christ's suffering and vulnerable nakedness? Could such a reimaging of nakedness move the pornography viewer from callousness to compassion, from objectification to identification, from domination to devotion? Nor does it seem implausible, precisely at this juncture, to link such meditational practices to the acts of penitential examination of conscience and satisfaction noted above. For example, apropos the examination of conscience in the sacrament of reconciliation as a tool against the sin of pornography, Morrow suggests that "naming [pornographic] thoughts, words, and actions as sins that are against the will of God and harm other persons is hence an important step in representing the human body as a human person and not an object."[48] As a counter-measure to the abstracting and objectifying tendencies of pornography, the act of meditating on the personal body of Jesus, precisely with the intention of compassionating his wounded and vulnerable body, his suffering nakedness, itself the victim of calloused objectification, might allow the penitent pornographer to feel the harm done in pornography and might also move such a one to genuine contrition. Morrow's proposal, that the sacrament of penance "re-presents the body" might well be helpfully expanded here in relation to such meditational practices. In this sacramental practice, Jesus "re-presents" his own body to us, a body both nakedly vulnerable, but also beautiful, and invites us to respond affectively to it in love and tender compassion, and by extension invites us to consider and treat all other bodies in the same way. The naked body of Christ becomes the site for practicing an "anti-pornographic gaze," one *not* of impersonal abstraction, but of intimate familiarity; *not* of transactional commodification, but of inter-subjective relation; *not* of callous objectification, but of compassionate identification.

47. See chapter 3 by William M. Struthers and Kyler Mulhauser in this volume.
48. Morrow, "Pornography and Penance," 76.

By incorporating these practices into the framework of sacramental reconciliation they would acquire the capacity to be more than simply human acts of "cognitive manipulation" (i.e., trying to think differently) and could become actual means of grace for those struggling with pornography. From this vantage point, there would seem to be considerable untapped potential in the traditional three-part understanding of penance, consisting of contrition, confession, and satisfaction. Penitential satisfaction, in particular, might be the appropriate sacramental location for the various meditational practices—especially those oriented toward meditation on the Passion—that are often advocated in the therapeutic literature on pornography. By considering meditation as an act of penitential satisfaction, it could be fruitfully incorporated into the sacramental life. There might even be a place for acts of voluntarily embraced suffering that contribute to healing and reforming a pornographic *sensus*. The believer's voluntary acceptance of wisely chosen disciplines of penitential satisfaction for the sin of pornography,[49] moreover, could well become a powerful means of therapeutic grace, yielding genuine and lasting fruitful repentance.[50]

Third, and even more daringly, the unavoidably erotic depictions of Christ's nakedness, and his interaction with both male and female beloved disciples (e.g., the two Marys, John, Francis depicted in the art work shared by Dianne Phillips [Fig. 6-12]), could model a kind of transformed eros, which could re-sensitize those who meditate on it. Does the nuptial or spousal gaze shared between Christ and his disciples, in which medieval Christians so obviously reveled, provide a way for us, not to run away from or avoid eros, but to see it reformed and transformed? Can those images teach us how properly to relate to the naked body, not just of Jesus, but of others too? Perhaps one contem-

49. Recommending specific practices here is of course a delicate and difficult matter, which may best be left to the discretion of (ideally) wise confessors.

50. "For, doubtless, these satisfactory punishments greatly recall from sin, and check as it were with a bridle, and make penitents more cautious and watchful for the future; they are also remedies for the remains of sin, and, by acts of the opposite virtues, they remove the habits acquired by evil living. Neither indeed was there ever in the Church of God any way accounted surer to turn aside the impending chastisement of the Lord, than that men should, with true sorrow of mind, practice these works of penitence." Council of Trent, *Penance and Extreme Unction*, 8.

porary strategy for dealing with our pornographic culture is to recover medieval practices of cultivating affective devotion to the sensuous, suffering body of Jesus.[51]

But there is a fourth point to be made here, which pertains in particular to married individuals. Liturgically encountered representations of Jesus' naked body are typically located behind the altar, in the direct visual field of the worshipper during the Eucharistic prayer. Accordingly, this moment of gazing upon Jesus' body is the *beginning* of a liturgical movement and sequence that leads the worshipper *beyond* this initial experience and affective gaze. This is an obvious but crucial point. In the context of the Eucharistic liturgy, the worshipper is led from the sight of Christ's naked body to direct contact with that very Body, to a unitive embrace of him in the Eucharist.[52] This liturgical sequence, it should be noted, coordinates, stepwise, with engagement of the other senses, from *hearing* the Word read and preached, to *smelling* incensed aroma, to *tasting* its bread-and-wine-like presence, and finally to the culmination in touch and union. The crucial point here is that the Eucharistic liturgy does not allow one simply to remain gazing affectedly at the body of Jesus, however therapeutic that might be in itself. Rather, the liturgy moves one from sight, through the other senses, finally to touch and communion.[53] The significance of this is that the act of touch, and all that it involves, is in a sense the opposite of the sense of sight. We are affected by both what we see and what we touch, but in very different ways. One can see without being seen, but one cannot touch without simultaneously being touched. Touch is inexorably bilateral and mutual, vulnerable and intimate,[54] while

51. It would be prudent, of course, to find strategies for monitoring and responding to the possibilities for self-deception in this regard.

52. At least in a context where Eucharistic communion and reception are practiced in both their sacramental and spiritual modalities, that is, where the sacraments are received *both* with proper affectivity *and* physically, both "sacramentally" and "spiritually," as Thomas Aquinas put it. See *ST*, III q. 80, a. 1.

53. Interestingly, many medieval descriptions of the spiritual life narrate a movement from seeing to touching God, since both physically and spiritually touch is union, and union with God is the ultimate goal.

54. This claim about touch would need to be nuanced in relation to the issue of sexual violence, which of course is quite germane to the topic of pornography, given the high frequency of aggression in popular porn videos, documented in the research of conference contributor Erica Scharrer. In one sense, of course, such violence is a form of physical touching, but clearly the opposite of what is intended here, especially the ab-

sight is often none of these.[55] Touch simultaneously and immediately affects both the one touching and the one touched. Touch implicates, so to speak, both subject and object in a way that sight does not. In direct physical contact, accordingly, there is both less objectification *of* the one touched and more vulnerability *to* the one touched. Tactile voyeurism is an oxymoron.

The implications for healing a pornographic sensibility are not far to seek. Pornography entails the *exclusive* cultivation of visual titillation, a stultifying dominance of the sense of sight, a remaining arrested in affected gaze, which both psychologically and even physically can inhibit one from having *real* contact with the *real* bodies of *real* spouses, in *real* sexual union.[56] Porn is the refusal, and ultimately the inability, to enter into real physical sexual relationships. It is premature closure, constricted affectivity, arrested experience; it is self-enclosed, unimplicated, invulnerable. The one caught in pornography can no longer touch and be touched. If so, then Eucharistic liturgy, which begins with affective vision but is inexorably consummated in unitive contact, enacts precisely what is missing in porn. Perhaps, accordingly, Eucharistic liturgy can function as a kind of therapeutic practice or exercise for relearning how to sense and relate to real bodies properly, in effect what James A. K. Smith has called "micropractices," "disciplinary formations that begin to reconfigure our relation to the wider world." The point here is not to sexualize the Eucharist, but rather to suggest a structural parallel, such that Eucharistic practice might be a sacramental strategy—a "microtraining that subtly and unconsciously trains us"[57]—for the reformation of a pornographic sensibility, to

---

sence of genuine mutuality of touch in such acts. This fact also makes the clerical abuse crisis all the more tragic as it impedes the possibility of a chaste touch.

55. Their respective modalities may be distinct as well. Note that the pattern here is from *visual consumption to tactile reception.* Is there a subtle but important distinction here? Obviously, at one level, both consumption and reception involve coming to have or possess something, but at another level they may entail very different ways of relating to that which is possessed. *Consumption* involves a measure of active control over its object, while *reception* entails a dimension of passivity, in the literal sense of undergoing or even suffering (*passio*) that consumption lacks.

56. As the essays in this volume by Jill Manning and William M. Struthers and Kyler Mulhauser explain.

57. James K. A. Smith, *Imagining the Kingdom: How Worship Works* (Grand Rapids, Mich.: Baker Academic, 2013), 143. Indeed, Smith suggests (143n86) that viewing

foster a change in the way one relates to other embodied persons, including a sexual relationship with one's spouse.

This, in sum, is the second meaning of the *sensus Christi*, sensing the body of Christ as object. The Eucharistic liturgy reforms the pornographic sensibility by first inviting us to gaze on Jesus's naked, suffering body and then to hear, touch, taste, and receive his body in communion. At the same time, the Eucharist helps to rewrite the pornographic narrative regarding the human body.

At this point, there is a Eucharistic convergence of the two meanings of *sensus Christi* considered thus far. As believers are drawn liturgically toward the Body of Christ as object of their loving, compassionate, meditative gaze (*sensus Christi* as objective genitive), which culminates in sacramental reception of and union with his Body, they increasingly share Christ's own mode of sensing, his own mode of viewing and experiencing and interacting with others—his ability to see others, including their bodies, rightly. That is, they come more and more to have "the mind of Christ" (*sensus Christi* as subjective genitive), as the Lord shifts from being the *object* of sense perception, to being in some sense the *subject* of it.

Sensus Christi 3: Sensing *in* the Body of Christ

In the liturgical context assumed here, the sacramental encounter with Christ is never an individualistic or private affair. Rather, it occurs communally and corporately *in* the Body of Christ, gathered around Christ its head, who is present in a unique way in their midst "when the church prays and sings, for he has promised 'where two or three are gathered together in my name there am I in the midst of them'" (Mt 18:20).[58] As Joseph Cardinal Ratzinger, later Pope Benedict XVI, once put the matter: "The most intimate mystery of communion between God and man is accessible in the sacrament of the Body of the Risen Lord; conversely, then, the mystery lays claim to our bodies and is realized in a Body."[59] Cardinal Ratzinger intimates that the pur-

---

pornography is itself such a "micropractice" in which one is "trained" "to construe women as objects available to be selected, viewed, touched, and enjoyed at the whim of the user."

58. Vatican Council II, *Sacrosanctum Concilium*, 7.

59. Joseph Cardinal Ratzinger, *Behold the Pierced One* (San Francisco, Calif.: Ignatius

suit of holiness by individual believers, and in their individual bodies, occurs most properly within the corporate Body of Christ. Indeed, Vatican II insisted that the grace of union with Christ in his paschal mystery, described above and so central to the therapeutic strategy here pursued, is received most fully in this ecclesial Body: "In that Body the life of Christ is poured into the believers who, through the sacraments, are united in a hidden and real way to Christ who suffered and was glorified."[60]

This may be expressed as a third form of *sensus Christi*, distinct from, but intimately related to the first two. For, properly understood, the experience of Christ—as *both* mystical subject *and* as therapeutic object of our own sensibility—is communal and corporate; neither one is ever experienced alone. Here, then, the *sensus Christi* means sensing *in* the Body of Christ, understood not just as Christ the individual, but as Christ the head of his body, the Church.[61] From this perspective, the third meaning of *sensus Christi* refers to the way the believer participates in a sensibility that is not only personally Christlike, but also communally ecclesial. With a nod to Ignatius of Loyola, what emerges here is both *sentire cum Christo* and *sentire cum ecclesia*—to sense with Christ and with the Church. Such a communal sacramental sensibility runs directly contrary to the *private, individualistic* character of the pornography sensibility. As Morrow insightfully notes, "given that pornography is not simply an individual problem, but one of broadly distributed cultural practices, an adequate response must offer an embodied, social, institutionally located alternative to abstraction and objectification, by which individuals can be formed and shaped toward a different set of ends within a different narrative."[62]

This third dimension of *sensus Christi* may also be coordinated

---

Press, 1986), 113. My thanks again to Fr. Robert Imbelli for bringing this text to my attention.

60. Vatican Council II, *Lumen Gentium*, 7.

61. "The Eucharist is never an event involving just two, a dialogue between Christ and me. Eucharistic Communion is aimed at a compete reshaping of my own life. It breaks up man's entire self and creates a new 'we.' Communion with Christ is necessarily also communication with all who belong to him: therein I myself become a part of the new bread he is creating by the resubstantiation of the whole of earthly reality." Joseph Cardinal Ratzinger, "Eucharist and Mission," in *Pilgrim Fellowship of Faith*, 78. Again, my thanks to Fr. Robert Imbelli for noting this text.

62. Morrow, "Pornography and Penance," 74.

helpfully with the liturgical movement. For the Eucharistic reception of Christ and union with Christ in the liturgy is a kind of pivot or hinge, which reverses the direction of liturgical movement. Having received Christ, the believer resumes his place in the Body of Christ along with the rest of the gathered community. Then, the individual within the community is sent out into the world to live out the universal vocation to holiness in the world.

> The liturgy in its turn moves the faithful, filled with "the paschal sacraments," to be "one in holiness" (Post-communion for both Masses of Easter Sunday); it prays that "they may hold fast in their lives to what they have grasped by their faith" (Collect of the Mass for Tuesday of Easter Week); the renewal in the Eucharist of the covenant between the Lord and man draws the faithful into the compelling love of Christ and sets them on fire. From the liturgy, therefore, and especially from the Eucharist, as from a font, grace is poured forth upon us; and the sanctification of men in Christ.[63]

In short, the "liturgy is the summit toward which the activity of the Church is directed," and "at the same time it is the font from which all her power flows."[64]

Given the oft-noted importance of "accountability groups" for assisting those struggling with pornography, from the perspective adopted here, the ecclesial and Eucharistic gathering could function as just such a group. Here is a single Body, with a single Head, striving together to share in the "mind of Christ" (*sensus Christi*)—seeking to participate in a sacramental sensibility; seeking to sense all of creation with a single, sanctified sensorium; and seeking to see the bodies of other human beings, as sacred, precious, and inviolable creatures to be cared for and cherished with the dignity proper to persons created in the image of God. More concretely, such support groups might benefit from more intentional and explicit integration of such practices as sacramental reconciliation, meditation (including on religious art and iconography, as treated elsewhere in this volume), and Eucharistic adoration into the actual structure of their meetings.[65] In this

63. Vatican Council II, *Sacrosanctum Concilium*, 10.

64. Vatican Council II, *Sacrosanctum Concilium*, 10.

65. This aspect of the *sensus Christi* intersects with the research findings among neuroscientists. As Struthers notes in this volume, "Research on breaking addictions indicates that two keys to success are a desire to end the compulsion and social support. Pornography usage is typically characterized by secrecy and feelings of shame, and

way, "having the mind of Christ" is truly a corporate and communal reality.

Conclusion: An Eschatological Coda

The approach to the sin of pornography here does not pretend to be sufficient in and of itself to overcome the problem. Rather, it seeks to provide an overarching theological framework within which to approach the matter. It also wishes to recommend an *ecclesial* context, a *liturgical* practice, and a *sacramental* orientation around and within which the various other strategies for overcoming pornography might find their place.

Finally, it would be pastorally important and sensitive to acknowledge that, consistent with the ultimately eschatological character of the Church in the world (as stressed by Vatican II), participation in these three dimensions of the *sensus Christi* must remain incomplete in this life. For many, the struggle with pornography will not be fully victorious until the complete restoration of all things in Christ. In this life, the believer clings to the cross especially, even as he strives in hope to live in the power of the Resurrection. In this respect, the enduring and ongoing posture of the believer who struggles with pornography is that of the perennially penitent. For, in its current pilgrimage toward eschatological fullness, toward *the full measure of the stature*—and *sensus—of Christ* (Eph 4:13), "the Church, embracing in its bosom sinners, at the same time holy and always in need of being purified, always follows the way of penance and renewal."[66]

---

users who desire to break their compulsion often attempt to do so alone so that their secrecy can be maintained. This, however, is almost always a recipe for failure. Social support is necessary, and the Christian community as the Body of Christ can play an essential role in sustaining people in recovery." See chapter 3, 80.

66. Vatican Council II, *Lumen Gentium*, 8.

NICHOLAS OGLE

12 ⇸ The Corporal Works of Mercy and the Sacramental Imagination

The allure of pornography in today's society derives in large part from our modern confusion about the telos or purpose of the human body. Modernity's exaltation of freedom over and against nature has resulted in the progressive evacuation of meaning and purpose from human embodiment.[1] It is no longer clear to us what value our bodies can have, other than that which we choose to confer upon them. In other words, the body has come to be viewed primarily as an object to be used for purposes extrinsic to it, rather than as a window into the intrinsic finality of the human person. In this context, the treatment of others' bodies is governed by purely formal principles, such as those of avoiding harm and respecting the rights of others. However, as the current pornography epidemic demonstrates, these principles are ultimately incapable of calling our misuse of the human body fundamentally into question, at least by themselves. That is to say, unless we situate them within a teleological vision of who we are and the end for which we were made, they will be ineffective in guarding against our sinful propensity towards pleasure- and power-seeking habits that objectify others. We simply cannot live in loving relationship with others without having some governing idea of the telos or purpose of our bodies.

Accordingly, in this chapter, I will examine one particular way that

1. Sarah Coakley has similarly noted in her recent work that there is "a striking contemporary confusion about 'desire' itself," which she seeks to address through "the recovery of a new vision of 'ascetic' life." In line with what I will argue in this chapter, she writes that "it is the complete intertwinement of physical and *spiritual* in desire that first has to be acknowledged afresh, as well as its moral and 'eschatological' goals, if we are to reverse the modern shrinkage of thought about desire." Sarah Coakley, *The New Asceticism: Sexuality, Gender and the Search for God* (London: Bloomsbury Continuum, an imprint of Bloomsburg Publishing, 2015), 4, 6–7.

the Church as the Body of Christ can help us recover a sense of the human body's intrinsic meaning. In a broad sense, the Church does this by virtue of its comprehensive theological vision, marked by a belief in the goodness of creation, our sinfulness and need for redemption, and our orientation toward the eternal enjoyment of God in the communion of saints. It is ultimately to this final beatitude that our bodies direct us, while also providing the means for our initial participation in this communion here and now. By living in accordance with the Catholic profession that we have been created *for* something—or rather, for *Someone*—the Body of Christ bears witness to a meaning inherent in the human body that transcends its capacity to be made into an object of pleasure or domination by another.

My aim in this chapter is to show how one particular ecclesial practice rooted in this theological vision of the human body can provide an antidote to the pornography epidemic—namely, the practice of the corporal works of mercy. The corporal works of mercy are known by most of us as the deeds listed in the parable of the sheep and the goats (Mt 25:31–46): feeding the hungry, giving drink to the thirsty, clothing the naked, ransoming the captive, sheltering the homeless, visiting the sick and the prisoner, and burying the dead. They are sacrificial acts performed with one's body for the service of another's body, which by their very nature communicate love and respect for the human person. In what follows, I will argue that the corporal works of mercy are a particularly effective antidote to the allure of pornography precisely because they consist in bodily practices and therefore can directly attend to the underlying cause of the pornography epidemic—that is, our confusion about the meaning and purpose of human embodiment.

In order to establish why these bodily acts are so important in our efforts to counter the pornography epidemic, we will begin by looking more closely at the nature of pornography, exploring the way in which it warps our imagination and undermines our capacity for loving relationship with others. Drawing on the work of Karol Wojtyła (later Saint Pope John Paul II), I will suggest that pornography exploits our modern confusion about the meaning and purpose of the body by instilling the belief that the value of a person is defined by his or her ability to become a source of pleasure for another. Wojtyła helps us see how this "pornographic" vision of the human body subverts the order of values proper to loving relationships, and how the recognition of the dignity of the human person is essential to the healing of our vision. Following this discussion, we will then consider one other recent theological response to the pornography epidemic, that of Reinhard Hütter. In his writing on this topic, Hütter argues that the pornography epidemic needs to be addressed at its hidden root, which he identifies as the vice of acedia or spiritual apathy. As a remedy to this spiritual sickness, Hütter recommends the intentional and communal practice of prayer, especially that of the Angelic Warfare Confraternity promoted by the Dominican order. In my analysis of Hütter's work, I will argue that while his account certainly helps us understand the psychology behind the widespread use of pornography, his response to the problem is ultimately incomplete because it offers a primarily spiritual solution that neglects the significance of our involvement in social practices that can deeply shape our vision of the human person. Thus, I will suggest that to overcome pornography's temptation, we need to draw closer to God not only through spiritual intimacy, but also bodily intimacy. This intimacy is realized, first and foremost, in the liturgy of the Eucharist, when we eat Christ's Body and drink his Blood. Yet, as St. Augustine and many other Church fathers recognized, it is also realized in our merciful response to Christ in the frail bodies of the poor, even if we are often unaware of whom it is that we meet in these encounters.[2]

Thus, I will argue that the ecclesial practice of the corporal works of mercy offers a way of releasing the grip of pornography on our imagination that is more effective than that proposed by Hütter, precisely because of the manner in which it instills in us a sacramental vision of the human body. In so doing, I will draw upon St. Augustine's theology of the works of mercy, which is perhaps the most profound exploration of any Church father on the sacramental character of these acts. As we will see, for Augustine, the works of mercy demonstrate the sacramental principle of the Incarnation—namely, that our

2. For a summary of the treatment of this theme in early Christianity, see Richard Finn, *Almsgiving in the Later Roman Empire* (New York: Oxford University Press, 2006), 183–84.

redemption lies not in fleeing the material world, but in following the Word made flesh, who in his life, death, and resurrection invites us to find eternal life by entering more deeply into our bodily existence.[3] Instead of seeing the body as a hindrance or as simply irrelevant to the spiritual healing necessary to overcome the allure of pornography, Augustine shows us how, by virtue of the Incarnation, the body is in fact the privileged means for such a renewal of our vision.

The Pornographic Imagination

One of the most insightful investigations into the pornographic imagination is that of Karol Wojtyła in *Love and Responsibility*. Although a proper treatment of this text in its entirety is not possible here, our understanding of the pornographic imagination can nevertheless be deepened by a brief consideration of Wojtyła's analysis of the phenomenon of "sensuality." By this, Wojtyła means the spontaneous movement of the passions elicited by the presence of someone of the other sex, such that his or her body is experienced as a possible object of use for one's own pleasure. Such a movement, Wojtyła explains, "is completely blind to the person and oriented only toward the sexual value linked to the 'body.'"[4] In other words, it is a sort of pre-personal reality of human interaction that functions on an almost instinctual level. Understood as such, sensuality is not in itself morally evil or morally good, but merely a natural phenomenon that arises spontaneously from contact between persons of different sexes.

While Wojtyła indeed acknowledges a natural goodness to sensuality, he nevertheless maintains that this goodness cannot be unequivocally affirmed, since its object—the human person—ultimately demands a different kind of relation than one of mere sensuality. As he puts it, sensuality "must be joined in a complete and mature relation to the person, since without this it is definitely not love."[5] Lacking

3. For an excellent treatment of this principle, see Carol Harrison, *Beauty and Revelation in the Thought of Saint Augustine* (New York: Oxford University Press, 1992). She writes: "The temporal, created realm is therefore not simply to be left to one side until man has purified himself, but is instrumental in his purification and needs to be turned towards and used by fallen man" (180).

4. Karol Wojtyła, *Love and Responsibility* (Boston, Mass.: Pauline Books and Media, 2013), 91.

5. Wojtyła, *Love and Responsibility*, 90.

such integration, it "threatens to devalue the person" by making him or her into merely an object of use.[6] According to Wojtyła, this integration involves the subordination of the sexual value of the person's body to the value of the person whose body it is. Such a subordination is necessary for a loving relationship because "every person of the other sex possesses above all the value as a person, and only then does he possess some sexual value."[7] In other words, the sexual value of the body is secondary to the value of the person because it pertains merely to a particular property of being, whereas the value of the person pertains to the entirety of his or her existence.

Although Wojtyła views the tendency to subvert this proper order as a manifestation of original sin, his exploration of the phenomenon of sensuality is more philosophical than theological, and thus pertains more to *how* this takes place than *why* it does. His analysis therefore focuses on how this kind of behavior results from the fact that the sexual value of the body and the value of the person are not recognized in the same way. Wojtyła writes, "the reaction to the value of the person cannot be something as direct as the reaction to the sexual value linked to the 'body' of this concrete person."[8] Unlike the sexual value of the body, the personhood of another "has an intellectual, conceptual character" and "is not the content of an impression."[9] That is to say, the recognition of the other as a person deserving of love does not arise in the immediate, almost instinctual way that sexual desire sometimes does. Unlike the movement of sensuality, respect for the dignity of another person requires a more concerted effort of the will. Thus, in order to be integrated into a loving relationship between persons, Wojtyła maintains that the impression made by the movement of sensuality needs to be "elevated to the truth that this being is a person."[10] And this truth can only be recognized and honored through the exercise of one's moral agency and responsibility, in which the movement of sensuality cannot be considered a sufficient basis for interaction with someone of the other sex.

6. Wojtyła, *Love and Responsibility*, 90.
7. Wojtyła, *Love and Responsibility*, 105.
8. Wojtyła, *Love and Responsibility*, 105.
9. Wojtyła, *Love and Responsibility*, 105.
10. Wojtyła, *Love and Responsibility*, 105.

To return now to the topic of the pornographic imagination, we should note how, in his analysis, Wojtyła is keenly aware that the movement of sensuality can be elicited even in the absence of any physical contact with another person. As he explains, "not only the exterior senses serve sensuality; the interior senses such as imagination and memory serve it as well. Through the mediation of each of them, one can establish contact even with the 'body' of a person physically absent by experiencing the value of that body inasmuch as it constitutes 'a possible object of use.'"[11] Wojtyła notes that this kind of engagement of the interior senses often happens spontaneously and does not require any external stimulus. At other times it occurs in the presence of another, but "when the body of the other person is not in the least treated as an object of use," such as when it is "an object of some research, study, or art."[12] In such cases, sensuality "attempts to pull into its orbit the entire relation to the body and to the person."[13] The interior experience of this sensual force, however, does not thereby determine one's entire relation to the other person. Rather, Wojtyła maintains that such an instinctive engagement of one's interior senses can be channeled into a loving relationship with the person whose body is viewed as an object of sexual desire, so long as this tendency is subordinated to respect for his or her dignity as a person.

However, in addition to this spontaneous engagement of the interior senses, Wojtyła is also concerned with how imagination and memory can be deliberately engaged in the service of sensuality through the consumption of pornography. This intentional use of the interior senses, Wojtyła argues, is morally evil because it devalues the person whose body is exposed and thus involves a distortion of the truth about human love. It is important to understand that, for Wojtyła, the nature of pornography cannot be fully explained in terms of its content alone. In order to adequately distinguish it from the exposure of the human body in the fine arts, it is necessary to recognize how pornography specifically "aims at evoking in the recipient of this work ... a conviction that the sexual value is the only essential value

11. Wojtyła, *Love and Responsibility*, 91.
12. Wojtyła, *Love and Responsibility*, 91.
13. Wojtyła, *Love and Responsibility*, 91.

of the person, and that love is nothing else but experiencing or co-experiencing this value."[14] In other words, pornography is defined by the fact that in its representation of the human body it intentionally seeks to elicit a movement of sensuality in its consumers by engaging their imagination and memory—by inviting them, as the *Catechism* puts it, to immerse themselves in "the illusion of a fantasy world."[15] In this way, pornography distorts our vision, instilling in us a pornographic imagination such that we begin to see others not as persons worthy of love and respect, but merely as possible objects of use for our own enjoyment.

To sum up this discussion, we might say that pornography represents the human being in such a way that it *reveals the body, while concealing the person*. The problem with pornography is therefore not that it shows too *much* of the person, but that it shows too *little*. It represents the human body with indifference towards the person, who becomes nothing more than an anonymous object. Though the body is exposed, the personal meaning and purpose inscribed in the body remains hidden. By emphasizing the sexual value of the body in a manner that eclipses the value of the person, pornography, as Wojtyła puts it, "destroys the complete image of this important fragment of human reality that consists in the love of a woman and a man."[16] The pornographic imagination determines the value of a human being according to the sexual value of his or her body, rather than according to his or her dignity as a person, thereby subverting the order of values proper to a loving relationship between persons. In this way, the pornographic imagination exploits our modern agnosticism of what the human body is for, instilling in us the conviction that a person is valuable only insofar as his or her body can become an object of use for another's pleasure.

Pornography and the Vice of Acedia

Among recent theological responses to the current pornography epidemic, one of the most compelling has been that of Reinhard Hüt-

14. Wojtyła, *Love and Responsibility*, 176.

15. *Catechism of the Catholic Church*, 2nd ed. (Washington, D.C.: United States Conference of Catholic Bishops, 2000), 2354.

16. Wojtyła, *Love and Responsibility*, 176.

ter. Drawing heavily upon the moral theology of St. Thomas Aquinas, Hütter's analysis of the widespread use of pornography is primarily psychological, concentrating on the spiritual and moral battle within the individual. Hütter stresses that while pornography appears to be concerned with the body, it is in fact a spiritual problem that is best dealt with using spiritual means. He writes, "One of the most pertinent lessons to be learned from Aquinas ... is that while the vice of lust has a carnal object, the root cause of this vice has a spiritual nature. It is one of the maladies of the soul. Thus, uprooting the vice of lust means attending to the spiritual nature of its root cause."[17] As Hütter goes on to explain, the hidden spiritual root of the lust that feeds the contemporary pornography epidemic is nothing other than the vice of acedia, commonly known as sloth, but perhaps better rendered as spiritual apathy.

According to Hütter, this vice manifests itself today as a collective state of spiritual apathy that issues in contempt for what is truly good. Such apathy undermines growth in the virtue of chastity by reinforcing social practices and institutions in which "the lust of the eyes and the flesh is both encouraged and easily facilitated."[18] The vice of acedia is therefore best understood not as mere laziness or sloth, but rather as an inward resistance and aversion to life with God. This attitude results from the fact that the Christian life involves an arduous struggle against engrained weaknesses and vices that can often be a cause for sorrow. As Aquinas puts it, "this divine good is a source of sadness for human beings because of the contrariety of the spirit to the flesh, since 'the flesh lusts against the spirit,' as the Apostle says in Gal 5:17. And so when desire of the flesh is dominant in human beings, they have distaste for spiritual good as contrary to their good."[19] In such a state, acedia can induce in one "the dislike, horror and detestation of the Divine good," ultimately resulting in the loss of the virtues of charity and hope.[20] And, as Hütter explains, in doing so, "*acedia* creates a void to

17. Reinhard Hütter, "The Virtue of Chastity and the Scourge of Pornography: A Twofold Crisis Considered in Light of Thomas Aquinas's Moral Theology," *The Thomist* 77, no. 1 (January 2013): 4.

18. Hütter, "The Virtue of Chastity," 23.

19. Thomas Aquinas, *De Malo*, q. 11, a. 3. For this translation, see *On Evil*, ed. Brian Davies, trans. Richard Regan (Oxford: Oxford University Press, 2003), 365–66.

20. Thomas Aquinas, *Summa Theologiae*, II-II q. 35, a. 3. For this translation, see

be filled not with what one has come to detest, the divine good, but with transient rushes of pleasure—primarily sexual pleasure—to ward off the *ennui* of life bereft of its *telos*, the divine good."[21]

But, as Hütter notes, "the *simulacra* that promise such rushes of pleasure betray."[22] That is, they only increase the void in our lives by intensifying our sense of craving. If left unchecked, acedia's aversion to life with God can result in a destructive despair. Concerning those in such a state, Aquinas writes that "due to the sadness conceived regarding spiritual goods, their minds then wander over the illicit things in which the carnal spirit takes pleasure. And in avoiding such sadness, we note the progression wherein human beings indeed first avoid spiritual goods and then attack them."[23] In other words, acedia can produce in us a sort of bored curiosity for illicit things, which is by no means innocent, but part of a process that can lead to contempt for friendship with God. In this respect, Hütter suggests that acedia has an affinity with the concepts of *Langeweile* and *ressentiment* developed in the phenomenological analyses of Martin Heidegger and Max Scheler.[24] As he puts it:

> The flight from sadness, which begins with avoiding and resisting spiritual goods and ends with attacking them, represents with uncanny accuracy the anti-Christian *ressentiment* typical of secular, post-Christian societies. The collective ideological, cultural, social, and political aversion to the divine good (previously received and embraced) might very well issue in a collective spiritual state of *acedia*.[25]

However, Hütter is clear that it is these modern concepts that need to be clarified in light of Aquinas's explicitly theological analysis of acedia, and not vice versa. He thus seeks to offer his account of the path acedia takes in bringing about these effects as a theological corrective that provides a more profound explanation of the pornography epidemic than its modern secular equivalents.

Fathers of the English Dominican Province, 5 vols. (Westminster, Md.: Christian Classics, 1948).

21. Hütter, "The Virtue of Chastity," 25–26.
22. Hütter, "The Virtue of Chastity," 26.
23. Aquinas, *De Malo*, q. 11, a. 4. For this translation, see *On Evil*, 370.
24. Hütter, "The Virtue of Chastity," 24–28.
25. Hütter, "The Virtue of Chastity," 26.

As a remedy to this downward spiral of the vice of acedia and the lust it breeds, Hütter proposes the communal practice of intercessory prayer. More specifically, he recommends the discipline of prayer practiced by the Angelic Warfare Confraternity promoted by the Dominican Order. Hütter regards this confraternity as "one of the most important spiritual initiatives that most directly addresses the problem of pornography."[26] According to Brian Mullady, OP, the confraternity "seeks to foster the connection between chastity and the other acquired and infused virtues, especially charity; which enables one to love and reverence [one's] own body as well as the bodies of others."[27] It does this through regular practices of prayer, such as the daily devotion:

> Dear Jesus, I know that every perfect gift and especially that of chastity depends on the power of your Providence. Without you, a mere creature can do nothing. Therefore, I beg you to defend by your grace the chastity and purity of my body and soul. And if I have ever imagined or felt anything that can stain my chastity and purity, blot it out, Supreme Lord of my powers, that I may advance with a pure heart in your love and service, offering myself on the most pure altar of your divinity all the days of my life. Amen.[28]

Through its exercise of the virtue of spiritual chastity, Hütter thinks that such a discipline of prayer "protects us most effectively from falling into spiritual apathy and its secular offspring, *ennui* and *ressentiment*."[29] "Far from being a convenient but inconsequential outlet of pious and prudish impulses," Hütter writes, "the Confraternity's practice of prayer reflects a pertinent theological truth about the efficaciousness of prayer."[30] While Hütter recognizes that such practices do not substitute for the kind of counseling or therapy needed in certain cases of pornography addiction, he nevertheless contends that "because the root of the problem is a spiritual one, the healing from the addictive behavior will ... ultimately be overcome only when the

26. Hütter, "The Virtue of Chastity," 36.

27. Fr. Brian T. Mullady, *The Angelic Warfare Confraternity*, 4th ed. (New Hope, Ky.: The St. Martin de Porres Lay Dominicans, 2006), 25. Cited in Hütter, "The Virtue of Chastity," 36–37.

28. Mullady, *Angelic Warfare Confraternity*, 32. Cited in Hütter, "The Virtue of Chastity," 37.

29. Reinhard Hütter, "Pornography and Acedia," *First Things* 222 (April 2012): 49.

30. Hütter, "The Virtue of Chastity," 37.

negative spiritual root [acedia] ... is eradicated."[31] And for this, he maintains, "an intentional discipline of prayer is essential."[32]

To suggest that someone who wishes to stop using pornography should seek to address the habit through the communal practice of prayer is fitting, insofar as the root of the pornography epidemic is indeed spiritual in nature. Hütter is correct to view this epidemic as a symptom of the *ennui* of a secular world that has lost its "transcendent calling to the love and friendship of God," leaving a void that our roaming spirit attempts to fill with pornography, only to find that all we have left, "when the act is completed, is a craving for stimulating a desire that will always remain unsatisfied."[33] But his recommendation of a communal practice of prayer as a spiritual remedy offers only a partial solution that, if considered by itself, risks trivializing the extent to which this spiritual root cause is intertwined with our bodily existence. Prudence, Hütter writes, is the helmsman of the ship of our moral agency, a helmsman who can only steer the ship rightly if properly formed in justice, courage, and temperance. More specifically, Hütter recognizes that prudence in sexual matters is realized only in chastity.[34] As Aquinas emphasized, however, our ship can reach its port in eternal beatitude with God only if our exercise of the cardinal virtues of prudence, justice, courage, and temperance is infused with the gift of the theological virtues of faith, hope, and charity. Charity is the virtue whereby we love God for his own sake and love in God our neighbor made in God's image. But loving our neighbor requires not only spiritual but also corporal acts. Hütter fails to give due attention to the fact that our state of spiritual apathy is ineradicably bound up with certain bodily practices, and that a change in these practices can be a means of receiving the grace necessary to live in charity and chastity as we reorient our lives toward our end of friendship with God. Of course, this is not to say that the discipline of prayer and the practice of the corporal works of mercy are somehow in competition with one another. Rather, what I am suggesting is that we recognize how these

31. Hütter, "The Virtue of Chastity," 36n66.
32. Hütter, "The Virtue of Chastity," 38.
33. Hütter, "Pornography and Acedia," 46–47.
34. Hütter, "Pornography and Acedia," 47–48.

spiritual and bodily practices can mutually reinforce one another, and ultimately bring about our healing in both body and soul.

Saint Augustine's Theology of the Corporal Works of Mercy

Turning now to consider the early Church's theology of the corporal works of mercy, we find in this practice a basis for a holistic response to the pornography epidemic. The Church fathers shared a deeply sacramental understanding of Christ's solidarity with the poor and suffering, rooted in a common reading of the parable of the sheep and the goats in Matthew 25. This parable was the focus of reflection in various theological treatises such as St. Cyprian's *Works and Almsgiving*, and the theme of the identification of Christ with the poor was memorialized in the Church's consciousness through such hagiographical works as Sulpitius Severus's *Life of St. Martin*.[35] In the *Life*, Severus famously writes of how St. Martin, after dividing his cloak in half to clothe a freezing beggar, received a nocturnal vision of Christ, who appeared to him wearing the same portion of the cloak that he had given away. Alluding to the passage from Matthew, Jesus says in the vision that "Martin, who is still but a catechumen, clothed me with his robe."[36] Accounts such as this indelibly stamped the Christological significance of the corporal works of mercy upon the early Christian imagination. Simply put, the works of mercy were considered by the early Church and the subsequent Christian tradition to be sacramental acts—that is, acts "that established a contact point between the believer and God."[37] This is visually evident in the oil on panel *The Seven Works of Charity* (AD 1504) attributed to the Master of Alkmaar in which Jesus Christ appears among those who are hungry, thirsty, naked, dead, strangers, sick, and imprisoned (Figs. 12-1, 12-2, 12-3, 12-4, and 12-5).

35. For a survey of this theme in early Latin Christian literature, see Boniface Ramsey, "Almsgiving in the Latin Church: The Late Fourth and Early Fifth Centuries," *Theological Studies* 43, no. 2 (June 1982): 226–30.

36. Sulpitius Severus, *On the Life of St. Martin*, chapter 3. For this translation, see vol. 11 of *The Nicene and Post-Nicene Fathers*, ed. Philip Schaff and Henry Wace (Peabody, Mass.: Hendrickson, 1994).

37. Gary Anderson, *Charity: The Place of the Poor in the Christian Tradition* (New Haven, Conn.: Yale University Press, 2013), 7.

Perhaps the most systematic and profound exploration of the sacramental nature of the corporal works of mercy is to be found in the work of St. Augustine. Augustine reflects upon the theological meaning of the works of mercy not only in his more theoretical works such as the *City of God* and *On The Trinity*, but also in many of his sermons and letters.[38] In one particular sermon on the humility of Christ, Augustine exhorts his congregation to

> fear Christ up above, recognize him down below. Have Christ up above lavishing bounty, recognize him here needing charity. Here he's poor, there he's rich. That Christ is poor for us here, he tells us himself: "I was hungry, thirsty, naked, a stranger, in prison." And to some he said "You helped me," to some "You didn't help me."[39]

In this passage, Augustine draws upon his doctrine of the *totus Christus* to shed light on the nature of Christ's ongoing earthly presence in the poor. In addition to emphasizing the sacramental unity of the Church and the hypostatic union of Christ's humanity and divinity, for Augustine, this important Christological doctrine also involves Jesus' solidarity with the suffering.[40]

Augustine understands this mystery of Christ's solidarity with the poor neither in a strictly spiritual sense nor in an exclusively corporal way. He is not simply exhorting his congregation to acknowledge

38. As Peter Brown comments, wealth and poverty were not considered proper topics for systematic exploration and were often dealt with in pastoral works. See *Through the Eye of a Needle: Wealth, the Fall of Rome, and the Making of Christianity in the West, 350–550 A.D.* (Princeton, N.J.: Princeton University Press, 2012), 55.

39. Augustine, *Sermo* 123.4. For this translation, see "Sermons 94A–147A," vol. 3, bk. 4 of *The Works of Saint Augustine: A Translation for the 21st Century*, ed. J. E. Rotelle, trans. E. Hill (Brooklyn, N.Y.: New City Press, 1992), 246. Hereafter this series is abbreviated as *WSA*.

40. Admittedly, it is not always clear whom Augustine has in mind when speaking about the poor with whom Christ identifies. Sometimes he will specify that this group consists only of those needy who are Christians, whereas at other times the opposite is implied. For discussion of this ambiguity in Augustine's doctrine of the *totus Christus*, see Kimberly Baker, "Augustine's Doctrine of the *Totus Christus*: Reflecting on the Church as Sacrament of Unity," *Horizons* 37, no. 1 (Spring 2010): 18. As Baker notes, in one place, Augustine explicitly extends Christ's solidarity to anyone who is poor, regardless of their membership in the visible Church: "Christ is destitute when any poor person is destitute" (*Sermo* 38.8). In light of this ambiguity, one might say that although the poverty with which Christ identifies always retains an ecclesial meaning for Augustine, it is not necessarily restricted to any particular category of people, such as those strictly within the visible Church.

that, because Christ was poor when he lived on earth, he is therefore in some sort of detached solidarity with the needy, despite the fact that he is now in heaven and no longer suffers himself. Nor is he asserting with a univocal literalism that the poor really *are* Christ nor that their suffering *is* his actual suffering. Rather, he conceives of this unity between Christ and the poor in terms of the Incarnation. The same love out of which Christ emptied himself and took the form of a servant is that by which he continues to be united with the weak and vulnerable among us. One might say that the poor constitute a sacrament of Christ's humanity, insofar as with the eyes of faith we recognize in their poverty—that is, in their bodily need—the mystery of the Incarnation. Thus, Augustine writes, "Understand that where weakness is displayed before your eyes, there godhead lies hidden."[41] And elsewhere: "You are all looking forward to greeting Christ seated in heaven. Attend to him lying under the arches, attend to him hungry, attend to him shivering with cold, attend to him needy, attend to him a foreigner."[42]

Underlying this pastoral instruction is the fundamental truth that while Christ's solidarity with the poor is essentially a spiritual solidarity, it is not thereby any less of a corporal solidarity. Indeed, it is perhaps best understood as a sacramental solidarity, in which one encounters Christ precisely by responding mercifully to the need of one's neighbor. From this sacramental perspective, the body is not seen as an obstacle to salvation, but precisely as the means God has chosen to bring about our healing. For Augustine, it is specifically through the practice of the works of mercy that we become active participants in this healing and thereby develop a sacramental imagination in which we begin to see the body rightly. In this respect, Augustine's theology of the works of mercy offers an incarnational perspective from which to address the pornography epidemic. That is to say, it recognizes that just as God accomplished his salvific work in Christ not by avoiding the flesh, but by becoming incarnate, so do we come to participate

41. Augustine, *Expositio* 40.1. For the English text, see "Expositions on the Psalms 33–50," vol. 3, bk. 16 of *WSA*, ed. J. E. Rotelle, trans. M. Boulding (Hyde Park, N.Y.: New City Press, 2000), 226.

42. Augustine, *Sermo* 25.8. For the English text, see "Sermons 20–50," vol. 3, bk. 2 of *WSA*, ed. J. E. Rotelle, trans. E. Hill (Brooklyn, N.Y.: New City Press, 1990), 86.

in our redemption by means of our bodily actions. Thus, while the pornography epidemic certainly has a spiritual root, this does not necessarily mean that the most appropriate solution is strictly spiritual in character. Rather, as Augustine suggests, the Incarnation reveals the opposite to be the case. Our spiritual acedia has resulted in actions that cause bodily harm, and it is through bodily acts of charity that our spiritual healing is accomplished.

One reason why merely spiritual approaches are so attractive is that it can seem overly simplistic to say that a particular action can bring about such a profound spiritual renewal. Surely what is needed is an interior conversion, not simply external conformity to some rule of behavior. To respond to this criticism, it is important to note how Augustine understands the practice of the works of mercy to involve more than the various exterior actions. As evident in the passage quoted above, Augustine thinks that the exterior actions also involve a corresponding interior recognition of Christ by faith. This is not to say that Augustine imagines there to be some kind of special knowledge given to those who perform works of mercy. He was well aware that most of our encounters with those in need are rather ordinary and mundane. While we may at times enjoy a kind of spiritual awareness that Christ is sacramentally present in the person we are serving, more often than not we are oblivious to this hidden reality, perhaps due to the overwhelming need of the other, or a sense of the futility of what seems to be an inconsequential action. Thus, when practicing works of mercy, we need not search for some sign of Christ's presence other than the poverty of our neighbor. Recall that in the parable in Matthew 25, not even those who practiced the works of mercy knew that in so doing they were serving Christ.[43] Augustine takes this to mean that our recognition of Christ comes through nothing other than our concrete response to the bodily need of the poor and suffering. Just as in the Gospel of Luke it is only in the breaking of the bread that Christ is recognized by the disciples who meet him on the road to Emmaus (Lk 24:13–35), so too Christ hidden in the poor is recognized only in the merciful act itself.

43. For an insightful reflection upon the ignorance of those serving Christ in the poor, see Simone Weil, *Gravity and Grace* (New York: Routledge, 2002), 45–46.

It is precisely through the practice of the works of mercy that our vision is transformed. This is because a charitable response to the poor costs us something—not merely our material wealth, but more fundamentally, our pride in our own material and spiritual self-sufficiency. In the implicit recognition of Christ in our suffering neighbor, we simultaneously recognize ourselves as poor, insofar as we share the same corporal existence and are always at risk of having insufficient means to provide for ourselves. In other words, we recognize our bodily existence itself as a kind of poverty. In practicing the works of mercy, the goal is therefore not to eliminate poverty, but, in a certain sense, to accept it, recognizing in it the way that God has prepared for us to enter into communion with him and one another. In this acceptance of poverty, we imitate the Word made flesh, who, as Paul says, "became poor although he was rich, so that by his poverty you might become rich" (2 Cor 8:9). Furthermore, alongside this material poverty, Augustine recognizes a corresponding spiritual poverty. He points out how even those of us who live now in material comfort stand with the destitute in equal relation to God, before whom we are all creatures who are poor in spirit. No matter our ability to care for our material well-being, we all must entreat our heavenly Father for the spiritual blessings only he can provide. Augustine suggests that the practice of the corporal works of mercy awakens us to this mystery in which we too find our own redemption.

This does not mean, however, that Augustine thinks such acts will in themselves be sufficient to meet our spiritual needs, apart from our participation in the sacramental life of the Church. According to Augustine, these needs can only be met by what he, in Book X of the *City of God*, calls "true sacrifice." "The true sacrifice," Augustine writes, "is every act done in order that we might cling to God in holy fellowship, that is, every act which is referred to the final good in which we can be truly blessed." Although when he speaks of true sacrifice Augustine is primarily thinking of Christ's sacrifice and our participation in it through the liturgy, he also uses the concept more broadly, claiming that "true sacrifices are works of mercy, whether shown to ourselves or shown to our neighbors, which are directed to God." However, Augustine is well aware that the merely exterior act of performing a work of mercy does not always involve true sacrifice. "Even the mercy which we extend to human beings," he writes, "is not a sacrifice if it is not done for God's sake."[44] On the one hand, Augustine means by this that practicing the works of mercy does not give one license to do evil or continue in sinful habits. As he puts it later on in the *City of God*, "People who are unwilling to give up their habitual evil and change for the better cannot be said to do works of mercy."[45] This is because one cannot cling to God by practicing works of mercy while simultaneously loving what separates one from Christ. Although the works of mercy can be a source of grace by which we become able to turn away from sin, they do not justify our persevering in it.

On the other hand, Augustine thinks that practicing the works of mercy for God's sake means that we should not think of practicing the corporal works of mercy as our own individual achievement but as an ecclesial action. The faith by which we recognize Christ in the poor is itself a gift that we have received through our participation in the sacramental life of the Church. It is through this sacramental participation that we are conformed to the mystery of God's merciful love, and thereby become capable of practicing the works of mercy as true sacrifices. In faith, we know that the mercy that we practice toward the hungry, thirsty, and naked, is not our own, but Christ's. Our actions are simply the ecclesial vehicle through which Christ is reconciling the world to himself. This insight into the ecclesial nature of the corporal works of mercy should inform our approach to them as an antidote to the pornography epidemic. In practicing the works of mercy, we should be attentive to the fact that our sacrificial actions are not merely instrumental for our own individual healing but already in themselves begin to bring about that communion in the Body of Christ to which we are all called. Our solidarity with those in need is a window, as it were, into the communion that the Church will share forever with Christ.

44. Augustine, *De Civitate Dei*, X.6. For the English text, see "The City of God: Chapters 1–10," vol. 1, bk. 6 of *WSA*, ed. B. Ramsey, trans. W. Babcock (Hyde Park, N.Y.: New City Press, 2012), 310–11.

45. Augustine, *De Civitate Dei*, XXI.27. For the English text, see "The City of God: Chapters 11–22," vol. 1, bk. 7 of *WSA*, ed. B. Ramsey, trans. W. Babcock (Hyde Park, N.Y.: New City Press, 2013), 490.

This theme is brought out explicitly in Augustine's insistence that it is by our works of mercy that we will be judged.[46] Reflecting on the day of judgment in Book I of *On the Trinity,* Augustine considers it particularly significant that in the parable of the sheep and the goats it is the "Son of Man" who comes to judge the nations. Augustine understands by this that Christ will appear in the last judgment not in "the form of God," but in "the form of man."[47] That is, he will appear in the form of his risen, wounded body. According to Augustine, Christ appears bodily so that he may be manifested to the just and the wicked alike: "Both good and bad, of course, are going to look upon the judge of the living and the dead, but the bad, we may be sure, will only be able to see him in the form by which he is the Son of man.... The form of God, however, in which he is equal to the Father, this the wicked will undoubtedly not see."[48] In accordance with the teaching of the beatitudes, Augustine maintains that this supreme gift is given only to the pure of heart. Thus, whereas for the just, the bodily sight of the Son of Man is an invitation to eternal rest, for the wicked it leads instead to their condemnation.

What is particularly of interest for us in this discussion is how Augustine accounts for this difference. Along with prior tradition, Augustine maintains that the wicked stand condemned due to their neglect of the poor. As the parable states rather starkly, they are convicted for failing to tend to Christ hidden in the hungry, naked, and homeless. Thus, in a rather forbidding tone, Augustine writes that "the day of judgment will arrive, and it will be an evil day for you if you have not understood about the needy, poor man."[49] But, on the other

46. It can perhaps be alarming to us how seriously Augustine took this message of Matthew 25. However, he was by no means alone in this strict interpretation. Almsgiving was widely considered by the Church Fathers to be a redemptive act that contributed in a singular way to making one acceptable before God. On this topic, see David J. Downs, *Charity, Reward, and Atonement in Early Christianity* (Waco, Tex.: Baylor University Press, 2016), 4–5. In addition, as Gary Anderson shows in *Sin: A History* (New Haven, Conn.: Yale University Press, 2009), the early Church "inherited this high valuation of alms from the Jews," who referred to it as "*the* commandment (*ha-mitsvah*) or the commandment that was on par with all others" (10). In Augustine, we find a similar assessment of the significance of almsgiving, albeit in a new Christological register.

47. Augustine, *De Trinitate,* I.29. For the English text, see "The Trinity," vol. 1, bk. 5 of *WSA*, ed. J. E. Rotelle, trans. E. Hill (Hyde Park, N.Y.: New City Press, 1991), 87–88.

48. Augustine, *De Trinitate,* I.28. For the English text, see *WSA*, vol. 1, bk. 5, 86–87.

49. Augustine, *Expositio* 40.2. For the English text, see WSA, vol. 3, bk. 16, 226.

hand, Augustine seems to suggest that those who have neglected to practice the works of mercy are also condemned by their aversion to Christ as he stands bodily before them. That is, they are judged by how they perceive him in his human form. Augustine writes in *On the Trinity*, "When the wicked see their judge, he will not seem good to them because the sight of him will not rejoice their hearts."[50] By this Augustine does not mean simply that the wicked will be saddened by Christ's judgment of their behavior. Rather, he means that the very bodily presence of Christ has this effect. The negative response of the wicked to the bodily presence of Christ therefore constitutes a self-condemnation, as it were. Their aversion to him is in itself a kind of judgment upon their lives.

But how do these two teachings relate to one another? Later on, in the same exposition of Psalm 40, we find Augustine making explicit their connection. There he writes concerning the practice of the works of mercy that "you are being invited to believe what you do not see, so that when you do see it you may not be shamed. Try to understand, then, about the needy, poor person; that is, about Christ."[51] This passage indicates that Augustine sees the practice of the works of mercy not simply as an objective standard by which we will be judged, but as something that subjectively determines how we will respond to the appearance of Christ on the last day. In other words, Augustine considers our ability to rejoice in the glory of Christ when he comes in the flesh to be wholly bound up with our experience of meeting him in the poor through the practice of the works of mercy. There are, as it were, two judgments, which both consist in our ability to recognize and rejoice at being in his presence. The first takes place now, insofar as Christ is sacramentally present in those around us who suffer. The second will occur at the last judgment, when Christ appears in his own crucified and risen flesh. The works of mercy are thus seen by Augustine as the privileged means by which our vision is transformed, making us capable of responding joyfully when the glory of Christ is finally revealed.

From this discussion of Augustine's theology of the corporal works

50. Augustine, *De Trinitate*, I.31. For the English text, see *WSA*, vol. 1, bk. 5, 89.
51. Augustine, *Expositio* 40.2. For the English text, see *WSA*, vol. 3, bk. 16, 227.

of mercy, two points are particularly important for our consideration of how this ecclesial practice can counteract the appeal of pornography. First, the way in which we will be judged by Christ is directly related to how we perceive the human body, both now and on the last day when Christ appears before us in the flesh. And second, an indispensable way in which we learn to behold the human body rightly is through the concrete practice of the works of mercy. If we fail to see the suffering bodies of others as proper occasions of extending love and mercy, we will ultimately be blind to the mercy of Christ when he appears bodily before us. However, if we conform ourselves to the mystery of Christ's self-emptying love through our bodily participation in the sacramental life of the Church and the practice of the works of mercy, we will readily rejoice when we look upon him in his human form. Instead of adopting a body-denying attitude, the Church invites us to see the body as the primary way by which to enter into communion with God and one another. In other words, the practice of the works of mercy instills in us a sacramental imagination by which we grow to recognize the dignity of our neighbors, some of whom may themselves have been exploited by the pornography industry.

Conclusion

In conclusion, I have argued that an indispensable way in which we cultivate a sacramental imagination is through the concrete practice of the works of mercy. In these encounters with Christ in the poor, we learn to see and relate to our bodies in a new way as gifts, which we have been mercifully given and through which we can communicate God's mercy to others. We learn to view the body not as something divided and separate from the person—that is, as an object to be managed, manipulated, and used—but as the particular mode of our existence as persons, which unites us to others and to God in Christ. As our discussion of Augustine's theology of the works of mercy has brought to light, Christ's healing of our spiritual separation from God is accomplished not only spiritually, but also corporally, in our bodies. The grace by which our relationship with God is renewed is not immaterial. Rather, it is Eucharistic. God calls us back to him both spiritually *and* physically. Like the Eucharist, the corporal works of mercy offer us a means of returning to God not only in spirit, but with all of who we are, body and soul. Moreover, through the corporal works of mercy, we not only receive healing from God, but also become active cooperators in God's healing of ourselves and others. As Gary Anderson puts it, in the practice of the works of mercy we not only "enact the miracle of God's grace" in our own lives, but also "assume the role of an active participant in the repair of the world."[52]

This active cooperation with God ultimately reveals to us the telos or purpose of the human body. In our discussion of the pornographic imagination, we noted how respect for others requires the elevation of our sensual experience to the truth that these others are in fact persons who deserve not to be used for our enjoyment, but to be loved. The works of mercy teach us how to integrate our sensuality into a loving relationship between persons by revealing to us that our bodies are made to give and receive God's mercy, not to be objects of domination and control. In this way, they instill in us a sacramental vision of the human body that, when rooted in the sacramental life of the Church and combined with disciplined practices of prayer, can most effectively serve to loosen the grip of pornography on our imagination.

52. Gary Anderson, *Charity*, 170.

PART 5

The Healing of Vision

JONAH

13 ⇜ "Neither Do I Condemn You" (Jn 8:11)

Seeing with the Eyes of Christ

My story begins when I was twelve. My seventh grade English class was reading a short story from a literary anthology, and the main character in the story, a young boy with leukemia, asked his mother for a *Playboy* magazine before a particularly hard day of treatment—as a sort of reward, I suppose. Everyone in my class laughed at that part of the story, except for me. I was oblivious. Later that day, out of curiosity, I googled *Playboy*, and, well, the rest is, sadly, history. By the eighth grade, I was addicted. This addiction took the form of increased obsession with sexual imagery, "needing'" porn to feel normal or to self-medicate difficult emotions, irritability, anger, jadedness in the spiritual life, conflicts with my parents, and despair.

In the initial months of pornography exposure, my prayer life improved, probably because I felt the need for God's intervention and saving power. After a while, however, it took a precipitous dive. God "refused" to help me, or so I thought. I felt hopeless and dirty, and, hey, it was a "normal" behavior, so why should I be stressing out so much, especially when it felt so good? Pornography causes us to forget, quite spectacularly, as it happens, that human beings are "created to praise, reverence, and serve God our Lord, and by means of this to save their souls."[1] It seizes upon the ultimate end for which we were created—eternal communion with perfect Love himself—and turns it on its head. Pornography lowers a man's gaze and convinces him that the highest good to which he should aspire is a cheap, neurochemical "high," a high earned off the backs of exploited and abused women (and men).

1. Ignatius Loyola, *The Spiritual Exercises*, trans. George E. Ganss (Saint Louis, Mo.: Institute of Jesuit Sources, 1992), 23.2 (p. 32).

Every porn video I have seen manifests the instrumental use of another person. I have never seen a video in which a man works for a woman, pursues her, sacrifices for her, or lays down his life for her. Women are always portrayed as insatiably carnal, thinking of nothing but sex, always desperate for more, willing to engage in even the most vulgar of actions for the man on the screen. In reality, this is not how women are at all: they are complex, multi-faceted, beautiful-beyond-compare creatures of God with wills, desires, and dreams of their own. They are not here for men to use. Rather, we are to sacrifice for them and steward creation together with them. Pornography mars our ability to see these truths and act on them.

Pope Saint John Paul II astutely observed that the human heart "has become a battlefield between love and concupiscence."[2] In this war, lust, which is aggressive, often overtakes, overpowers, and ousts the more fragile love, subjecting men to yet another of pornography's evils: the enslavement of the human will and aspirations. Pornography does *not* enhance our freedom, which, John Paul II explains, is properly understood not just as freedom from coercion but as the freedom of self-mastery that is indispensable for one to become a gift to another, "the freedom that finds its fullness in love" and new life and works according to the Spirit.[3]

It is in the midst of this spiritual tug-of-war between love and lust —played out upon the vast, digital fields of the internet—that our view of ourselves, of the opposite sex, of our own sex, of humanity as a whole, of the sex act itself, and of the proper use of the sexual powers is warped and debased. Pornography obscures the truth of three beautiful realities. First, that we are children of the Father, co-heirs with his Son in whom we are redeemed, and sanctified by their Holy Spirit; we are "temples of the Holy Spirit" (1 Cor 6:19), and it is within our very hearts that the Father and Son make their indwelling of pure, self-giving love. Second, we are creatures made in the image of God for relationship and communion. Third, the use of the sexual faculties within the loving bond of marriage, ordered toward the twofold end

2. John Paul II, *Man and Woman He Created Them: A Theology of the Body*, trans. Michael Waldstein (Boston, Mass.: Pauline Books and Media, 2006), 258.

3. John Paul II, *Man and Woman He Created Them*, 186, 340.

of the good of the spouses and procreation, turns the sexual powers outward in love of others.

Pornography, for me, anyway, was and remains (to a lesser degree nowadays, praise God) a Trojan horse of sin. Its arrival first appeared to offer good things but in the final analysis revealed itself to be a source of nothing but misery, pain, and disintegration. It robbed me of my time, my peace of mind, my ability to connect with others, my basic sense of innocence and trust in other people, my relationships with my parents and my three younger brothers, my conception of love, my ability to give and receive love, and my faith in a loving God. It negatively impacted every single facet of my existence and did so in direct proportion to the intensity of the pornography that I sought out and the duration of my consumption (which trended inexorably toward ever-greater forms of deviancy and ever-longer chunks of time). I was indeed a slave, led by the nose by my fleshly passions, no matter the consequences—eternal or otherwise. This experience is a common one for those entangled in pornography.

Yet, pornography can never *truly* obliterate the innate goodness of the sex act. As the porn addict sinks ever deeper into his addiction—his "harem of imaginary brides," as C. S. Lewis terms it[4]—he is constantly and consistently reminded of that for which he longs (perhaps even only subconsciously) and conspicuously lacks. This tension—the desperate clawing for something that is wholly illusory and therefore fundamentally incapable of satisfying the addict—paradoxically aids in sending him back on his way to God. But in the depths of compulsion and illusion, where is our cause for hope?

It is to be found in the unchangeable and awesome reality that *God loves us no matter what.* As St. Paul says: "Neither death, nor life, nor angels, nor rulers, nor things present, nor things to come, nor powers, nor height, nor depth, nor anything else in all creation, will be able to separate us from the love of God in Christ Jesus our Lord" (Rom 8:38–39). Do not misunderstand me: as someone who has lived (and still lives) the horrid life of addiction, I am not saying that God excuses

4. C. S. Lewis, "Letter to Keith Masson," March, 6, 1956, in *Narnia, Cambridge, and Joy 1950–1963*, vol. 3 of *The Collected Letters of C. S. Lewis*, ed. Walter Hooper (San Francisco, Calif.: Harper, 2007), 758.

our actions or covers them up, nor would I wish that God would do so; rather, God's love enflames us. It inspires us. It spurs us to make amends, to repent for our sinful lives. It calls us beyond ourselves, just as Christ was called beyond himself—as were all those he encountered.

"For mortals it is impossible, but for God all things are possible" (Mt 19:26). To address the magnitude of pornography, we must first recognize that the problem is bigger and more powerful than any of us, even all of us acting in concert, and that if we neglect to include God in our response, all our efforts will be for naught. If we spurn God's saving help, we will be like the "foolish man who built his house on sand" (Mt 7:26).

The reason that we can be hopeful is because Christ has "redeemed" us, but what does this really mean? Pope Benedict illuminates this reality beautifully in his encyclical *Spe Salvi*: "Through [Jesus] we have become certain of God, a God who is not a remote 'first cause' of the world, because his only-begotten Son has become man and of him everyone can say: 'I live by faith in the Son of God, who loved me and gave himself for me' (Gal 2:20)."[5] So in the most real sense, God truly works from *within* our lives, not from without, evidenced by the realities of the Incarnation of the Son of God in Jesus Christ and his saving Passion. The suffering servant (Is 53) enters into our human condition and transfigures the torment and anguish that he finds there, not by erasing their terrible sting but by reordering our lives in cooperation with his perfectly meritorious, redemptive suffering, conferring upon our lives meaning beyond themselves, and thus rewriting them into "hymns of praise." So, we can be supremely confident in God because his Word made flesh (Jn 1:14) "descended into 'Hell' and is therefore close to those cast into it, transforming their darkness into light."[6] *He will not abandon us.*

The Jesuits who minister at my university make a conscious effort through a Daily Examen to recognize the Holy Spirit at work in each of our lives, which means noticing little things. Even tragedy and loss and heartbreak can be God speaking to us, albeit in a mysterious way.

5. Benedict XVI, Encyclical Letter *Spe Salvi* (November 30, 2007), 26.
6. Benedict XVI, *Spe Salvi*, 41.

On the day of my conversion, like Saint Ignatius, I received spiritual consolation. "By [this kind of] consolation," Ignatius wrote, "I mean that which occurs when some interior motion is caused within the soul through which it comes to be inflamed with love of its Creator and Lord. As a result it can love no created thing on the face of the earth in itself, but only in the Creator of them all."[7] I was truly on fire (and I mean that almost literally). I made my first confession in over four years through the mediation of the Jesuit priest who was for a time my spiritual director, and I was back home. When I gaze upon Caravaggio's *Calling of Saint Matthew*, I'm convinced that my experience parallels his in some fundamental way (Fig. 13-1). It inspires me to this day and refreshes me when I fall.

God is always with us, even to the end of the world (Mt 28:20), and God loves us and wills our salvation more fervently than we can possibly imagine. How is it, then, that God intends for the pandemic of pornography to be solved? Because pornography is the cause of such grave ruptures within personal lives, families, and humanity more broadly—communities both great and small—it is to be confronted and challenged by and through that which it principally devastates: community. Communities of faith challenge us, support us, and stand as a bulwark against narcissism, because those living in Christian community serve one another. This safeguards our identity by anchoring it in a corporate body with an origin in the Blood of Christ.[8] Pornography renders us incapable, even deeply ashamed, of accepting community and the refreshing and healing balms it is capable of offering us at the time when our sin-sick souls need it most desperately. In Christ, however, we who are sinners are brought together in a bond of communion created by the sinless one who gave his life on our behalf, and in this bond our hearts are changed.[9]

How can communities of faith support persons who have been lured into pornography? We must first take great pains not to white-

7. Ignatius, *Spiritual Exercises*, 316.1–2 (p. 122).

8. Vatican Council II, *Lumen Gentium* (December 7, 1965), 9.

9. On this point, see John C. Cavadini, "Spousal Vision: Seeing the Church with *Lumen Gentium*" (Documents of Vatican II Lecture Series, St. Procopius Abbey, Lisle, Ill., September 16, 2014), accessed October 20, 2018, https://www.youtube.com/watch?v=D-7iP7Ir8i4.

wash pornography. No one is served by the incorrect, dangerous, and, sadly, all-too-common notion that "porn isn't that bad." We need to be firm and call it what it is: a sin that offends God deeply. But we must also be careful not to adopt a self-righteous "holier than thou" attitude, missing the opportunity to visit compassion on the suffering souls in our midst so very in need of Christ.

In all this, women have a very special role to play. Pornography, it is no secret, caters to the so-called "desires" of men. The industry has, unfortunately, discovered how men's brains are wired and has exploited this biological fact relentlessly—succeeding, via this perverse social engineering, at shifting what men find alluring. It is also a sad fact that many, many men are hooked on (or at least overly friendly with) pornography. Women, being somewhat more (though by no means completely) insulated, must be available to help their brothers fight their distorted desires. They too must support them in charity and call them to higher things, and they have a special way of doing that: men love heroism and adventure and danger. Give a man a task with great import, and he will do it. Women must make the choice: to stand or not to stand together with their brothers. And men in turn must make the choice to stand with their sisters. To stand is to fight, and to fight is to have a chance.

We must also take pains not to promulgate intangible theories, abstract theologies, and remote commandments as though they were a silver bullet. These components of our faith are incredibly important and do most definitely have their place; they provide the religious superstructure within which we operate from day-to-day. But they must not come at the expense of opportunities to administer concrete words and actions of love. If we give "book knowledge" precedence over love, we risk behaving like a preacher who exhorts his flock to feed and clothe the poor even as he ignores a homeless man across the street who is begging for help from passersby. We risk forgetting that the Church is not a museum for saints but is, in Pope Francis's words, a "field hospital after battle."[10]

It is very unlikely that even a well-intentioned addict will respond

10. Antonio Spadaro, "A Big Heart Open to God: The Exclusive Interview with Pope Francis," *America Magazine* 209, no. 8 (September 20, 2013): 24.

positively to lots of words, especially when those words so often fall harshly on the ears. I know that I would not have responded to harsh words. My Jesuit spiritual director Father Matthew (pseud.) recognized this and proceeded to direct me in a loving and merciful manner. He was never soft on the fact that my pornography usage had to stop, but he also understood the struggles and failures that so often accompanied my journey toward freedom and was always hopeful that the day would come when Christ would liberate me—even when I was (to put it mildly) somewhat less than optimistic. Through his actions, he gave authentic testament to that which God desires that we all know about ourselves at the deepest level of our being, namely that, "*it is good that you exist*."[11] And now, by the grace of God, I believe that.

In sum, we must recognize God's primary role in the salvation of pornography users, abusers, and addicts; we must work to strengthen ties between men and women; and we must rebuild community in a loving manner that neither unhelpfully harps on the sin nor gives it a free pass—but simply loves, that is, wills the ultimate good of the sinner. We can look to the life of Christ for a model in this endeavor, particularly to the story of the woman caught in adultery. In this story, the scribes and the Pharisees bring a woman who was caught in adultery into the middle of a crowd in the Temple area. They are using her for their own end of testing Jesus in the hope of bringing a charge against him (Jn 8:6).

"In the law," they state, "Moses commanded us to stone such women. So what do you say?" (Jn 8:5). Christ, Truth itself, beholds the woman, and what does he do? He bends down and writes on the ground with his finger. When the scribes and the Pharisees continue questioning him, he stands and says: "Let the one among you who is without sin be the first to throw a stone at her" (Jn 8:7). In response, the people who have formed a crowd walk away, one by one, leaving Christ alone with the woman. "Where are they?" he asks her. "Has no one condemned you?" (Jn 8:10). She replies "No one, sir." Then, he sends her on her way with the words that pornography users long to

11. Joseph Cardinal Ratzinger, *Principles of Catholic Theology: Building Stones for a Fundamental Theology*, trans. Mary Frances McCarthy (San Francisco, Calif.: Ignatius Press, 1987), 80–81.

hear: "*Neither do I condemn you. Go your way, and from now on do not sin again*" (Jn 8:11).

Christ enters into the shame and suffering of the adulteress, meets her where she is, and calls her and all the characters in the story, none of whom are without sin, to something greater. His actions create a space in which Christ, the woman caught in adultery, the scribes, the Pharisees, and the crowd—and by extension every pornography addict—can together share a vulnerable moment: one filled with love, mercy, tenderness, and hope. We can learn from this story what love truly is, after so much time of either running from it, avoiding it, or not being able to recognize it. Jesus does not go soft on the sin, but he recognizes that harsh judgment is not the answer. He names sin in the context of a compassion so strong that it has the power to transform an attempt to shame and entrap into a moment of conversion.

I will conclude with two more short passages. Joseph Cardinal Ratzinger, who became Pope Benedict, writes: "Of ourselves, we cannot come to terms with ourselves. Our 'I' becomes acceptable to us only if it has first become acceptable to another 'I.' We can love ourselves only if we have first been loved by someone else."[12] Christ has loved us, and others who channel his love can share in that reality by also loving us, and when we recognize this, we can joyfully join our voices with his holy mother Mary and say: "The Mighty One has done great things for me, and holy is his name" (Lk 1:49).

12. Ratzinger, *Principles of Catholic Theology*, 79–80.

JENNIFER NEWSOME MARTIN

14 ⋘ Beauty as Paradigm for Resistance

Against the Pornographic Age

The year 2017 was a landmark year for opening up a national conversation in America about sexual misconduct. Hundreds of high-profile men across various industries were accused of sexual, physical, or verbal harassment, abuse, and assault in the wake of Hollywood producer Harvey Weinstein's dramatic fall from grace.[1] The nature and extent of these accusations reveal toxic, predatory, and misogynistic attitudes and behaviors directed toward women that, in my view, cannot be separated from the pervasive availability and use of pornography in Western culture. In general, pornography normalizes and encourages the narrative of the commodification of and subsequent violence against women where consent, if given at all, is only notional or merely simulated within an economy of exploitation and coercion that routinely preys upon the poor and the addicted. Often the performers are young people who, seeing no other genuine alternatives for survival, are recruited to the pornography industry from economically underprivileged classes. Many are also deeply traumatized by abuses of power, depression, prescription and street drug addiction, the psychological and the physical pain of having multiple abortions, STDs, suicidal tendencies, and damage to their reproductive organs. Under

1. A sampling of the news coverage might include Jodi Kantor and Megan Twohey, "Harvey Weinstein Paid Off Sexual Harassment Accusers for Decades," *New York Times* (October 5, 2017), accessed October 15, 2018, https://www.nytimes.com/2017/10/05/us/harvey-weinstein-harassment-allegations.html; Megan Twohey, "Harvey Weinstein Is Fired After Sexual Harassment Reports," *New York Times* (October 8, 2017), accessed October 15, 2018, https://www.nytimes.com/2017/10/08/business/harvey-weinstein-fired.html; Sarah Almukhtar, Michael Gold, and Larry Buchanan, "After Weinstein: 71 Men Accused of Sexual Misconduct and Their Fall from Power," *New York Times* (updated February 8, 2018), accessed October 15, 2018, https://www.nytimes.com/interactive/2017/11/10/us/men-accused-sexual-misconduct-weinstein.html.

these conditions, there is no genuine possibility of actual free consent.

These appalling realities of the pornography industry and the grip it has on sexual culture in America require a full-blown reformation of habits of the broad cultural and theological imagination—certainly not as a sufficient condition for attenuating the damaging effects of pornography, but perhaps as a necessary one. I am not naïve enough to assume that what follows in my largely theological and aesthetic account approaches the degree of concrete practicality necessary for solving the public health crisis of pornography addiction.[2] It does seem to me, however, that at least a partial antidote to the escalating violence that begins in a deformation of vision might at least tentatively begin in vision's reformation. An imaginative reconsideration of the nature of beauty, perception, and the dignity of human personhood is necessary to inoculate both men and women against the pervasive images of pornography that not only have seeped into popular culture but have altogether overdetermined it. To that end, I will appeal to certain resources in the work of Roman Catholic theologian Hans Urs von Balthasar, known as the author of what is perhaps the canonical version of contemporary theological aesthetics, which may create a conceptual space for ameliorating the negative effects of pornography. Recourse to elements in Balthasar's theological aesthetics can be antidotal to symptoms of a pornographic culture constitutively characterized by a disabled conception of beauty, the constriction of perception, and a manifestly destructive anthropology.

In the first volume of his aesthetics, Hans Urs von Balthasar writes

2. A more immediately concrete resource for breaking the addictive patterns of pornography consumption is the non-profit group, "Fight the New Drug," accessible at https://fightthenewdrug.org/. For a more pastorally inclined document, consult the United States Conference of Catholic Bishops, "Create in Me a Clean Heart: A Pastoral Response to Pornography" (Washington, D.C.: United States Conference of Catholic Bishops, 2015): http://www.usccb.org/issues-and-action/human-life-and-dignity/pornography/upload/Create-in-Me-a-Clean-Heart-Statement-on-Pornography.pdf. As part of this USCCB effort, a number of Catholic and other Christian resources, including videos, books, support groups, counseling, and internet filtering tools are listed at: http:// www.foryourmarriage.org/help-for-men-and-women-struggling-with-pornography-use-or-addiction/. For a highly recommended, child-appropriate read-aloud book that assists parents in facilitating early, proactive conversations about the addictive and damaging effects of pornography, see Kristen A. Jenson and Gail Poyner, *Good Pictures, Bad Pictures: Porn-Proofing Today's Young Kids* (Richland, Wash.: Glen Cove Press, 2016).

that "the fundamental human sense of the eye and its act of seeing is precisely the fact that ... [the] 'other' becomes visible to oneself *as person* and is seen by one as person. *All seeing is inhuman if it does not comprise this kind of seeing*."[3] In the immediate context of this text, the first volume of *The Glory of the Lord*, Balthasar's notion of "inhuman seeing" is not connected directly with the pornographic gaze or with pornographic consumption, but the applications are clear enough. Pornographic seeing is a thoroughly inhuman seeing, which is predicated on a series of distanciations, the cumulative effect of which is depersonalization, an act of violence that creates at least the capacity for escalation to other acts of violence, both against the performers as well as among pornography's consumers who become more likely to commit sexual or domestic abuse.[4]

In what follows, I will begin by reviewing the violence both implicit and explicit in pornography before considering two distinct but related sites of possible antidotes against "inhuman seeing." These antidotes might include: (1) Balthasar's rehabilitation of a (transcendental, theologically specified) beauty connected inextricably to Being itself, which is both resistant to profit-driven commodification and exceeds decisively the truncated category of exhibition valuc, and (2) his interest in recovering an alternative—biblical, not philosophical—theological anthropology that weds embodiment, materiality, and spirituality, privileging the totality of human persons by reconnecting the physical sensorium with spiritual perception.[5]

3. Hans Urs von Balthasar, *Seeing the Form*, vol. 1 of *The Glory of the Lord: A Theological Aesthetics*, ed. Joseph Fessio and John Riches, trans. Erasmo Leiva-Merikakis (San Francisco, Calif.: Ignatius Press, 1982), 382; emphasis added.

4. Gail Dines describes a phenomenon of distanciation in which women are never named as women but rather dehumanized with abusive names and attributes. She terms this a kind of "verbal segregation," the function of which, she says, is "to erode any empathy that many men may have for the women in porn ... [in order to] clearly demarcate them from the women men know and love." See Gail Dines, *Pornland: How Porn Has Hijacked Our Sexuality* (Boston, Mass.: Beacon Press, 2010), 64. On the link between pornography consumption and violence against women, see also Catherine A. Simmons, Peter Lehmann, and Shannon Collier-Tennison, "Linking Male Use of the Sex Industry to Controlling Behavior in Violent Relationships: An Exploratory Analysis," *Violence against Women* 14, no. 4 (2008): 406–17.

5. See Boyd Taylor Coolman's "*Sensus Christi:* A Liturgico-Sacramental Therapy for a Pornographic Sensibility," also in this volume.

Extraction(s)

In early 2015, the once notoriously vulgar comedic actor Russell Brand —an unlikely anti-pornography spokesman by any measure—denounced the corrosive effects of pornography in a short online video; at present count, it has garnered over 2.9 million views. In this extraordinarily salient, honest, and impassioned critique, Brand recounts: "I heard a quote from a priest that said, 'Pornography is not a problem because it shows us too much; it's a problem because it shows us too little.'"[6] Brand's interpretation of this incisive diagnosis (unattributed in Brand's comments but said by Pope Saint John Paul II) is that pornography reduces the sexual experience to what he calls "a kind of *extracted* physical act." That he chooses this particular word—"extraction"—to describe pornography is revealing on three counts: first, the language of extraction suggests essentially that pornographic sex gets removed from its more proper contexts either of expressing love or of procreating, basically what the Catholic tradition calls the unitive and the procreative dimensions of sexual intercourse.[7] Brand's observation that pornography isolates or extracts sex from context is made more explicit in the distinction in the contemporary pornographic industry between the subgenres of "features" and "wall-to-wall," or "gonzo," porn.[8] While the former category might at least nominally resemble Hollywood movies insofar as they have a plot and dialogue between established characters, the latter category dispenses altogether with the pretension of plot such that the entire production consists of context-less sex scenes. This type of pornography in particular has received criticism—even from within the porn industry—not only for its lack of context but also for the detrimental

6. Russell Brand, "Russell Brand Talks Sex, Softcore & Hardcore Porn," originally published on the YouTube channel of actor/comedian Russell Brand; republished on YouTube by Fight the New Drug on February 23, 2015, accessed October 25, 2018, https://www.youtube.com/watch?v=5kvzamjQW9M.

7. Paul VI, Encyclical Letter, *Humanae Vitae* (July 25, 1968), §12.

8. For this distinction, see Ana J. Bridges and Robert Jensen, "Pornography," in *Sourcebook on Violence against Women*, 2nd ed., ed. Claire M. Renzetti, Jeffrey L. Edleson, and Raquel Kennedy Bergen (Los Angeles, Calif.: Sage Publications, 2010), 138; Dines, *Pornland*, xxii.

effects it is having on women's bodies routinely forced to endure hours of sexual use and abuse.[9]

Second, the culture of pornography is predicated not only upon extracting a physical act from its proper context, but upon a whole set of reductive extractions, all of which proceed from an insufficient anthropology that treats persons not as persons but as objects for use and as capital for profit. In pornographic images, physical bodies are extracted from whole persons, who are rightly the indissoluble union of body-spirit. This extraction reduces the sexual act, with no accounting for the complexity of personhood or genuine relations between persons. Pornography extracts physical bodies from persons: yet the reduction is not only to the physical, but also to function, as persons are reduced to parts of bodies and even to functions of these parts as purely sexual stimuli.[10] Indeed, the contraction required in pornography appears to be a nearly infinite one, from person to body, to body part, to function, to capacity of that material sexual organ, such that the activity regresses toward complete extraction and even liquidation of the full humanity and dignity of the person. In pornography, the other's visibility precisely as an (exceptional, particular, whole) person is elided. There is no genuine encounter among any of the parties involved. The pornographers see the performers through a camera lens as objects. The consumers of pornography see the performers through a screen, even further removed from the reality of the actual persons playing the roles.

The final connotation to the language of "extraction" may be more subtextual than explicit, but it implicates the reductive and actual violence inherent in pornographic expression. It is not insignificant that force and violence are implicit in the very definition of "extraction" (teeth, petroleum, etc.). The performers meet not with reciprocity and mutuality, but in a mode that appears phenomenologically more

9. Erik Jay, "Gonzo: Taking a Toll," XBIX News, September 10, 2007, http://xbiz.com/articles/83870. Cited in Dines, *Pornland*, xxvii and 171n23.

10. As Gail Dines puts it in the transcript to her DVD "Pornland," the ideal man in porn is "a life-support system for an erect penis. He's got no emotions, he's got no connections, nothing." *Pornland: How the Porn Industry Has Hijacked Our Sexuality* (North Hampton, Mass.: Media Education Foundation, 2014), DVD. Her statement can be found on page 10 of a transcript of the film, accessed September 20, 2018, at: http://www.mediaed.org/transcripts/Pornland-Transcript.pdf.

like sexual assault than any expression of love.[11] The escalating levels of sexual viciousness, brutality, and abuse are detailed in Gail Dines's *Pornland.*[12] Even without the pretense of particular narrative, as in "gonzo" porn, assumptions consistently presuppose that women are sexual objects for use, control, or domination. These assumptions are symptoms of pornography's drive to commodification because, as Dines points out, "porn images are produced by an industry and are hence scripted, formulaic, and genre-bound representations."[13] In this narrative of pornography, women exist only to be penetrated. The female characters, Dines writes, are "one-dimensional women who are nothing more than collections of holes;"[14] they are reduced "to orifices and body parts, bled dry of soul, personality, history, and future."[15] Elsewhere she says emphatically that women in pornography are represented as "f*** objects who are deserving of sexual use and abuse."[16] They are depicted as enthusiastic participants in sexual activity "irrespective of how painful, humiliating, or harmful the act is," and they "have no sexual imagination of their own,"[17] preferring instead to capitulate to the powerful male characters who express "nothing but contempt and hatred for them."[18] The most fundamental problem with pornography, then, is not *merely* a reductive objectification or commodification of persons (a phenomenon just as readily observed on Tinder), but also the normalization of sexualized violence against women that emerges from these prior reductions. Indeed, alarming levels of sexualized violence, degradation, verbal abuse, and brutal humiliations have become increasingly mainstreamed in modern pornographic material.[19] The damaging narrative provided or assumed is that these women in the films are of a certain type who are always available for sex, and who desire it not in spite of, but in direct pro-

11. Dines, *Pornland,* xxvii.
12. Dines, *Pornland,* 68–75.
13. Dines, *Pornland,* xxiii.
14. Dines, *Pornland,* xxiv.
15. Dines, *Pornland,* xvi.
16. Dines, *Pornland,* 63.
17. Dines, *Pornland,* xxiii.
18. Dines, *Pornland,* xxiv.
19. See, for instance, Ana J. Bridges et al., "Aggression and Sexual Behavior in Best-Selling Pornography Videos: A Content Analysis Update," *Violence against Women* 16, no. 10 (October 2010): 1065–85.

portion to the cruelty, aggression, and brutal abuse they suffer. The dangerous myth of this narrative is somehow perpetrated among pornography consumers even when the female performers are clearly depicted crying, vomiting, and in physical pain at the same time that they must enthusiastically affirm verbally whatever it is that the man in the film demands or performs, complicating—among other things—the concept of consent.

Faces

In his essay "Nudities," the Italian philosopher Giorgio Agamben recalls a brief exchange in one of Plato's dialogues, the *Charmides*. In this dialogue, the following conversation takes place when Charmides, an exceptionally handsome young man, enters the room in which Socrates is seated:[20]

> They all gazed at him as if he were a statue. Then Chaerephon called me and said—How does the youth strike you, Socrates? Has he not a fine face?
>
> Immensely so, I replied.
>
> Yet if he would consent to strip, he said, you would think he had no face [*aprosopos*], he has such perfect beauty of form.[21]

The Greek text is *aprosopos*: the word "face" or *prosopon* proceeded by an alpha privative. Chaerephon's suggestion is thus perhaps stronger than it appears in English: if this character were to be seen naked, observers would think he was *aprosopos*: "no face." Once they turn an objectifying gaze upon the body, his face, here a synecdoche of his personal identity, ceases to register as having any sort of meaning or relevance; Charmides is no longer a particular person. That this naked form happens to be Charmides is perfectly indifferent under this objectifying gaze.

Agamben's essay "Nudities" goes on to suggest that beauty, especially the beauty of a woman's face, has in the modern era of late capitalism been evacuated of its depth: think of the impassive, bored, dis-

20. Giorgio Agamben, "Nudity," in *Nudities*, trans. David Kishik and Stefan Pedatella (Stanford, Calif.: Stanford University Press, 2011), 89.

21. Plato, *Charmides*, in vol. 8 of *Plato in Twelve Volumes*, Loeb Classical Library No. 201, trans. W. R. M. Lamb (Cambridge, Mass.: Harvard University Press, 1955), 154d, accessed online October 15, 2018, http://www.perseus.tufts.edu/hopper/text?doc=Perseus%3Atext%3A1999.01.0176%3Atext%3DCharm.%3Asection%3D154d.

interested—sometimes outright hostile—non-expression that comes down high-fashion runways or is featured in magazine ads of the top fashion houses. Agamben calls this often aggressive absence of expression the "nihilism of beauty." He diagnoses but does not necessarily object categorically to this notion, since for him expressions of nihilism and profanation can function as sites of possibility and hope. He describes this "nihilism of beauty" as the deliberate reduction of

> one's own beauty to pure appearance and then exhibiting this appearance with a sort of remote sadness, stubbornly denying the idea that beauty can signify something other than itself. But it is precisely the very lack of illusions about itself—*this nudity without veils* that beauty thus manages to achieve—that furnishes the most frightful attraction. This disenchantment of beauty, this special nihilism, reaches its extreme stage with the mannequins or the fashion models, who learn before all else to erase all expression from their faces. In so doing, *their faces become pure exhibition value*, and, as a result, acquire a particular allure.[22]

The principle of the nihilism of beauty is that true beauty is incredibly strict: it does not allow the supplement of friendliness or emotional expressiveness, only a stark kind of beauty in its barest instantiation. For Agamben, part of the enchantment of a beautiful face is because of and not in spite of this mode of aggressive superficiality: it is a celebration of the possibilities of appearance at the surface-level alone, vacated even of animating expression. For Agamben, this antagonistic lack of illusion about the revelatory capacity of beauty actually becomes part of beauty's legitimate attraction.

Elsewhere, in the essay "In Praise of Profanation," Agamben continues his diagnosis of late capitalism through the apparatus of pornography, again invoking the category of "exhibition value."[23] He observes that when a woman becomes aware that she is the object of a gaze her face tends to lose its expression, noting that it is "brazen-faced indifference that fashion models, porn stars, and others whose profession it is to show themselves must learn to acquire: they show nothing

22. Agamben, "Nudity," 88; italics added.

23. The term "exhibition value" (*Ausstellungswert*) is suggested by Walter Benjamin in 1935 as an addition to Marx's notions of "use-value" and "exchange-value." See Giorgio Agamben, "In Praise of Profanation," in *Profanations*, trans. Jeff Forth (New York: Zone Books, 2007), 90.

but the showing itself."[24] He makes particular mention of the French porn actress Chloë des Lysses, who displays an exaggerated mode of this detachment between face and body overtly in her films. As she is filmed or photographed performing even the lewdest sexual acts, she keeps her face in the foreground of the frame, studiously void of any expression. As Agamben continues, "instead of simulating pleasure, as dictated by the conventions of the genre, she affects and displays—like fashion models—the most absolute indifference, the most stoic ataraxy. . . . Her impassive face breaks every connection between lived experience and the expressive sphere; it no longer expresses anything but shows itself as a place without a hint of expression."[25] For Agamben, in contrast to Balthasar, the diagnosis of the inexpressive face in fashion houses and pornographic films is not made in a register of lament. Agamben's position does not censure pornography as such as a reprehensible industry; rather, for him pornography is a site of profanation *par excellence*, which he sees counterintuitively as a possible good insofar as it "neutralizes what it profanes. Once profaned, that which was unavailable and separate loses its aura and is returned to use."[26] Agamben thinks, then, that expressionless but beautiful faces reduced to their exhibition value alone (even or especially in pornography) might indeed be the entrance to "new use . . . a new form of erotic communication,"[27] were it not for the absolute manner in which these images are consumed. That is, it is the "solitary and desperate [that is, masturbatory] consumption of the pornographic image" that frustrates whatever potential of new use there might be.[28] We see, then, that it is the excessive consumption of late capitalism rather than pornography as such that is the direct object of Agamben's censure. For him, capitalist consumption has placed everything into a field "where all use becomes and remains impossible."[29] What compels him to employ pornography in this manner—that is, to illustrate issues of class, economics, or politics or else to show the fragility of

24. Agamben, "In Praise of Profanation," 90.
25. Agamben, "In Praise of Profanation," 91.
26. Agamben, "In Praise of Profanation," 77.
27. Agamben, "In Praise of Profanation," 90.
28. Agamben, "In Praise of Profanation," 91.
29. Agamben, "In Praise of Profanation," 81.

human happiness—is more the abstract "logic" of the pornographic industry and not necessarily its concrete practice.

Agamben's emphasis on commodification in pornography is well-placed given the fact that pornography is a counterfeit representation of sex constructed almost unilaterally according to profit-driven parameters.[30] His critique, however, is not nearly damning enough. It is not clear whether abstracting the logic of pornography is actually possible, and it is not clear whether such abstraction may further commodify, economize, or further exploit actual sex workers whose actual bodies are being treated harshly by excessive, usually violent sexual acts.[31] Furthermore, Agamben's discussion of exhibition value suggests that there is nothing inherently transgressive about the object of pornographic images (the sex act itself) but rather that the transgressive element lies primarily in the photographic or cinematic representation of an otherwise intimate moment presented without any actual intimacy.[32] Whatever the virtues and limitations of Agamben's analysis, his valuation of exhibition remains incommensurate with a theological anthropology in which the human person is created in the image and likeness of God.

Antidotes

For Balthasar, unlike Agamben, the separation of a beautiful form from its depths (or, analogously, the separation of face and expres-

30. See Dines, "Introduction: Porn and the Industrialization of Sex" and "From the Backstreet to Wall Street: The Big Business of Porn," in *Pornland*, xv–xxxi and 47–58.

31. Agamben's co-opting of pornography and the symbol of the inexpressive female face to offer political critique is certainly not uncontroversial. For a clear discussion of and constructive response to the various criticisms levied at Agamben's references to pornography, including his inattention to the injurious effect of the sex industry on concrete individuals, see Sergei Prozorov, "Pornography and Profanation in the Political Philosophy of Georgio Agamben," *Theory, Culture & Society* 28, no. 4 (July 2011): 71–95.

32. Agamben here quotes Walter Benjamin: "If there is anything sexually arousing here," Benjamin writes, "it is more the idea that a naked body is being exhibited before the camera than the sight of nakedness itself." In a comparable vein, Prozorov reflects: "what makes plausible pornography's claim to transgression is not its subject matter, *which transgresses nothing whatsoever*, but its promise to bring this subject matter to representation without losing its authentic reality." See Walter Benjamin, "Eduard Fuchs: Collector and Historian," in vol. 3 of *Selected Writings, 1935–1938*, ed. Howard Eiland and Michael W. Jennings, trans. Edmond Jephcott (Cambridge, Mass.: Belknap Press, 2002), 300n71. Cited in Agamben, "In Praise of Profanation," 89–90; Prozorov, "Pornography and Profanation," 81, emphasis added.

sion) is nothing other than deeply lamentable. Authentic beauty in Balthasar's theological aesthetics resists absolutely commodification and transcends exhibition value. When beauty becomes impoverished in the way that it has in modern visual culture, when it is no longer understood as revelatory of Being, it is no indifferent matter: to disengage from beauty denatures the human perception of the good and the true. Balthasar writes, in an analysis similar to Agamben's in diagnosis, if not in prescription:

> We no longer dare to believe in beauty and we make of it a mere appearance in order the more easily to dispose of it. Our situation today shows that beauty demands for itself at least as much courage and decision as do truth and goodness.... We can be sure that whoever sneers at her name as if she were the ornament of a bourgeois past ... *can no longer pray and soon will no longer be able to love.*[33]

The ability to perceive the wholeness of a truly beautiful form has—from lack of use—become atrophied and vestigial. The denial of the wholeness or even the existence of forms as such creates a culture in which people feel disfigured, incapable of seeing themselves and others as images of God.[34] These assumptions about image and representation leak into the formation of self-identity, especially hazardous for impressionable young women who have been saturated with a media culture that demeans and objectifies them, habituating them to the reality of sexual violence. If there are no other measures than a (usually sexualized) physical appearance, identity gets tied very deeply to it. In her chapter, "Visible or Invisible: Growing Up Female in a Porn Culture," Dines draws back the curtain on what it is like for young women, formed by what she calls "cultural constructions of idealized femininity," who have been informed (or, rather, deformed) by a hypersexualized culture, saturated with images that have eclipsed any alternative modes of being female.[35] These hypersexualized images, inherited at least partially from pornographic culture, influence not only clothing fashions (revealing, tight, or low-cut), and a homogenous "ideal" body type (white, blonde, heavy make-up, free of all body

33. Balthasar, *Glory of the Lord*, I:18.
34. Balthasar, *Glory of the Lord*, I:25–26.
35. Dines, *Pornland*, 101–2, 105.

hair, fit, and much thinner than the national average),[36] but also attitudes and behaviors towards casual hook-ups and degrees of sexual adventurousness, which masquerade as power but are only its counterfeit. A cultural inability to see the ontological, objective status of beauty and the self as an image of such ontological, objective beauty is not just a vaguely regrettable aesthetic problem—a lack of taste—but an existential crisis of moral, spiritual, and cultural life that is affecting an entire generation of young people.

With its objectivity and depth-dimension, beauty as reimagined in Balthasar's aesthetics might be called upon as a powerful restorative force for healing human vision and, effectively, to imaging the self as an embodied self that matters, and is matter, without being mere matter. Perhaps this announcement of the ameliorating power of beauty seems naïve, precious, and indefensible. Certainly, in modern aesthetics from Baumgarten and Kant forward, the idea of beauty has been contracted to the merely subjective and phenomenal. It has come to mean something that reflects only taste or preference; this concept of beauty, however, is far too insubstantial to defy pornography's regressive drive toward reductive extraction of personhood and the violence that reduction can engender. Our first task, then, is to rehabilitate a definition of beauty robust enough to counter the devastating effects of pornography. Modernity relegated beauty to a merely subjective concept, and much of Balthasar's theological project is a conscious recovery of the ancient and medieval notion of beauty as an objective reality, a transcendental unified with goodness and truth. As a transcendental property of being, beauty is not simply ornamental, but rather is the first and the last, forming and informing all of reality from creation to final salvation. Its encounter is an encounter with the luminously mysterious—and for Balthasar, trinitarian—depths of Being itself.

36. Dines writes, "The bodies of the women we see in magazines and on television are actually very unusual in their measurements and proportions, with long necks, broad shoulders, and high waists. Yet because these are more or less the only images we see, we take them to be the norm rather than the exception and assume that the problem lies with us and not the fashion and media industries that insist on using a very specific body type. This is what the media do: They take the abnormal body and make it normal by virtue of its visibility, while making the normal bodies of real women look abnormal by virtue of their invisibility." Dines, *Pornland*, 110.

The theological analogue to beauty for Balthasar is *doxa*, or "glory," which he defines in the foreword to the first volume of *Herrlichkeit* simply as "transcendental beauty,"[37] or beauty connected to being. More than having this metaphysical status, the category of "glory" in Balthasar's theological aesthetics is at the same time Christological: it has taken flesh. As Balthasar writes, "the 'glory' of Christian transfiguration is in no way less resplendent than the transfiguring glory of worldly beauty, but the fact is that the glory of Christ unites splendor and radiance with solid reality, as we see pre-eminently in the Resurrection and its anticipation through faith in Christian life."[38] Thus, the "weight" of a glory in which the infinite finds absolutely perfect expression in the finite (through the Incarnation and Resurrection) exceeds by an absolute order of magnitude thoroughly immanentized, earthly beauty.

Indeed, the central form of beauty for Balthasar is Christ. It is Christ—the absolutely singular and perfectly concrete instance of the infinite expressed in the finite in a genuine flesh-taking—who is the "Ur-form" of beauty.[39] It is Christ who, as the full expression of infinite in finitude, is "God's greatest work of art" and functions absolutely generatively for all other beautiful things.[40] Because of the Incarnation of the Word of God in Christ—Beauty made flesh—other finite forms, whether in nature, art, literature, language, poetry, and especially the form of the human being, are capacitated to participate in this mystery, where the supernatural acts as a kind of leavening agent all throughout the "natural," such that in a physical world invigorated with divine presence, it becomes impossible to demarcate the natural and the supernatural into two hermetically sealed spheres.[41] With Christ as the form of forms and the model that can imprint it-

37. Balthasar, *Glory of the Lord*, I: "Foreword" (unnumbered pagination). This notion will be extended biblically across both the Hebrew Bible and the New Testament in volumes 6 and 7 of Balthasar's *The Glory of the Lord*.

38. Balthasar, *Glory of the Lord*, I:124.

39. Balthasar, *Glory of the Lord*, I:29.

40. Hans Urs von Balthasar, "Revelation and the Beautiful," in *The Word Made Flesh*, vol.1 of *Explorations in Theology*, trans. A. V. Littledale with Alexander Dru (San Francisco, Calif.: Ignatius Press, 1989), 117.

41. Hans Urs von Balthasar, *A Theological Anthropology* (Eugene, Ore.: Wipf & Stock, 2010), 226. See also Balthasar, "Revelation and the Beautiful," 120.

self upon human lives, human beings are called to make themselves, in Balthasar's language, "into God's mirror and seek to attain to that transcendence and radiance that must be found in the world's substance if it is indeed God's image and likeness—his word and gesture, action and drama."[42]

For Balthasar, beauty has both a concrete, bodily manifestation visible to the physical senses and a (concomitantly veiled and unveiled) depth-dimension. This conception of beauty is always embodied, but it is not only body. It is in perceptible media that, as Balthasar says, with a likely nod toward Plato's *Symposium*, "the lightning-bolt of eternal beauty [can] flash,"[43] but this fact does not mean that eternal beauty has been restricted or domesticated to the mundane or the corporeal alone. Beauty is located objectively at the intersection of (in language borrowed from scholasticism) form or *species* and splendor or *lumen*. Neither form nor splendor can be present without the other. For Balthasar, the relation between "form," that is, the shape of something, and "splendor,"[44] or its interior luminosity, is simultaneous and complementary: in the perception of beauty there is a concurrent beholding of the form and the luminous quality that "shines forth" from within its interior.[45] This indissolubility of form is critical. We have identified pornography's violent logic of extraction and reduction, where the part is cleaved from the whole such that it is not illumined by it at all. But the concept of beauty Balthasar sought to rehabilitate is a transcendental of being and is thus by necessity an experience of the whole. Beautiful forms are beautiful because they reflect and embody that which *is*, an expression of the depths of reality—that is, God.

We see this point of form and splendor expanded in Russian Orthodox theologian Vladimir Soloviev, whose influence can be felt especially in Balthasar's aesthetics. Soloviev, like Balthasar, understands beauty to be irreducible either to its material expression or its subjective evaluation.[46] He consistently uses the example of the diamond,

42. Balthasar, *Glory of the Lord*, I:22.

43. Balthasar, *Glory of the Lord*, I:32.

44. Balthasar, *Glory of the Lord*, I:120.

45. Balthasar, *Glory of the Lord*, I:20.

46. Vladimir Soloviev, *Heart of Reality: Essays on Beauty, Love, and Ethics* (Notre Dame, Ind.: University of Notre Dame Press, 2003), 32.

which, as crystallized carbon, materially has the same constitution as ordinary coal.[47] The primary difference is its lucidity, the dynamic contribution of photons of light, what he calls "a supra-material, ideal agent,"[48] which interacts with the carbon in such a way that "the material element, embodying in itself ideal content, is transformed and becomes resplendent."[49] A diamond's beauty is located in neither the chemical material composition of the diamond nor the light refracted through it, but rather is the product of their transformative interaction. The concrete form must mediate the light, "form" and "splendor" presenting together.

It is not that perceivers see form *with* the splendor but rather that they see form *as* the splendor.[50] We have seen that beauty is proper to the whole (and to the wholeness of Being); it is the composite of the luminous form and the interior luminosity proper to it. As Balthasar suggests, "Visible form not only 'points' to an invisible, unfathomable mystery: form *is* the apparition of this mystery, and reveals it while . . . *at the same time protecting and veiling it*."[51] Especially when considered against the backdrop of pornographic images, Balthasar's notion of preserving veiledness as a precondition for beauty is significant. Recall the way in which Agamben spoke of the exhibition value of a beautiful but vacuous face: "It is precisely the very lack of illusions about itself—*this nudity without veils* that beauty thus manages to achieve—that furnishes the most frightful attraction."[52] Pornography exposes the naked body; the stripping of expression exposes the naked face. On the one hand, pornographic images have no veil because of this aggressive exposure of hypersexualized flesh: nothing is left to the imagination. In this manner, these images might well be said to show too much. On the other hand, pornographic images have no veil because they do not allow for the metaphysical luminousness of splendor to animate physical forms. The physical is all there is. In this manner,

47. Soloviev, *Heart of Reality*, 31–32.

48. Soloviev, *Heart of Reality*, 36.

49. Soloviev, *Heart of Reality*, 37

50. "We 'behold' the form," Balthasar writes, "but, if we really behold it, it is not as a detached form, rather in its unity with the depths that make their appearance in it. We see form as the splendor, as the glory of Being." Balthasar, *Glory of the Lord*, I:119.

51. Balthasar, *Glory of the Lord*, I:151; italics added.

52. Agamben, "Nudity," 88.

pornographic images show far too little. Elsewhere, Balthasar helpfully connects the symbol of the veil to love and mystery. He writes:

> In the end, only something endowed with mystery is worthy of love. It is impossible to love something stripped of mystery; *at best it would be a thing one uses as one sees fit, but not a person whom one could look up to.* Indeed, no progress in knowledge, not even when it occurs in love, may lift the veil from the beloved. Love itself demands, not only possession and unveiling, but just as forcefully reverence and, therefore, veiling. . . . If love is to endure to the very end, then unveiling must not be ultimate, but only penultimate . . . True love is so full of the true mystery of being's intimacy that it need never stagnate. Love remains vital because in its eyes the object itself, even apart from what love might add, is always ever greater and never wholly comprehensible.[53]

Because the pornographic gaze operates with a disordered vision that cannot see human beings as they truly are—deep, unutterable mysteries with infinite intrinsic worth—it sees them in a restrictive way as manipulatable things that "one uses as one sees fit." This mode of vision is inscribed with violence in its very operation even before concrete acts of violence ensue.

Balthasar's commitment to the indissolubility of form-content in his aesthetics has an analogue in his theological anthropology, which stipulates the unified soul-body composition of the human being. While it is certainly possible to describe a human being by his or her attributes, whether physical or nonphysical, any amalgamation of these component parts cannot communicate the essential mystery of human personhood. As Balthasar puts it, evoking Matthew's parable:

> Truly, it would not be worthwhile being human if man were but the amalgamation of such "material," if the one thing necessary, the irreplaceable pearl, were not a reality for the sake of which we would sell everything else. This precious "pearl" . . . alone is worthy of claiming our life unconditionally, the one thing that lends value to whatever we might be by allowing us to participate in its own intrinsic worth.[54]

As someone formed deeply in the tradition of Ignatian meditation during his twenty-one years as a Jesuit, Balthasar was certain-

53. Hans Urs von Balthasar, *Truth of the World*, vol 1. of *Theo-Logic: Theological Logical Theory*, trans. Adrian J. Walker (San Francisco, Calif.: Ignatius Press, 2000), 209–10; italics added.

54. Balthasar, *Glory of the Lord*, I:26–27.

ly accustomed to deploying imaginative resources for entering more concretely into spiritual practice. Ignatian meditation is not, however, simply a subjective therapy or strategy for the healing of vision but rather "unconditionally, an interior realization of the *objective* mystery of salvation *which transforms even the sensory disposition.*"[55] Ultimately, the sensory disposition is meant to be transformed into the sensory disposition of Christ. We will turn briefly now to our second substantive "antidote" to pornographic culture: namely, a reflection upon the cultivation of the spiritual senses in the context of reimagining theological anthropology.

Biblical Anthropology and the Sensorium

Balthasar considers four different examples of thinkers who have surprising levels of convergence: Karl Barth, Romano Guardini, Gustav Siewerth, and Paul Claudel. He deploys these four particular thinkers in order to demonstrate concrete lines of what he terms "biblical anthropology," called such to distinguish it from Greek philosophical conceptions of the human being, which both Barth and Balthasar worry have been over-determined by abstract categories of "essence."[56] For Balthasar, biblical anthropology includes the following characteristics: (a) human beings experience both God and the world from the concrete unity of the body-soul; that is, there is a fundamental unity of the physical and spiritual *sensorium*; (b) it is deeply relational, both horizontally and vertically; and (c) Christology provides the conditions of the possibility not only for the anthropological claims, but for the genuine healing of human vision.

Perception, Balthasar suggests, is "a fully human act of encounter" that prioritizes the physical sensorium; there is no other way, after all, that human beings interact with God and the world.[57] In Balthasar's discussion on the spiritual senses as part of his broader project of theological aesthetics, however, he writes that the divorce between the physical senses and the spirit "makes the relationship of human perception to all its objects and contents both improper and

55. Balthasar, *Glory of the Lord*, I:375; italics added.
56. Balthasar, *Glory of the Lord*, I:382.
57. Balthasar, *Glory of the Lord*, I:365.

abnormal."[58] In biblical anthropology, the senses are not merely physical but are thoroughly comprehensive categories.[59] Balthasar makes a particular point of the fact that the aim of Ignatian contemplative practice is not propositional knowledge of any order but rather the cultivation of a certain kind of subjective experience. This practice does not divorce internal and external experiences but rather understands them as unified phenomena.

Secondly, biblical anthropology is relational, both horizontally (human to human) and vertically (human to God). Especially in Barth's deeply covenantal and Christological theology, Balthasar sees an anthropology that is neither individualistic nor a rationalization of "essence" but a theology of the human marked most characteristically by relatedness to other persons and relatedness to God. This character of "being for" finds its very archetype in the person of Christ, and the experience of the other as a "Thou" is constitutive for personal identity.[60] Indeed, for Barth, a human being is "'a being in which one [person] looks the other in the eye.'"[61] Balthasar's gloss of Barth follows: "We see the Thou with *real bodily eyes*, and indeed *not as a thing* but in all its exceptionalness and particularity as person."[62] Here, then, is the absolute inverse of the "inhuman seeing" of the pornographic gaze. This alternative anthropology also is relational on the vertical axis. We see because God first sees us. From Paul Claudel in particular, Balthasar draws the idea of human creatureliness as a precondition for relation, with creatureliness described as "the reality of not being God, as the oscillation of relationships, as coexistence through abandonment to the other, as knowledge of the First Cause through one's

58. Balthasar, *Glory of the Lord*, I:388. See also I:391.

59. Balthasar finds Barth especially helpful on this point. See Balthasar, *Glory of the Lord*, I:380–89. For Barth's own marvelously detailed treatment of the (always Christologically undergirded) claim that the human being is the unity of soul and body, see Karl Barth, "Man as Soul and Body," in *Church Dogmatics III.2: The Doctrine of Creation*, eds. G. W. Bromiley and T. F. Torrance (London: T&T Clark, 2004), 325–436, especially the sections "Jesus, Whole Man," 325–44, and "Soul and Body in Their Interconnexion," 366–94.

60. Balthasar, *Glory of the Lord*, I:381–82.

61. Barth, *Church Dogmatics*, III/2:250; quoted by Balthasar in *Glory of the Lord*, I:382.

62. Balthasar, *Glory of the Lord*, I:382; emphasis added.

limits."[63] Seeing, then, is not an exercise of power but rather its relinquishing, which is on balance the more powerful act.

Finally, Christ is the precondition for this healing of vision. We have already seen that one of the goals of Ignatian meditation is to receive and let one's vision be transformed by a reality greater than oneself; indeed, it is to learn to take on the very subjective disposition of Christ. Moreover, this healing of vision effected by Christ is both subjective and objective, having to do both with the individual person's capacity for perception, but also with the entire "sensory environment" in which we live and move and have our being (Acts 17:28).[64] That is:

> If Christ is the image of all images, it is impossible that he should not affect all the world's images by his presence, arranging them around himself. There is no such thing as an isolated image; every image appears against a background of fellow-images.... But what Christ brings with him is not primarily his historical environment, but the world of creation and of redemption as a whole.... [The human being's] sensory environment, in which he lives and with which he is apparently wholly familiar, is through and through determined by the central image and event of Christ, so that, by a thousand open and hidden paths, his wholly real and corporeal sense-experiences bring him into contact with that central point.[65]

Balthasar notes that Christ is uniquely present in the Church, in the liturgy, and uniquely in the image of other human beings.[66] Especially in the image of our neighbor (understood broadly as in the Lucan parable of the good Samaritan), perceivers are confronted with someone who has the same complexity, depth, and freedom as themselves, someone who is likewise the recipient of the extravagant love of the trinitarian God and is known by God, someone who is called ultimately to divinity. Being able to recognize this truth about every other person may make us more inclined to see other people in all their particularity. According to Balthasar, it is precisely in the love of neighbor wherein the human being receives conclusively his or her spiritual senses, which, he says, "are none 'other' than his bodily sens-

63. Balthasar, *Glory of the Lord*, I:399.
64. Balthasar, *Glory of the Lord*, I:419–20.
65. Balthasar, *Glory of the Lord*, I:419–20.
66. Balthasar, *Glory of the Lord*, I:420–24.

es, but these senses in so far as they have been formed according to the form of Christ."[67]

Encounters

As an absolute inverse to pornographic modes of vision, encounters with transcendental beauty are events with the capacity to demonstrate what human beings are in our fullness and, moreover, what we shall be eschatologically. According to Balthasar's aesthetics, this encounter brings perceivers to the point of moral transformation.[68] It would not be too much to say that it is confrontation: to see a Caravaggio or read Zosima's conversion narrative in Dostoevsky's *The Brothers Karamazov* or hear Dvořák's ninth symphony or watch Terrance Malick's *Tree of Life* or listen to any of the rich compositions of Arvo Pärt is simultaneously to behold and to be enraptured, both of which are conditions of the possibility for the other. In the perception of beautiful form there is an element of surprise or shock, a sort of rupture or interruption of being taken aback, called to attention, sometimes even transported into rapture.[69] For Balthasar, too, the encounter with genuine beauty has a consequent moral call: the confrontation is an ethical summons, demanding a free "yes" or a "no." In this context, Balthasar recalls the very last lines of Rilke's erotic—though manifestly non-pornographic—poem, "The Archaic Torso of Apollo." Witnessing the suffused beauty of the broken torso implicates us: *for here*, it says, there is no place that does not see you. You must change your life.[70]

One concrete "form" to which Balthasar alludes briefly in his theological aesthetics is that of sacramental marriage, which may prove especially salient in the context of a discussion of pornography.[71] In this case the form calls the married persons to moral and spiritual transformation in a very particular way. "Marriage," Balthasar writes,

67. Balthasar, *Glory of the Lord*, I:424.

68. Here consider, perhaps, Fr. Julián Carrón's book, *Disarming Beauty: Essays on Faith, Truth, and Freedom* (Notre Dame, Ind.: University of Notre Dame Press, 2017).

69. On this point, Joseph Ratzinger's 2002 message to the Communion and Liberation community in Rimini is especially instructive. See Joseph Cardinal Ratzinger, *The Feeling of Things, the Contemplation of Beauty* (August 24–30, 2002).

70. Balthasar, *Glory of the Lord*, I:23; "Revelation and the Beautiful," 107.

71. On marriage, see chapter 9 in this volume by Ann W. Astell entitled "Memory, the Sacrament of Marriage, and the Song of Songs."

is that indissoluble reality which confronts with an iron hand all existence's tendencies to disintegrate, and it compels the faltering person to grow, beyond himself, into real love by modeling his life on the form enjoined. When they make their promises, the spouses are not relying on themselves—the shifting songs of their own freedom—but rather on the form that chooses them because they have chosen it, the form to which they have committed themselves in their act as persons. As persons, the spouses entrust themselves not only to the beloved "thou" and to the biological laws of fertility and family; they entrust themselves foremost to a form with which they can wholly identify themselves even in the deepest aspects of their personality because this form extends through all the levels of life—from its biological roots up to the very heights of grace and life in the Holy Spirit.[72]

Love as represented by sacramental marriage can serve as an antidote to the culture and assumptions of pornography insofar as it brings erotic love to its fulfillment. Sexual expression in a marriage is different from sexual acts in pornographic film because it requires and demands the fullness and mutuality of a love—full of context—that resists extraction and the violence of sheer exhibition value.

Alongside the sense of transformative encounter in art or in sacramental marriage is often a wish to prolong or repeat the experience, to be outside of or beyond time. Those places and moments at which the "lightning flash of eternal beauty" breaks through seem to complexify our sense of time, drawing the experience out of the here and now and pointing the beholder towards the infinite. In this Johannine flash of eternity in an instant, we sometimes want time to stop, or else slow down, to repeat or savor the experience. This is a strange and wonderful thing, what amounts to a seemingly impossible thing, this nostalgia for the Infinity for which we are made and toward which we are ever oriented. True beauty is thus eschatologically calibrated: it calls us to become what we already are and what we shall be. While Soloviev, as we have seen, uses the image of the diamond to illustrate the depth dimension of beauty, and Matthew employs the image of the pearl of great price in his Gospel (Mt 13), Gerard Manley Hopkins uses the image of the diamond to integrate anthropology and Christology, and to identify the luminous nature of true human selves:

72. Balthasar, *Glory of the Lord*, I:27–28.

In a flash, at a trumpet crash,
I am all at once what Christ is, since he was what I am, and
This Jack, joke, poor potsherd, patch, matchwood, immortal diamond,
Is immortal diamond.

Genuine beauty is essentially proleptic, charged with hope, at this strange intersection of past, present, and future. Beauty functions prophetically, non-didactically: it is a sign of contradiction in the world, a grasping after but also a participation now in the infinite and a prophetic anticipation of the life that is to come. As Soloviev puts it, "*every tangible representation of any object and phenomenon from the point of view of its final, definitive status, or in the light of the world to come, is artistic work.*"[73] The revelation of real beauty is the same as that of Christ who is the form of beauty, the perfect and perfectly singular concurrence of finite humanity and luminously infinite divinity, the first and the last, the expression and Incarnation of trinitarian love that envelops and suffuses the entire world from creation to that which is to come. The call of the beautiful is no abstract imperative for empty gratification, as in the pornographic image, but a concrete, singular invitation: Jesus Christ—the Beauty who will save the world—calls us (priceless pearl, immortal diamond!) to himself.

In the conclusion to her exposé on pornography's "hijacking" of modern sexuality, Gail Dines advocates for grassroots efforts that provide "a way to envisage a sexuality that is based on equality, dignity, and respect. Part of this inevitably means *organizing against the commodification of human needs and desires.*"[74] She calls for a reimagination of sexuality that rebuffs the "plasticized," profit-driven images provided in pornographic content, exchanging them with new images that support a way of relating to one another with mutual dignity. What effect might it have on this culture, over-determined by the crassness and reductivity of pornographic images, if both women and men could substitute the damaging self-images from media culture with a self-image that knows oneself unconditionally to be unutterable mystery, a particular, unrepeatable someone so inimitable as to be an absolutely irreplaceable pearl of great price for which an entire

73. Soloviev, *Heart of Reality*, 76.
74. Dines, *Pornland*, 164; empahsis added.

kingdom and all earthly possessions might justly be sold? This way of thinking about the self—as unrepeatable, unnameable mystery, a riddle even to the self, and the recipient of the extravagant love of God—puts into stark contrast all the counterfeit measures of selfhood to which society has made us accustomed. When the domain of the innermost self is preserved as a mystery of unfathomable depth, there is no sense in which self-formation can be dependent upon these false measures.

Beauty—the Beauty made flesh in the Incarnation—saves us from the devastating fiction that selfhood has anything at all to do with the things that we produce or contribute, with anything at all that can be commoditized or exchanged for profit. True beauty, like Angelus Silesius's rose, is "without 'why'"; it is gratuitous, and thus not subject to an economy of crass exchange. In Wendell Berry's poem, "Manifesto: The Mad Farmer Liberation Front," he entreats his audience,

> So, friends, every day do something
> that won't compute. Love the Lord.
> Love the world. Work for nothing.
> Take all that you have and be poor.
> Love someone who does not deserve it.[75]

These acts of gratuitous non-computation are small openings toward resisting the industrialization of sexuality that makes pornography so pervasive in modern culture. One such act of non-computation might include the practice of "wasting" otherwise productive time in a regular practice of Eucharistic adoration, a sign of contradiction in the world that intimates that God always sees before being seen—human beings are both adoring and adored. In Eucharistic adoration, the perceiver does not exert power over or dominate its object of inspection; rather, he or she is confronted with a mysterious reality to which he or she must surrender.[76] This practice thus challenges the modern, contracted understanding of what it means to see something. Seeing is far more than the scrutiny of an object with the physical senses; human beings see, simultaneously, "with the eyes of the heart."

75. Wendell Berry, "Manifesto: The Mad Farmer Liberation Front," in *The Country of Marriage*, 14–15 (Berkeley, Calif.: Counterpoint Press, 2013).

76. Balthasar makes a similar distinction in his discussion of Romano Guardini's *The Senses and Religious Knowledge* in Balthasar, *Glory of the Lord*, I:391.

If beauty is to heal, the modern person—who no longer has eyes to see—must take account of the Crucified One and, as Balthasar puts it, "experience the unclassifiable, total otherness of Christ as the outshining of God's sublimity and glory," which is to say, "to learn to see again."[77] But the kind of beauty we must learn to see exceeds the visual reception of proportion, color, symmetry, harmony, and so on: to perceive even worldly beauty is a great mystery. Balthasar writes, "In order to read even a form within the world, *we must see something invisible as well, and we do in fact see it*."[78] This visible invisibility is a paradox, and the habit and the lie that pornography perpetuates culturally is mistaking this paradox for a contradiction: it dictates that there is *only* the visible to be seen. Being converted and attuned to this invisible, luminous beauty, to attend to the splendor invisibly revealed and concealed in the form, is to inveigh against this lie, to inoculate ourselves, at least aesthetically, against this pervasive constriction of imagination and to preserve us against the sickness unto death that is a life forfeited of true beauty. More than this, however, attunement to Beauty, whether in art, nature, human relationships, spiritual practices, or in the sacramental life of the Church, ushers the human being into the full liveliness of the radically and authentically erotic dimension offered only by the God who is love.[79]

77. Balthasar, *Theo-Logic*, I:20.

78. Balthasar, *Glory of the Lord*, I: 444.

79. I am grateful to Elizabeth Antus, Elizabeth Groppe, Jay Martin, and Joe Nolan for reading and commenting helpfully upon previous drafts of this chapter.

JOHN C. CAVADINI

15 ⪻ *The Price of Pleasure* and the Power of Love Crucified

The Perversion of Manhood and the Healing Power of the *Anastasis*

What does it mean to be a man?[1] The pornographers whose work we have considered in this volume would perhaps scoff at the notion that they are addressing such a lofty question, but the portrayal of masculinity in pornographic films suggests an answer. A man is someone who enjoys himself most and knows himself best in degrading, humiliating, and debasing women. A man is most himself as a man, has the climax experience of manhood, in robbing women of their human dignity and rendering them half-human. According to an old Roman saying, "a man loses half his soul the day he becomes a slave."[2] The pornographers would have us believe that a man is someone who enjoys himself by taking half of the soul away from a woman and then celebrates this accomplishment with other men. For example, they give us the image of a miserable woman, an actress, with semen from six different men on her face;[3] this is an inverse image of those men, a community of men who have defined themselves as men by their "joy" in taking half of the soul away from a woman, who is left with the other half of her soul so that she has enough left to know that she has been degraded. Even without the explicit aggression that is

1. The author wishes to express his gratitude to the Catholic University of America Press editor John Martino for his contributions to this chapter.

2. Quoted in an essay about affliction by Simone Weil, *Waiting for God* (Abingdon, Oxon: Routledge, 2010), 50.

3. As seen in the documentary film *The Price of Pleasure: Pornography, Sexuality, and Relationships* (Northhampton, Mass.: Media Education Foundation, 2008), DVD.

now common in pornographic films,[4] the sexual acts they depict are acts that attempt to take joy in contempt, domination, subordination, and degradation. The physical violence that enters into many of the images is simply a natural outgrowth, an exterior sign of an interior attitude. Pornography is a kind of anti-sacrament, a visible sign that makes powerfully present the essence of male sexual "enjoyment" as the pornographers would have us men experience it.[5]

One might reply that this violence and contempt exists only in fantasy. I would reply that the very idea that this is a fantasy is a function of the attempt to depict pornographic acts on screen. The fantasy is that no one is actually being degraded, and that this is just a "representation" or an "image," the product of "acting." It is easy for the viewer to forget that what he is enjoying is not a drawing or an artist's rendition of women being degraded, but real live women who have been physically violated again and again. The male viewer is not truly enjoying a fantasy degradation of the image of a woman, but the real degradation of a real woman, screened as though it were just a movie, just a play, just acting. In reality, when the man watching the screen joins in the action through his own pursuit of sexual gratification, his own most intimate bodily member becomes a member of this community of contempt. In the most sinister way possible, fantasy and reality are joined, and the male viewer experiences his most intimate sexual self as part of a real, not fantasy, community of exploitation and degradation. Perhaps the most sinister part is that he does not (hopefully) consciously will this. The male viewer commits himself to a fantasy, which turns out to be a deadly serious reality under the guise of a fantasy. It is a fantasy one watches in order to enjoy it, and if one repeatedly subjects one's most intimate feelings of pleasure and enjoyment to these fantasies, then one is learning to take pleasure in being part of the real degradation that is actually taking place. Perhaps, and I am speaking to men here, you have or have had a glimmer of a suspicion that the

4. Ana J. Bridges et al., "Aggression and Sexual Behavior in Best-Selling Pornography Videos: A Content Analysis Update," *Violence against Women* 16, no. 10 (2010): 1065–85.

5. I speak throughout this essay primarily of the male enjoyment of women depicted in pornography; of course, there are other variants of pornographic films and viewers, but those about which I speak are the most pervasive ones.

expansive feeling of sexual arousal was a kind of longing for something beautiful, an enlargement of the soul so that one could experience joy in an elevated state of gratitude and wonder at the mutual sharing of love and respect. But that is not what the fantasy in the pornographic image depicts, to which a man is expected to bind his sense of pleasure in enjoying it.

But this means that, in participating in this way in an act of soul-theft, you are actually losing half of your own soul as well. It becomes harder and harder to remember the suspicion that the expansive feeling of sexual arousal is properly a call to joy in the enlargement of one's soul in humility and wonder and gratitude, that indeed there is any telos for sexual desire beyond pleasure-taking in degradation. Instead one's soul increasingly becomes as coarse as the pornographer's cynicism, and one doesn't even notice it happening, because, after all, it's "only a fantasy."[6] Pornography coarsens the souls of men so that they recognize themselves as men only in the shared pleasures of contempt. That is the price of pornographic pleasure.

Young male readers—are you going to accept that as an adequate account of what it means to be a man? Must we give up the designation "man," and refer to ourselves with the neutral descriptor "penised persons," a term suggested by another recent commentator on pornography, because being a man really *means* being what is depicted in pornography? Are we really reducible not only to our bodies, but even to just one part of our body, a bodily member whose only telos is to take pleasure in the degradation of a woman who is soul-robbed and dismembered by the anti-sacrament of pornography?

I call pornography an "anti-sacrament" because, by analogy to a genuine sacrament, it is more than a mere symbol—it efficaciously

6. Pornography's defenders maintain that viewers can distinguish their own reality from the images of actors and actresses on a screen. This was not true for Michael Leahy, who writes autobiographically that in his undergraduate experience in a school in the Pacific Northwest "porn was THE status symbol for independent male living." Michael participated in this porn culture and soon found that he needed to "score" sexually "even if it came at another person's expense. . . . I needed it [sex] to feel a sense of worth and significance, to feel good about myself and who I was. To be a real man in the way I always saw real men portrayed in porn. That was my ideal, to become fulfilled and satisfied as a sexual conqueror of women." Michael Leahy, *Porn University: What College Students Are Really Saying about Sex on Campus* (Chicago, Ill.: Northfield Publishing, 2009), 21, 23.

makes present that which it signifies.[7] The Eucharist, for example, makes truly present the person of Christ and brings about the unity of the Church, which is also his Body. In the anti-sacrament of pornography, the viewing of visual representations of women being degraded efficaciously makes present a real sexual arousal and a perverse unity among the viewers. Pornography is the efficacious sign of the loss of the souls of both men and women. It is not a neutral fantasy.

Even if we recognize this loss, how do we recover our souls? The title for this chapter comes from the *The Price of Pleasure*, a documentary film that is intended as a critique of the pornography industry but that left me with the question of whether there can actually *be* an objective documentary on pornography that does not itself, in its turn, become pornographic.[8] The filmmakers seem to have assumed that everyone watching was used to seeing pornography. The illustrative film clips came up without warning and so they participated in the violence of pornography itself, because if you hadn't seen such pornography before, as I had not, you would not know what was coming. But part of the sick, frightened, and frozen feeling the documentary left me with was due not simply to the shock at the pornography I saw, but also to the commentary, which seemed to leave me with no alternative to the pornographers' depiction of what it means to be a man. To that extent, the documentary participated in the anti-sacrament of pornography itself, for it presented no account of the meaning of masculinity other than one that identifies manliness with the subordination and degradation of women, and so it participated, even if at arm's length, in the false joy of the robbing of women's souls. For example, though there was one undergraduate man interviewed, and he was willing to speak, somewhat wistfully, about the unwelcome intrusion of pornographic images into his actual attempts at sexual intimacy, there were no first-person stories of men who had recovered from the addiction to pornography, though there was an extensive in-

7. *Catechism of the Catholic Church*, 2nd ed. (Washington, D.C.: United States Conference of Catholic Bishops, 2000), 1131: "The sacraments are efficacious signs of grace, instituted by Christ and entrusted to the Church, by which divine life is dispensed to us. The visible rites by which the sacraments are celebrated signify and make present the graces proper to each sacrament. They bear fruit in those who receive them with the required dispositions."

8. *The Price of Pleasure.*

terview with a woman who was an ex-porn star. There was a depiction of counseling available to women, but no depiction of counseling available to men, or support groups of and for men trying to recover from an addiction to pornography. There was no depiction of friendship among men forged through mutual support in recovering from the addictive coarsening of pornography. The documentary left the male viewer with no viable community of men as an alternative to the virtual, anti-community defined by the shared "enjoyment" of the robbing of women's souls. There was not in this particular documentary even a single depiction of a group of people devoted to political action against pornography. Such men and women were represented only in "fantasy" too, that is, only in the cynical comment made by one of the pornographers interviewed, who called such organized protests "impotent," pun surely intended.

This failure is itself pornographic, because it leaves any man watching the film feeling that what is depicted in pornography about women is false, but that what is depicted about men is true, and not only in the sense, horrific enough, that the male actors are enjoying themselves while the women are not. The documentary seems to imply that men should restrain their masculinity for the good of women, but not for their own good and happiness. With the sole exception of the slightly wistful undergraduate man, no one was allowed to speak who might have even hinted that there is another way to look at human sexuality, one that gives a meaning to being men and women that does not involve taking pleasure in soul-stealing. The dramatic rise in pornography that we have seen in the last thirty years, the documentary implied, is what we must expect as the natural outcome of a system in which capitalism and patriarchy are intertwined. Capitalism commodifies anything it can lay its hands on, and patriarchy offers women the unforgivingly cold embrace of capitalism as nothing but patriarchal cultural constructs, ready-made for domination and consumption by men.

I agree that a consumerist culture—in which there is no higher value than a cash value—commodifies anything it can, meaning anything vulnerable, and so will necessarily be a pornographic culture. But there are other narratives to consider that the documentary was not willing to entertain. One could argue, for example, that it is the pervasive acceptance of the separation of sex from procreation that is being so efficaciously represented in the anti-sacrament of our consumerist culture, pornography. Procreation has to be captured and commodified, made into production, and for that it has to be separated from an intimacy that is irreducibly personal. The severing of the fathering and raising of children from bodily masculinity unleashes a powerful force that then expresses itself in less-than-loving ways. Some will argue that Pope Paul VI's letter *Humanae Vitae* warned us in 1968 that a contraceptive culture would be one whose hallmark was the instrumentalization of women. I'm not, at present, arguing that the documentary proves the truth of these alternative narratives as explaining the proliferation of pornography, but rather that it is significant that nothing of the kind was represented in the film. To use a metaphor coined by Andrea Dworkin, who was a prominent feminist critic of pornography in the 1980s, pornography is evidence of the "homelessness" of women in our society.[9] Homelessness, she explains, in the literal sense, is a social condition of impoverishment that creates a population of women who can be prostituted. In the metaphorical sense, homelessness is a metaphor of the condition of all women in a society in which one in three girls is sexually abused before the age of eighteen and one in two married women is beaten by her husband.[10] "I think," she writes, "that women are dispossessed of a place to live that is safe."[11] It may seem strange to cite Dworkin to support a claim about the instrumentalization of women made by Pope Paul VI, who would not usually be described as a "radical feminist."[12] But both secu-

9. For instance, Andrea Dworkin, "Prostitution and Male Supremacy," *Michigan Journal of Gender and Law* 1, no. 1 (1993): 1–12. While the context of that article was prostitution, Dworkin was a fierce critic of pornography in her own way. See Andrea Dworkin, *Pornography: Men Possessing Women* (New York: Perigee, an imprint of G. P. Putnam's Sons, 1981).

10. Dworkin, "Prostitution and Male Supremacy," 5. She cites Diana E. H. Russell, *Sexual Exploitation: Rape, Child Sexual Abuse, and Workplace Harassment* (Newberry Park, Calif.: Sage Publications, 1984), 193–94; Nancy Gibbs, "'Til Death Do Us Part," *Time* 141, no. 3 (January 18, 1993): 38, 41.

11. Dworkin, "Prostitution and Male Supremacy," 5.

12. Dworkin, of course, was as much an advocate of contraception as she was an opponent of pornography. See Dworkin, *Heartbreak: The Political Memoir of a Feminist Militant* (New York: Perseus Books, 2002), 23. On the other hand, she does note that the

lar feminists and Catholics are interested in developing some vision of human sexuality that is different—and truer—than that of the pornographers, a vision of homecoming rather than homelessness. For Paul VI, this vision is one in which a man and a woman perfect one another in a specific and exclusive "mutual gift of themselves," lovingly make a home for each other, are open to receiving the gift of children, and learn to feel the soul-affirming and soul-building pleasures and joy of being with one another.[13]

Such a view of sexuality requires something surprisingly absent from the documentary itself—the human couple. Most of the scenes consisted of blurred-out clips of partially glimpsed men (plural, usually) doing various things to a woman. Almost none of the clips depicted the male actors as human persons with faces—the faces were not blurred, they simply were not shown—nor did the clips portray the human couple, a man and a woman together. I realize that the intention of this is to highlight, without the mystification that sex provides, the degradation and humiliation of the women involved, and this indeed was very effective. Nor do I wish to lobby for any more pornographic images than the documentary, unfortunately, already contains. But I wonder if there is another, more hidden motive for leaving out a scene of a man and woman, specifically. The human couple is something intrinsically beautiful. Even in its most perverted and degraded manifestations or depictions, the couple still retains, even if by contrast, a glimmer of its original beauty as an original sign of hope, of new life. Depicting only various gang-rape perversions of this means depicting not simply the degradation of women but the degradation of the human couple, of the family, and so of an ideal of men and women together.

Evil, according to the Catholic tradition, is parasitic on the good and gets its power from whatever good remains. Hell is hell because it is the inversion and perversion of an ideal, to which it still bears some reference, as in Dante's *Inferno*. The power of pornography is partly that it perverts the authentic longing of the human heart for divine and human love. That very longing, however corrupted and impugned, is

---

state has used contraception in a way that treats non-white poor women and children as expendable. Dworkin, *Right-wing Women* (New York: Perigee, 1978), 149–50.

13. Paul VI, Encyclical Letter *Humanae Vitae* (July 25, 1968), 8.

present in a perverted way in pornography and gives pornography its power. The documentary's removal of the man, paradoxically, is a part of its failure to offer a counter-ideal, a wider framework in which one could even recognize and mourn pornography's twisting and perverting of the goodness of human longing and desire.[14] In that sense, the pornography proved so irresistible that the documentary could not resist moving one degree farther away from any possible memory of a framework in which sex has a telos. And so one left the documentary with a feeling of disempowerment, of helplessness, and, if you are a man, with the alternatives of either renouncing the pleasure of being a man or else embracing the soul destroying, spirit-coarsening spirituality depicted by the pornographers, which is really an anti-spirituality.

The alternative is to envision the true meaning of masculinity. This requires, among other things, that we counter pornography, a system of visual representation degrading reality and yet masquerading as fantasy, with another system of visual representation that speaks truthfully of and participates in the reality that it signifies. Of course, much more goes into building a true community of men ecclesially and socially than just visual images. But a system of visual representation that conveys grace and love can invite conversion from our own complicity in the culture of pornography and contribute to a process of healing one's imagination from its seeming nakedness and helplessness before the deceits of the pornographer. This alternative system of visual representation is the traditional iconography of the Church, centered on Jesus Christ, "the revelation of the mystery of the Father and His love," who "fully reveals man to man himself and makes his supreme calling clear."[15]

The icon of the *Anastasis*, which depicts the descent of Christ into Hades, appears on the cover of this volume. I have in mind another exemplar of this type from the Chora Church of the Holy Savior in Istanbul, Turkey (Fig. 15-1). Recall the micro-parable of the strong man from the Gospel of Mark: "No man can enter into a strong man's house, and spoil his goods, except he will first bind the strong man; and then

14. Nor did any of the academic commentators on the documentary that I have seen do much to offer an alternative either.

15. Vatican Council II, *Gaudium et Spes* (December 7, 1965), 22.

he will spoil his house" (Mk 4:27). The icon depicts this spoliation of the strong man's house, the house of death, or Hades. You can see the "strong man" bound at the bottom of the icon. His house has been plundered. All of the instruments of imprisonment, the locks, the keys, and bars are knocked into fragments and the captives liberated from captivity to death. In the words of Paul Evdokimov's commentary:

> At the center of the icon, we see Christ the lightning-bolt as he breaks into Hades; he is a brilliantly shining light, the master of life, charged with the dynamism of the Holy Spirit, and shining with the divine energies. But his face, as though immobilized by his infinite tenderness, royally masters and dominates this liberating whirlwind. . . . The power of his gesture, this violence that grabs hold of the heavens and flashes across the firmament, is reinforced by Christ's flowing and floating tunic. . . . He is the Lord, but his only power is Love crucified.[16]

Christ is the "stronger man" here. He is unarmed. His powerful physical frame represents the strength of his person, which, as Evdokimov put it, is the strength of love, powerful but not on the same terms as the "strong man" is powerful. This is the power of love of one so free as to empty himself and, though sinless, to join in solidarity with sinners to the point of fully accepting the lot of sinners, which is death. He did not claim special privilege or status but rather persisted in solidarity even to the point of death, and so he transformed all human solidarity away from sin and death, inviting all men and women to become sons and daughters of God. "So you are," writes Paul to the Galatians, "no longer a slave but a son, and if a son then also an heir, through God" (Gal 4:7). Adam and Eve, the primal couple, are raised, liberated, and joined in Christ; their fellowship—their solidarity—is restored and refigured according to this love. Looking at this figure of "the stronger man," one could not imagine him using his strength to engage in the acts of exploitation and violence depicted in pornography. Instead his strength is used to solidify and heal the relationship between Adam and Eve.

This icon has something to offer all Christians in its interpretation of the descent into Hades by Love itself, but perhaps it has something

16. Paul Evdokimov, *The Art of the Icon: A Theology of Beauty*, trans. Steven Bigham (Redondo Beach, Calif.: Oakwood, 1990), 324.

extra to offer a man who feels as though the only way to be a man is to participate in the culture of domination and degradation, tendered by the anti-sacrament of pornography. Icons are not, strictly speaking, sacraments, but they are channels of grace for those who contemplate them and in so doing, contemplate the mysteries they depict. An icon such as the *Anastasis* could be a visual aid around which to focus the attention of men who are healing from addiction to pornography. It invites them, at once, to see a larger horizon for what it means to be a man, and, at the same time, to grasp the hand of Love crucified, grace himself, and never let go.

ELIZABETH T. GROPPE

Pastoral Coda

Rop tú mo Baile—"Be thou my vision." Thus begins an Irish hymn of the *lorica* genre—a prayer for protection—dated to sometime between AD 950 and 1000. The symbols of a battle-shield and sword invoked in the verses that follow echo Paul's letter to the Ephesians, which speaks of the shield of faith and the sword of the Spirit (Eph 6:16–17). At the heart of the scholarly reflection in this volume is a pastoral care and concern for the protection of those whom pornography threatens and the healing of those whom pornography has harmed. This coda revisits some of the themes of the chapters with particular attention to pastoral and ecclesial practice.[1] It incorporates reflections by readers who generously agreed to comment on a draft of the manuscript, including several current or former students at two Catholic universities and several members of the Saint Augustine Men's Group, a lay apostolate in the diocese of Fort Wayne-South Bend, Indiana, with a mission to support men in living in chastity and freedom from pornography.[2] Some of those who shared comments elected to be identified by name and others simply by their affiliations.

Such is the power of images that the portion of this book most prominent in your memory may well be the inset of color plates, and perhaps this has rendered the impression that the overarching thesis of this volume is that we can heal our imagination of pornography simply through the incorporation of Christian imagery in our homes, schools, and churches. Perhaps you consider such a hypothesis to be simplistic, and I would concur. To be sure, the character of our visual

1. In conjunction with the publication of the pastoral statement "Create in Me a Clean Heart," the USCCB has compiled pastoral resources including videos, books, support groups, counseling, and internet filtering tools at http://www.foryourmarriage.org/help-for-men-and-women-struggling-with-pornography-use-or-addiction/, accessed November 8, 2018.

2. See http://staugustinefwsb.org/about-us, accessed November 8, 2018.

culture is of real consequence. Marketing firms do not spend millions of dollars on internet pop-up ads, billboards, and television commercials because they desire to spend money without result. These expenditures are based on evidence of the conscious and subconscious effects of images on the human psyche and human behavior.[3] Even just the presence of Christian visual imagery in the horizon of one's daily routine can be a salutary reminder of the character of God's love and the baptismal vocation to holiness—mysteries that can be obscured by the many counter-veiling images that saturate our culture. Even more so can an intentional contemplation of sacred images—a mystagogical practice of *visio divina* akin to the tradition of *lectio divina,* the contemplative reading of Scripture—contribute to the formation of a sacramental imagination.[4]

As the contributors to this volume have written, however, the cultivation of a sacramental imagination is a matter not only of *what* we see but also *how* we see. It concerns not only the character of the images we behold in our homes, churches, schools, places of employment, and digital screens, but also the mode of our perception and the community and context in which we see and interpret visual imagery. The production and consumption of pornography, John C. Cavadini explains in chapter 15, is a kind of anti-sacrament, an act that is the inverse of the Eucharist. It efficaciously makes present that which it signifies, placing us in relation to other real human persons within a community of actual exploitation and degradation.[5] To see with the eyes of the heart (Eph 1:18), in contrast, is to participate through the power of the Holy Spirit in the very Body of Christ. This communion in Christ's Body is both an unearned, unmerited grace and a responsibility that requires much of us, including a practice of learning to see. The discipline of learning to see was at one time an explicit part of Christian mystagogy.[6] Saint Ambrose (AD 337–97), for example, wrote to catechumens

3. Mara Einstein, *Advertising: What Everyone Needs to Know* (New York: Oxford University Press, 2017), 57.

4. On the practice of *visio divina*, see Barbara Sutton, *Seeing the Word: Program Manual* (Collegeville, Minn.: Liturgical Press, 2011), 20–23

5. John C. Cavadini, chapter 15, 283–84.

6. See Georgia Frank, "'Taste and See': The Eucharist and the Eyes of Faith in the Fourth Century," *Church History* 70, no. 4. (December 2001): 619–43.

preparing for baptism that they must learn to see not only with the eyes of the body but also with the eyes of the heart (*oculos cordis*). Just as Jesus' application of mud to the eyes of the blind man healed his sight, so too the eyes of the neophyte's heart will gradually be opened as the preparation for baptism progresses.[7] The catechetical lectures of John Chrysostom (d. AD 407) anticipated the fuller sensorial experience (*pleiona tēn aisthēsin*) that awaited catechumens when they were welcomed to their first Eucharist after learning to see through spiritual eyes.[8] Chrysostom described these eyes as inseparable from the eyes of the body and yet the means of a distinct kind of vision: "God has made for us two kinds of eyes: those of the flesh and those of faith.... The eyes of the body see the body emerging from the water; the eyes of faith see the new man come forth brightly shining from that sacred purification."[9] Chrysostom's mystagogical instruction is part of a tradition of reflection on the spiritual senses first attested in the writings of Origen of Alexandria (ca. AD 185–254) and continued in our own era by theologians including Karl Rahner and Hans Urs von Balthasar.[10] In Balthasar's approach, the spiritual eyes of the human person who is a body-soul unity are inseparable from the physical eyes and receive the graced capacity to behold the *lumen* of the glory of God in and through Christ. The spiritual senses, Jennifer Newsome Martin explains in chapter 14, are none other than the bodily senses "in so far as they have been formed according to the form of Christ."[11]

What mystagogical and ascetic practices might help us to learn to see with spiritual eyes the *lumen* of the glory of God? The contributors to this volume have identified a number of spiritual disciplines and

7. Ambrose, *De sacramentis* 4.4.14–20; see also 6.1.2. Cited in Frank, "'Taste and See,'" 620.

8. Chrysostom's term *pleiona tēn aisthēsin*, Orthodox theologian and Greek scholar Silviu Bunta explains, does not mean "fuller perception" as some translations would have it. "*Aisthesis* involves experiences by the senses rather than a sheer activity of the intellect. Even when the intellect is involved, *aisthesis* is still sensorial, experiential." Correspondence with Silviu Bunta, December 16, 2019.

9. Chrysostom, Cat. 3.3.9–22. Cited in Frank, "'Taste and See,'" 635.

10. See Paul L. Gavrilyuk and Sarah Coakley, eds., *The Spiritual Senses: Perceiving God in Western Christianity* (Cambridge: Cambridge University Press, 2012); Mark McInroy, *Balthasar on the Spiritual Senses: Perceiving Splendour* (New York: Oxford University Press, 2014).

11. Jennifer Newsome Martin, chapter 14, 275–76.

practices that can contribute to the cultivation of sacramental vision. These include the practice of chastity of the eyes, the tending of the dovecotes of memory, cultivation of an iconic gaze, the practice of the corporal works of mercy, and active participation in the sacramental and corporate life of the ecclesial body that culminates in the praise and glorification of God.

The Practice of Chastity of the Eyes

In an age of pornography, a foundational dimension of learning to see with the eyes of the heart is the discipline of chastity of the eyes. "Avoid images," David W. Fagerberg emphasizes in chapter 7, "that would corrupt your imagination. . . . Be attentive and thoughtful about the object on which your light-beam falls, because you are never going to unsee the thing."[12] This wisdom from the Christian ascetical tradition finds support in twenty-first century neuroscience, from which we learn that images cannot be willfully erased from our memories. If a curious toddler ingests a mothball that rolled out of a linen closet, one can rush the child to an emergency room where charcoal can be administered to absorb the poisonous substance Naphthalene. But if a ten-year-old playing on a computer is locked into a mouse-trap of pornographic images, there is no comparable way to cleanse the imagination. "I still have in my head vivid recollections of specific scenes in pornographic films I saw 25 years ago," writes Robert Jensen, who viewed pornography occasionally in his 20s and subsequently critiqued the pornography industry as a professor of journalism. "I still struggle against those forces. I have to work to bracket out of my mind—to the degree possible—those images."[13] A member of the Saint Augustine Men's Group corroborates: "Having viewed porn and then been given a way out of seeing more of it, I realized the memories of images continued to cause problems related to compulsions and emotional immaturity."[14] He advises parents to help their children to

12. David W. Fagerberg, chapter 7, 150.

13. Robert Jensen, *Getting Off: Pornography and the End of Masculinity* (Cambridge, Mass.: South End Press, 2007), 41–42.

14. Correspondence with a member of the Saint Augustine Men's Group, February 2018.

understand "how harmful images stay in their psyche long after they casually view them on their electronic devices."[15]

Images prevalent in the media, writes Randi Sider-Rose in chapter 4, may evoke involuntary responses. Some responses can be willfully resisted, but it is better not to be exposed in the first place, not to "set a worthless thing before your eyes" (Ps 103:2)."[16] The disciplines of an ascetic life, she continues, are not an abrogation of human freedom; to the contrary, the asceticism of the eyes enables freedom from involuntary responses and prepares us to behold the glory of God in creation and in every human being. Dr. Kevin Skinner outlines steps that one can take upon encountering a pornography teaser to execute a "U-Turn" of attention to interrupt the activation sequence of triggers, emotions, thoughts, and chemical releases that can lead to viewing pornography.[17] The "Can Do Plan" presented by Kristen A. Jenson and Gail Poyner in *Good Pictures, Bad Pictures: Porn-Proofing Today's Young Kids* is a version of this protective turning that parents can teach children through this picture book intended to be read by parents and children together.[18]

Another form of parental chastity of the eyes that mothers and fathers can exercise on behalf of our children is the placement of filtering software on computers, phones, and other electronic devices. Maria Morrow, a mother of young children and author of the University of Dayton MA thesis *Pornography and Penance*, recommends that parents "delay giving a smartphone to a child as long as possible, always provide at-home filters for your children's internet, check up on how your child is spending time online, limit screen time, encourage and enable independence with outdoor activities, get to know your

15. Correspondence with a member of the Saint Augustine Men's Group, February 2018.

16. Randi Sider-Rose, chapter 4, 95–96.

17. Kevin Skinner, *Treating Pornography Addiction* (Provo, Utah: Growth Climate, 2005). Cited in Matthew Fradd, *The Porn Myth: Exposing the Reality behind the Fantasy of Pornography* (San Francisco, Calif.: Ignatius Press, 2017), 182–85.

18. Kristen A. Jenson and Gail Poyner, *Good Pictures, Bad Pictures: Porn-Proofing Today's Young Kids* (Richland, Wash.: Glen Cove Press, 2016). See also China Weil, "How to Talk to Young People about the Dangers of Pornography," *Church Life Journal* (February 6, 2017), accessed October 30, 2018, http://churchlife.nd.edu/2017/02/06/the-dangers-of-pornography/.

children's friends and invite them into your home."[19] Rob, a member of the Saint Augustine Men's Group, counsels: "Monitor, oversee, and be protective! Speak matter-of-factly of the truth and beauty of virginity of both the eyes and the body. Point out the 'soft core porn' of TV shows, commercials, and printed media. Speak clinically about the harms of pornography—the lives lost and damaged."[20]

No matter how vigilant a parent may be, however, it is almost impossible to fully protect a child or young adult from encounter with pornography. "Do not assume that your precious child has not been exposed," Rob continues.[21] Filtering software is imperfect and may be beyond the financial means of parents with low-wage employment who face hard economic choices. And, even if a parent filters the family electronics, another child with a mobile device at school or on a playground can easily break the shield of protection a parent has attempted to construct. The frequency of involuntary exposure is one of the reasons that the pastoral statement by the United States Conference of Catholic Bishops, "Create in Me a Clean Heart," describes pornography in our internet age as a structure of sin. "It is so pervasive in sectors of our society," they write, "that it is difficult to avoid, challenging to remove, and has negative effects that go beyond any one person's actions."[22] Initial exposure may lead to a habitual or even compulsive practice. Morrow chose pornography as the focus of her MA thesis "because I had heard so many stories of young Christian men who truly believed that pornography was sinful and yet found it very difficult to avoid.... Christian men were struggling with it and failing so easily, despite their intellectual convictions against it. These were well-intentioned, kind young men who wanted to live good and holy lives but found it very difficult in a society where pornography was readily available and even acceptable."[23]

Personal virtue is a necessary but insufficient response to social

19. Correspondence with Maria Morrow, March 20, 2018. In addition to the MA thesis, Morrow is also the author of "Pornography and Penance," in *Leaving and Coming Home: New Wineskins for Catholic Sexual Ethics*, ed. David Cloutier, 62–84 (Eugene, Ore.: Cascade Books, an imprint of Wipf and Stock, 2010).

20. Correspondence with Rob of the Saint Augustine Men's Group, January 2018.

21. Correspondence with Rob of the Saint Augustine Men's Group, January 2018.

22. United States Conference of Catholic Bishops, *Create in Me a Clean Heart*, 8.

23. Correspondence with Maria Morrow, March 20, 2018.

sin, which requires social action and social transformation. One student effort to develop a corporate form of the practice of chastity of the eyes is the initiative of Students for Child-Oriented Policy (SCOP) at the University of Notre Dame. They organized White Ribbon against Pornography (WRAP) week, which concluded with the circulation of a petition calling upon Notre Dame to filter the university Wi-Fi to block pornographic websites. "We're hoping that a block, if it goes through," said senior Maria Kunath, "gives people pause and they say, 'Okay, why is that? . . . We're hoping that the filter is a moment for a lot of people to pause and think and say, 'What's porn? Why am I using it? Why does Notre Dame think it's bad?'"[24]

On the civic scale, *The Catechism of the Catholic Church* calls for civil authorities to "prevent the production and distribution of pornographic materials."[25] There was a time, according to political science Professor James R. Stoner, when public policy in the United States was more protective than is currently the case. In the aftermath of the development of radio technology, the Communications Act of 1934 affirmed that there was to be no censorship over radio communication and no interference with the right of free speech but also that "no person within the jurisdiction of the United States shall utter any obscene, indecent, or profane language by means of radio communication."[26] In the 1957 case of *Roth v. United States*, the Supreme Court reaffirmed that the First Amendment does not protect obscenity. However, the verdict occurred in a context in which *Playboy* magazine had begun publication and become immediately popular, and the ruling became a precedent for an interpretation of the term "obscenity" in a manner that allowed for the publication and public airing of content that once would have been classified as obscene.[27]

24. Ciara Hopkinson, "Students Look to Implement Wi-Fi Filter to Limit Pornography Use," *The Observer* (October 30, 2017), accessed March 21, 2018, https://ndsmcobserver.com/2017/10/students-look-to-implement-wi-fi-filter-to-limit-pornography-use/.

25. *Catechism of the Catholic Church*, 2nd ed. (Washington, D.C.: United States Conference of Catholic Bishops, 2000), no. 2354.

26. The Federal Communications Act of 1934, Public Law No. 416, June 19, 1934, 73rd Congress, http://www.criminalgovernment.com/docs/61StatL101/ComAct34.html, cited in James R. Stoner Jr., "Freedom, Virtue, and the Politics of Regulating Pornography," in *The Social Costs of Pornography: A Collection of Papers*, edited by James R. Stoner Jr. and Donna M. Hughes (Princeton, N.J.: The Witherspoon Institute, 2010), 168.

27. Stoner, "Freedom, Virtue, and the Politics of Regulating Pornography," 169.

In 1983, Minneapolis legislators therefore challenged pornography on other grounds. A city ordinance was passed that identified pornography as a violation of the civil and human rights of women, which are protected by the Fourteenth Amendment to the Constitution, and the city of Indianapolis and other polities soon followed suit.[28] In Minneapolis, however, the mayor vetoed the ordinance, and the Indianapolis legislation was struck down in 1985 by the U.S. Court of Appeals as an infringement of free speech.[29] In 1996, Congress passed the Communications Decency Act (CDA) that was signed into law by President Clinton as part of the Telecommunications Act. The CDA prohibited the transmission of obscene or indecent communication to children and youth under the age of eighteen. The CDA was challenged in *Reno v. ACLU*, and the Supreme Court ruled that the Act was too broadly construed; its means of protecting minors would also suppress speech to which adults have a constitutional right.[30] Notably, writes Terry Schilling, Executive Director of the American Principles Project, this ruling leaves open the door for more defined forms of restriction. There are several legally and constitutionally feasible ways to protect minors from pornography in the United States, he explains, including a "zoning" of the internet in which pornography would be limited to an .xxx domain that users could not access without adult age verification, or a filtering of the internet at the Internet Service Provider (IPS) level.[31] This later approach is now in effect in Great Britain. There, Internet Service Providers filter content such that the default version of their internet service is pornography-free. In contrast to the United States, where one must "opt out" of pornography by installing a filter on one's personal computer or phone, Britain requires anyone who wants to access pornography to "opt in" by requesting to bypass the ISP filter after verifying their adult age. "This is, quite simply," British Prime Minster

28. For the proceedings, see Catharine A. MacKinnon and Andrea Dworkin, eds., *In Harm's Way: The Pornography Civil Rights Hearings* (Cambridge, Mass.: Harvard University Press, 1997).

29. American Booksellers v. Hudnut, 771 F.2d 323 (7th Cir. 1985). Cited in MacKinnon and Dworkin, *In Harm's Way*, 17 and 17n54.

30. Terry Schilling, "How to Regulate Pornography," *First Things* (November 2019), accessed December 12, 2019, https://www.firstthings.com/article/2019/11/how-to-regulate-pornography.

31. Schilling, "How to Regulate Pornography."

David Cameron stated when making the 2013 announcement, "about how we protect our children and their innocence."[32]

Tending the Dovecotes of Memory

There has been a decline in the presence of sacred imagery in Catholic churches and homes, Danielle Peters observes in chapter 5, at the same time as there has been an exponential increase in other forms of imagery in our media and digital culture.[33] Catholics can be more intentional about the visual culture of our parishes and homes in awareness that this culture forms memory and contributes to the shaping of our wills, emotions, and desires. In the Middle Ages, Nathaniel Peters explains in chapter 10, the training of memory was approached not only as a means of storing information but also as a matter of ethics and character. William of Saint Thierry urged his readers to fill the storehouse or "dovecotes" of their memories with holy things that imprint signs of God's love on the consciousness.[34]

A memory replete with sacred images cultivates what philosopher Charles Taylor terms a "social imaginary"—a constellation of expectations, norms, and assumptions—that is fundamentally different from the social imaginary generated by pornography. Today's pornography, for example, commonly portrays the male as a dominating and aggressive figure and the female as a subordinate object of intercourse or violence. In the fresco of the Resurrection in the Chora Church of the Holy Savior, in contrast, Cavadini observes, the strong man is one who is unarmed and whose face radiates an infinite tenderness as he breaks the bonds of sin and death through the power of love (Fig. 15-1).[35] In chapter 5, Peters highlights imagery of East and West in which Mary is a strong and free woman who uses her agency to say "yes" to God, a mediator and intercessor between humanity and God, an eminent examplar of the Christian life and a symbol of the universal call to holiness, a maternal presence, and a victorious Queen of Heaven.[36]

32. "Online Pornography To Be Blocked by Default, P. M. Announces," *B.B.C. News* (July 22, 2013), accessed October 15, 2018, http://www.bbc.com/news/uk-23401076.

33. Danielle M. Peters, chapter 5, 98.

34. Nathaniel Peters, chapter 10, 192 and 199.

35. Cavadini, chapter 15, 289.

36. This is not to suggest that Jesus Christ is an exemplar only for men and Mary

Mary also appears in Catholic visual culture as the grieving mother of the Pietà. In the best-selling pornographic films analyzed by Ana Bridges and her colleagues in a study cited in several chapters in this volume, the faces of actresses in brutally aggressive scenes typically express neutrality or even pleasure, obscuring the reality of the violence that these women are experiencing.[37] In contrast, the Pietà images discussed by Danielle Peters and Dianne Phillips portray realistically the agony of Christ crucified. In Michele Giambono's *Imago Pietatis* (Fig. 6-16), Christ's anguish is palpable; blood streams in rivulets from his crown of thorns and frames his contorted face. In Carlo Crivelli's *Lamentation over the Dead Christ*, the faces of the disciples are etched in grief (Fig. 6-17). Mary, Phillips observes, gazes deeply into the eyes of Christ, tenderly measuring the breadth of the wound in his lanced side, recalling to our memories the prophecy of the piercing she will suffer with her beloved son. Dovecotes of memory that harbor a version of the Pietà will shape a realistic imagination aware of both the terrible consequences of human sin and violence and the mystery that the Incarnate Word of God assumes this suffering in an act of unfathomable love.

Mary appears in Catholic visual culture not only as the grieving mother of the Pietà but also as a strong and protective woman who shelters the vulnerable in the *Schutzmantelmadonna* tradition that was a popular *topos* in German-speaking countries in the Middle Ages (Fig. 5-7). *Our Lady of Recovery*, a contemporary interpretation of this tradition by Suzann Miriello of the New Guild Studio, appears on a prayer card that I received from a member of the Saint Augustine Men's Group (Fig. 16-1). According to Catholic clinician Peter Kleponis, one of the roots of pornography usage is our human condition of woundedness.[38] The neurochemical "high" that pornography can stimulate temporarily blocks from consciousness the pain of rejection,

only for women. All the baptized are members of the body of Christ and Mary is a model and exemplar for all Christians.

37. Ana J. Bridges et al., "Aggression and Sexual Behavior in Best-Selling Pornography Videos: A Content Analysis Update," *Violence against Women* 16, no. 10 (October 2010): 1065–85. See also Eran Shor, "Age, Aggression, and Pleasure in Popular Online Pornographic Videos," *Violence Against Women* 25, no. 8 (2019): 1018–36.

38. Peter C. Kleponis, *Integrity Restored: Helping Catholic Families Win the Battle against Pornography* (Steubenville, Ohio: Emmaus Road, 2014), 229–31.

neglect, conflict, or abuse that many of us have experienced in relation to parents, siblings, spouses, peers, or others. Dovecotes of memory that include images from the Pietà and *Schutzmantelmadonna* traditions remind us that we are members of an ecclesial body formed in broken-hearted response to the crucifixion of a beloved child and that the Church, of whom Mary is a type and exemplar, must be fiercely committed to the compassionate protection of those who are suffering and vulnerable. "The most helpful to me in healing the imagination," explains the member of the Saint Augustine Men's Group who sent me the prayer card on which *Our Lady of Recovery* appears, "has been seeing my brokenness held by mother Mary."[39]

The visual culture of pornography implies that it is our desire to be reduced *ad absurdum* from the body-soul unity of the human person to an extracted physical body, to parts or organs of this body, and even to functions of these organs.[40] In contrast, the imagery from the high medieval and early modern period, elucidated by Phillips in chapter 6, unites body and soul, enlisting "the sensual dimensions of human bodily existence to visualize the passionate love God has for his creatures and the human yearning for fulfillment in life with God." The sacred works she shares employ marital and erotic motifs to express and inspire this love. "Christian faith, especially as lived in the Catholic tradition, employs both [hunger/thirst and sexual desire] as a way to think and speak about human relationship to God: about how God loves and desires us, how we respond to that love, and how we find completion in it."[41] In the biblical text of the Songs of Songs and its exegetical and artistic interpretation, Ann W. Astell observes in chapter 9, we find "the memory of a deeply personal love, mutually shared and capable of surviving periods of absence and seasonal change; of that love's propensity toward fruitfulness; and, ultimately, of God, the source of all love, especially of a love 'strong as death' (Song 8:6)."[42] Interpretations of the Song of Songs in the Christian tradition express in multivalence the mysteries of Christian initiation, the spiritual mar-

39. Correspondence with a member of the Saint Augustine Men's Group, February 2018.

40. See Martin, chapter 14, 261.

41. Diane Phillips, chapter 6, 120.

42. Ann W. Astell, chapter 9, 187.

riage of Christ the bridegroom and the Church, the joy of vowed religious or monastic life or the sacrament of marriage, and God's love for each and every beloved.

Dovecotes of memory that are carefully tended store images such as the *Schutzmantelmadonna*, *Hodegetria*, or *Anastasis* that can be brought to awareness as needed. A female graduate student at a Catholic university who read this book in manuscript form shares: "During the time I was reading this manuscript, I picked up a document from a printer in the library and there amidst my own pages was a print of a pornographic image. It was very unnerving to think that someone in the computer lab at that very moment was looking at a woman in this way. I felt degraded and ashamed. I recalled to mind the illumination of the icon of the *Theotokos of Tenderness* (Fig. 4-7) by the iconographer who explained the process of how she makes icons, which I thought was so interesting, and it was helpful to focus my attention on this. To hold in mind an image of a woman portrayed with strength and sanctity gave me a completely different sense of my own identity than the image of the woman that I was holding in my hand."[43]

Once, after a day immersed in literature about pornography, I went to an Orthodox church and sat in full view of the iconostasis, a wall of icons that marks the boundary between the nave and the sanctuary. I allowed its iconography to permeate my imagination and the dovecotes of my memory. No one, the icons of holy women and men expressed visually, was created to be the object of a "gang-bang." My nieces are not "teen f*** holes." My female students are not anyone's "slut #1," "slut #2," or "slut #3." My son and my nephews are not "bubble butts." My male students are not "beaver hunters."[44] My husband is not a "life-support system for a male organ," as pornography would have it,[45] but a person who is a body-soul unity, a man who through the sacrament of marriage is committed to me in sickness and in health and who is a loving and caring father to our son. We are creatures made male and female in the image and likeness of God (Gn 1:26–27), invit-

43. Correspondence with Catholic university student, February 2018.

44. These are all terms used in pornography. See Groppe, chapter 1, 39–40, and 34.

45. I refer here to Gail Dines's account of pornography's portrayal of the ideal man cited in Martin, chapter 14, 261n10, and to a pornography commentator's description of men cited in Cavadini, chapter 15, 283.

ed through Christ and the love of the Holy Spirit to the transfiguring deification evident in Sider-Rose's juxtaposition of the photo and icon of Saint Maria of Paris (Figs. 4-2 and 4-3).

Tending the dovecotes of memory in an age of pornography is not simply a matter of overlaying memories of pornographic pictures with sacred images, covering them with a blanket of Christian symbolism. Nor is it a matter of breaking or forcibly overpowering pornographic scenes with Christian iconography. As Anglican theologian Sarah Coakley observes, "the impetus simply to smash and bury an idolatrous image must face the charge that such violence may leave the broken shards curiously and remainingly powerful; a subtler approach, more cognizant of the psychology of the imagination—and its capacity for plasticity and transformation—is demanded."[46] What Christian conversion requires and sacramental grace can enable is a purgation of human desires that have become distorted and the engrafting of human desire into the very desire of God. In the Holy Spirit, we may desire as God desires and see as God "sees." To see with sacramental vision, Fagerberg writes, citing John Chrysostom's homilies on Ephesians, is to see with God's own heart.[47]

Cultivating an Iconic Gaze

To desire as God desires is to behold another in an iconic gaze transpierced by the *lumen* of God. An iconic gaze, Kimberly Hope Belcher reflects in chapter 8 with reference to the work of Emmanuel Levinas and Jean-Luc Marion, is a gaze free of idolatries and the projections of our own self-serving desires. It is a gaze that transcends the self-consciousness of our own flesh with its pains and its pleasures and "feels the feeling flesh" of another. How is this possible? "Through the work of Jesus Christ," Belcher explains, "human beings are offered the experience of sharing, not only with God, but with one another, the one divine and human feeling-flesh of the Word Incarnate."[48] Participants in the sacrament of baptism are mystagogically invited to cultivate this iconic vision by the liturgical "you" that refers simul-

46. Sarah Coakley, *God, Sexuality and the Self: An Essay "On the Trinity"* (Cambridge: Cambridge University Press, 2013), 20.

47. Fagerberg, chapter 7, 142.

48. Kimberly Hope Belcher, chapter 8, 168.

taneously to the baptizand—stripped of old garments of sin, anointed with oil, clothed in a royal robe—and to the assembly. The words of the rite and the language of baptismal homilies, such as those of Cyril of Jerusalem, cultivate "an empathetic gaze, which attempts to share the feeling flesh of those who have been baptized."[49] This empathetic gaze beholds the Eucharistic communion line as a joyous procession of the baptized streaming toward heaven. In nuptial form within the sacrament of marriage, the iconic gaze comes to see in the exposed flesh of the lover the "revelation of God the lover of the world."[50] The Christian erotic gaze, Belcher explains, "neither elevates nor evades sexuality, but sees in the human body the gift of the ineradicable desire and capacity for love," a love that "is a participation in the trinitarian perichoretic dance."[51]

The Orthodox tradition of iconography described by Sider-Rose may help Western Christians to cultivate the iconic gaze that Belcher describes. In a culture dominated by depersonalizing images, writes Benedictine Jeana Visel in *Icons in the Western Church*, the Catholic Church could be enriched by incorporating the Orthodox practice of icon veneration in a manner adapted to our own liturgical and devotional traditions.[52] "I think learning to pray with icons is one of the strongest spiritual weapons we have for counteracting the evils of using people as objects," she reflects.[53] An icon, Sider-Rose explains, is not a portrait of a person but a visual form that can be composed only through rigorous training and spiritual disciplines including prayer and fasting. Once completed, an icon is not hung upon a wall as an adornment but carefully placed in a reserved space in a church or home where it is neither looked "at" nor worshiped idolatrously but venerated. One who venerates an icon approaches with a bodily prostration, a sign of the cross, and a kiss. The icon makes present the person who is venerated in a manner that fits neither the Western theological category of "sacrament" nor that of "sacramental." Unlike

49. Belcher, chapter 8, 164.

50. Belcher, chapter 8, 169.

51. Belcher, chapter 8, 169.

52. Jeana Visel, *Icons in the Western Church* (Collegeville, Minn.: Liturgical Press, 2016), 106–7.

53. Correspondence with Jeana Visel, Aug 9, 2018.

the sacraments of the Church, Visel explains, the icon is not efficacious *ex opere operato*, but, unlike a sacramental, it can bear the real presence of Christ, Mary, or the saint who is signified.[54] The practice of venerating icons cultivates a receptivity to the Holy Spirit in whom our vision can be transfigured. Orthodox theologian Leonid Ouspensky reflects:

> The icon is an image not only of a living but also of a deified prototype ... this is why grace, characteristic of the prototype, is present in the icon. In other words, it is the grace of the Holy Spirit which sustains the holiness of both the represented person and of his [or her] icon.... the icon participates in the holiness of its prototype and, through the icon, we in turn participate in this holiness in our prayers.[55]

On the 1200th anniversary of the Second Council of Nicaea, Pope Saint John Paul II's apostolic letter *Duodecimum Saeculum* encouraged the practice of the veneration of icons.[56] Incorporation of this practice in Roman Catholic homes and churches, Visel reflects, would require instruction in the meaning and history of the Orthodox tradition and attention to the proper placement of icons within Western liturgical space to mitigate against possible abuse.[57] Introduced with due care, the practice of the veneration of icons could contribute to Roman Catholic mystagogical formation in the discipline of learning to see.

In *Image and Presence: A Christological Reflection on Iconoclasm and Iconophilia*, Natalie Carnes shares a poignant story about her visit to St. Anthony's Coptic monastery on the Red Sea. This seventeen hundred-year-old community is home to some of the oldest Christian iconography in the world, and the monks shellac prints of icons onto wooden bases to create replicas affordable to all. "I watched," Carnes writes, "a monk give an icon copy to a young boy, perhaps three or four years old, teaching him to kiss it and hold it with reverence, similar to the way he might treat an authentic, hand-written icon. The small icon copy almost disappeared into the monk's beard as he brought it care-

54. For Visel's reflection in this regard, see *Icons in the Western Church*, 80–81.

55. Leonid Ouspensky, *Theology of the Icon* (Crestwood, N.Y.: St. Vladimir's Seminary Press, 1978), 191.

56. Visel, *Icons in the Western Church*, 84–85.

57. Visel, *Icons in the Western Church*, 84–95.

fully to his lips. He opened his eyes and took the boy's hands, helping him to imitate his gesture."[58] The hope expressed by this action, she continues, is the merciful gift of the God who is present to us through unanticipated forms "without ceasing to be the invisible God."[59]

Practicing the Corporal Works of Mercy

One who practices the veneration of icons is not automatically immune to the lure of pornography. Today, every Christian denomination, including the Orthodox, faces pastoral challenges in this regard. The formative power of media culture and the blindness of human sin are obstacles to sacramental vision among Orthodox Christians just as among Roman Catholics, Episcopalians, and Protestants. Jim Forest, co-Secretary with his wife Nancy of the Orthodox Peace Fellowship of the Protection of the Mother of God, observes, "it is not only icons that are censed [with incense] by the deacon or priest but each person standing in the church. If we are indifferent to the image of God in other people, we won't find that image in icons."[60]

When a woman named Maria sought spiritual counsel from an Orthodox priest, he advised, "'Do not go out and buy icons. Go downtown and look at Christ in the faces of the poor.'"[61] Rublev's icon of the Trinity (Fig. 4-13) is part of an Orthodox iconographic tradition that takes its inspiration from the narrative of the hospitality of Sarah and Abraham (Gn 18), as Randi Sider-Rose explains in chapter 4. Dorothy Day, cofounder with Peter Maurin of the Catholic Worker, was inspired by this Genesis story of Sarah and Abraham's welcoming of three strangers who were ultimately revealed to be the Lord God and two angels. Like the artist of *The Seven Works of Charity* (Fig. 12-1), Day took the words of Jesus in Matthew's Gospel in their clear and plain sense: "For I was hungry and you gave me food, I was thirsty and you gave me drink, a stranger and you welcomed me, naked and you clothed me, ill and you cared for me, in prison and you visited me" (Mt

58. Natalie Carnes, *Image and Presence: A Christological Reflection on Iconoclasm and Iconophilia* (Stanford, Calif.: Stanford University Press, 2018), 186.
59. Carnes, *Image and Presence*, 187.
60. Jim Forest, *Praying with Icons* (Maryknoll, N.Y.: Orbis, 1997), 42.
61. Forest, *Praying with Icons*, 42.

25:35–36).[62] Day welcomed the hungry and homeless of the city of New York into her heart and was often asked: How can you see Christ in people? "We only say," she responded:

> It is an act of faith, constantly repeated. It is an act of love, resulting from an act of faith. It is an act of hope, that we can awaken these same acts in their hearts, too, with the help of God, and the Works of Mercy, which you, our readers, help us to do, day in and day out over the years.... In that last glorious chapter of St. Luke, Jesus told His followers, "Why are you so perturbed? Why do questions arise in your minds? Look at My hands and My feet. It is I Myself. Touch Me and see. No ghost has flesh and bones as you can see I have." They were still unconvinced, for it seemed too good to be true. "So He asked them, 'Have you anything to eat?' They offered Him a piece of fish they had cooked which He took and ate." The mystery of poverty is that by sharing in it, making ourselves poor in giving to others, we increase our knowledge of and belief in love.[63]

Among the works of mercy practiced by Day and depicted in the *Seven Works of Charity* attributed to the Master of Alkmaar is the clothing of the naked (Fig. 12-4). Ending the production of pornography, observes a member of the Saint Augustine Men's Group, is a work of mercy that will clothe those who have been made publicly naked and reduce the number of children and youth who are trafficked by the commercial sex industry.[64] One can also imagine ecclesial initiatives that reach out to women and men who believe they have no economic alternatives to the sex industry—works of mercy that support them in accessing education, job-training, and employment.

Clothing the naked is the corporal work of mercy most directly germane to pornography, but former Catholic Worker staff member Nicholas Ogle reflects in chapter 12 that the practice of all of the corporal works of mercy can contribute to the formation of a sacramental imagination. Through these corporeal actions, we may learn to see the

62. On some other works of art in this tradition, see Federico Botana, *The Works of Mercy in Italian Medieval Art (c. 1050–c. 1400)*, Medieval Church Studies 20 (Turnhout, Belgium: Brepols, 2011).

63. Dorothy Day, "The Mystery of the Poor," in *The Catholic Worker* (April 1964), accessed October 15, 2018, http://www.catholicworker.org/dorothyday/articles/189.html.

64. Correspondence with a member of the Saint Augustine Men's Group, February 2018. On the relation of some pornography production to human trafficking, see Dawn Hawkins, "It Can't Wait: Exposing the Connections between Forms of Sexual Exploitation," *Dignity: A Journal on Sexual Exploitation and Violence* 2, no. 2 (2017): 1–12.

bodies of others not with a voyeuristic eye that pleasures itself in the exposure of another but with an eye cleansed through baptism to see in human nakedness and need our own vulnerability and the grace of God. "It is precisely through the practice of the works of mercy," Ogle explains, "that our vision is transformed. This is because a charitable response to Christ in the poor costs us something—not merely our material wealth, but more fundamentally, our pride in our own material and spiritual self-sufficiency."[65] To see those who are hungry, thirsty, and naked with the eye of the heart is to see that all of us by virtue of our creaturely corporal existence are utterly dependent upon God.[66] It is to participate in the mystery of a shared creatureliness, and it is only in awareness of this that we can truly be receptive to the grace of adoption and the pledge of an inheritance toward redemption as God's children in Christ (Eph 1).

Seeing in the Body of Christ: *Sentire cum Christo* and *cum Ecclesia*

To see sacramentally, Boyd Taylor Coolman writes in chapter 11, is to see with the grace of Christ's own sensibility (*sensus Christi*, subjective genitive). To see *in* Christ is to see as a member of the Body of Christ; it is not an individual but a corporate act. This liturgical and ecclesial form of vision is exercised in the sacrament of the Eucharist, in the sacrament of penance and reconciliation, and in the life of the Christian community. Strong Christian communities have in many cases proven indispensable to the practice of learning to see anew after sustained exposure to pornography. Although the Barna Group study *The Porn Phenomenon* found that filtering software is helpful as a quick form of intervention for persons with pornography habits, the study's analysis of Protestant pastoral care emphasized that a quick technological fix alone is inadequate. The study strongly recommends gender-specific support groups: "for long-term recovery, the relational component seems to be key."[67] Psychology Professor William M.

65. Nicholas Ogle, chapter 12, 241.

66. Ogle, chapter 12, 241.

67. Barna Group, *The Porn Phenomenon: The Impact of Pornography in the Digital Age* (Ventura, Calif.: Barna Group, in partnership with Josh McDowell Ministry, 2016), 114.

Struthers and his former graduate assistant Kyler Mulhauser corroborate: "Users who desire to break their compulsion often attempt to do so alone so that their secrecy can be maintained. This, however, is almost always a recipe for failure. Social support is necessary, and the Christian community as the Body of Christ can play an essential role in sustaining people in recovery."[68] Dr. Peter C. Kleponis's clinical experience with Catholic men who are fighting addictions has convinced him of the importance of an active sacramental life integrated with participation in a Catholic men's group or twelve-step program.[69]

A member of the Saint Augustine Men's Group affirms the importance of this sacramental and ecclesial approach: "I believe any literature wanting to help with porn addiction needs to include references to Catholic 12-step approaches. I have been helped by the literature and videos of Fr. Emmerick Vogt available through 12-Step Review.org. His lens of recovery is his own experience and that of the Eucharistic liturgy and the lives of the saints."[70] A Catholic university student comments that finding a support group may be more easily said than done. "For this reason," the student recommended after reading this book in manuscript form, "I think it would be important to mention things like online forums, helpful apps like the *Victory* app, podcasts like *Integrity Restored*, conferences, or pastoral movements like *The Porn Effect* or *The Chastity Project* so that a reader has a safe space to make connections and feel empowered."[71]

A Christian community, explains a member of the Saint Augustine Men's Group, can foster accountability, provide support in practice of the virtues, and shape and nurture relationships to other persons and to God in a sacramental and ecclesial response to the human heart's desire to love and to be loved, which pornography can never sate. The drug-like effect of internet pornography, Catholic clinician Kleponis writes, can temporarily overpower the insecurity or loneliness of someone who longs for but does not have the gift of true friendships

68. William M. Struthers and Kyler Mulhauser, chapter 3, 80.

69. Kleponis, *Integrity Restored*, 229–31.

70. Correspondence with a member of the Saint Augustine Men's Group, February 2018.

71. Comments of a student at a Catholic university, February 2018.

or the intimacy and love of marital and familial life.[72] But the privacy sought for the practice of a pornography habit can beget even more loneliness, particularly in someone who feels shame in doing something he or she knows to be wrong. When Audrey Assad first encountered a pornographic broadcast on a television in her family home, the shame she felt was so great she could not even bring this to God. "It drove me into a pit of isolation."[73]

Assad had the strength of character to stop viewing pornography of her own accord at the age of seventeen after unintentional exposure led to two years of compulsive consumption. Yet, she writes, "I was still dying inside. My heart was broken by my own actions.... And I still didn't know how to process the addiction. I didn't understand the core issues behind it. Two years of striving and I had successfully stopped the symptoms, but the illness remained."[74] A turning point came when peers at her college in South Florida invited her to share her musical gifts with a Bible study group at their Baptist church. "It was the first time," she writes, "I allowed myself to wonder if maybe I had a role in the church, even with my past. Nobody there was aware of my interior battle, but they welcomed me with open arms. Healing began there, among those ten or twelve college students; singing songs of worship to God, the conception of redemption began forming in my heart."[75] Youth will not be moved, Jonah advises in chapter 13, by harsh words, but by the experience of authentic Christian communion within an ecclesial family that welcomes us with joy and compassion to conversion in a Church that is a field hospital after battle.

72. Kleponis, *Integrity Restored*, 42–44. For one testimony of a young man for whom pornography served as an alternative to the awkwardness, rejection, and pain of real human relationships, see Jacob Turnrose, "I Wanted to Become a Catholic. But First I Had to Give Up the Eucharist—and Porn" *America Magazine* 219, no.1 (July 9, 2018): 34–35.

73. Audrey Assad, "Freedom and Fullness," in *Delivered: True Stories of Men and Women Who Turned from Porn to Purity*, ed. Matt Fradd (San Diego, Calif.: Catholic Answers Press, 2013), 35.

74. Assad, "Freedom and Fullness," 38.

75. Assad, "Freedom and Fullness," 39.

Ecstasis and the Glorification of God

Joel Hesch, a Protestant lawyer and founder of the nonprofit organization Proven Men Ministries, emphasizes that the pastoral counsel to say "no" to pornography will likely be ineffectual unless accompanied by heart-work that addresses the underlying motivations that lead someone to seek it out. These motivations, he writes, include not only the human woundedness emphasized by Kleponis but also the pride and selfishness that are intertwined with lust. "That's where the battle must be fought and won. These twin sins of pride and selfishness cause a man to become so consumed with his rights that he loses sight of the real prize of true intimacy with God or a spouse."[76] To behold one's own naked humanity in a baptismal stripping (see chapter 8)—and then to see with the eyes of Rogier van der Weyden (Figs. 6-13 and 8–9) that human nakedness has been assumed by the Word of God in a kenotic mystery of redemption—may shatter the prideful self-curvature and *libido dominandi* that is part of our human condition and a root of some pornography consumption.

Christian visual culture at its best allures us with a beauty that has the power to carry us beyond the self. Bishop Robert Barron testifies to the way in which the very architecture of cathedrals like Amiens (Fig. 1-9) invites the ecstasy of a *sortie-de-soi*.[77] Joseph Cardinal Ratzinger found in Plato's *Phaedrus* evidence of beauty's power to enkindle ecstasis: "Plato contemplates the encounter with beauty as the salutary emotional shock that makes man leave his shell and sparks his 'enthusiasm' by attracting him to what is other than himself."[78] In like vein, writes Newsome Martin in chapter 14, Balthasar emphasizes that encounter with transcendental beauty can interrupt the beholder and carry him or her to a state of rapture that becomes a point of moral transformation.[79] This encounter can be mediated by music or literature or by paintings such as those of Caravaggio,

76. Joel Hesch, cited in Barna Group, *The Porn Phenomenon*, 78.

77. Robert Barron, *Heaven in Stone and Glass: Experiencing the Spirituality of the Great Cathedrals* (New York: Crossroad, 2000), 29.

78. Joseph Cardinal Ratzinger, "*The Feeling of Things, the Contemplation of Beauty*": *Message to the Communion and Liberation Meeting at Rimini* (August 24–30, 2002).

79. Martin, chapter 14, 276.

whose *Calling of Saint Matthew* (Fig. 13-1) has been important in Jonah's conversion and ongoing journey of healing. A member of the Saint Augustine Men's Group shares: "All Catholics should be shown ways to appreciate true beauty, whether in art, poetry, or music. As Saint Paul said, 'Whatever is true, whatever is honorable, whatever is just, whatever is pure, whatever is lovely, whatever is gracious, if there is any excellence and if there is anything worthy of praise, think about these things' (Phil 4:8). Holiness should not exclude sensual experiences, but transform them."[80]

When Eugène-Emmanuel Viollet-le-Duc was a child, Bishop Barron recounts, his mother took him to Notre-Dame Cathedral in Paris, and when this young boy, who would become a great nineteenth-century artist, beheld the great rose window in the north transept (Fig. 16-2) he cried out, *Maman, écoute, c'est le rosacea que chante!* ("Listen, Mama, it is the rose that is singing!")[81] There is a liturgical *synaesthesis* between sight, sound, and the other senses in which a stained glass window can "sing." Music, a member of the Saint Augustine Men's Group shares, has been important to him in living in freedom from the visual culture of pornography. Songs and hymns that have been particularly meaningful to him include: "Balm in Gilead," "They that Wait upon the Lord," "Holy Is Thy Name," "On Eagle's Wings," "Our God Reigns," "Amazing Grace," "You Are Mine," and "Holy Darkness." Worship in song with other college youth was a turning point in the life of Audrey Assad.[82] She now brings beauty into the lives of others as a Catholic vocal artist, and one of the songs in her 2016 album *Inheritance* is the Irish *lorica* "Be Thou My Vision":

> Be Thou my vision, O Lord of my heart
> Naught be all else to me, save that Thou art
> Thou my best thought, by day or by night
> Waking or sleeping, thy presence my light.[83]

80. Correspondence with a member of the Saint Augustine Men's Group, February 2018.

81. Barron, *Heaven in Stone and Glass*, 29.

82. Assad, "Freedom and Fullness," 39.

83. Assad's album is available at: https://store.audreyassad.com/, accessed October 15, 2018.

This light, mystics testify, is a luminous darkness, a night of excessive brilliance that is both purgative and healing, a seeing that is a "not seeing" of the face of God. This is God who sees us in the Incarnate Word and the Spirit of Love in infinite compassion with the eyes of the divine heart.

ILLUSTRATIONS: CREDITS AND NOTES

Credits

Cover. *The Anastasis.* Icon by the hand of Randi Sider-Rose. Photo credit: Christopher Humphrey. Used with permission.

Figure 1-1. Replica of the interior of the Second Synagogue of Dura-Europos (west wall). Museum of the Diaspora, Tel Aviv, Israel. Photo credit: Princeton University Press/Art Resource, N.Y. Used with permission.

Figure 1-2. Church Baptistery wall painting: procession of women. ca. 240–45, paint on plaster, Dura-Europos, Syria. Yale University Art Gallery, accession number 1932.1201c. Photo public domain courtesy of Yale University Art Gallery.

Figure 1-3. Tommaso Masolino da Panicale, *Curing the Crippled and the Raising of Tabitha.* 1424–28, fresco, Brancacci Chapel, Santa Maria del Carmine, Florence, Italy. Photo credit: Scala/Art Resource, N.Y. Used with permission.

Figure 1-4. Masaccio (Maso di San Giovanni), left wall of the Brancacci Chapel. 1424–26, fresco, Brancacci Chapel, Santa Maria del Carmine, Florence, Italy. Photo credit: Scala/Art Resource, N.Y. Used with permission.

Figure 1-5. Masaccio, interior of the Brancacci Chapel. 1424–26, Brancacci Chapel, Santa Maria del Carmine, Florence, Italy. Photo credit: Scala/Art Resource, N.Y. Used with permission.

Figure 1-6. Masaccio, Saint Peter baptizing the new converts. 1424–26, fresco, Brancacci Chapel, Santa Maria del Carmine, Florence, Italy. Photo credit: Scala/Art Resource, N.Y. Used with permission.

Figure 1-7. Haitian artists, Sanctuary of Holy Trinity Cathedral. 1949–51, murals, Holy Trinity Cathedral of the Episcopal Church, Port-au-Prince, Haiti. Photo credit: Ron Mayhew, www.ronmayhewphotography.com. Used with permission.

Figure 1-8. Haitian artists, *Wedding Feast at Cana.* 1949, mural, Holy Trinity Cathedral of the Episcopal Church, Port-au-Prince, Haiti. Photo credit: Ron Mayhew, www.ronmayhewphotography.com. Used with permission.

Figure 1-9. Intersection of nave and apsis, Notre-Dame d'Amiens Cathedral. Thirteenth century, Amiens, France. Photo credit: Erich Lessing/Art Resource, N.Y. Used with permission.

Figure 4-1. *The Transfiguration.* School of Theophanes the Greek. ca. 1403, tempera on wood, from the Cathedral of the Transfiguration of the Savior, Pereslavl-Zalessky. Tretyakov Gallery, Moscow, Russia. Photo credit: Scala/Art Resource, N.Y. Used with permission.

Figure 4-2. Photograph of Saint Maria Skobtsova of Paris. From the archives of Hélène Arjakovsk. Used with permission.

Figure 4-3. *Saint Maria of Paris.* Icon by the hand of Randi Sider-Rose. Photo credit: Christopher Humphrey. Used with permission.

Figure 4-4. Progressive stage of the painting of the *Theotokos of Tenderness.* Icon by the hand of Randi Sider-Rose. Photo credit: Christopher Humphrey. Used with permission.

Figure 4-5. Progressive stage of the painting of the *Theotokos of Tenderness.* Icon by the hand of Randi Sider-Rose. Photo credit: Christopher Humphrey. Used with permission.

Figure 4-6. Progressive stage of the painting of the *Theotokos of Tenderness.* Icon by the hand of Randi Sider-Rose. Photo credit: Christopher Humphrey. Used with permission.

Figure 4-7. *Theotokos of Tenderness.* Icon by the hand of Randi Sider-Rose. Photo credit: Christopher Humphrey. Used with permission. The icon is in the tradition of a *Virgin Eleousa* attributed to Angelos Akotantos (ca. 1450) in the collection of the Cleveland Museum of Art, Cleveland, Ohio, accession number 2010.154.

Figure 4-8. *Crucifixion with Virgin Mary and John the Evangelist.* Thirteenth century, tempera on wood. Icon Gallery, Ohrid, Macedonia. Photo credit: Erich Lessing/Art Resource, N.Y. Used with permission.

Figure 4-9. *The Virgin of Vladimir.* Byzantine icon. Tretyakov Gallery, Moscow, Russia. Photo credit: Scala/Art Resource, N.Y. Used with permission.

Figure 4-10. *The Holy Face* or *Acheiropoletos.* Twelfth century. Tretyakov Gallery, Moscow, Russia. Photo credit: Scala/Art Resource, N.Y. Used with permission.

Figure 4-11. Geometry of *The Holy Face.* Randi Sider-Rose. Photo credit: Christopher Humphrey. Used with permission.

Figure 4-12. *The Nativity* with geometry. Icon by the hand of Randi Sider-Rose. Photo credit: Christopher Humphrey. Used with permission.

Figure 4-13. *Old Testament Trinity.* Icon by the hand of Andrei Rublev. ca. 1411–27, tempera on wood. Tretyakov Gallery, Moscow, Russia. Photo credit: Scala/Art Resource, N.Y. Used with permission.

Figure 5-1. *Theotokos Enthroned.* Ninth century, mosaic, apse of Hagia Sofia (Church of the Divine Wisdom), Istanbul, Turkey. Photo credit: © Vanni Archive/Art Resource, N.Y. Used with permission.

Figure 5-2. *Theotokos Enthroned,* close-up. Ninth century, mosaic, apse of Hagia Sofia (Church of the Divine Wisdom), Istanbul, Turkey. Photo credit: De Agostini Picture Library/L. Romano/Bridgeman Images. Used with permission.

Figure 5-3. *Panagia.* Nineteenth century, wall painting over the doorway between the narthex and nave, Church of Our Lady of the Pastures, Asinou, Cyprus. Photo credit: Sonia Halliday Photographs/Bridgeman Images. Used with permission.

Figure 5-4. Giovanni di Paolo, *Madonna of Humility*. ca. 1442, tempera on panel, Siena, Italy. Museum of Fine Arts, Boston, Mass., Maria Antoinette Evans Fund, accession number 30.772. Photograph © 2019 Museum of Fine Arts, Boston, Mass. Used with permission.

Figure 5-5. *Vierge ouvrante* (closed state). ca. 1400, statue of Virgin and Child with Trinity, limewood and polychrome paint, Germany. Musée national du Moyen Âge-Thermes de Cluny, Paris, France. Photo credit: Michel Urtado, © RMN-Grand Palais/Art Resource, N.Y. Used with permission.

Figure 5-6. *Vierge ouvrante* (open state). ca. 1400, statue of Virgin and Child with Trinity, limewood and polychrome paint, Germany. Musée national du Moyen Âge-Thermes de Cluny, Paris, France. Photo credit: Michel Urtado, © RMN-Grand Palais/Art Resource, N.Y. Used with permission.

Figure 5-7. Michael Erhart or Friedrich Schramm, *Ravensburger Schutzmantelmadonna*. ca. 1480, wood carving, Liebfrauenkirche, Ravensburg, Germany. Sculpture Collection and Museum of Byzantine Art, Staatliche Museen zu Berlin, Germany. Photo credit: Antje Voigt, Berlin, © Skulpturensammlung und Museum für Byzantinische Kunst der Staatlichen Museen zu Berlin-Preußischer Kulturbesitz. Used with permission.

Figure 5-8. Lisa Fracica, *African Madonna*. Oil and gold leaf on canvas. Photo credit: Lisa Fracica. Used with permission.

Figure 5-9. Brother Michael O'Neill McGrath, *Baltimore Holy Family*. Digital image. Used with permission.

Figure 5-10. Rev. John B. Giuliani, *Guatemalan Annunciation*. Photo credit: http://www.jbgicon.com. Used with permission.

Figure 5-11. Rev. John B. Giuliani, *Guatemalan Mother and Child*. Photo credit: http://www.jbgicon.com. Used with permission.

Figure 5-12. Unknown artist, *Japanese Madonna*. Twentieth century, painting on textile, Japan. Marian Library, University of Dayton, Dayton, Ohio. Photo credit: Ryan O'Grady. Used with permission.

Figure 5-13. In (Clara) Jeong-ok, *Madonna and Child*. 2007, Korean paper, Seoul, South Korea. Marian Library, University of Dayton, Dayton, Ohio. Photo credit: Ryan O'Grady. Used with permission.

Figure 5-14. Studio of Father Damien Higgens, *Our Lady of Chaminade (Ke Lede o Kaminaka)*. Chaminade University, Honolulu, Hawaii. Icon © Chaminade University. Photo credit: Island Digital Imaging. Used with permission.

Figure 5-15. *The Virgin Hodegetria*. Late sixteenth century. Benaki Museum, Athens, Greece, accession number ΓΕ 2986. Photo credit: Benaki Museum. Used with permission.

Figure 5-16. Johann Georg Melchior Schmittner, *Mary, Untier of Knots*. ca. 1700, Saint Peter am Perlach Church, Augsburg, Germany. Photo credit: Artothek/Bridgeman Images. Used with permission.

Figure 6-1. Sienese artist, *The Triumph of Saint Thomas Aquinas.* Fourteenth century, Santa Caterina, Pisa, Italy. Photo credit: Scala/Art Resource, N.Y. Used with permission.

Figure 6-2. Gian Lorenzo Bernini, *The Ecstasy of Saint Teresa of Avila,* 1647–52, marble, stucco, and gilt bronze sculpture, Cornaro Chapel, Santa Maria della Vittoria, Rome, Italy. Photo credit: Scala/Art Resource, N.Y. Used with permission.

Figure 6-3. "Initial O" from the Song of Songs, *Alardus Bible,* Ms. 10, Fol. 113. Eleventh century, parchment, Saint-Amand-les-Eaux, Nord-Pas-de-Calais, France. Bibliothèque municipale, Valenciennes, Nord-Pas-de-Calais, France. Photo credit: Visual Resources Collection–History of Art, University of Michigan, image 070385. Used with permission.

Figure 6-4. Christ and the Sponsa, *Rothschild Canticles,* Ms. 404, Fol. 18v. ca. 1300, parchment, Flanders or the Rhineland. Photo credit: General Collection, Beinecke Rare Book and Manuscript Library, Yale University, image ID 18v: 1011525. Used with permission.

Figure 6-5. Christ at the Column and the Cross, *Rothschild Canticles,* Ms. 404, Fol. 19r. ca. 1300, parchment, Flanders or the Rhineland. Photo credit: General Collection, Beinecke Rare Book and Manuscript Library, Yale University, image ID 19r: 1011526. Used with permission.

Figure 6-6. Studio of Niccolò di Giacomo da Bologna, The Annunciation, *Meditations on the Life of Christ: Fol. 8r, Annunciation.* 1380, tempera and gold leaf on parchment. The Snite Museum of Art, University of Notre Dame, Notre Dame, Ind., 1985.025.008.a. Used with permission.

Figure 6-7. Rogier van der Weyden, *The Annunciation.* ca. 1434, central panel of a triptych, oil on oak. Musée du Louvre, Paris, France. Photo credit: Gérard Blot, © RMN-Grand Palais/Art Resource, N.Y. Used with permission.

Figure 6-8. Lippo Memmi, *Madonna and Child,* and Simone Martini, *Pietà of Christ.* 1326–28, diptych, tempera on wood. Horne Museum, Florence, Italy, inventory numbers 55 and 56. Used with permission.

Figure 6-9. *Cupid and Psyche.* Marble statue, Rome. Uffizi Gallery, Florence, Italy. Photo credit: Scala/Art Resource, N.Y. Used with permission.

Figure 6-10. Workshop of Robert Campin, *The Virgin and Child in an Interior.* Before 1432, oil on oak, Tournai, South Netherlands. The National Gallery, London. Used with permission.

Figure 6-11. Peter Paul Rubens, *The Holy Family with Saints Elizabeth and John the Baptist.* ca. 1615, oil on panel, Flanders, Belgium. The Art Institute of Chicago, Major Acquisitions Fund, reference number 1967.229. Photo credit: The Art Institute of Chicago/Art Resource, N.Y. Used with permission.

Figure 6-12. Ugolino di Nerio, *The Deposition.* ca. 1325–28, egg tempera on poplar, fifth of seven scenes of Christ's Passion in the predella of the high altarpiece of Santa Croce, Florence, Italy. The National Gallery, London. Used with permission.

Figure 6-13. Workshop of Rogier van der Weyden, *Pietà.* ca. 1465, oil with egg tempera on oak, Brussels, Belgium. The National Gallery, London. Used with permission.

Figure 6-14. Adriatic School, *Imago Pietatis* or *Cristo in pietà con la Vergine dolente.* Horne Museum, Florence, Italy, inventory number 70. Used with permission.

Figure 6-15. Pseudo-Jacopino di Francesco, *Polyptych of the Presentation in the Temple with Pietà and Twelve Figures of Saints.* 1335–40, tempera and oil on panel. Pinacoteca Nazionale, Bologna, Emilia-Romagna, Italy. Photo credit: Mondadori Portfolio/Electa/ Sergio Anelli/Bridgeman Images. Used with permission.

Figure 6-16. Michele Giambono, *Imago Pietatis (Man of Sorrows).* ca. 1430, tempera and gold on wood, Venice, Italy. Metropolitan Museum of Art, New York, Rogers Fund, 1906, accession number 06.180. Used with permission.

Figure 6-17. Carlo Crivelli, *Lamentation over the Dead Christ.* 1485, tempera on panel. Museum of Fine Arts, Boston, Mass. Anonymous Gift and Julia Bradford Huntington James Fund, accession number 02.4. Photograph © 2019 Museum of Fine Arts, Boston, Mass. Used with permission.

Figure 6-18. Titian, *Noli me Tangere.* ca. 1514, oil on canvas, Venice, Italy. National Gallery, London, bequeathed by Samuel Rogers, 1856. Used with permission.

Figure 6-19. *Christ and Saint John.* ca. 1320, oak, Germany, Upper Swabia. Skulpturensammlung und Museum für Byzantinische Kunst, Staatliche Museen, Berlin, Germany, inv. 7950. Photo credit: Johannes Laurentius/Art Resource, N.Y. Used with permission.

Figure 6-20. Francisco Ribalta, *Saint Francis Embraces the Crucified Christ.* ca. 1620, oil on canvas, Capuchin Convent of Valencia. Museu de Belles Arts de València. Used with permission.

Figure 6-21. Michelangelo Merisi da Caravaggio, *Saint Francis of Assisi in Ecstasy.* ca. 1595–96, oil on canvas, Rome, Italy. Wadsworth Atheneum Museum of Art, Hartford, Conn., Ella Gallup Sumner and Mary Catlin Sumner Collection Fund. Photo credit: Nimatallah/Art Resource, N.Y. Used with permission.

Figure 6-22. Daniel Bonnell, *The Young Holy Family.* 2011, oil on canvas, Savannah, Georgia. Photo credit: Daniel Bonnell. Used with permission.

Figure 6-23. Neilson Carlin, *The Holy Family.* 2014, commissioned for the 2015 World Meeting of Families in Philadelphia, Pa. by the Archdiocese of Philadelphia. Photo credit: Office of Divine Worship, Archdiocese of Philadelphia. Used with permission.

Figure 8-1. Ambrogio Lorenzetti, *Madonna del Latte.* ca. 1325–48, tempera on panel, Oratorio di San Bernardino e Museo Diocesano, Siena, Italy. Photo credit: Fine Art Images/Alinari Archives, Firenze, Italy. Used with permission.

Figure 8-2. Jan van Eyck, *The Lucca Madonna.* ca 1437, tempera and oil on wood. Städtische Galerie im Städelschen Kunstinstitut, Frankfurt am Main, Germany. Photo credit: Fine Art Images/Alinari Archives, Firenze, Italy. Used with permission.

Figure 8-3. Hans Memling, *Virgin and Child.* 1485–90, oil on panel, Netherlands. Art Institute of Chicago, Ill., Mr. and Mrs. Martin A. Ryerson Collection, reference number 1933.1050. Photo credit: Art Institute of Chicago/Art Resource, N.Y. Used with permission.

Figure 8-4. Master of Frankfurt, *Holy Family with Music-Making Angels.* ca. 1505, oil on panel. Walker Art Gallery, Liverpool, England, bequeathed by P. H. Rathbone, 1905, accession number WAG 1020. Photo courtesy National Museums Liverpool, Walker Art Gallery. Used with permission.

Figure 8-5. Jan and Hubert van Eyck, Adam and the offerings of Cain and Abel, interior of the left-hand wing of the *Ghent Altarpiece.* 1432, oil on panel, Saint Bavo Cathedral, Ghent, Belgium. Photo credit: Maeyaert /Iberfoto/Alinari Archives, Firenze, Italy. Used with permission.

Figure 8-6. Jan and Hubert van Eyck, Eve and the murder of Abel by Cain, interior of the right-hand wing of the *Ghent Altarpiece.* 1432, oil on panel, Saint Bavo Cathedral, Ghent, Belgium. Photo credit: Maeyaert /Iberfoto/Alinari Archives, Firenze, Italy. Used with permission.

Figure 8-7. Jan and Hubert van Eyck, *Ghent Altarpiece.* 1432, oil on panel. Saint Bavo Cathedral, Ghent, Belgium. Photo credit: Fine Art Images/Alinari Archives, Firenze, Italy. Used with permission.

Figure 8-8. Rogier van der Weyden, *Last Judgment Altarpiece.* ca. 1445–50, oil on oak panels, Hôtel-Dieu, Beaune, France. Photo credit: Erich Lessing/Art Resource, N.Y. Used with permission.

Figure 8-9. Rogier van der Weyden, *Altarpiece of the Virgin (Miraflores Altarpiece).* ca. 1435, oil on oakwood, post-restoration. Gemaeldegalerie, Staatliche Museen, Berlin, Germany, inv. 534 A. Photo credit: bpk Bildagentur/Staatliche Museen/Jörg P. Anders/ Art Resource, N.Y. Used with permission.

Figure 10-1. *Christ Pantocrator.* Sixth century, encaustic on panel, Monastery of Saint Catherine, Mount Sinai, Egypt. Photo credit: © Zev Radovan/Bridgeman Images. Used with permission.

Figure 12-1. Master of Alkmaar, Polyptych with *The Seven Works of Charity.* 1504, oil on panel. Rijksmuseum, Amsterdam, Netherlands, purchased with the support of the Vereniging Rembrandt and the Commissie voor Fotoverkoop, object number SK-A-2815. Photo: public domain courtesy of Rijksmuseum.

Figure 12-2. Master of Alkmaar, "Feed the Hungry," first panel of *The Seven Works of Charity.* 1504, oil on panel. Rijksmuseum, Amsterdam, Netherlands, purchased with the support of the Vereniging Rembrandt and the Commissie voor Fotoverkoop, object number SK-A-2815–1. Photo: public domain courtesy of Rijksmuseum.

Figure 12-3. Master of Alkmaar, "Give Drink to the Thirsty," second panel of *The Seven Works of Charity.* 1504, oil on panel. Rijksmuseum, Amsterdam, Netherlands, purchased with the support of the Vereniging Rembrandt and the Commissie voor Fotoverkoop, object number SK-A-2815–2. Photo: public domain courtesy of Rijksmuseum.

Figure 12-4. Master of Alkmaar, "Clothe the Naked," third panel of *The Seven Works of Charity.* 1504, oil on panel. Rijksmuseum, Amsterdam, Netherlands, purchased with the support of the Vereniging Rembrandt and the Commissie voor Fotoverkoop, object number SK-A-2815–3. Photo: public domain courtesy of Rijksmuseum.

Figure 12-5. Master of Alkmaar, "Care for the Sick," sixth panel of *The Seven Works of Charity*. 1504, oil on panel. Rijksmuseum, Amsterdam, Netherlands, purchased with the support of the Vereniging Rembrandt and the Commissie voor Fotoverkoop, object number SK-A-2815–6. Photo: public domain courtesy of Rijksmuseum.

Figure 13-1. Michelangelo Merisi da Caravaggio, *Calling of Saint Matthew*. 1599–1600, oil on canvas, Contarini Chapel, San Luigi dei Francesi, Rome, Italy. Photo credit: Scala/Art Resource, N.Y. Used with permission.

Figure 15-1. *The Anastasis*, fresco in the Parrecclesion. Fourteenth century, fresco, Chora Church (Kariye Camii), Istanbul, Turkey. Photo credit: Album/Art Resource, N.Y. Used with permission.

Figure 16-1. Suzann Miriello, New Guild Studio, *Our Lady of Recovery*. Braddock, Pa. Photo credit: Anton Miriello. Used with permission.

Figure 16-2. North transept rose window (the Virgin Mary surrounded by figures from the Old Testament), Notre-Dame, Paris, France. Thirteenth century, stained glass. Photo credit: © Vanni Archive/Art Resource, N.Y. Used with permission.

Notes

Figures 1-7 and 1-8 In 1949, Episcopal bishop Alfred Voegli commissioned Haitian artists to paint biblical scenes on the interior walls of Holy Trinity Episcopal Cathedral, which had been established in 1861 in Port-au-Prince, Haiti. The murals that were completed between 1950 and 1951 were a vibrant expression of Haitian faith, art, and culture. In January 2010, a catastrophic earthquake killed more than 300,000 people in Haiti and left another 1.3 million homeless. Among the buildings destroyed was Holy Trinity Cathedral.

Figures 4-2 and 4-3 Mother Maria Skobtsova sheltered Jews during the Nazi occupation of Europe and died in Ravensbrück concentration camp in 1945. She was glorified by the Church of Constantinople in 2004 and is commemorated in the Orthodox Church on July 20.

Figures 4-4, 4-5, 4-6, and 4-7 These images show the stages of illumination of the icon of the *Virgin Elousa* or *Theotokos of Tenderness* by the hand of Randi Sider-Rose. The icon is inspired by an exemplar of the *Elousa* attributed to Angelos Akotantos and on view in the Cleveland Museum of Art. In the *Elousa* tradition, the three stars on the Virgin's cloak symbolize her chastity and the blue cap covering her hair is a sign of her modesty. The scroll held by the Christ child is a symbol of the Gospels. See http://www.clevelandart.org/art/2010.154.

Figures 5-1 and 5-2 *Theotokos Enthroned* is a ninth century Byzantine mosaic in the apse of Hagia Sophia (Church of the Divine Wisdom). Hagia Sophia was commissioned by Emperor Justinian and constructed by Anthemius of Tralles and Isidore of Miletus between AD 537–48. Following the conquest of Constantinople by the Ottomans in 1453, Hagia Sophia was used as a mosque. The medallions visible in the photo feature the names of the Prophet Muhammad (left) and Allah (right). Since 1935, Hagia Sophia has served as a museum open to the public.

Figure 5-8 Lisa Fracica, painter of *African Madonna*, writes of her work: "Some of the elements I strive for in my artistic practice are beauty, symbolic content, and narrative. These elements I value as an artist have been influenced by studying the works of late Medieval and early Renaissance painters as well as the work of contemporary figurative painters, icon painters, and painters of illuminated manuscripts." For more about the artist and her work, see https://lisafracica.com/home.html.

Figure 5-9 *Baltimore Holy Family* is an original image by Brother Michael O'Neill McGrath. For more on his work, see his website www.bromickeymcgrath.com.

Figures 5-10 and 5-11 *Guatemalan Annunciation* and *Guatemalan Mother and Child* are both works of Rev. John Giuliani. He describes his work as a celebration of the prophetic sign and spiritual presence of the native peoples of Central and North America. His artistic style has been described as a hybrid of Orthodox iconography and Italian Renaissance naturalism. For more on his work, see http://www.jbgicon.com/.

Figure 5-14 *Ke Lede o Kaminaka*, or *Our Lady of Chaminade*, was commissioned by Dr. David Coleman and the Humanities and Fine Arts division of Chaminade University to mark the 125th anniversary of the Marianist presence in the Island of Hawaii. The design depicting Mary and Christ with Polynesian characteristics was developed in conversation with Father Damien Higgins of the Ukrainian Catholic Church and painted in his studio in Augusta, Georgia on aged poplar boards covered with old altar linens and layers of gesso. The icon was painted with 23k gold leaf, red bole, and egg tempera and then varnished with *olifa*. It is based on the prototype of *Our Lady of Kykkos* (ca. 1668). The International Marian Research Institute (IMRI) at the University of Dayton provides this commentary: "Mary wears the insignia of an *Ali'i*, a noble Hawaiian woman with royal associations. She is dressed in a wide wrap of Kapa cloth imbued with patterns of plants associated with Hawaiian culture and spirituality. The first set of patterns is the Kukui Nut, or the Tree of Light, an association with Christ as the 'light of the world' (John 8:12), the next is the taro, the staple or 'bread' of the Hawaiian people. The next is the bread fruit, which is a symbol of healing, and finally, the white hibiscus as a symbol of beauty and purity. Mary rests on top of the Pacific Ocean on a Cherubim floating at her feet. Two angels with kahili stand at attention on either side as the heavenly hosts witness the mystery of God becoming human. Above them are the sun and the moon representing not only the heavens but all of creation. They are commonly used in Byzantine hymnography to express the feelings and yearnings of the material world created by God. In the two circles above the sun and moon are the monograms for the Mother of God, *Theotokos*, with the stars directly above which are traditionally placed on the outside of her veil representing the miraculous nature of her giving birth and remaining a virgin before, during and after giving birth. The two side panels of the triptych include the founders of the Marianist Community: Father William Joseph Chaminade, Mother Adele de Batz de Trenquelleon, and Marie Therese Charlotte de Lamourous. Included with each founder are scrolls expressing their faith in the Incarnation. As an extension of this faith, Father Chaminade is accompanied by the images of Chaminade University of Honolulu with its roots in St. Louis College. The women are accompanied by the images and symbols of the Immaculate Heart of Mary and the people of France they served and inspired. They too are set in the waters of the sea which connect the diverse parts of the world together in one human family." See https://udayton.edu/imri/mary/o/our-lady-of-chaminade.php.

Figure 6-22 "My art," writes Daniel Bonnell in his artist's statement, "is a direct reflection of a Franciscan ethos that sees life through the lens of interpreting love through the teachings of Jesus Christ. This personal interpretation is enabled through producing art that is a direct response to periods of contemplation and prayer. These visual interpretations seek to take a point of reflection and take it beyond the written words themselves allowing the essence of the teaching, Scripture or parable to embrace a sacred and interior realm of understanding. My path of following a Franciscan ethos and following the teachings of Jesus is also demonstrated in seeking to serve the disenfranchised and underprivileged within society directly through teaching art to inner city African Americans, with the goal of demonstrating love to them first, and allowing art to embrace them as a result." For more on his work, see his website http://www.bonnellart.com/home.

Figure 6-23 Neilson Carlin was commissioned to paint an image of the Holy Family for the 2015 World Meeting of Families held in the Archdiocese of Philadelphia. Working for months under the guidance of The Most Reverend John McIntyre, Auxiliary Bishop of the Archdiocese of Philadelphia, he created *The Holy Family* that was unveiled by Archbishop Charles Chaput on September 7, 2014 at the Cathedral Basilica of Sts. Peter and Paul. The painting was blessed by His Holiness Pope Francis during the Cathedral Mass at the World Meeting of Families on September 26, 2015. See https://www.neilsoncarlin.com/world-meeting-of-families.

Figures 12-1, 12-2, 12-3, 12-4, and 12-5 *The Seven Works of Charity* (1504) is a polyptych of panels that still stand in their original frame. Similar polyptypchs were often found in almhouses in the fifteenth and sixteenth centuries. In these works, inspired by the Gospel account of the Last Judgment (Mt 25:31–46, supplemented by Tb 1:17), the presence of Jesus Christ in each scene illustrates that "whatever you did for these least brothers of mine, you did for me" (Mt 25:40). This particular version of *The Seven Works of Charity* may have been commissioned by the regents of the Holy Spirit Almshouse in Alkmaar, who are perhaps the three men in the right foreground of the panel *Visiting the Sick* (Fig. 12-5). Whether or not the work was ever installed in the Holy Spirit Almhouse, which closed in 1575, is unknown, but the presence of the polyptych in Saint Laurenskerk is attested in 1582 and it remained there into the early twentieth century behind the baptismal font and below the main organ. The work was seriously damaged with a knife in a period of Protestant iconoclasm in 1566 or 1572 and these scars remain. A church warden chronicles that in 1582 the work was also defaced with black paint. Nonetheless, even when Saint Laurenskerk became a Protestant place of worship, *The Seven Works of Charity* remained in place as an encouragement to leave alms for the poor, perhaps in a nearby collection box. Although the work is attributed to the Master of Alkmaar, no effort to identify the artist has proven satisfactory.

Figure 16-1 *Our Lady of Recovery* is a sacred image available as a holy card or plaque from the New Guild Art and Design Studio. This guild of artists in Braddock, Pennsylvania affirm the power of sacred art to give form to humanity's quest for the divine and awaken us to the eternal.

BIBLIOGRAPHY

Christian Theology and Christian Visual Culture

Agostino, G. "Chi e Maria per il popolo?" *La Madonna* 32 (1984): 5–6, 66–70.

Ahlborn, Mel and Ken Arnold, eds. *Visio Divina: A Reader in Faith and Visual Arts.* Leeds, Mass.: Leader Resources, 2009.

Alexander of Hales. *Glossa in quatuor libros Sententiarum Petri Lombardi.* Bibliotheca Franciscana scholastica medii aevi 12–15. Quaracchi, Florence: Collegium S. Bonaventurae, 1951–57.

———. *Quaestiones disputatae "antequam esset frater."* Bibliotheca Franciscana scholastica medii aevi 19–21. Quaracchi, Florence: Collegii S. Bonaventurae, 1960.

Anderson, Gary. *Sin: A History.* New Haven, Conn.: Yale University Press, 2009.

———. *Charity: The Place of the Poor in the Christian Tradition.* New Haven, Conn.: Yale University Press, 2013.

Asiedu, F. B. A. "The Song of Songs and the Ascent of Soul: Ambrose, Augustine, and the Language of Mysticism." *Vigiliae Christianae* 55, no. 3 (2001): 299–317.

Astell, Ann W. *The Song of Songs in the Middle Ages.* Ithaca, N.Y.: Cornell University Press, 1990.

Athanasius. *On the Incarnation.* Crestwood, N.Y.: St. Vladimir's Orthodox Theological Seminary, 1982.

Augustine. *On Christian Doctrine.* Translated by D. W. Robertson Jr. Indianapolis, Ind.: Bobbs-Merrill Educational Publishing, 1958.

———. "The City of God: Chapters 1–10." Vol. 1, bk. 6 of *The Works of Saint Augustine: A Translation for the 21st Century.* Edited by B. Ramsey. Translated by W. Babcock. Hyde Park, N.Y.: New City Press, 2012.

———. "The City of God: Chapters 11–22." Vol. 1, bk. 7 of *The Works of Saint Augustine: A Translation for the 21st Century.* Edited by B. Ramsey. Translated by W. Babcock. Hyde Park, N.Y.: New City Press, 2013.

———. *Confessions.* Translated by Henry Chadwick. Oxford: Oxford University Press, 2008.

———. "Expositions on the Psalms 33–50." Vol. 3, bk. 16 of *The Works of Saint Augustine: A Translation for the 21st Century.* Edited by J. E. Rotelle. Translated by M. Boulding. Hyde Park, N.Y.: New City Press, 2000.

———. "On Genesis." Vol. 1, bk. 13 of *The Works of Saint Augustine: A Translation for the 21st Century.* Edited by John E. Rotelle. Translated by Edmund Hill. Hyde Park, N.Y.: New City Press, 2002.

———. "Sermons 20–50." Vol. 3, bk. 2 of *The Works of Saint Augustine: A Translation for the 21st Century.* Edited by J. E. Rotelle. Translated by E. Hill. Brooklyn, N.Y.: New City Press, 1990.

———. "Sermons 94A–147A." Vol. 3, bk. 4 of *The Works of Saint Augustine: A Trans-*

lation for the 21st Century. Edited by J. E. Rotelle. Translated by E. Hill. Brooklyn, N.Y.: New City Press, 1992.

———. *Sermons on the Liturgical Season*. New Rochelle, N.Y.: New City Press, 1993.

———. *Treatises on Marriage and Other Subjects*. Translated by Charles T. Wilcox. Washington, D.C.: The Catholic University of America Press, 1999.

———. "The Trinity." Vol. 1, bk. 5 of *The Works of Saint Augustine: A Translation for the 21st Century*. Edited by J. E. Rotelle. Translated by E. Hill. Hyde Park, N.Y.: New City Press, 1991.

Awi Mello, Alexandre. *Ela é minha Mãe! Encontros do Papa Francisco com Maria*. São Paulo: Edições Loyola Jesuitas, 2014.

Baker, Kimberly. "Augustine's Doctrine of the *Totus Christus*: Reflecting on the Church as Sacrament of Unity." *Horizons* 37, no. 1 (Spring 2010): 7–24.

Balthasar, Hans Urs von. *Parole et mystère chez Origène*. Paris: Les Éditions du Cerf, 1957.

———. *Seeing the Form*. Vol. 1 of *The Glory of the Lord: A Theological Aesthetics*. Edited by Joseph Fessio and John Riches. Translated by Erasmo Leiva-Merikakis. San Francisco, Calif.: Ignatius Press, 1982.

———. "Revelation and the Beautiful." In *The Word Made Flesh*. Vol. 1 of *Explorations in Theology*. Translated by A. V. Littledale with Alexander Dru. San Francisco, Calif.: Ignatius Press, 1989.

———. *Truth of the World*. Vol. 1 of *Theo-Logic: Theological Logical Theory*. Translated by Adrian J. Walker. San Francisco, Calif.: Ignatius Press, 2000.

———. *A Theological Anthropology*. Eugene, Ore.: Wipf & Stock, 2010.

Barbagallo, Sandro. *St. Joseph in Art: Iconology and Iconography of the Redeemer's Silent Guardian*. Translated by Adam Elgar. Vatican City: Edizioni musei vaticani, 2014.

Barron, Robert. *Heaven in Stone and Glass: Experiencing the Spirituality of the Great Cathedrals*. New York: Crossroad, 2000.

Barth, Karl. *Church Dogmatics III.2: The Doctrine of Creation*. Edited by G. W. Bromiley and T. F. Torrance. London: T&T Clark, 2004.

Bauer, Walter. *A Greek-English Lexicon of the New Testament and Other Early Christian Literature*. 3rd ed. Chicago, Ill.: University of Chicago Press, 2001.

Baxandall, Michael. *Painting and Experience in Fifteenth Century Italy: A Primer in the Social History of Pictorial Style*. 2nd ed. Oxford: Oxford University Press, 1988.

Beinert, Wolfgang. *Maria-eine ökumenische Herausforderung*. Regensburg: Friedrich Pustet, 1984.

Belting, Hans. *Likeness and Presence: A History of the Image before the Era of Art*. Translated by Edmund Jephcott. Chicago: University of Chicago Press, 1994.

Benedict XVI. *Deus Caritas Est*. Encyclical Letter. December 25, 2005.

———. *Spe Salvi*. Encyclical Letter. November 30, 2007.

———. *Homage to the Immaculate at the Spanish Steps*. Address. December 8, 2008.

———. *Address to Artists*. Address. November 21, 2009.

Bernard of Clairvaux. *On the Song of Songs 1*. Translated by Kilian Walsh. Kalamazoo, Mich.: Cistercian Publications, 1971.

———. *On the Song of Songs 3*. Translated by Kilian Walsh and Irene M. Edmonds. Kalamazoo, Mich.: Cistercian Publications, 1979.

Boersma, Hans. *Seeing God: The Beatific Vision in Christian Tradition*. Grand Rapids, Mich.: Eerdmans, 2018.

Botana, Federico. *The Works of Mercy in Italian Medieval Art (c. 1050–c. 1400)*. Medieval Church Studies 20. Turnhout, Belgium: Brepols, 2011.

Brown, Peter. *Through the Eye of a Needle: Wealth, the Fall of Rome, and the Making of Christianity in the West, 350–550 A.D.* Princeton, N.J.: Princeton University Press, 2012.

Bryer, Anthony, and Judith Herrin, eds. *Iconoclasm*. Birmingham: University of Birmingham, 1997.

Bunge, Gabriel. *The Rublev Trinity: The Icon of the Trinity by the Monk-Painter Andrei Rublev*. Translated by Andrew Louth. Crestwood, N.Y.: St. Vladimir's Seminary Press, 2007.

Calloway, Donald. *No Turning Back*. Stockbridge, Mass.: Marian Press, 2010.

Cannon, Joanna. *Religious Poverty, Visual Riches: Art in the Dominican Churches of Central Italy in the Thirteenth and Fourteenth Centuries*. New Haven, Conn.: Yale University Press, 2013.

Carnes, Natalie. *Image and Presence: A Christological Reflection on Iconoclasm and Iconophilia*. Stanford, Calif.: Stanford University Press, 2018.

Carrón, Julián. *Disarming Beauty: Essays on Faith, Truth, and Freedom*. Notre Dame, Ind.: University of Notre Dame Press, 2017.

Carruthers, Mary J. *The Craft of Thought: Meditation, Rhetoric, and the Making of Images, 400–1200*. Cambridge Studies in Medieval Literature 34. Cambridge: Cambridge University Press, 2000.

———. *The Book of Memory: A Study of Memory in Medieval Culture*. New York: Cambridge University Press, 2008.

Catechism of the Catholic Church. 2nd ed. Washington, D.C.: United States Conference of Catholic Bishops, 2000.

Cavadini, John C. "Spousal Vision: Seeing the Church with *Lumen Gentium*." Documents of Vatican II Lecture Series, St. Procopius Abbey, Lisle, Ill., September 16, 2014. https://www.youtube.com/watch?v=D-7iP7Ir8i4.

Cavadini, John C., and Danielle M. Peters, eds. *Mary on the Eve of the Second Vatican Council*. Notre Dame, Ind.: Notre Dame Press, 2017.

Chesterton, G. K. *Heretics*. Vol. 1 of *G. K. Chesterton Collected Works*. Edited by David Dooley, 39–207. San Francisco, Calif: Ignatius Press, 1986.

Chidester, David. *Word and Light: Seeing, Hearing, and Religious Discourse*. Urbana, Ill.: University of Illinois Press, 1992.

Clayton, David. "What Is the Place of the Nude in Sacred Art?" In *The Beauty of God's House: Essays in Honor of Stratford Caldecott*, edited by Francesca Aran Murphy, 232–54. Eugene, Ore.: Cascade Books, an imprint of Wipf and Stock, 2014.

Coakley, Sarah. *God, Sexuality and the Self: An Essay "On the Trinity."* Cambridge: Cambridge University Press, 2013.

———. *The New Asceticism: Sexuality, Gender and the Quest for God*. London: Bloomsbury Continuum, an imprint of Bloomsbury Publishing, 2015.

Congregation for Divine Worship. *Saltatio Religiosa* [On Dance in the Liturgy]. *Notitiae* 11 (1975): 202–5.

Corry, Maya. "The Alluring Beauty of a Leonardesque Ideal: Masculinity and Spirituality in Renaissance Milan." *Gender and History* 25, no. 3 (2013): 565–89.

Council of Trent. *Decree on Justification*. January 13, 1547.

———. *Decree on the Most Holy Sacraments of Penance and Extreme Unction*. November 25, 1551.

———. *Decree on the Holy Eucharist*. October 11, 1551.

———. *Doctrine Touching the Sacrifice of the Mass*. September 17, 1562.

Crouzel, Henri. *Origen*. Translated by A. S. Worrall. San Francisco, Calif.: Harper & Row, 1989.

Cutrone, Emmanuel J. "Sacraments." In *Augustine through the Ages: An Encyclopedia*, edited by Allan D. Fitzgerald, 741–47. Grand Rapids, Mich.: Eerdmans, 1999.

Cyprian. "Epistle 31." In *Letters 28–54*. Vol. 2 of *The Letters of St. Cyprian of Carthage*. Translated by G. W. Clarke. New York: Newman Press, 1984.

Cyril of Jerusalem. "The Mystagogical Lectures." Vol. 2 of *The Works of Saint Cyril of Jerusalem*. Translated by Leo P. McCauley and Anthony A. Stephenson. Fathers of the Church 64. Washington, D.C.: The Catholic University of America Press, 1970.

———. *Lectures on the Christian Sacraments*. Edited by Maxwell E. Johnson. Yonkers, N.Y: St. Vladimir's Seminary, 2017.

Daniélou, Jean. "The Canticle: A Song of Sacraments." *Orate Fratres* 25, nos. 3–4 (1951): 97–103, 161–65.

Dante Alighieri. *Paradiso*. Edited by Robert Hollander. Translated by Jean Hollander and Robert Hollander. New York: Doubleday, 2007.

Davis, John. "Catholic Envy: The Visual Culture of Protestant Desire." In *The Visual Culture of American Religions*, edited by David Morgan and Sally Promey, 105–28. Berkeley, Calif.: University of California Press, 2001.

Day, Dorothy. "The Mystery of the Poor." *The Catholic Worker*. April 1964. http://www.catholicworker.org/dorothyday/articles/189.html.

Debby, Nirit Ben-Aryeh. "*Nel mio bel San Giovanni, fatti per loco de' battezzatori*: Baptismal Fonts in Tuscany." In *The Visual Culture of Baptism in the Middle Ages: Essays on Medieval Fonts, Settings and Beliefs*, edited by Harriet M. Sonne de Torrens and Miguel A. Torrens, 11–30. Burlington, Vt.: Ashgate, 2013.

Demarest, Donald. "Guadalupe Cult in the Lives of Mexicans." In *A Handbook on Guadalupe*, edited by Franciscan Friars of the Immaculate, 112–15. Waite Park, Minn.: Park Press, 1996.

Derbes, Anne. *Picturing the Passion in Late Medieval Italy: Narrative Painting, Franciscan Ideologies, and the Levant*. New York: Cambridge University Press, 1996.

Downs, David J. *Charity, Reward, and Atonement in Early Christianity*. Waco, Tex.: Baylor University Press, 2016.

Drever, Matthew. *Image, Identity, and the Forming of the Augustinian Soul*. New York: Oxford University Press, 2013.

Durand, William. "Rationale of the Divine Offices." In Vol. 2 of *A Documentary History of Art*, edited by Elizabeth Gilmore Holt, 120–29. New York: Doubleday, 1957.

Duricy, Michael, and Vincenzina Krymow. "The Black Madonna: Past and Present." *Marian Studies* 57, Article 10 (2006): 190–241. http://ecommons.udayton.edu/marian_studies/vol57/iss1/10.

Duricy, Michael. "The Life of Mary in Film: Marian Films in the Twentieth Century."

Marian Studies 60, Article 14 (2009): 275–86. https://ecommons.udayton.edu/cgi/viewcontent.cgi?referer=https://www.google.com/&httpsredir=1&article=1230&context=marian_studies.

Eusebius. *The History of the Church from Christ to Constantine*. Translated by G. A. Williamson. Middlesex, England: Penguin, 1965.

Evdokimov, Paul. *The Art of the Icon: A Theology of Beauty*. Translated by Steven Bigham. Redondo Beach, Calif.: Oakwood, 1990.

Fagerberg, David W. *On Liturgical Asceticism*. Washington, D. C.: The Catholic University of America Press, 2013.

———. *Consecrating the World: On Mundane Liturgical Theology*. Kettering, Ohio: Angelico Press, 2016.

Farhadian, Charles E., ed. *Christian Worship Worldwide: Expanding Horizons, Deepening Practices*. Calvin Institute of Christian Worship Liturgical Studies Series. Grand Rapids, Mich.: Eerdmans, 2007.

Fine, Steven. *Art and Judaism in the Greco-Roman World: Toward a New Jewish Archaeology*. New York: Cambridge University Press, 2010.

Finn, Richard. *Almsgiving in the Later Roman Empire*. New York: Oxford University Press, 2006.

Forest, Jim. *Praying with Icons*. Maryknoll, N.Y.: Orbis, 1997.

Fowl, Stephen E. *Ephesians: A Commentary*. Louisville, Ky.: Westminster John Knox, 2012.

Fox, Michael V. *The Song of Songs and the Ancient Egyptian Love Songs*. Madison, Wis.: University of Wisconsin Press, 1985.

Fraeters, Veerle. "*Visio*/Vision." In *The Cambridge Companion to Christian Mysticism*, edited by Amy Hollywood and Patricia Z. Beckman, 178–88. New York: Cambridge University Press, 2012.

Francis. *Misericordiae Vultus*. Bull of Indiction for the Extraordinary Holy Year of Mercy. April 11, 2015.

Frank, Georgia. "'Taste and See': The Eucharist and the Eyes of Faith in the Fourth Century." *Church History* 70, no. 4 (December 2001): 619–43.

Fulton, Rachel. *From Judgment to Passion: Devotion to Christ and the Virgin Mary, 800–1200*. New York: Columbia University Press, 2002.

Gambero, Luigi. *Mary and the Fathers of the Church*. San Francisco, Calif.: Ignatius Press, 1999.

Gavrilyuk, Paul L. and Sarah Coakley, eds. *The Spiritual Senses: Perceiving God in Western Christianity*. Cambridge: Cambridge University Press, 2012.

Gibson, David. "Jesus Was Not a Bottle Baby: What Happened to Maria Lactans?" *Commonweal Magazine* (December 11, 2012): https://www.commonwealmagazine.org/jesus-was-not-bottle-baby-what-happened-maria-lactans.

Giorgi, Rosa. *Saints: A Year in Faith and Art*. New York: Abrams, 2006.

Grabar, André. *Christian Iconography: A Study of Its Origins*. Princeton, N.J.: Princeton University Press, 1968.

Grant, Daniel. "'I Don't Want That Crap in My Gallery': Why the Art World Frowns on Expressions of Faith." *Commonweal Magazine* (March 6, 2017): https://www.commonwealmagazine.org/i-dont-want-crap-my-gallery.

Gregory the Great. *Life and Miracles of St. Benedict: Book Two of the Dialogues*. Translated by Odo J. Zimmermann and Benedict R. Avery. Collegeville, Minn.: St. John's Abbey Press, 1949.

Gregory the Great. "Epistle CV, To Serenus, Bishop of Massilia." In vol. 13 of *Nicene and Post-Nicene Fathers: Second series.* Edited by Phillip Schaff and Henry Wace. Translated by James Barmby. Grand Rapids, Mich.: Eerdmans, 1978.

Gregory of Nyssa. *The Life of Moses.* Translated by A. J. Malherbe and E. Ferguson. The Classics of Western Spirituality. New York: Paulist Press, 1978.

Griffiths, Paul J. *Song of Songs: Brazos Theological Commentary on the Bible.* Grand Rapids, Mich.: Brazos Press, 2011.

Hall, Marcia B., and Tracey E. Cooper, eds. *The Sensuous in the Counter-Reformation Church.* New York: Cambridge University Press, 2013.

Hamburger, Jeffrey F. *The Rothschild Canticles: Art and Mysticism in Flanders and the Rhineland circa 1300.* New Haven, Conn.: Yale University Press, 1990.

———. *St. John the Divine: The Deified Evangelist in Medieval Art and Theology.* Berkeley, Calif.: University of California Press, 2002.

Hammarskjold, Dag. *Markings.* New York: Alfred A. Knopf, 1964.

Harrison, Carol. *Beauty and Revelation in the Thought of Saint Augustine.* New York: Oxford University Press, 1992.

———. "Spiritual Senses." In *Augustine through the Ages: An Encyclopedia.* Edited by Allan D. Fitzgerald, 767–68. Grand Rapids, Mich.: Eerdmans, 1999.

Herrin, Judith. *Byzantium: The Surprising Life of a Medieval Empire.* Princeton, N.J.: Princeton University Press, 2007.

The Holy Bible. Translated from the Latin Vulgate: Douay Rheims Version, 1899. Reprinted Rockford, Ill.: Tan Books, 1971.

The Holy Bible. Revised Standard Version, Catholic Edition. San Francisco, Calif.: Ignatius Press, 1966.

Honorius Augustodunensis. *Expositio in Cantica Canticorum.* Patrologiae cursus completus, series latina. Edited by Jacques Paul Migne. Paris: Migne, 1857–66.

Hopkins, Clark. *The Discovery of Dura-Europos.* New Haven, Conn.: Yale University Press, 1979.

Hugh of St. Victor. *De scripturis et scriptoribus.* Patrologiae cursus completus, series latina. Edited by Jacques Paul Migne. Paris: Migne, 1857–66.

Ignatius Loyola. *The Spiritual Exercises.* Translated by George E. Ganss. Saint Louis, Mo.: Institute of Jesuit Sources, 1992.

International Commission on English in the Liturgy. *Rite of Christian Initiation of Adults: Study Edition.* Chicago, Ill.: Liturgy Training Publications, 1988.

Jacob the Deacon. "The Life of St. Pelagia the Harlot." In *Vitae Patrum.* Translated by Benedict Baker. Online publication, last updated July 12, 2004. http://www.vitae-patrum.org.uk/page46.html.

Jansen, Katherine Ludwig. *The Making of the Magdalene: Preaching and Popular Devotion in the Later Middle Ages.* Princeton, N.J.: Princeton University Press, 2000.

Jensen, Robin Margaret. *Understanding Early Christian Art.* London: Routledge, 2000.

———. *The Substance of Things Seen: Art, Faith, and the Christian Community.* Grand Rapids, Mich.: Eerdmans, 2004.

———. *Face to Face: Portraits of the Divine in Early Christianity.* Minneapolis, Minn.: Fortress, 2005.

———. *Baptismal Imagery in Early Christianity: Ritual, Visual, and Theological Dimensions.* Grand Rapids, Mich.: Baker Academic, 2012.

Jerome. *Prologus in Hiezechielem.* Corpus christianorum series latina 75. Edited by Francis Glorie. Turnhout: Brepols, 1964.

The Jewish Annotated New Testament, 2nd ed. Edited by Amy-Jill Levine and Marc Zvi Brettler. New York: Oxford University Press, 2017.

John Chrysostom. "Homily on Ephesians 1:1–2." In vol. 13 of *Nicene and Post-Nicene Fathers: Series One*, edited by Phillip Schaff, Oxford translation revised by Gross Alexander, 53–54. Peabody, Mass. Hendrickson, 1994.

John of Damascus. *On the Divine Images: Three Apologies against Those Who Attack the Divine Images.* Crestwood, N.Y.: St. Vladimir's Seminary Press, 2000.

John Paul II. *Familiaris Consortio.* Apostolic Exhortation. November 22, 1981.

———. *Redemptoris Mater.* Encyclical Letter. March 25, 1987.

———. *Mulieris dignitatem.* Apostolic Letter. August 15, 1988.

———. *Evangelium Vitae.* Encyclical Letter. March 25, 1995.

———. *Homily on Easter Sunday.* April 4, 1999.

———. *Letter to Artists.* April 4, 1999.

———. *Theotókos: Woman, Mother, Disciple: A Catechesis on Mary, Mother of God.* Boston, Mass.: Pauline Books & Media, 2000.

———. *Man and Woman He Created Them: A Theology of the Body.* Translated by Michael Waldstein. Boston, Mass.: Pauline Books and Media, 2006.

Johnson, Maxwell E. *The Rites of Christian Initiation: Their Evolution and Interpretation.* Revised and expanded edition. Collegeville, Minn.: Liturgical Press, 2007.

Kentenich, Joseph. *Reply to the Report on the Canonical Visitation of the Apostolic Movement of Schoenstatt from February 19–28, 1949.* Manuscript. May 31, 1949.

———. *Aus dem Glauben leben.* [Sermons at St. Michael's Parish, Milwaukee, Wis. between 1962–65.] Vol. 14. Vallendar-Schönstatt: Patris, 1986.

Kingsmil, Edmée. *The Song of Songs and the Eros of God: A Study in Biblical Intertextuality.* Oxford: Oxford University Press, 2009.

Kloos, Kari. *Christ, Creation, and the Vision of God.* Leiden: Brill, 2011.

Kolb, Karl. "Typologie der Gnadenbilder." In vol. 2 of *Handbuch der Marienkunde*, edited by Wolfgang Beinert and Heinrich Petri, 449–81. Regensburg: Friedrich Pustet, 1997.

Lavin, Marilyn Aronberg, and Irving Lavin. *The Liturgy of Love: Images from the Song of Songs in the Art of Cimabue, Michelangelo, and Rembrandt.* Lawrence, Kans.: Spencer Museum of Art, University of Kansas, 2001.

Leclercq, Jean. *Monks and Love in Twelfth-Century France: Psycho-historical Essays.* Oxford: Clarendon Press, 1979.

Lewis, C. S. *The Great Divorce.* In *The Complete C. S. Lewis Signature Classics.* San Francisco, Calif.: Harper, 2002.

———. *Narnia, Cambridge, and Joy 1950–1963.* Vol. 3 of *The Collected Letters of C. S. Lewis.* Edited by Walter Hooper. San Francisco, Calif.: Harper, 2007.

Lossky, Vladimir. *In the Image and Likeness of God.* Edited by John H. Erickson and Thomas E. Bird. Oxford: A. R. Mowbray, 1974.

Lundbom, Jack R. "Mary Magdalene and Song of Songs 3:1–4." *Interpretation* 49, no. 2 (1995): 172–75.

Madeleva, Sister M. *My First Seventy Years*. New York: Macmillan, 1959.
Magesa, Laurenti. *Anatomy of Inculturation: Transforming the Church in Africa*. Maryknoll, N.Y.: Orbis, 2004.
Maguire, Henry. *The Icons of Their Bodies: Saints and Their Images in Byzantium*. Princeton, N.J.: Princeton University Press, 1996.
Mandell, Gail Porter. "Beauty Is God's Visibility: The Educational Philosophy of Sister M. Madeleva Wolff, C.S.C." Paper presentation, "Seeing with the Eyes of the Heart" conference. Saint Mary's College, Notre Dame, Ind. March 27, 2015.
Marion, Jean-Luc. *God without Being: Hors-Texte*. Translated by Thomas A. Carlson. Chicago, Ill.: University of Chicago Press, 1991.
———. *In Excess: Studies of Saturated Phenomena*. New York: Fordham University Press, 2002.
———. *Prolegomena to Charity*. New York: Fordham University Press, 2002.
———. *The Erotic Phenomenon*. Chicago, Ill.: University of Chicago Press, 2007.
———. "Seeing, or Seeing Oneself Seen: Nicholas of Cusa's Contribution in *De visione Dei*." Translated by Stephen E. Lewis. *Journal of Religion* 96, no. 3 (2016): 305–31.
Matter, E. Ann. *The Voice of My Beloved: The Song of Songs in Western Medieval Christianity*. Philadelphia, Pa.: University of Pennsylvania Press, 1990.
Maximus the Confessor. "The Four Hundred Chapters on Love." In *Maximus Confessor: Selected Writings*. Translated by George C. Berthold, 33–98. The Classics of Western Spirituality. New York: Paulist Press, 1985.
McGann, Mary E. *A Precious Fountain: Music in the Worship of an African American Catholic Community*. Virgil Michel Series. Collegeville, Minn.: Liturgical Press, 2004.
McGinn, Bernard. *The Growth of Mysticism*. New York: Crossroad, 1994.
McInroy, Mark. *Balthasar on the Spiritual Senses: Perceiving Splendour*. New York: Oxford University Press, 2014.
Miles, Margaret R. *Image as Insight: Visual Understanding in Western Christianity and Secular Culture*. Boston, Mass.: Beacon Press, 1985.
———. *A Complex Delight: The Secularization of the Breast, 1350–1750*. Berkeley, Calif.: University of California Press, 2008.
Milliner, Matthew J. "The Sexuality of Christ in Byzantine Art and in Hypermodern Oblivion." Religion and Culture Web Forum, The Martin Marty Center for the Advanced Study of Religion, University of Chicago Divinity School. January 2014. http://docplayer.net/26299398-The-sexuality-of-christ-in-byzantine-art-and-in-hypermodern-oblivion.html.
Morgan, David. *Protestants & Pictures: Religion, Visual Culture, and the Age of American Mass Production*. New York: Oxford University Press, 1999.
———. *The Sacred Gaze: Religious Visual Culture in Theory and Practice*. Berkeley, Calif.: University of California Press, 2005.
Mullady, Brian T. *The Angelic Warfare Confraternity*. 4th ed. New Hope, Ky.: The St. Martin de Porres Lay Dominicans, 2006.
Murphy, Francesca Aran. *Christ the Form of Beauty: A Study in Theology and Literature*. Edinburgh: T & T Clark, 1995.
Neff, Amy. "The Pain of *Compassio*: Mary's Labor at the Foot of the Cross." *Art Bulletin* 80, no. 2 (1998): 254–73.

Niehaus, Jonathan. *Schoenstatt's Covenant Spirituality*. Waukesha, Wis.: Schoenstatt Editions, 1992.

O'Brien, Peter T. *The Letter to the Ephesians*. Grand Rapids, Mich.: Eerdmans, 1999.

Oliana, Guido. "African Language, Drum, and Dance." In vol. 2 of *God and Popular Culture*, edited by Stephen Butler Murray and Aimée Upjohn Light, 225–44. Santa Barbara, Calif.: ABC-CLIO, 2015.

Osborne, Mary Pope. *The Life of Jesus: In Masterpieces of Art*. New York: Viking, 1998.

Ouellet, Marc. "The Beauty of Being Christians." In *The Beauty of Being a Christian: Movements in the Church. Proceedings of the Second World Congress of the Ecclesial Movements and New Communities, Rocca di Papa, 31 May–2 June 2006*, edited by The Pontifical Council on the Laity, 41–57. Rome: Libreria editrice vaticana, 2007.

Ouspensky, Leonid. *Theology of the Icon*. Crestwood, N.Y.: St. Vladimir's Seminary Press, 1978.

Ouspensky, Leonid and Vladimir Lossky. *The Meaning of Icons*. Translated by G. E. H. Palmer and E. Kadloubovsky. Boston, Mass.: Boston Book and Art Shop, 1969.

Paul VI. *Populorum Progressio*. Encyclical Letter. March 26, 1967.

———. *Humanae Vitae*. Encyclical Letter. July 25, 1968.

———. *Discourse to the Mariological Congress*. May 16, 1975.

Pelikan, Jaroslav. *The Illustrated Jesus through the Centuries*. New Haven, Conn.: Yale University Press, 1999.

———. *Imago Dei: The Byzantine Apologia for Icons*. Princeton, N.J.: Princeton University Press, 2011.

Pentcheva, Bissera V. *The Sensual Icon: Space, Ritual, and the Senses in Byzantium*. University Park, Pa.: Pennsylvania State University Press, 2010.

Peppard, Michael. *The World's Oldest Church: Bible, Art, and Ritual at Dura-Europos, Syria*. New Haven, Conn.: Yale University Press, 2016.

Peters, Nathaniel. "The Composer of Silence." *The Catholic Herald* (October 5, 2017): https://catholicherald.co.uk/magazine/the-composer-of-silence/.

Phillips, Dianne. "Leo Steinberg's Artistic Vision." *First Things* 218 (December 2011): 35–39.

Pius X. *Ad Diem Illum Laetissimum*. Encyclical Letter. February 2, 1904.

Pius XI. *Casti Connubii*. Encyclical Letter. December 31, 1930.

Pötzl, Walter. "Marianisches Brauchtum an Wallfahrtsorten." In vol. 2 of *Handbuch der Marienkunde*, edited by Wolfgang Beinert und Heinrich Petri Regensburg, 483–553. Regensburg: Friedrich Pustet, 1997.

Pseudo-Dionysius. "The Mystical Theology." In *Pseudo-Dionysius: The Complete Works*, translated by Colm Luibheid, 133–41. The Classics of Western Spirituality. New York: Paulist Press, 1987.

Pseudo-John Damascene. *Homilie 2 "in Annuntiationem."* Patrologiae cursus completus series graeca 96. Edited by Jacques Paul Migne. Paris: Migne, 1928–36.

Radler, Gudrun. *Die Schreinmadonna "Vierge ouvrante": von den bernhardinischen Anfängen bis zur Frauenmystik im Deutschordensland: mit beschreibendem Katalog*. Frankfurt am Main: Kunstgeschichtliches Institut der Johann Wolfgang Goethe-Universität, 1990.

Rahner, Karl. "Theology of the Symbol." In *More Recent Writings*. Vol. 4 of *Theological Investigations*, translated by Kevin Smyth, 221–52. Baltimore, Md.: Helicon, 1966.

———. "The Doctrine of the 'Spiritual Senses' in the Middle Ages." In *Experience of the Spirit: Source of Theology*. Vol. 16 of *Theological Investigations*, translated by David Moreland, 109–28. New York: Crossroad, 1979.

Ramsey, Boniface. "Almsgiving in the Latin Church: The Late Fourth and Early Fifth Centuries." *Theological Studies* 43, no. 2 (June 1982): 226–59.

Ratzinger, Joseph Cardinal. *Behold the Pierced One*. San Francisco, Calif.: Ignatius Press, 1986.

———. *Principles of Catholic Theology: Building Stones for a Fundamental Theology*. Translated by Mary Frances McCarthy. San Francisco, Calif.: Ignatius Press, 1987.

———. "*The Feeling of Things, the Contemplation of Beauty*." Message to the Communion and Liberation Meeting at Rimini. August 24–30, 2002.

———. *Pilgrim Fellowship of Faith: The Church as Communion*. San Francisco, Calif.: Ignatius Press, 2005.

Reddaway, Chloë. "Reading Hermeneutic Space: Pictorial and Spiritual Transformation in the Brancacci Chapel." In *ReVisioning: Critical Methods of Seeing Christianity in the History of Art*, edited by James Romaine and Linda Stratford, 146–65. Cambridge: Lutterworth Press, 2014.

Roten, Johann G. "Vierge Ouvrante or Shrine Madonna." "All about Mary" website. International Marian Research Institute, University of Dayton. https://udayton.edu/imri/mary/v/vierge-ourvante-what-is.php.

———. "How Can Spirituality Be Marian?" *Marian Studies* 52, Article 5 (2001): 7–52. http://ecommons.udayton.edu/marian_studies/vol52/iss1/5.

———. "From Epinal to Plateau D'Assy: Religious Art and the Marian Century." In *Mary on the Eve of the Second Vatican Council*, edited by John C. Cavadini and Danielle M. Peters, 79–110. Notre Dame, Ind.: University of Notre Dame Press, 2017.

———. "Popular Religion and Marian Images." *Marian Studies* 45, Article 9 (1994): 62–120. http://ecommons.udayton.edu/marian_studies/vol45/iss1/9.

Rougé, Matthieu. *Doctrine et experience de l'eucharistie chez Guillaume de Saint-Thierry*. Paris: Beauchesne, 1999.

Sacchetti, Franco. *Le Trecento Novelle*. Edited by Michelangelo Zaccarello. Florence: SISMEL, 2014.

Sahas, Daniel, ed. *Icon and Logos: Sources in Eighth Century Iconoclasm*. Toronto: University of Toronto Press, 1986.

Schoemperlen, Diane. *Our Lady of the Lost and Found: A Novel*. New York: Viking, 2001.

Schönborn, Christoph. *God's Human Face: The Christ-Icon*. Translated by Lothar Krauth. San Francisco, Calif.: Ignatius Press, 1994.

Shuve, Karl. *The Song of Songs and the Fashioning of Christian Identity in Early Latin Christianity*. Oxford: Oxford University Press, 2016.

Siegel, Lee. "Pope Francis and the Naked Christ." *The New Yorker* (December 17, 2013): https://www.newyorker.com/books/page-turner/pope-francis-and-the-naked-christ.

Smith, James K. A. *Imagining the Kingdom: How Worship Works*. Grand Rapids, Mich.: Baker Academic, 2013.

Smith, Jeffrey Chipps. *Sensuous Worship: Jesuits and the Art of the Early Catholic Reformation in Germany*. Princeton, N.J.: Princeton University Press, 2002.

Soloviev, Vladimir. *Heart of Reality: Essays on Beauty, Love, and Ethics.* Notre Dame, Ind.: University of Notre Dame Press, 2003.

Spadaro, Antonio. "A Big Heart Open to God: The Exclusive Interview with Pope Francis." *America Magazine* 209, no. 8 (September 20, 2013): 14–18, 20, 22, 24, 26, 28, 30, 32, 34, 36, 38.

Steinberg, Leo. *The Sexuality of Christ in Renaissance Art and in Modern Oblivion.* 2nd rev. ed. Chicago, Ill.: University of Chicago Press, 1996.

Sulpitius Severus. *On the Life of St. Martin.* In vol. 11 of *The Nicene and Post-Nicene Fathers.* Edited by Philip Schaff and Henry Wace. Peabody, Mass.: Hendrickson, 1994.

Sutton, Barbara. *Seeing the Word: Program Manual.* Collegeville, Minn.: Liturgical Press, 2011.

Taylor, Walter F. *Ephesians: Augsburg Commentary on the New Testament.* Minneapolis, Minn.: Augsburg, 1985.

Thomas Aquinas. *Summa Theologiae.* Translated by the Fathers of the English Dominican Province. 5 vols. Westminster, Md.: Christian Classics, 1948.

———. *On Evil.* Edited by Brian Davies. Translated by Richard Regan. Oxford: Oxford University Press, 2003.

Toniolo, E. M. "La figura di Maria nei canti popolari." *La Madonna* 26 (1978): 32–60.

Travis, John. *In Defense of Faith: The Theology of Patriarch Nikephoros of Constantinople.* Brookline, Mass.: Hellenic College Press, 1984.

Tugwell, Simon, ed. *Early Dominicans: Selected Writings.* The Classics of Western Spirituality. New York: Paulist Press, 1982.

Turner, Victor. *Image and Pilgrimage in Christian Culture: Anthropological Perspectives.* New York: Columbia University Press, 1978.

Uzukwu, E. Elochukwu. *Worship as Body Language: Introduction to Christian Worship: An African Orientation.* Collegeville, Minn.: Liturgical Press, 1997.

Vassilaki, Maria, ed. *Mother of God: Representations of the Virgin in Byzantine Art.* Milan: Skira, 2000.

Vatican Council II. *Sacrosanctum Concilium.* December 4, 1963.

———. *Lumen Gentium.* November 21, 1964.

———. *Gaudium et Spes.* December 7, 1965.

Verdeyen, Paul. *La théologie mystique de Guillaume de Saint-Thierry.* Paris: FAC-éditions, 1990.

Visel, Jeana. *Icons in the Western Church.* Collegeville, Minn.: Liturgical Press, 2016.

Vrudny, Kimberly J. and Wilson Yates, eds. *Arts, Theology, and the Church: New Intersections.* Cleveland, Ohio: Pilgrim Press, 2005.

Ward, Benedictine. *Harlots of the Desert: A Study of Repentance in Early Monastic Sources.* Kalamazoo, Mich.: Cistercian Publications, 1987.

Ware, Kallistos. "Eastern Christendom." In *The Oxford Illustrated History of Christianity,* edited by John McManners, 123–61. New York: Oxford University Press, 1992.

Weil, Simone. *Gravity and Grace.* New York: Routledge, 2002.

———. *Waiting for God.* Abingdon, Oxon: Routledge, 2010.

Welsh-Asante, Kariamu, ed. *African Dance: An Artistic, Historical, and Philosophical Inquiry.* Trenton, N.J.: Africa World Press, 1996.

William of Saint Thierry. *Aenigma fidei.* In *Guillelmi a Sancto Theodorico omnia opera pars V: Opuscula adversus Petrum Abaelardum et de fidei*, edited by Paul Verdeyen. Turnhout: Brepols, 2007.

———. *The Enigma of Faith*. Translated by John D. Anderson. Washington, D.C.: Cistercian Publications, 1974.

———. *Epistola ad Fratres de Monte Dei*. In *Guillelmi a Sancto Theodorico omnia opera pars III: Opera didactica et spiritualia*, edited by Stanislaus Ceglar and Paul Verdeyen. Turnhout: Brepols, 2003.

———. *The Golden Epistle*. Translated by Theodore Berkeley. Kalamazoo, Mich.: Cistercian Publications, 1971.

———. *Meditatio*. In *Guillelmi a Sancto Theodorico omnia opera pars IV: Meditationes devotissimae (Meditativae orations)*, edited by Paul Verdeyen. Turnhout: Brepols, 2005.

———. *Meditations*. In *On Contemplating God, Prayer, Meditations*. Translated by Penelope Lawson. Kalamazoo, Mich.: Cistercian Publications, 1970.

———. *De natura et dignitate amoris*. In *Guillelmi a Sancto Theodorico omnia opera pars III: Opera didactica et spiritualia*, edited by Stanislaus Ceglar and Paul Verdeyen. Turnhout: Brepols, 2003.

———. *The Nature and Dignity of Love*. Translated by Thomas X. Davis. Kalamazoo, Mich.: Cistercian Publications, 1981.

———. *De sacramento altaris*. In *Guillelmi a Sancto Theodorico omnia opera pars III: Opera didactica et spiritualia*, edited by Stanislaus Ceglar and Paul Verdeyen. Turnhout: Brepols, 2003.

Wojtyła, Karol. *Love and Responsibility*. Boston, Mass.: Pauline Books and Media, 2013.

Wolf, Peter. *Ein Bild geht um die Welt: 1915–2015*. Vallendar: Schönstatt, 2015.

———. *A Picture Goes Around the World, 1915–2015: Schoenstatt's Marian Image*. Translated by Margaret Gründing. Waukesha, Wis.: Schoenstatt Editions USA, 2019.

Yarnold, Edward. *The Awe-Inspiring Rites of Initiation: The Origins of the R.C.I.A.* Collegeville, Minn.: Liturgical Press, 1994.

Zachman, Randall C. *Image and Word in the Theology of John Calvin*. Notre Dame, Ind.: University of Notre Dame Press, 2007.

Pornography

Allen, Mike, Tara Emmers, Lisa Gebhardt, and Mary A. Giery. "Exposure to Pornography and Acceptance of Rape Myths." *Journal of Communication* 45, no. 1 (1995): 5–26.

Barrett, Paul M. "The New Republic of Porn." *Bloomberg Businessweek*, no. 4285 (June 21, 2012): 58–64.

Bergner, Raymond M., and Ana J. Bridges. "The Significance of Heavy Pornography Involvement for Romantic Partners: Research and Clinical Implications." *Journal of Sex & Marital Therapy* 28, no. 3 (2002): 193–206.

Brand, Russell. "Russell Brand Talks Sex, Softcore & Hardcore Porn." Originally published on the YouTube channel of actor/comedian Russell Brand; republished on YouTube by Fight the New Drug on February 23, 2015. https://www.youtube.com/watch?v=5kvzamjQW9M.

Bridges, Ana J., Raymond M. Bergner, and Matthew Hesson-McInnis. "Romantic

Partners' Use of Pornography: Its Significance for Women." *Journal of Sex & Marital Therapy* 29, no. 1 (2003): 1–14.

Bridges, Ana J., and Robert Jensen. "Pornography." In *Sourcebook on Violence against Women*, 2nd ed., edited by Claire M. Renzetti, Jeffrey L. Edleson, and Raquel Kennedy Bergen, 133–49. Los Angeles, Calif.: Sage Publications, 2010.

Bridges, Ana J., Robert Wosnitzer, Erica Scharrer, Chyng Sun, and Rachel Liberman. "Aggression and Sexual Behavior in Best-Selling Pornography Videos: A Content Analysis Update." *Violence against Women* 16, no. 10 (October 2010): 1065–85.

Carroll, Jason S., Laura M. Padilla-Walker, Larry Nelson, Chad Olson, Carolyn McNamara Barry, and Stephanie D. Madsen. "Generation XXX: Pornography Acceptance and Use among Emerging Adults." *Journal of Adolescent Research* 23, no. 1 (2008): 6–30.

Cebulko, Susan. *The Impact of Internet Pornography on Married Women: A Psychodynamic Perspective*. Youngstown, N.Y.: Cambria Press, 2007.

Cooper, Al, David L. Delmonico, and Ron Burg. "Cybersex Users, Abusers, and Compulsives: New Findings and Implications." *Sexual Addiction & Compulsivity* 7 (2000): 5–29.

Davis, Kelly Cue, Jeanette Norris, William H. George, Joel Martell, and Julia R. Heiman. "Men's Likelihood of Sexual Aggression: The Influence of Alcohol, Sexual Arousal, and Violent Pornography." *Aggressive Behavior* 32, no. 6 (2006): 581–89.

DeKeseredy, Walter S., and Marilyn Corsianos. *Violence against Women in Pornography*. New York: Routledge, an imprint of the Taylor & Francis Group, 2016.

Dines, Gail. *Pornland: How Porn Has Hijacked Our Sexuality*. Boston, Mass.: Beacon Press, 2010.

———. *Pornland: How the Porn Industry Has Hijacked Our Sexuality*. North Hampton, Mass.: Media Education Foundation, 2014, DVD. Transcript published online at http://www.mediaed.org/transcripts/Pornland-Transcript.pdf.

———. "Growing Up with Porn: The Developmental and Societal Impact of Pornography on Children." *Dignity: A Journal on Sexual Exploitation and Violence* 2, no. 3 (2017): https://digitalcommons.uri.edu/dignity/vol2/iss3/3/.

Dworkin, Andrea. *Right-wing Women*. New York: Perigee, 1978.

———. *Pornography: Men Possessing Women*. New York: Perigee, an imprint of G. P. Putnam's Sons, 1981.

———. "Prostitution and Male Supremacy." *Michigan Journal of Gender and Law* 1, no. 1 (1993): 1–12.

———. *Heartbreak: The Political Memoir of a Feminist Militant*. New York: Perseus Books, 2002.

Eberstadt, Mary, and Mary Anne Layden. *The Social Costs of Pornography: A Statement of Findings and Recommendations*. Princeton, N.J.: The Witherspoon Institute, 2010.

Fight the New Drug. "What's the Average Age of a Child's First Exposure to Porn?" Fight the New Drug website. August 20, 2019. https://fightthenewdrug.org/real-average-age-of-first-exposure/.

———. "These Sixteen States Passed Resolutions Recognizing Porn as a Public Health Issue." Fight the New Drug website. May 9, 2019. https://fightthenewdrug.org/here-are-the-states-that-have-passed-resolutions/.

———. “10 Ex-Porn Performers Reveal the Brutal Truth behind Their Most Famous Scenes.” Fight the New Drug website. September 3, 2019. https://fightthenewdrug.org/10-porn-stars-speak-openly-about-their-most-popular-scenes/.

Flood, Michael, and Clive Hamilton. *Youth and Pornography in Australia: Evidence on the Extent of Exposure and Likely Effects*. Discussion Paper Number 52. Canberra: The Australia Institute, 2003.

Grubbs, Joshua B., and Samuel L. Perry. “Moral Incongruence and Pornography Use: A Critical Review and Integration.” *Journal of Sex Research* 56 (2019): 29–37.

Grudzen, Corita R., Danielle Meeker, Jaqueline M. Torres, Qingling Du, R. Sean Morrison, Ronald M. Anderson, and Lillian Gelberg. “Comparison of the Mental Health of Female Adult Performers and Other Young Women in California.” *Psychiatric Services* 62, no. 6 (2011): 639–45.

Hald, Gert Martin, Neil M. Malamuth, and Carlin Yuen. “Pornography and Attitudes Supporting Violence against Women: Revisiting the Relationship in Nonexperimental Studies.” *Aggressive Behavior* 26 (2010): 14–20.

Halverson, Haley. “Report: The Gender-Based Torture Found in the Pornography Industry.” Washington, D.C.: The National Center on Sexual Exploitation, 2016. http://endsexualexploitation.org/wp-content/uploads/NCOSE_Report_UN_Final.pdf.

Hamann, Stephan. “Sex Differences in the Responses of the Human Amygdala.” *The Neuroscientist* 11, no. 4 (2005): 288–93.

Hawkins, Dawn. “It Can’t Wait: Exposing the Connections between Forms of Sexual Exploitation.” *Dignity: A Journal on Sexual Exploitation and Violence* 2, no. 2 (2017): 1–12.

Jensen, Robert. *Getting Off: Pornography and the End of Masculinity*. Cambridge, Mass.: South End Press, 2007.

Jenson, Kristen A., and Gail Poyner. *Good Pictures, Bad Pictures: Porn-Proofing Today’s Young Kids*. Richland, Wash.: Glen Cove Press, 2016.

Kasper, T. E., M. B. Shor, and A. C. Milam. “Narcissism and Internet Pornography Use.” *Sex & Marital Therapy* 41, no. 5 (2015): 481–86.

Kühn, Simone, and Jürgen Gallinat. “Brain Structure and Functional Connectivity Associated with Pornography Consumption: The Brain on Porn.” *JAMA Psychiatry* 71, no. 7 (2014): 827–34.

Lafavor, Carole. “Testimony XXX.” In *In Harm’s Way: The Pornography Civil Rights Hearings*, edited by Catharine A. MacKinnon and Andrea Dworkin, 147–49. Cambridge, Mass.: Harvard University Press, 1997.

Laier, Christian, Frank P. Schulte, and Matthais Brand. “Pornographic Picture Processing Interferes with Working Memory Performance.” *Journal of Sex Research* 50, no. 7 (October 2013): 642–52.

Layden, Mary Anne. “Pornography and Violence: A New Look at the Research.” In *The Social Costs of Pornography: A Collection of Papers*, edited by James R. Stoner Jr. and Donna M. Hughes, 57–68. Princeton, N.J.: The Witherspoon Institute, 2010.

Leahy, Michael. *Porn University: What College Students Are Really Saying about Sex on Campus*. Chicago, Ill.: Northfield Publishing, 2009.

Lenhart, Amanda. “Teens and Sexting: How and Why Minor Teens Are Sending Sexually Suggestive Nude or Nearly Nude Images via Text Messaging.” Washington,

D.C.: Pew Research Center, 2009. http://www.pewinternet.org/2009/12/15/teens-and-sexting/.

Ley, David, Nicole Prause, and Peter Finn. "The Emperor Has No Clothes: A Review of the 'Pornography Addiction' Model." *Current Sexual Health Reports* 6 (February 2014): 94–105.

Linz, Daniel. "Exposure to Sexually Explicit Materials and Attitudes toward Rape: A Comparison of Study Results." *Journal of Sex Research* 26, no. 1 (February 1989): 50–84.

Löfgren-Mårtenson, Lotta and Sven-Axel Månsson. "Lust, Love and Life: A Qualitative Study of Swedish Adolescents' Perceptions and Experiences with Pornography." *The Journal of Sex Research* 47, no. 6 (2010): 568–79.

Love, Todd, Christian Laier, Matthias Brand, Linda Hatch, and Raju Hajela. "Neuroscience of Internet Pornography Addiction: A Review and Update." *Behavioral Sciences* 5, no. 3 (2015): 388–433.

MacKinnon, Catharine A., and Andrea Dworkin, eds. *In Harm's Way: The Pornography Civil Rights Hearings*. Cambridge, Mass.: Harvard University Press, 1997.

MacKinnon, Catharine A., "Pornography as Trafficking." In *Pornography: Driving the Demand in International Sex Trafficking*, edited by David E. Guinn with Julie DiCaro, 31–42. Los Angeles, Calif.: Captive Daughters Media, 2007.

Malamuth, Neil M., Tamara Addison, and Mary Koss. "Pornography and Sexual Aggression: Are There Reliable Effects and Can We Understand Them?" *Annual Review of Sex Research* 11, no. 1 (2000): 26–94.

Manning, Jill C. "The Impact of Internet Pornography on Marriage and the Family: A Review of the Research." *Sexual Addiction & Compulsivity* 13, no. 2/3 (2006): 131–65.

———. *What's the Big Deal about Pornography? A Guide for the Internet Generation.* Salt Lake City, Utah: Shadow Mountain, 2008.

———. "The Impact of Pornography on Women: Social Science Findings and Clinical Observations." In *The Social Costs of Pornography: A Collection of Papers*, edited by James R. Stoner Jr. and Donna M. Hughes, 69–87. Princeton, N.J.: The Witherspoon Institute, 2010.

Mesch, Gustavo S. "Social Bonds and Internet Pornographic Exposure among Adolescents." *Journal of Adolescence* 32, no. 3 (2009): 601–18.

Monet, Melissa. "Pornography Does Not Harm Those Involved in Its Production." In *Pornography: Opposing Viewpoints*, edited by Melissa Monet, 63–69. San Diego, Calif.: Greenhaven Press, 2002.

Mulhauser, Kyler R. W., Willliam M. Struthers, Joshua N. Hook, Benjamin A. Pyykkonen, Stephanie D. Womack, and Mark MacDonald. "Performance on the Iowa Gambling Task in a Sample of Hypersexual Men." *Sexual Addiction & Compulsivity* 21, no. 2 (2014): 170–83.

National Center on Sexual Exploitation (NCOSE). Introduction to "Pornography: A Public Health Crisis. A Collection of Papers from Symposium Held at the U.S. Capitol on July 14, 2015." Washington, D.C.: National Center on Sexual Exploitation, 2015. https://endsexualexploitation.org/publichealth/.

———. "Pornography & Public Health: Research Summary." NCOSE website, Septem-

ber 8, 2016. https://endsexualexploitation.org/wp-content/uploads/NCOSE_PornographyPH_RESEARCH-SUMMARY_9-8-16.pdf.
Ogas, Ogi and Sai Gaddam. *A Billion Wicked Thoughts: What the World's Largest Experiment Reveals about Human Desire.* New York: Dutton, an imprint of the Penguin Group, 2011.
Owens, Eric W., Richard J. Behun, Jill C. Manning, and Rory C. Reid. "The Impact of Internet Pornography on Adolescents: A Review of the Research." *Sexual Addiction & Compulsivity* 19, no. 1/2 (2012): 99–122.
Park, Brian Y., Gary Wilson, Jonathan Berger, Matthew Christman, Bryn Reina, Frank Bishop, Warren P. Klam, and Andrew P. Doran. "Is Internet Pornography Causing Sexual Dysfunctions? A Review with Clinical Reports." *Behavioral Sciences* 6, no. 3 (2016): 1–25.
Paul, Pamela. "The Porn Factor." *TIME Magazine* 163, no. 3 (January 19, 2004): 99–101.
———. *Pornified: How Pornography Is Transforming Our Lives, Our Relationships, and Our Families.* New York: Times Books, an imprint of Henry Holt, 2005.
Perry, Samuel L. "Pornography Consumption as a Threat to Religious Socialization." *Sociology of Religion* 76, no. 4 (2015): 436–58.
Peter, Jochen, and Patti M. Valkenburg. "Adolescents' Exposure to a Sexualized Media Environment and Their Notions of Women as Sex Objects." *Sex Roles* 56, no. 5/6 (2007): 381–95.
———. "Adolescents' Exposure to Sexually Explicit Internet Material and Notions of Women as Sex Objects. Assessing Causality and Underlying Processes." *Journal of Communication* 59, no. 3 (2009): 407–33.
Power to Decide (formerly, The National Campaign to Prevent Teen and Unplanned Pregnancy). *Sex and Tech: Results from a Survey of Teens and Young Adults.* Washington, D.C.: The National Campaign to Prevent Teen and Unplanned Pregnancy, 2008. https://powertodecide.org/sites/default/files/resources/primary-download/sex-and-tech.pdf.
The Price of Pleasure: Pornography, Sexuality, and Relationships. DVD. Northhampton, Mass.: Media Education Foundation, 2008.
Qualls, Roxanne. Remarks at "Set Free Global Summit." Greensboro, N.C. April 2016. https://setfreesummit.org/monday/the-porn-phenomenon-david-kinnaman-roxanne-stone/.
Reavill, Gil. *Smut: A Sex Industry Insider (and Concerned Father) Says Enough Is Enough.* New York: Sentinel, an imprint of the Penguin Group, 2005.
Riddell, Jenny. "Desire and Memory: The Impact of Internet Pornography on the Couple Relationship, and Processing of Early Trauma in Therapy." In *Love in the Age of the Internet: Attachment in the Digital Era,* edited by Linda Cundy, 81–97. London: Karnac Books, 2015.
Rothbart, Davy. "He's Just Not That Into Anyone." *New York Magazine* 44, no. 4 (January 30, 2011): http://nymag.com/news/features/70976/.
Rupp, Heather A., and Kim Wallen. "Sex Differences in Response to Visual Sexual Stimuli: A Review." *Archives of Sexual Behavior* 37, no. 2 (2008): 206–18.
Russell, Diana E. H. *Dangerous Relationships: Pornography, Misogyny, and Rape.* Thousand Oaks, Calif.: SAGE Publications, 1998.

Schneider, Jennifer P. "Effects of Cybersex Addiction on the Family: Results of a Survey." *Sexual Addiction & Compulsivity* 7, no. 1/2 (2000): 31–58.

Shor, Eran. "Age, Aggression, and Pleasure in Popular Online Pornographic Videos." *Violence Against Women* 25, no. 8 (2019): 1018–36.

Simmons, Catherine A., Peter Lehmann, and Shannon Collier-Tennison. "Linking Male Use of the Sex Industry to Controlling Behavior in Violent Relationships: An Exploratory Analysis." *Violence against Women* 14, no. 4 (2008): 406–17.

Stack, Steven, Ira Wasserman, and Roger Kern. "Adult Social Bonds and Use of Internet Pornography." *Social Science Quarterly* 85, no. 1 (2004): 75–88.

State of Arkansas, 91st General Assembly, "House Resolution 1042: Recognizing and Finding that the Proliferation and Accessibility of Pornography Has Created a Public Health Crisis Leading to a Broad Spectrum of Individual and Public Health Impacts and Societal Harms." Regular Session 2017. http://www.arkleg.state.ar.us/assembly/2017/2017R/Bills/HR1042.pdf.

Steffens, Barbara A., and Robyn L. Rennie. "The Traumatic Nature of Disclosure for Wives of Sexual Addicts." *Sexual Addiction & Compulsivity* 13, no. 2/3 (2006): 247–67.

Stoner, James R. Jr. "Freedom, Virtue, and the Politics of Regulating Pornography." In *The Social Costs of Pornography: A Collection of Papers*, edited by James R. Stoner Jr. and Donna M. Hughes, 165–84. Princeton, N.J.: The Witherspoon Institute, 2010.

Stroller, R. J., and I. S. Levine. *Coming Attractions: The Making of an X-Rated Video.* New Haven, Conn.: Yale University Press, 2007.

Struthers, William. *Wired for Intimacy: How Pornography Hijacks the Male Brain.* Downers Grove, Ill.: Intervarsity Press, 2009.

Sun, Chyng, Ana Bridges, Jennifer A. Johnson, and Matthew B. Ezzell. "Pornography and the Male Sexual Script: An Analysis of Consumption and Sexual Relations." *Archives of Sexual Behavior* 45 (2016): 983–94.

Tarrant, Shira. *The Pornography Industry*. New York: Oxford University Press, 2016.

Tsitsika, Artemis, Elena Critselis, Georgios Kormas, Eleftheria Konstantoulaki, Andreas Constantopoulos, and Dimitrios Kafetzis. "Adolescent Pornographic Internet Site Use: A Multivariate Regression Analysis of the Predictive Factors of Use and Psychosocial Implications." *CyberPsychology & Behavior* 12, no. 5 (2009): 545–50.

Walter, Martin, Felix Bermpohl, Harold Mouras, Kolja Schiltz, Claus Tempelmann, Michael Rotte, Hans Jochen Heinze, Bernard Bogerts, and Georg Northoff. "Distinguishing Specific Sexual and General Emotional Effects in fMRI—Subcortical and Cortical Arousal during Erotic Picture Viewing." *Neuroimage* 40, no. 4 (2008): 1482–94.

Whitty, Monica Therese. "Pushing the Wrong Buttons: Men's and Women's Attitudes toward Online and Offline Infidelity." *CyberPsychology & Behavior* 6, no. 6 (December 2003): 569–79.

Wolak, Janas, Kimberly Mitchell, and David Finkelhor. "Unwanted and Wanted Exposure to Online Pornography in a National Sample of Youth Internet Users." *Pediatrics* 119, no. 2 (February 2007): 247–57.

Wright, Paul J. "U.S. Males and Pornography, 1973–2010: Consumption, Predictors, Correlates." *Journal of Sex Research* 50, no. 1 (2013): 60–71.

Wright, Paul J., and Robert S. Tokunaga. "Men's Objectifying Media Consumption, Objectification of Women, and Attitudes Supportive of Violence against Women." *Archives of Sexual Behavior* 45, no. 4 (2016): 955–64.

Yang, Doug-ouk, and Gahyun Youn. "Effects of Exposure to Pornography on Male Aggressive Behavioral Tendencies." *The Open Psychology Journal* 5 (2012): 1–12.

Ybarra, Michele L. and Kimberly J. Mitchell. "Exposure to Internet Pornography among Children and Adolescents: A National Survey." *CyberPsychology & Behavior* 8, no. 5 (2005): 473–86.

Ybarra, Michele L., Kimberly J. Mitchell, Merle Hamburger, Marie Diener-West, and Philip J. Leaf. "X-Rated Material and Perpetration of Sexually Aggressive Behavior among Children and Adolescents: Is There a Link?" *Aggressive Behavior* 37, no. 1 (2011): 1–18.

Zillman, Dolf. "Influence of Unrestrained Access to Erotica on Adolescents' and Young Adults' Dispositions toward Sexuality." *Journal of Adolescent Health* 27, no. 2/1 (2000): 41–44.

Theological and Pastoral Responses to Pornography

Archdiocese of Kansas City. "My House" Initiative. https://www.archkck.org/myhouse/.

Assad, Audrey. "Freedom and Fullness." In *Delivered: True Stories of Men and Women Who Turned from Porn to Purity*, edited by Matt Fradd, 33–42. San Diego, Calif.: Catholic Answers Press, 2013.

Barna Group. *The Porn Phenomenon: The Impact of Pornography in the Digital Age*. Ventura, Calif.: Barna Group, in partnership with Josh McDowell Ministry, 2016.

Bransfield, J. Brian. *Overcoming Pornography Addiction: A Spiritual Solution*. New York: Paulist Press, 2013.

Fradd, Matt. *The Porn Myth: Exposing the Reality behind the Fantasy of Pornography*. San Francisco, Calif.: Ignatius Press, 2017.

Fradd, Matt, and Cameron Fradd. *Restored: True Stories of Love and Trust after Porn*. El Cajon, Calif.: Catholic Answers Press, 2015.

Garris, April. "Beauty for Ashes." In *Delivered: True Stories of Men and Women Who Turned from Porn to Purity*, edited by Matt Fradd, 59–70. San Diego, Calif.: Catholic Answers Press, 2013.

Hopkinson, Ciara. "Students Look to Implement Wi-Fi Filter to Limit Pornography Use." *The Observer* (October 30, 2017): https://ndsmcobserver.com/2017/10/students-look-to-implement-wi-fi-filter-to-limit-pornography-use/.

Hütter, Reinhard. "Pornography and Acedia." *First Things* 222 (April 2012): 45–49.

———. "The Virtue of Chastity and the Scourge of Pornography: A Twofold Crisis Considered in Light of Thomas Aquinas's Moral Theology." *The Thomist* 77 (January 2013): 1–39.

Kleponis, Peter C. *Integrity Restored: Helping Catholic Families Win the Battle against Pornography*. Steubenville, Ohio: Emmaus Road, 2014.

Mike and Anne. "To Hell and Back." In *Delivered: True Stories of Men and Women Who Turned from Porn to Purity*, edited by Matt Fradd, 71–88. San Diego, Calif.: Catholic Answers Press, 2013.

Morrow, Maria C. "Pornography and Penance." In *Leaving and Coming Home: New*

Wineskins for Catholic Sexual Ethics, edited by David Cloutier, 62–84. Eugene, Ore.: Cascade Books, an imprint of Wipf and Stock, 2010.
Schilling, Terry. "How to Regulate Pornography." *First Things* (November 2019): https://www.firstthings.com/article/2019/11/how-to-regulate-pornography.
Scruton, Roger. "The Abuse of Sex." In *The Social Costs of Pornography*, edited by James R. Stoner Jr. and Donna M. Hughes, 113–26. Princeton, N.J.: The Witherspoon Institute, 2010.
Skinner, Kevin. *Treating Pornography Addiction*. Provo, Utah: Growth Climate, 2005.
Smith, John. "Confessing My Porn Addiction: A Priest Learns to Ask for Help." *America Magazine* 216, no. 7 (April 3, 2017): 32–36.
Snyder, Jon. *The Mighty Man Manual: Victory and Freedom over Lust, Pornographic, and Sexual Addictions*. Edgemont, Pa.: Jon Snyder and Mighty Man Ministries, 2009.
Struthers, William M. "Living in a Hyper-Sexualized Culture." Wheaton College Chapel Message, Wheaton, Ill. March 28, 2011. https://www.youtube.com/watch?v=uQq3-YPEmQM.
———. "Wired for Intimacy." Pure Passion Media Presentation, 2012. https://www.youtube.com/watch?v=sWXqSFuIXSc.
Turnrose, Jacob. "I Wanted to Become a Catholic. But First I Had to Give Up the Eucharist—and Porn." *America Magazine* 219, no. 1 (July 9, 2018): 34–35.
United States Conference of Catholic Bishops. "Create in Me a Clean Heart: A Pastoral Response to Pornography" and "*Crea in mí un Corazón puro: Una respuesta pastoral a la pornografía*." Washington, D.C.: United States Conference of Catholic Bishops, 2015.
Weil, China. "How to Talk to Young People about the Dangers of Pornography." *Church Life Journal* (February 6, 2017): http://churchlife.nd.edu/2017/02/06/the-dangers-of-pornography/.

Additional Sources Cited

Ackerman, Diane. *A Natural History of the Senses*. New York: Vintage Books, 1990.
Agamben, Giorgio. *Profanations*. Translated by Jeff Forth. New York: Zone Books, 2007.
———. *Nudities*. Translated by David Kishik and Stefan Pedatella. Stanford, Calif.: Stanford University Press, 2011.
Almukhtar, Sarah, Michael Gold, and Larry Buchanan. "After Weinstein: 71 Men Accused of Sexual Misconduct and Their Fall from Power." *The New York Times* (updated February 8, 2017): https://www.nytimes.com/interactive/2017/11/10/us/men-accused-sexual-misconduct-weinstein.html.
American Psychiatric Association. *Diagnostic and Statistical Manual of Mental Disorders*, 5th ed. Arlington, Va.: American Psychiatric Publishing, 2013.
Berry, Wendell. "Manifesto: The Mad Farmer Liberation Front." In *The Country of Marriage*, 14–15. Berkeley, Calif.: Counterpoint Press, 2013.
Brodersen, Kai, ed. and trans. *Reiseführer zu den Sieben Weltwundern: Philon von Byzanz und andere antike Texte*. Frankfurt am Main: Insel, 1992.
Chaucer, Geoffrey. "The Merchant's Tale." In *The Riverside Chaucer*, 3rd ed., edited by Larry D. Benson. Boston, Mass.: Houghton Mifflin, 1987.

Einstein, Mara. *Advertising: What Everyone Needs to Know*. New York: Oxford University Press, 2017.

Hart, Donna and Robert W. Sussman. *Man the Hunted: Primates, Predators, and Human Evolution*. Boulder, Colo.: Westview, 2009.

Hopkins, Gerard Manley. *Gerard Manley Hopkins: A Critical Edition of the Major Works*. Edited by Catherine Philips. New York: Oxford University Press, 1986.

Horowitz, Alexandra. *Being a Dog: Following the Dog into a World of Smell*. New York: Scribner, 2016.

Josephus. *The Jewish War*. Translated by Martin Hammond. New York: Oxford University Press, 2017.

Kantor, Jodi, and Megan Twohey. "Harvey Weinstein Paid Off Sexual Harassment Accusers for Decades." *New York Times* (October 5, 2017): https://www.nytimes.com/2017/10/05/us/harvey-weinstein-harassment-allegations.html.

Kristeva, Julia. *Tales of Love*. Translated by Leon S. Roudiez. New York: Columbia University Press, 1987.

Lyon, M. L., and J. M. Barbalet. "Society's Body: Emotion and the 'Somatization' of Social Theory." In vol. 2 of *Embodiment and Experience: The Existential Ground of Culture and Self*, edited by Thomas Csordas, 48–66. New York: Cambridge University Press, 1994.

Monáe, Janelle. "Q.U.E.E.N." Official music video featuring singer Erykah Badu, directed by Alan Ferguson. Published online May 1, 2013. https://www.youtube.com/watch?v=tEddixS-UoU.

Peitz, Chelsea. *Talking in Pictures: How Snapchat Changed Cameras, Communication, and Communities*. Chelsea Peitz, 2017.

Plato. *Charmides*. In vol. 8 of *Plato in Twelve Volumes*. Loeb Classical Library No. 201. Translated by W. R. M. Lamb. Cambridge, Mass.: Harvard University Press, 1955.

Prozorov, Sergei. "Pornography and Profanation in the Political Philosophy of Georgio Agamben." *Theory, Culture & Society* 28, no. 4 (July 2011): 71–95.

Rogers, Adam. "The Science of Why No One Agrees on the Color of this Dress." *Wired* (February 26, 2015): https://www.wired.com/2015/02/science-one-agrees-color-dress/.

Romer, John, and Elizabeth. *The Seven Wonders of the World: A History of the Modern Imagination*. New York: Barnes & Noble Books, 2005.

Shiner, Larry. *The Invention of Art: A Cultural History*. Chicago, Ill.: University of Chicago Press, 2001.

Taylor, Charles. *Modern Social Imaginaries*. Durham, N.C.: Duke University Press, 2004.

Turner, Jacob. "Sex and the Spectacle of Music Videos: An Examination of the Portrayal of Race and Sexuality in Music Videos." *Sex Roles* 64 (2011): 173–91.

Twohey, Megan. "Harvey Weinstein Is Fired After Sexual Harassment Reports." *New York Times* (October 8, 2017): https://www.nytimes.com/2017/10/08/business/harvey-weinstein-fired.html.

Vernallis, Carol. *Experiencing Music Video: Aesthetics and Cultural Context*. New York: Columbia University Press, 2004.

Wittgenstein, Ludwig. *Tractatus Logico-Philosophicus*. Translated by D. F. Pears and B. F. McGuinness. London: Routledge & Kegan Paul, 1961.

CONTRIBUTORS

Ann W. Astell is a professor of theology at the University of Notre Dame. Her research focuses on medieval literature and spirituality. She is the author of six books including *The Song of Songs in the Middle Ages* (1990) and *Eating Beauty: The Eucharist and the Spiritual Arts of the Middle Ages* (2006). Her numerous articles have appeared in journals including *Journal of Medieval and Early Modern Studies, Franciscan Studies,* and *Contagion: Journal of Violence, Mimesis, and Culture.*

Kimberly Hope Belcher is associate professor of theology at the University of Notre Dame, where she teaches sacramental and liturgical theology and ritual studies. She is the author of *Efficacious Engagement: Sacramental Participation in the Trinitarian Mystery* (2011) and "The Givenness of Thanks and the Eucharist: Marion, Acknowledgements, and Anaphora" in *Louvain Studies* (2017). Her current work explores how approaching the worship of the Church as a human ritual enhances an understanding of worship as the work of God and how the renewal of pneumatology in the West can contribute to a fully trinitarian theology of sacrament.

John C. Cavadini is professor of theology and the McGrath-Cavadini Director of the McGrath Institute for Church Life at the University of Notre Dame. His main areas of research and teaching are patristics and the biblical spirituality of the fathers of the church, with a special focus on the theology of St. Augustine. He is the author or editor of nine books and over ninety articles or book chapters on a wide array of topics. He was appointed by Pope Benedict XVI to a five-year term on the International Theological Commission and named a member of the Order of the Knights of St. Gregory the Great. He has served as a consultant to the USCCB Committee on Doctrine since 2006.

Boyd Taylor Coolman is professor of theology at Boston College where he is a scholar and teacher of medieval theology. His research interests lie in the twelfth and early thirteenth centuries with a focus on the Victorine and early Franciscan traditions, the emergence of scholastic theology, and medieval mystical theologies. He is the author of three books: *Knowledge, Love, and Ecstasy in Thomas Gallus* (2017), *The Theology of Hugh of St. Victor: An Interpretation* (2010), and *Knowing God by Experience: The Spiritual Senses in the Theology of William of Auxerre* (2004). His articles appear in journals including *The Thomist, Pro Ecclesia,* and *Franciscan Studies.*

David W. Fagerberg is professor of liturgical theology at the University of Notre Dame. He first explored how the church's *lex orandi* (law of prayer) is the foundation of its *lex credendi* (law of belief) in *Theologia Prima* (2003). To this he integrated the Orthodox understanding of asceticism as preparing the liturgical person (*On Liturgical Asceticism*, 2013). He now wants to see how this affects our daily life (*Consecrating the World*, 2016) and our spiritual life (*Liturgical Mysticism*, 2019). He returned to engagement with Orthodox theologian Alexander Schmemann in *Liturgy outside Liturgy* (2018).

Elizabeth T. Groppe is professor of religious studies at the University of Dayton, where she teaches systematic theology. In 2015, she served as a consultant to the Division for Mission of Saint Mary's College, Notre Dame, Indiana, to coordinate the conference "Seeing with the Eyes of the Heart," funded by a grant from the Our Sunday Visitor Institute. Her books include *Yves Congar's Theology of the Holy Spirit* (2004). Her articles appear in journals including *Modern Theology*, *Theological Studies*, and *Worship*.

Jonah is the pseudonym of a young man who was an undergraduate student at a North American university at the time of the composition of his chapter in this volume in which he shares his own story of habitual pornography consumption, conversion, and healing.

Jill Manning is a marriage and family therapist who specializes in research and clinical work related to pornography, sex addiction, and betrayal trauma. She has practiced in a variety of settings including hospitals, community mental health clinics, schools, and private practice. In 2005, she served as a visiting social science fellow at the Heritage Foundation in Washington, D.C., and, as a result of her research there, testified before a Senate subcommittee on the impact of pornography on marriage and the family. She is the author of *What's the Big Deal about Pornography? A Guide for the Internet Generation* (2008) and numerous peer-reviewed articles. She currently serves on the board of directors for Enough Is Enough.

Jennifer Newsome Martin is associate professor in the Program of Liberal Studies (Great Books) at the University of Notre Dame with a concurrent appointment in the Department of Theology. She is a systematic and historical theologian with areas of specialization in twentieth-century Roman Catholic systematic theology. Following the publication of her first book *Hans Urs von Balthasar and the Critical Appropriation of Russian Religious Thought* (2015), she was honored with the 2017 Manfred Lautenschlaeger Award for Theological Promise. She is co-editor of *An Apocalypse of Love: Essays in Honor of Cyril J. O'Regan* (2018) and is the author of research articles in peer-reviewed journals including *Modern Theology* and *Communio: International Catholic Review*.

Kyler Mulhauser is a doctoral candidate in clinical psychology at Saint Louis University. His research investigates neuropsychological functioning and addiction processes with a focus on the role of executive functions and decision making in substance use disorders, gambling disorder, and hypersexuality. He earned a bachelor's degree in studio art and a master's degree in clinical psychology from Wheaton College.

Nicholas Ogle is a doctoral candidate in moral theology at the University of Notre Dame. His research focuses on retrieving the ethical insights of pre-modern theologians and bringing them to bear on current moral debates. He is currently writing a dissertation entitled "Ignorance in Action: A Thomistic Theory of Moral Culpability," which analyzes Christian theological reflection on the erroneous conscience from a perspective informed by the ethical thought of Thomas Aquinas. As a master's student, he was a staff member in residence at the St. Peter Claver Catholic Worker in South Bend, Indiana.

Danielle M. Peters earned her doctorate of sacred theology with a specialization in Marian studies from the International Marian Research Institute in 2008. She is the author of *Ecce Educatrix Tua: The Role of the Blessed Virgin Mary for a Pedagogy of Holiness in the Thought of John Paul II and Father Joseph Kentenich* (2009) and a contributor to *Mary, God-Bearer to a World in Need* (2013). She is co-editor with John C. Cavadini of *Mary on the Eve of the Second Vatican Council* (2017). She has served as professor and coordinator of academic programs at the Pontifical International Marian Research Institute (IMRI) in Dayton, Ohio, as a post-doctoral research fellow at the McGrath Institute for Church Life at the University of Notre Dame, and as vice president and president of the Mariological Society of America.

Nathaniel Peters is the executive director of the Morningside Institute and a lecturer at Columbia University. He is currently working on an English translation of the letters of William of Saint-Thierry, and his articles and reviews can be found in numerous journals including *Religious Studies Review*, *America*, *Commonweal*, *First Things*, and *Plough Quarterly*.

Dianne Phillips obtained her PhD in the history of art from Yale University and currently is an independent scholar specializing in late medieval religious art. Her doctoral dissertation was a study of the fourteenth-century Italian illuminated manuscript *Meditations on the Life of Christ* in the Snite Museum of Art at the University of Notre Dame, a preliminary summary of which was published in Jill Mann and Maura Nolan (eds.), *The Text in the Community: Essays on Medieval Works, Manuscripts, Authors, and Readers* (2006). Her publications also include the article "Leo Steinberg's Artistic Vision" in *First Things* (2011). She is a frequent guest lecturer in theology classes at the University of Notre Dame and has given presentations on religious art for various audiences in South Bend, Indiana.

Randi Maria Sider-Rose studied iconography at the Mt. Angel Abbey Iconography Institute in Oregon and with various other teachers in the United States. She lived in Russia and Latvia for two and a half years, first as a student and then as a Fulbright Scholar. She now paints and teaches iconography in Pittsburgh, Pennsylvania. She serves the church under the name Immanuel Icons: "Iconographers do not sign our names to the icons because we are mere vessels, not artistic geniuses or masters. I use the name 'Immanuel Icons' so you can find me at *www.immanuelicons.org* and because Christ is truly the 'Icon' (literally: image) of 'God-with-Us.' Alleluia!"

William M. Struthers earned his doctorate in biopsychology and is now professor of psychology at Wheaton College. His publications include *Wired for Intimacy: How Pornography Hijacks the Male Brain* (2009), "Pornography Addiction" in *Addictions and Substance Abuse*, and numerous journal articles. His clinical research is in the area of compulsive sexuality and pornography use. His theoretical interests include neuroethics, the biological bases of spirituality and personhood, and the dialogue between science and religious faith. He speaks internationally as an advocate against various forms of sexual exploitation including pornography, prostitution, and sex trafficking. In 2014, he was named a visiting research fellow to Biola University's Center for Christian Thought for his work on the impact of sexual exploitation on spirituality.

INDEX

Seeing with the Eyes of the Heart: Cultivating a Sacramental Imagination in an Age of Pornography was designed in Warnock with Scala Sans display type and composed by Kachergis Book Design of Pittsboro, North Carolina. It was printed on 60-pound House Natural Smooth and 80-pound House White Matte and bound by Sheridan Books of Chelsea, Michigan.